Flyfisher's Guide to™
PENNSYLVANIA

Titles Available in This Series

Flyfisher's Guide to Colorado

Flyfisher's Guide to Idaho

Flyfisher's Guide to Michigan

Flyfisher's Guide to Montana

Flyfisher's Guide to Northern California

Flyfisher's Guide to Northern New England

Flyfisher's Guide to Oregon

Flyfisher's Guide to Washington

Flyfisher's Guide to Wyoming

Flyfisher's Guide to™
PENNSYLVANIA

Dave Wolf

Wilderness
Adventures
Press™

Belgrade, Montana

Published by Wilderness Adventures Press
45 Buckskin Road
Belgrade, MT 59714
800-925-3339
Website: www.wildadv.com
email: books@wildadv.com

10 9 8 7 6 5 4 3 2 1

Library of Congress Cataloging-in-Publication Data

Wolf, Dave, 1947–
   Flyfisher's guide to Pennsylvania / Dave Wolf
     p.   cm.
   Includes index
   ISBN 1–885106–58–0
   1. Fly fishing—Pennsylvania—Guidebooks. 2. Pennsylvania—Guidebooks. I. Title
SH541.W66   2000
799.1'24'09748—dc21
                                      99-59790
                                          CIP

To my wife and life partner, AnGel,
for her dedication and help with this book and life

To our children and to all of those who have helped
nurture our resources for our use now
and for our children and their children in the future

And to my grandmother who had the patience
and insight to teach me how to fish at the age of six

Table of Contents

Acknowledgments xi

Introduction xiii

Major Roads and Rivers of Pennsylvania (map) xiv

Pennsylvania Facts xv

Explanation of Special Regulations 1

Pennsylvania's Coldwater Fisheries 3

Northeast Pennsylvania 7
   Delaware River 8
   West Branch Delaware River 13
   Lackawanna River 19
   Lackawaxen River 21
   Roaring Brook 23
   Dyberry Creek 25
   Big Bushkill Creek 28
   Brodhead Creek 29
   Hickory Run 32
   Hayes Creek 33
   Mud Run 35
   Fishing Creek 37
   Mehoopany Creek 41
   Approved Trout Waters and Special Regulations 44
   Northeast Hub Cities 50

Southeast Pennsylvania 55
   Little Lehigh Creek 57
   Lehigh River 59
   Monocacy Creek 63
   White Clay Creek 63
   Saucon Creek 64
   Cedar Creek 65
   French Creek 66
   Ridley Creek 67
   Valley Creek 68
   Brandywine Creek 71
   Octoraro Creek 75
   Donegal Creek 77
   Tulpehocken Creek 79
   Little Schuylkill River 83
   Approved Trout Waters and Special Regulations 84
   Southeast Hub Cities 89

Northcentral Pennsylvania 95
   Allegheny River 99
   Oswayo Creek 103
   Lyman Run 107
   Lyman Lake 107
   Genesee River 113
   Pine Creek 113

Northcentral Pennsylvania *(continued)*
Little Pine Creek 116
Cedar Run 119
Slate Run 120
Francis Branch 121
Gray's Run 122
Elk Creek 124
Muncy Creek 126
Loyalsock Creek 129
White Deer Creek 132
Young Woman's Creek 135
Penns Creek 137
Cherry Run 140
Fishing Creek 143
Spring Creek 147
Lick Run 151
Spruce Creek 151
Cross Fork Creek 155
Kettle Creek 158
First Fork Sinnemahoning Creek 161
Driftwood Branch Sinnemahoning Creek 164
Hunts Run 171
Big Mill Creek 173
Clarion River 177
Approved Trout Waters and Special Regulations 179
Northcentral Hub Cities 188

Southcentral Pennsylvania 195
Clarks Creek 199
Stony Creek 203
Shermans Creek 203
Yellow Breeches Creek 205
The Letort 213
Big Spring Creek 217
Green Spring Creek 218
Codorus Creek 219
Muddy Creek 222
Conewago Creek 223
Falling Springs Branch Creek 225
East Branch Antietam Creek 229
Little Juniata River 229
Canoe Creek 233
Frankstown Branch Juniata River 235
Bald Eagle Creek 239
Raystown Branch Juniata River 243
Tuscarora Creek 247
Honey Creek 249
Manada Creek 251
Quittapahilla Creek 253
Approved Trout Waters and Special Regulations 257
Southcentral Hub Cities 264

Northwest Pennsylvania 271
   Oil Creek 273
   Caldwell Creek 277
   West Branch Caldwell Creek 279
   Little Sandy Creek 279
   Neshannock Creek 281
   Cool Spring Creek 284
   Steelhead Fishing 285
      Lake Erie Tributaries 285
         Steelhead Streams West Side 289
         Steelhead Streams East Side 293
      Lake Erie 294
   Approved Trout Waters and Special Regulations 296
   Northwest Hub Cities 300
Southwest Pennsylvania 305
   Little Mahoning Creek 307
   Chest Creek 309
   Clear Shade Creek 312
   Loyalhanna Creek 315
   Laurel Hill Creek 317
   Youghiogheny River 319
   Dunbar Creek 324
   Camp Run and Indian Creek 327
   Meadow Run 329
   Approved Trout Waters and Special Regulations 330
   Southwest Hub Cities 335
Coldwater Fly Box 339
Pennsylvania's Warmwater Fisheries 349
   Delaware River 351
   Schuylkill River 361
   Lake Wallenpaupack 368
   Blue Marsh Lake 371
   West Branch Susquehanna River 374
   North Branch Susquehanna River 380
   Susquehanna River 389
   York Haven Dam/Lake Frederic 403
   Safe Harbor Dam/Lake Clarke 405
   Holtwood Dam/Lake Aldred 407
   Conowingo Reservoir 408
   Pinchot (Conewago) Lake 409
   Driftwood Branch Sinnemahoning Creek 411
   George B. Stevenson Dam 413
   Juniata River 415
   Raystown Lake 422
   Opossum Creek Lake 424
   French Creek 427
   Allegheny River 429
   Kinzua Dam 440
   Lake Erie 443

Pennsylvania's Warmwater Fisheries *(continued)*
Presque Isle Bay... 447
Pymatuning Lake.. 449
Conneaut Lake.. 451
Lake Arthur.. 452
Keystone Lake 454
Ohio River... 455
Monongahela River... 458

Big Bass Program 464

Warmwater Fly Box... 466

Fly Shops by Region 470

Pennsylvania Fish and Boat Commission Regional Headquarters................. 479

Tackle and Equipment.. 480

Pennsylvania Fish Species... 486

Pennsylvania's Wild Trout Streams................................... 495

Afterword.. 512

Index.. 515

Acknowledgments

First to my wife and partner, AnGel, who I met and subsequently married after I had contracted to write this book. She shared in the research, editing, and gathering of materials. She relentlessly pursued the locations of streams on maps to help find their beginning and end. She even took photos for the book...obviously the honeymoon was extremely short. Without her, this book would not have been completed.

I would also like to thank Darren Brown of Wilderness Adventures Press, who stood firm in his belief that this would be a good and timely book. His patience, congenial attitude, and willingness to work with me were an enlightening and refreshing experience. A special thanks to Bob Butz for introducing me to Chuck Johnson and Wilderness Adventures Press.

To Bob Clouser, Clouser's Fly Shop; Pete Ryan; Harry Redline; Alan Bright; Spruce Creek Outfitters; Paradise Ranch; Phil Baldachinno; Kettle Creek Tackle; Raymond "Skip" Gibson and Dan Bailey's for making my wading easier with their breathable waders; Cortland Line Company for supplying the fly lines for all species pursued during this project; Tom Eggler, owner of the Phillips Lure/Gaines Company, a Pennsylvania manufacturer of popping cork popping bugs; Delorme, Publishers of the *Pennsylvania Atlas & Gazetteer*; and Vivid Publishing for Professor Higbee's *Streams of Pennsylvania*.

To Karl Power, Mike Bleech, Carol Sipos, Mike Simmons and countless other members of the Pennsylvania Outdoor Writer's Association; Pennsylvania Fish and Boat Commission; Pennsylvania Department of Environmental Resources; Pennsylvania Bureau of Forestry and Parks; Federal Fish and Wildlife Service; Trout Unlimited; and countless tourist promotion agencies and visitors centers that helped so graciously, I can only say thank you to all of you.

To all of those with whom I have swapped fishing stories and information, all of those who have shared the waters of Pennsylvania with me, and to those who will in the future. You know who you are...those who leave the water in the same manner that it was found or improved by a simple turn of a boulder or by picking up another's litter.

Last, but not least, to all the family, friends, and longtime fishing buddies like Wayne Foust with whom I have been unable to spend time in order to complete this book. Thank you all for your time, patience, and understanding. Now we will find the time to fish the streams, rivers, and lakes of Pennsylvania again, and most important, have fun pursuing whatever fish is the order of the day.

Dave Wolf

Introduction

I have known Dave Wolf for close to 20 years. In that time we have fished together only once, for bass of course, on my home waters, the Susquehanna River. However, we have talked more than we have fished. We have met often in flyfishing circles throughout the state. I have attended his slide programs and lectures, and he has attended mine.

Dave is someone who is more than a flyfisherman—he is a conservationist through and through. He has labored hard and long through the years to spread the word through his writing that flyfishing requires clean water and stringent catch-and-release regulations so that fishing will survive for future generations to enjoy.

He has been embroiled in the controversy over changes in creel limits and size restrictions that we all realize are needed to protect and preserve our natural resources. He has not backed away from his strong opinions, no matter what the cost.

We talk frequently over the phone, and although the conversations begin with water levels and color and fishing success, they always end on a serious note. Dave and I think alike when it comes to our water resources, be they cold or warm. One can never err on the side of safety, if and when we ever have an overabundance of a species of fish. That is a problem easily resolved. When we lose year classes of fish, they cannot be replaced.

Both of us have fished the Susquehanna River for years, and we are old enough to recall the stringers of small fish taken here when the size limit was much lower. We have seen a significant change since the "Big Bass Regulation" was been put into place, along with an increased and renewed interest in flyfishing the river.

I know that Dave has written this book with the intent of bringing others into the realm of flyfishing. He also has penned these words with a lot of wading beneath his feet and with the continual beat of a conservationist within his heart. Use these places wisely, release what you catch, and leave the land the way you found it. In doing so, the time he has spent on this endeavor will not be wasted. It might even help secure the future of flyfishing in Pennsylvania.

Bob Clouser
Middletown, Pennsylvania

Major Roads and Rivers of Pennsylvania

© Wilderness Adventures Press

Pennsylvania Facts

Nickname	Keystone State (during colonial times, Pennsylvania was the middle colony of the original 13 colonies, holding the colonies together like the "keystone" in a window or door arch)
Flower	Mountain laurel
Tree	Hemlock
Bird	Ruffed grouse
Animal	White-tailed deer
Insect	Firefly
Fish	Brook trout
Area	45,888 square miles
Rank	32nd in nation
Width	310 miles east to west
Length	180 miles north to south
Highest point	Mt. Davis, Somerset County, 3,213 feet
Lowest point	Delaware River
Capital	Harrisburg
Counties	67
Population	12,009,000
Lakes	50 natural lakes (over 20 acres) and 2,500 manmade lakes
Rivers	45,000 miles
State Parks	116 (282,500 acres)
State Forests	20 (2,200,000 acres)
State Game Lands	294 (1,379,002 acres)

Fish Species

American eel	Green sunfish	Redear
American shad	Golden trout	Redfin
Bluegill	Hybrid bass	Rockbass
Black crappie	Lake trout	Sauger
Brook trout	Lamprey	Smallmouth bass
Brown trout	Largemouth bass	Steelhead
Brown bullhead	Longnose gar	Striped bass
Burbot	Muskie	Tiger muskie
Carp	Paddlefish	Walleye
Chain Pickerel	Rainbow trout	White perch
Channel catfish	Redbreast	Yellow perch
Flathead catfish		

Explanation of Special Regulations

Selective Harvest Program
- Flies and artificial lures only
- Open to fishing year-round (no closed season)
- The minimum size is 12 inches for brown trout and 9 inches for other trout
- The daily limit is 2 trout (combined species) except during the period from-midnight Labor Day to 8AM on the opening day of regular trout season when no trout may be killed or had in possession

All Tackle Selective Harvest
- Artificial lures, flies, and natural bait
- The minimum size is 12 inches for brown trout and 9 inches for other trout
- The limit is two trout (combined species) from 8AM on the opening day of regular trout season to midnight Labor Day, except during the period from the day after Labor Day to 8AM on the opening day of regular trout season of the following when no trout may be kill or had in possession
- Open to fishing year-round (no closed season)

Delayed Harvest Flyfishing Only (DHFFO)
- Flyfishing only
- Fishing hours: 1 hour before sunrise to 1 hour after sunset
- Minimum size: 9 inches, caught from 1 hour before sunrise on June 15 to 1 hour after sunset on Labor Day
- Daily creel limit: 3 combined species (creel limit is 0 from the day after Labor Day until 1 hour before sunrise on June 15
- Open to fishing year-round (no closed season)

Heritage Trout Angling
- Flyfishing only
- Barbless hooks required
- Fishing hours: 1 hour before sunrise to 1 hour after sunset
- No trout may be killed or had in possession
- Open to fishing year-round (no closed season)

Catch-and-Release
- Flies or lures only
- Barbed hooks are prohibited; fishing may be done with barbless hooks only
- Fishing hours: 1 hour before sunrise to 1 hour after sunset
- No trout may be killed or had in possession
- Open to fishing year-round (no closed season)

Delayed Harvest Artificial Lures Only (DHALO)
- Flies or lures only
- Fishing hours: 1 hour before sunrise to 1 hour after sunset.
- Minimum size: 9 inches, caught from 1 hour before sunrise on June 15 to 1 hour after sunset on Labor Day
- Daily creel limit: 3 combined species (creel limit is 0 from the day after Labor Day until 1 hour before sunrise on June 15)
- Open to fishing year-round (no closed season)

Trophy Trout Projects
- Flies or lures only
- Minimum size: 14 inches, caught from 8AM on the opening day of regular trout season to midnight Labor Day
- Daily creel limit: 2 trout, combined species (from midnight Labor Day to 8AM on the opening day of regular trout season of the following year no trout may be killed)
- Open to fishing year-round (no closed season)

All Tackle Trophy Trout
- Flies, lures, or bait
- Minimum size: 14 inches, caught from 8AM on the opening day of regular trout season to midnight Labor Day
- Daily creel limit: 2 trout, combined species (from midnight Labor Day to 8AM on the opening day of regular trout season of the following year no trout may be killed)
- Open to fishing year-round (no closed season)

Conservation Lakes: Special Regulations Warmwater and Coolwater Species
- Bass: 15-inch minimum, 2 per day
- Muskie: 36-inch minimum, 1 per day
- Northern pike: 28 inches minimum, 1 per day

Approved Trout Waters
Defined as any stream, lake, pond, or reservoir that meets the criteria qualifying them to be stocked with trout by the Fish and Boat Commission. They are open to trout fishing during the "extended season," which includes all approved trout waters and their downstream areas and all lakes and ponds, January 1 to midnight February 28, and September 7 to midnight December 31.

Pennsylvania's Coldwater Fisheries

The value of a trout stream is being discovered throughout the Commonwealth of Pennsylvania. You will find few coldwater resources within the state that do not have caretakers in one form or another. Pennsylvania is a heavily populated state, and home to all types of industry. With its dense population comes the need for work places, housing, shopping, dining, entertainment, and recreation.

It has been said that for every action there is a reaction, and that holds true on the Commonwealth's trout streams, defined by the Pennsylvania Fish & Boat Commission (PFBC) as coldwater streams. The premise is that coldwater streams will hold trout, and while that is true, those on the "Approved Trout Waters" list, although deemed suitable for stocking, do not necessarily hold trout year-round—in fact, most do not.

Delayed Harvest regulations are designed for waters with "thermal pollution." In some circles it is called the lack of oxygenated waters, which basically means the same thing—trout water that rises into and stays in the 70s for any length of time. When coldwater streams rise to the mid-70s and stay there for a period of a week or more, trout either perish or move to coldwater sanctuaries. This is most apparent on freestones, where constant flow fluctuations occur with each passing storm.

The June 15 date set for the delayed harvest of stocked trout is, at times, premature. I am personally of the catch-and-release persuasion, in the hope that trout might find coldwater springs or migrate upstream to the mouths of tributaries or into the headwaters themselves, a place where cold water is most often found.

I have been fishing for trout almost my entire life, and while living and operating a fly shop on the First Fork of the Sinnemahoning in the 1970s to early 1980's, I fished an average of five days per week. In that span of time, I fished freestones almost exclusively, and the Fork was primarily where I did most of my fishing. Here, as on most freestones, trout moved whenever the water became warm. Brown trout were, by far, the most adaptable, and they moved into the mouths of tributaries and into pools that were springfed.

Rainbows and browns disappeared quickly by mid-June to early July, and it is a rare occurrence in this state to find rainbows that reproduce in freestone streams. Brook trout are known to be susceptible to the hook, and they are believed to be the first removed after being stocked.

Pennsylvania's hatchery system operates on the basis of mass production of fish. For many streams, including the famed Yellow Breeches, a prolific limestone in Cumberland County, could not sustain a fishery without the addition of stocked fish. It has been tried and has usually failed.

The streams of the state have been stripped of the hemlock forests that grew in many areas here as virgin timber. Roadways, timber, oil, gas, coal, and other industries have spoiled many a coldwater stream. In this book, I cover the streams that are stocked and wild. Many of the stocked streams have wild trout and native brook trout in their colder tributaries.

Trout fishing in the Commonwealth is on the upswing as more and more organizations have taken on the responsibility of protecting our coldwater resources. Dams with topwater releases, which allows the sun-warmed water of the surface to spill into cold water, have degraded many streams as well, and the advantages of bottom-release dams are now fully understood.

An educated angling public has been trying to spread the word for years that we all need clean, cold water, often butting heads with the industries that claimed the cost was prohibitive. The Army Corps of Engineers, once the most organized and persuasive group in favor of dams for flood control, now helps oppose building more of them.

Trout water can be as variable as the silt-laden Letort to a clean and clear freestone. The ideal trout stream provides shade and streamside vegetation for cover and has boulders to provide resting areas for trout. Its bottom would be covered with pea-sized gravel and free of silt, providing ideal spawning grounds in which eggs don't become smothered. A stream such as this would have a good pool-to-riffle ratio, thus allowing the depths in which to hide, and the oxygen needed to sustain life.

Food sources in a trout stream would be varied and have an abundance of hatches. Anglers would not need to moan silt was burying some species of nymphs. Of course, there would be undercut banks and woody debris along the banks and dangling into the flow, providing protection from land-roving and avian predators.

If flyfishers had their way, there would only be a handful of anglers casting to the abundance of trout residing there. Trout waters should be easily found after reading this book. Finding the best locations usually entails using a stream thermometer and doing some exploring.

Today we are regaining trout streams faster than we ever have before, but even as progress is made, others streams are being degraded. As flyfishers, it is important that we all do our part.

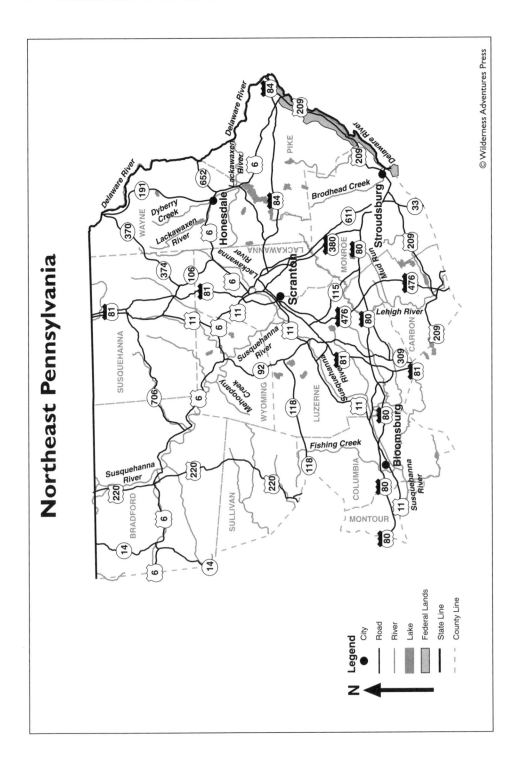

Northeast Pennsylvania

Legend
- City
- Road
- River
- Lake
- Federal Lands
- State Line
- County Line

N

Northeast Pennsylvania

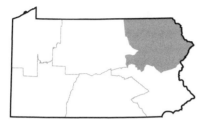

This is a beautiful region of the state, with steep mountains canopied by hardwoods and ever-greens, awesome plateaus, and steep canyon-like cliffs. It is filled with trout water, rushing and tumbling over falls on the way to major arteries of the Delaware River, which forms the eastern boundary of the state and is itself a beautiful river.

At one time, this rugged and desolate country was home mostly to fishing and hunting camps and had almost no industry and therefore little pollution. Anglers came seeking the native brook trout in these untainted streams. Pennsylvania's native jewel, brook trout are actually a member of the char family.

Today, brown trout and large rainbows that haunt the upper Delaware are what attract throngs of flyfishers. And anglers are also pursuing shad, a long forgotten aspect of the flyfishing art, as well as striped bass coming up from Delaware Bay.

Lodging here is nearly as abundant as trout, from rooms with swimming pools and champagne-glass whirlpools to neatly kept cabins that are remnants of the past or the modern log cabins that are meant to blend in with the land.

The region's rivers and lakes also contain bass, stripers, and muskie, providing nearly year-round flyfishing, beginning with spring shad and running until early winter when the waters become laced with ice. However, if there is a trace of open water in the depths of winter, flyfishers can be found casting to fish with great hopes and expectations—at least those on the fanatical fringe of the sport.

The northeast's expanding economy is due to tourist trade from neighboring New York and New Jersey, something the region has long sought and now enjoys. But the reality is bittersweet-in return for the tourist dollars, land has been purchased that has become unavailable to the public, blocking access to many good streams.

Private fishing clubs that are steeped in tradition have stood their ground for the most part, despite the phenomenal prices that have been offered for their land. To many, these clubs are as much a part of the landscape as the white-tailed deer and black bear that live here. They certainly seem more appropriate than the resorts and shopping malls that are springing up, but it all depends on a person's perspective. It is evident that the future of this region's flyfishing is tied to good planning for controlling and monitoring commercial expansion.

But on the bright side, there are still plenty of unpaved and narrow winding blacktop roads leading to plenty of fishing opportunities, and the Delaware River is making a strong comeback. Shad runs are increasing as are runs of striped bass, and they are expected to improve in the coming years. Trout fishing on the Delaware will depend on coldwater releases from dams in New York State. An optimistic viewpoint is that this region's flyfishing will continue improving, and that's the view I would most likely take.

DELAWARE RIVER

The Delaware River travels 280 miles from its conception in southeastern New York's Catskill Mountains where the East and West Branches meet at Hancock. It flows southeast along the New York-Pennsylvania border to Port Jervis, then between Pennsylvania and New Jersey to Delaware Bay.

Reservoirs and dams on the river's headwaters provide flood control and supply water to New York City. The diversion of large amounts of water from the upper Delaware has increased the salinity of Delaware Bay. The Delaware River Basin Compact was formed in 1961 to regulate water use in the entire river basin.

It is difficult to find or even imagine a river with the wealth of fishing opportunities contained in the Delaware. Consider the following:

- Trout that are measured in pounds rather than inches
- Browns of 5 pounds or more are a daily possibility
- Tremendous runs of American shad that can be fished from the bank and that rise to a dry fly when spawning is completed
- Bringing a muskie or striped bass to hand by working a saltwater streamer through deep pools
- Hooking into a smallmouth bass that dances over stillwater pools or silver threaded riffles

What more could one fishery offer?

In its upper reaches near where the branches join, this large river can be tough to wade, but wading is necessary to reach fish. It's always wise to have a wading stick on this section, and the current should never be underestimated.

It was my good fortune to have Leon Reed, commissioner of the Pennsylvania Fish and Boat Commission, offer to take me fishing on the Delaware. Besides being a commissioner, Leon is an excellent flyfisher who has fished this river longer than he cares to admit. Since access to the upper reaches is difficult to find, a guide is needed here probably more than anywhere else in the state.

Leon had a friend from the New York side who took us to the river. Fortunately, Pennsylvania and New York have a reciprocal license agreement that allows anglers from either state to fish the Delaware, regardless of where the river is entered. New Jersey and Pennsylvania also have the same agreement that allows anglers access farther downstream.

We were fishing in mid-June, and tan caddis were bringing fish to the surface in a constant ring of rises. Leon had tried to convince me that nothing smaller than a 5X tippet would hold fish here. I feel strongly that drag-free floats are easier to accomplish with light tippets, but I compromised and quietly clipped my leader back from 7X to 6X. While I did hook a lot of fish (many good trout and a number of shad) with a size 16 caddis, I lost well over 75 percent of them. When dam releases from both branches are good for fishing, wading doesn't allow one to follow a fish very far, and some fish simply snapped me off with one turn of the head.

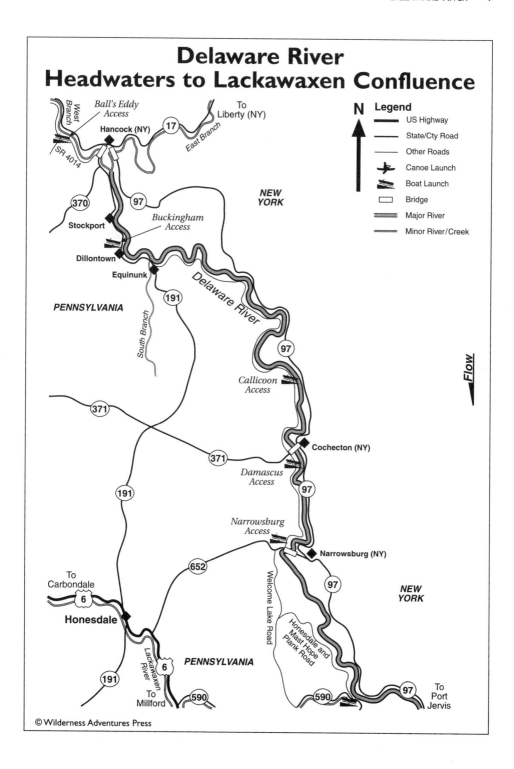

Delaware River
Headwaters to Lackawaxen Confluence

N

Legend

▬▬▬	US Highway
────	State/Cty Road
───	Other Roads
✈	Canoe Launch
⛴	Boat Launch
▭	Bridge
▬▬▬	Major River
▬▬▬	Minor River/Creek

West Branch

Ball's Eddy Access

To Liberty (NY)

Hancock (NY) 17

East Branch

SR 4014

370 97

NEW YORK

Stockport

Buckingham Access

Dillontown

Equinunk

191

Delaware River

PENNSYLVANIA

South Branch

97

Callicoon Access

371

Cochecton (NY)

371

Damascus Access

97

191

Narrowsburg Access

Narrowsburg (NY)

652

To Carbondale

6

97

NEW YORK

Honesdale

Welcome Lake Road

Honesdale and Mast Hope Plank Road

Lackawaxen River

6

PENNSYLVANIA

191

To Millford

590

To Port Jervis

590

97

Flow

© Wilderness Adventures Press

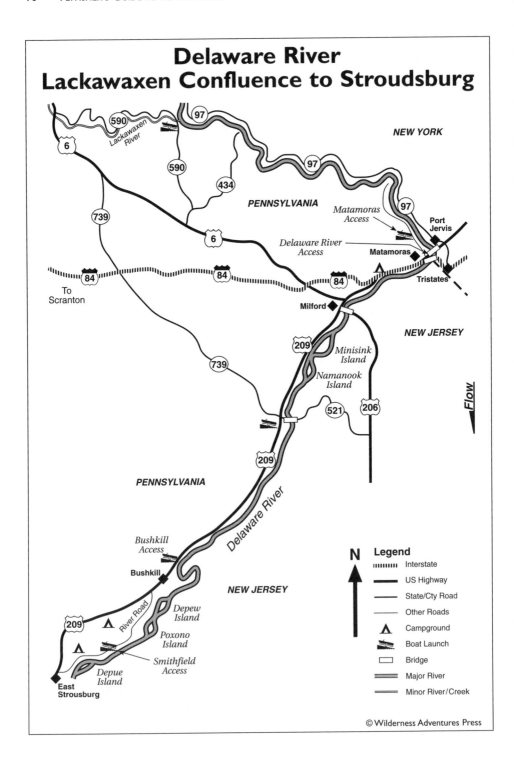

Delaware River
Lackawaxen Confluence to Stroudsburg

NEW YORK

Lackawaxen River

590

97

6

590

434

97

PENNSYLVANIA

Matamoras
Access

Port
Jervis

739

6

Delaware River
Access

Matamoras

84

84

84

Tristates

To
Scranton

Milford

NEW JERSEY

209

Minisink
Island

739

Namanook
Island

521

206

209

Flow

PENNSYLVANIA

Delaware River

Bushkill
Access

N   Legend

Bushkill

Interstate

US Highway

River Road

NEW JERSEY

State/Cty Road

Depew
Island

Other Roads

209

Poxono
Island

Campground

Smithfield
Access

Boat Launch

Depue
Island

Bridge

East
Strousburg

Major River

Minor River/Creek

© Wilderness Adventures Press

Boat anglers fishing the Delaware River.

In this part of the river, fish are large and 6-weight lines are not out of question. I did fine with a 5-weight, 9-foot rod and a medium-sized CFO reel until the second day when I found a good fish rising in a deep pool. Leon told me there was a gravel bar out there somewhere, but reaching it from the Pennsylvania side was impossible without a boat. I found a large boulder some two feet beneath the surface that allowed me to present the fly to the continuously rising trout. The tan caddis imitation was taken without hesitation, but that meant little. The large brown headed for New York and took refuge along the far streambank, shaking his head from time to time. My spool was stripped one wind away from all fly line and 50 feet of backing — something I normally consider enough for most trout fishing.

Clambering off the rock, I stumbled my way down the Pennsylvania bank, gathering line as I worked below the now nonresident brown that was holding in backwaters shallow enough to see his length, literally a state away. Once below the fish, I forced the large trout to fight both man and current by staying downstream from him. Someone came running with a net and someone else with a camera as the fish came within rod length, but with one last shake of the head, he was gone.

The owner of the land on which we were fishing called the following week to tell me that he thought he hooked and landed the same trout from the same rock. It went close to 30 inches, and he estimated the weight at over 7 pounds before releasing it.

The author with a big water brown from the Delaware River.

There can be fantastic fishing on the Delaware's upper reach, however it is dependent on water releases from dams on the East and West Branches. Drought has been predominant during the last few years, and trout fishing has been declining. However, that could change in the blink of an eye.

The entire river is considered navigable, so if you can get in the water either by wading or by boat, you can fish anywhere. However, access to the river is the key, so to avoid trespassing on private property, make sure you get landowner permission. If you don't have a lot of time to find access and gain permission, you may be disappointed. If access is a problem, there are guides who have access and can get you on the water.

Regulations governing trout fishing here should be carefully noted: the season begins the first Saturday after the 11th of April and closes at midnight September 30th. The creel limit is one trout per day over 14 inches north of I-84 and 5 below it with no minimum size limit. With the amount of pressure on all Pennsylvania streams, it is highly recommended that all trout be released.

The river's upper portions contain a mix of rainbow, browns, and a sprinkling of brook trout. No adult trout stocking takes place here, so this is considered a wild trout fishery. Many come to find large rainbows that are not prevalent elsewhere in the state, but the brown trout fishery shouldn't be overlooked.

Entering Pennsylvania in Wayne County, management of the Delaware is shared by Pennsylvania and New York. The better trout fishing exists within the boundaries

The upper Delaware River.

of Wayne County and Pike Counties before the river turns into a warmwater fishery. Access to the river area is gained from SR 191.

WEST BRANCH DELAWARE RIVER

The West Branch Delaware River is a wonderful trout stream that depends on reservoir water releases to maintain a healthy trout fishery. When I first fished this branch, it had plenty of long glides and a good pool-to-riffle ratio and was filled to the brim with wild trout: browns, rainbows, and brookies. It was an easy stream to wade and allowed plenty of casting room, which made it about as ideal a trout stream as one can get.

However, when I returned, the stream was a skeleton of its former self, and water levels were so low that the stream's inhabitants were few and far between. During my first visit, willing fish were plentiful, and on my return, I had to search to find a few.

The West Branch can be a superb place to fish, however, the health of its trout fishery depends on release from Cannonsville Reservoir as well as the Downsville Reservoir on the East Branch. The two branches join below Hancock, New York, to form the Delaware River. Both branches and their water levels are extremely important to the health of Pennsylvania's trout fishery.

As it is on the Delaware itself, access is limited on the West Branch, and you will need landowner permission or a guide who has permission to get on the water.

Guides and Fly Shops for the Delaware River and West Branch

Northeast Flyfishers
93 Main Street
Honesdale, PA 18431
570-253-9780

Windsor's Sport Shop
348 North 9th Street
Stroudsburg, PA 18360
570-424-0938

Al Caucci Flyfishing
38 Chestnut Ridge
Tannersville, PA 18372
570-629-2962

Delaware River Anglers
228 Davisville Road
Willow Grove, PA 19090
215-830-9766

Ray Peewee Serfass
P.O. 194, Heath Lane
Pocono Summit, PA 18346
570-839-7736

Dunkelbergers Sports Outfitters
585 Main Street and 6th
Stroudsburg, PA 18360
570-421-7950

River Essentials
HC1 Box 1025
Starlight, PA 18461
570-635-5900

Delaware River Fly Shop, Inc.
HC1 Box 1061
Starlight, PA 18461
570-635-5983

Starlight Lodge
Box 86
Starlight, PA 18461
570-798-2350

Delaware River Access Sites

Wayne County; 60 miles
Species: Bass, Muskie, Panfish, Shad, Pickerel, Trout, Walleye

Balls Eddy Access (PFBC); West Branch, two miles east of Winterdale on SR 4037; can be reached by SR 191
- Limited to small motors and nonpowered boats
- Perfect for float trips with canoes or light motors
- Suitable for small boats only
- Shallow draft, lightweight fishing boats, canoes, and inflatables
- Boat fishing and float trips
- Beach-type ramp
- Parking available

Buckingham Access (PFBC); three miles north of Equinunk
- Suitable for small boats only
- Small motors and nonpowered boats
- Perfect for float trips with canoes or light motors
- Shallow draft, lightweight fishing boats, canoes, and inflatables
- Boat fishing and float trips
- Beach-type ramp
- Parking Available

Callicoon Access (PFBC); west of Callicoon, NY; can be reached by SR 191
- Sanitary facilities
- Limited to small motors and nonpowered boats
- Perfect for float trips with canoes or light motors
- Suitable for small boats only
- Shallow draft, lightweight fishing boats, canoes, and inflatables
- Boat fishing and float trips
- Beach-type ramp
- Parking available

Damascus Access (PFBC); in borough of Damascus, SR 371
- Sanitary facilities
- Suitable for small boats only
- Shallow draft, lightweight fishing boats, canoes, and inflatables
- Boat fishing and float trips
- Beach-type ramp
- Parking available

Narrowsburg Access (PFBC); opposite Narrowsburg, NY, on SR 652
- About a 150-acre pool for power boating and perfect for float trips
- Suitable for small boats only
- Moderate draft fishing boats, sailboats, and recreational runabout boats
- Boat fishing and float trips
- Beach-type ramp
- Parking available

Pike County: 67 miles
Species: Muskie, Panfish, Shad, Pickerel, Suckers, Trout, Walleye

Matamoras Access (PFBC); on Delaware Drive, about one mile north of US 209 bridge
- Sanitary facilities
- Shallow draft, lightweight fishing boats, canoes, and inflatables
- Boat fishing and float trips
- Surfaced ramp
- Parking available

Delaware River (National Park Service); US 6 & 209
- Shallow draft, lightweight fishing boats, canoes, and inflatables
- Boat fishing and float trips
- Beach-type ramp
- Parking available

Bushkill Access; one mile north of Bushkill, off US 209 within Delaware Water Gap National Recreation Area
- Suitable for small boats
- Shallow draft, lightweight fishing boats, canoes, and inflatables
- Boat fishing and float trips
- Surfaced ramp
- Parking available

DELAWARE RIVER MAJOR HATCHES

Insect	J	F	M	A	M	J	J	A	S	O	N	D
Blue Quill #18				■								
Quill Gordon #14				■								
Hendrickson #14				■	■							
Caddis #14 & 16 (grannom, olive, gray)				■	■							
Tan Caddis #16					■	■	■	■				
Sulphur #16					■	■						
March Brown #14					■							
Green Drake #12, 3X long (Spinner, Coffin Fly, 3X long)						■						
Light Cahill #14						■						
Brown Drake #12, 3X long						■						
Blue-winged Olive #18 & 20								■	■			
Tricos #24 (sporadic)								■	■	■		
Ants #16–20; Beetles #12–18; Grasshoppers #10–14							■	■	■			
Caterpillars #12, 3X long						■	■	■				

Lackawanna River

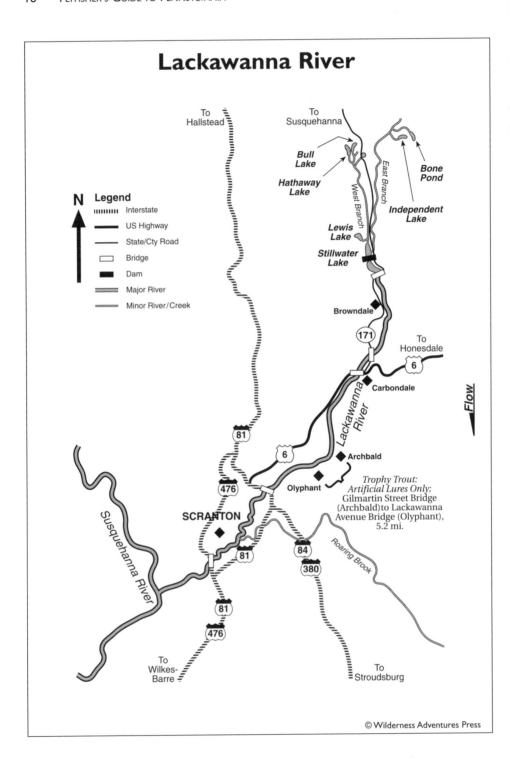

Legend

N

|||||||| Interstate

——— US Highway

——— State/Cty Road

▭ Bridge

■ Dam

═══ Major River

——— Minor River/Creek

To Hallstead

To Susquehanna

Bull Lake

Hathaway Lake

West Branch

East Branch

Bone Pond

Independent Lake

Lewis Lake

Stillwater Lake

Browndale

171

To Honesdale

6

Carbondale

Lackawanna River

Flow

81

6

Archbald

476

Olyphant

*Trophy Trout:
Artificial Lures Only;
Gilmartin Street Bridge
(Archbald) to Lackawanna
Avenue Bridge (Olyphant),
5.2 mi.*

SCRANTON

Susquehanna River

81

84

380

Roaring Brook

81

476

To Wilkes-Barre

To Stroudsburg

© Wilderness Adventures Press

LACKAWANNA RIVER

The Lackawanna, which runs through a coal mining area, is an excellent example of how a stream can be brought back to life through the efforts of dedicated cold-water fishing enthusiasts. This trout fishery has been slowly on the mend for years and is now returning to its former glory and getting better with age. The river isn't completely healed, especially in its lower reaches as it nears its confluence with the Susquehanna River. Acid mine drainage is still a problem but the river is holding its own and making progress in reducing damage from this pollutant.

A river with over 11 miles designated as wild trout water is nearly unheard of, but from the upper Carbondale city line downstream to SR 347, this stream is a wild trout fishery. A Trophy Trout project protects 5.2 miles of the wild trout water from the Gilmartin Street bridge in Archbald downstream to the Lackawanna Avenue bridge (SR0347) in Olyphant, with the exception of 0.7 miles from Deport Street bridge in Jessup, downstream to foot bridge in Robert Mellow Park.

Below the wild trout water, the Lackawanna is stocked by the PFBC. The river offers many faces, beginning as a scenic waterway with wild trout in a beautiful setting and then becoming an urban waterway. In Susquehanna County, the river provides excellent fishing. Its East and West Branches start in this county, flowing into Stillwater Lake, where the main stem begins. From there it parallels SR 171 to Browndale, at which point SR 1003 follows the road to Carbondale.

The special regulations section and wild trout water begin in Carbondale. To follow the stream to Archbald, take SR 1023 to Washington Avenue. Follow Main Street from Archbald to Scranton and then take US 11, which allows access via secondary roads. The Lackawanna empties into the Susquehanna near Upper Pittston.

The river is stocked in all the counties it flows through, except its very last leg in Luzerne County, where it enters the Susquehanna River. A large river, approximately 20 miles in length, this is one of the premier trout streams in the northeast, and offers good fishing throughout the year.

Depending on where you fish, a 5-weight rod is ideal for the majority of the river. Waders are necessary, and wading can be extremely treacherous in areas. My favorite sectors of this stream are found from Archbald upstream to the source.

Hatches are good here, but their numbers and species differ. The hatch chart is a overview of the hatches that occur in many sectors. Call ahead for more specific details about hatches and water conditions.

Lackawaxen River and Dyberry Creek

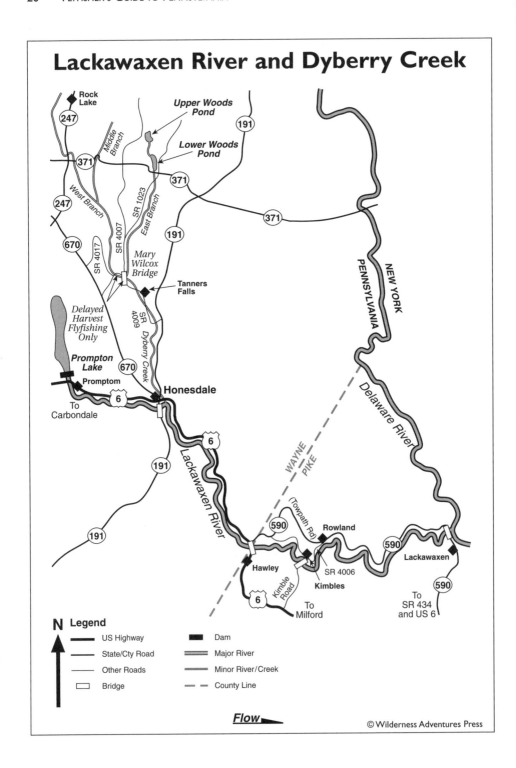

LACKAWAXEN RIVER

This famed river in its glory years had good numbers of wild trout and is still a river well worth checking out. The Lackawaxen is large, has plenty of room for fishermen, and travels through some of the most beautiful country in Pennsylvania.

Although the river warms up as it nears its confluence with the Delaware River, it is heavily stocked in both Wayne and Pike Counties by the PFBC. Many portions of the river are stocked with trout in both spring and fall. Unfortunately, despite the beauty of the area and the presence of wild and carryover trout, none of the approximately 30 miles of stream has any special regulations placed upon it.

Sections of the river with heavy canopy hold trout longer than would usually be expected in a river this size. Where the Lackawaxen's many coldwater tributaries enter the river, fishing remains good late into the season.

Beginning near Prompton in Wayne County, the river flows west to Honesdale before dropping southwest to enter Pike County. Access to the river is found on US 6 as it parallels the river to Hawley, situated on the county line. From Hawley, the stream runs west to join the Delaware River at the town of Lackawanna. From Kimbles to the mouth, SR 4006 runs next to the river through Pike County. Near Rowland SR 4006 meets Towpath Road and continues to follow the river to its mouth.

An angler hauls in a trout on a northeastern stream.

This is big water, where one can wade and cast at ease in many sectors, although wading can be difficult in some areas. I prefer a 9-foot for a 5-weight here, and waders are a must. The stream is often crowded in the spring of the year, but there are miles upon miles of water to test. This is one fine stream in spring, and when the foliage begins to warn of the approaching winter, it is unbeatable.

The Lackawaxen has some excellent hatches, particularly during the early season. However, I prefer to wait for the crowds to disperse, and although the elm span worm is nearly history now, a good imitation does bring trout to the surface. As the season progresses, a stream thermometer helps find the most productive water.

LACKAWANNA/LACKAWAXEN RIVER MAJOR HATCHES

Insect	J	F	M	A	M	J	J	A	S	O	N	D
Blue Quill #18				▬								
Quill Gordon #14				▬								
Hendrickson #14				▬								
Blue-winged Olive #14					▬							
Tan Caddis #16					▬▬▬▬							
Cream Cahill #18					▬			▬▬				
Light Cahill #14					▬							
March Brown #12					▬							
Sulphur #16					▬▬							
Green Drake, 3X long (Coffin Fly Spinner, sparse hatch)					▬							
Blue-winged Olive #20					▬▬▬							
Ants #16–20; Beetles #12–18; Grasshoppers #10–14							▬▬▬▬					
Caterpillars #12, 3X long							▬▬▬					
Other												
Floating Nymphs #16 & 18 (green, yellow, white)						▬▬▬▬▬						
Yellow Adams #14 & 16							▬▬▬▬					
Mosquito #12 & 14							▬▬▬▬					
Terrestrials and caterpillar patterns should always be in your fly box.												

ROARING BROOK

Roaring Brook defies the odds by being a Class A wild trout stream, despite the fact that it flows through Hollister Dam, then goes a short 3.9 miles before entering another impoundment, Elmhurst Reservoir.

Between the two reservoirs, there is a catch-and-release section, and there should be another on its upper reaches. From Elmhurst Reservoir downstream to the Lehigh River, Roaring Brook is heavily stocked with trout in both spring and fall by the PFBC.

There aren't too may places that can boast over 7 miles of wild trout water. Roaring Brook has an added bonus in that Elmhurst Reservoir protects streambred trout from mixing with the stocked trout below the dam. Like most wild trout streams, Roaring Brook varies from small to medium-sized and can easily be fished in hip boots in its upper reaches, although I prefer waders for fishing here. For those who like larger trout, the section below the dam will do nicely.

Roaring Brook's headwater is south of Hollister Dam near Henry Lake. The East Branch flows out of a small, unnamed lake located just over the line in Wayne County and joins Roaring Brook below Hollister Dam, which can be reached on secondary roads off SR 435. Below the dam, SR 435 parallels the creek to the catch-and-release area and Elmhurst Reservoir until it joins I-380 near Scranton. Roaring Brook ends where it joins the Lackawanna River in downtown Scranton. Watch for posted areas while fishing here.

In its upper and middle reaches, Roaring Brook is heavily canopied, so be sure to take inchworm and caterpillar patterns along. For rods, 7½- to 9-foot rods will do, and many prefer the shorter length on Roaring Brook.

ROARING BROOK MAJOR HATCHES

Insect	J	F	M	A	M	J	J	A	S	O	N	D
Blue Quill #18				■								
Quill Gordon #14				■								
Hendrickson #14				■								
Blue-winged Olive #14					■							
Tan Caddis #16					■	■	■	■				
Cream Cahill #18					■				■			
Light Cahill #14					■							
March Brown #12					■							
Gray Fox #12					■							
Midges #20–24 (all colors)					■	■	■	■				
Ants #16–20; Beetles #12–18; Grasshoppers #10–14							■	■	■			
Caterpillars #12, 3X long							■	■	■			
Other												
Floating Nymphs #16 & 18 (green, yellow, white)						■	■	■	■	■		
Yellow Adams #12 & 16							■	■	■	■		
Mosquito #12 &14							■	■	■	■		

*Terrestrials and caterpillar patterns should always be in your fly box.

DYBERRY CREEK

Beautiful scenery and cold, trout-filled water characterize this region. Many of the streams are small, prancing down steep mountainsides at breakneck speed and tumbling over breathtaking waterfalls. Streams that make it into the valleys slow down and widen, creating long glides and pools, and offer the angler a respite from the hiking and brush beating that many of the state's better streams require.

But some streams have become too wide due to the clearing of land in the valleys. The nature of a freestone stream is to take an ever-changing course as high volumes of water from spring runoffs erode streambanks over time, allowing the stream to take the easiest path. Between land being developed for commercial purposes and road building, we have pushed streams around to suit our needs rather than letting the streams find their own course.

By changing the nature of freestones and allowing them to widen, the water has become warmer and smallmouth bass have taken over the lower reaches. Although I love bass fishing, finding them in what had been coldwater streams is a sign that things are wrong. Small bronzebacks seldom achieve the growth rate they do in larger streams and lakes where the food supply is more abundant. Anglers, in turn, seldom fish for bass in these creeks, which have long been held in high esteem as coldwater fisheries.

The end result is that we have neither a top-notch bass nor a trout fishery—we have something in between that may well be considered borderline fishing. Streams stocked with trout confuse the issue since many anglers feel that a trout stream is a trout stream and a bass river is a bass river, and the two don't mix. But they do, and Dyberry could be a prime example. The severe droughts we have experienced at the end of this century may decide the fate of many streams, especially freestones.

Dyberry Creek is just one example of what has taken place on hundreds of coldwater streams in Pennsylvania. Better ways of handling urban sprawl need to be developed so that streamside vegetation and timber can be retained rather than stripped and replaced after great expense in time and money.

Dyberry Creek is a good stream, filled with deep pools and with plenty of room to cast freely. It is considered by many to be an early season stream that relies heavily upon stocking. However, some portions of the stream do hold fish throughout much of the season.

Dyberry begins at Tanner's Falls, where the East and West Branches meet to form the main stem. Dyberry is stocked heavily in the spring and fall by the PFBC. The better flyfishing lies within the DHFFO area located from the Mary Wilcox Bridge on SR 4007 upstream for 1 mile. There is good fishing to be found on the mile stretch that lies between the special regulations area and Tanner's Falls.

Dyberry flows approximately 7 miles to Honesdale, where it enters the Lackawaxen River. The East Branch is also stocked by the PFBC and finds its origin at a coldwater lake named Upper Woods Pond. Here, in the more canopied State Game

Drought has plagued Pennsylvania in recent years.

Lands, a fair number of wild browns can be found, as well. To reach the lower portion of the stream, take SR 4007. From there, SR 1023 then parallels the stream to Lower Woods Pond. The Branch is approximately 6 miles in length.

The West Branch is also stocked water beginning north of the town of Rock Lake. Access is available from SR 247 and 4017. Access here is more difficult and will require some hiking in to certain areas of the stream.

The Middle Branch is not stocked water and flows under SR 317 before joining the West Branch. The Middle Branch is just over a mile in length and does have some wild trout, but not enough to classify it as a Class A wild trout stream.

The main stem follows SR 191 north from Honesdale. Turn onto SR 4009 to reach SR 4007 near Tanner's Falls. The stream and its branches offer a good variety of fishing at least until mid-June, and then it picks up again in October.

To fish Dyberry, take 4- and 5-weights, and because the water runs thin in many places, I like leaders with light tippets at least 9 feet in length.

DYBERRY CREEK MAJOR HATCHES

Insect	J	F	M	A	M	J	J	A	S	O	N	D
Blue Quill #18				▪								
Quill Gordon #14				▪								
Hendrickson #14				▪								
Gray Fox #12					▪							
Tan Caddis #16					▪▪▪▪▪▪							
Cream Cahill #18					▪				▪▪			
Light Cahill #14					▪							
March Brown #12					▪							
Ants #16–20; Beetles #12–18; Grasshoppers #10–14						▪▪▪▪▪▪						
Caterpillars #12, 3X long						▪▪▪▪▪▪						
Other												
Floating Nymphs #16 & 18 (green, yellow, white)					▪▪▪▪▪▪▪▪							
Yellow Adams #14 & 16							▪▪▪▪					
Mosquito #12 & 14						▪▪▪▪▪▪						
Terrestrials and caterpillar patterns should always be in your fly box.												

BIG BUSHKILL CREEK

Found in Monroe County, Big Bushkill Creek is a spectacular sight and an important tributary of the Delaware River. The stream is 12 miles in length and managed for trout. Six miles of the stream are managed under DHFFO regulations, all on the Resica Falls Scout Reservation property. Restrictions do not apply to 200 yards of water above and below a picturesque waterfall on the property.

The water here is absolutely beautiful and the fishing is good, however, it is an early season stream and warms considerably by July 4th. Access is limited and parking is available on the reservation. Registration at the Boy Scout Headquarters is required.

Hiking is required to get on the stream's lower reaches, so it is important to bring suitable footwear. I prefer felt-soled waders for spring fishing and suggest a wader bag for those willing to walk. The bag may then be used for storing hiking boots.

The stream is heavily stocked and appears to hold carryover browns. A wading staff is suggested, both for hazardous wading conditions and for hiking into the area.

Big Bushkill is accessible from SR 402 where it crosses above Resica Falls.

BIG BUSHKILL CREEK MAJOR HATCHES

Insect	J	F	M	A	M	J	J	A	S	O	N	D
Blue Quill #18				▄								
Quill Gordon #14				▄								
Hendrickson #14				▄▄								
Tan Caddis #16					▄▄▄▄							
Gray Fox #12					▄							
March Brown #12						▄						
Light Cahill #14						▄						
Cream Cahill #18								▄▄				
Ants #16–20; Beetles #12–18; Grasshoppers #10–14							▄▄▄					
Caterpillars #12, 3X long							▄▄▄					
Other												
Floating Nymphs #16–24 (green, yellow, white)												
Yellow Adams #16 & 18							▄▄▄					

Floating nymphs and beadheads in a variety of colors—include them in your fly box.

BRODHEAD CREEK

What may be the wave of the future of quality trout water has taken place on the Brodhead. Like Spruce Creek and other named streams within the state, private waters have begun to spring up. Private clubs and private access through guides or fly shops are scattered throughout the Pocono region of the state.

The once famous Brodhead is posted extensively, leaving the Brodhead a wonderful stream to fish by members, but a stream with shrinking mileage open to the public with each passing year. The Pocono Region of the state is experiencing tremendous growth that is ever encroaching on the waters of the region.

As a recreational community, the growth here has been phenomenal, but the recreational opportunities are now so varied that it does not create a tremendous amount of overcrowding on area trout streams after the first week of the season.

The stream begins near Spruce Mountain, the Middle Branch near Mt. Wismer, just east of 447. The Middle Branch is considered Class A wild trout water, but access is limited. The two streams join near Coveville, and 447 parallels the stream to within the outer limits of East Stroudsburg, where Rt. 191 follows it to I-80.

The Brodhead has always been a famed stream, and anglers from all over the world came to it in the 1950s and 1960s to test its water. It is a stream with character, with medium size to large boulders marking its runs. As the private water increases and Stroudsburg expands, there may be less water open to the public than now, as I pen this book. However, the stream has prolific hatches and, if anglers follow it north from Stroudsburg, they will find open water that holds some excellent fishing for carryover and stocked trout.

Certainly wild trout do exist with the influence of coldwater streams that enter the flow along its path. The fishing can be excellent, and the Brodhead should be added to your list of streams to fish when in the Poconos. Because I am unwilling to commit myself to the amount of water that will be open to public fishing within the next few years, it is best to follow the stream north of East Stroudsburg and fish it wherever a No Trespassing sign is not encountered. You should still be able to find miles of good water to fish.

You will need waders, at least a long sleeved shirt, and a rod matched to a 4- or 5-weight line.

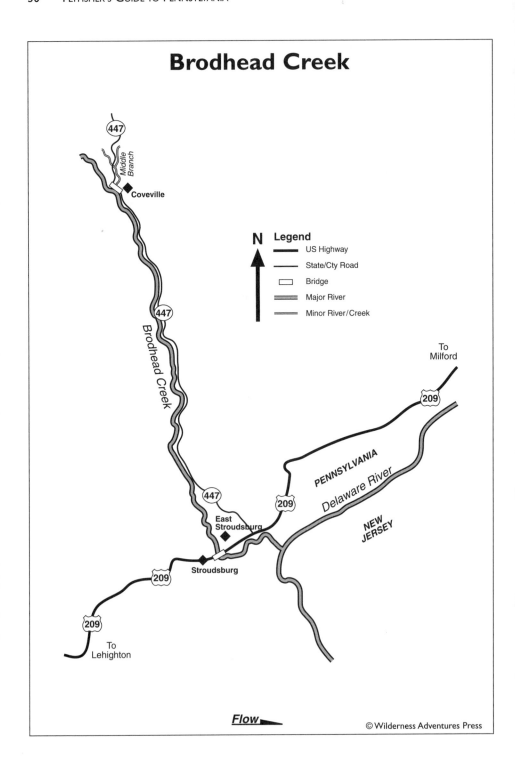

Brodhead Creek

447

Middle Branch

◆ Coveville

N

Legend
US Highway
State/Cty Road
Bridge
Major River
Minor River/Creek

447

Brodhead Creek

To
Milford

209

PENNSYLVANIA

Delaware River

447

209

East
Stroudsburg ◆

NEW
JERSEY

209 ◆ Stroudsburg

209

To
Lehighton

Flow

© Wilderness Adventures Press

BRODHEAD CREEK MAJOR HATCHES

Insect	J	F	M	A	M	J	J	A	S	O	N	D
Blue Quill #18				▬								
Quill Gordon #14				▬								
Hendrickson #14			▬									
Blue-winged Olive #14					▬							
Tan Caddis #16					▬	▬	▬	▬				
Cream Cahill #18					▬				▬			
Light Cahill #14					▬							
March Brown #12					▬							
Gray Fox #12					▬							
Sulphur #16					▬							
Ants #16–20; Beetles #12–18; Grasshoppers #10–14							▬	▬	▬			
Caterpillars #12, 3X long							▬	▬	▬			
Other												
Floating Nymphs #16 & 18 (green, yellow, white)					▬	▬	▬	▬	▬	▬		
Yellow Adams #14 & 16							▬	▬	▬			
Mosquito #12 & 14							▬	▬	▬			

HICKORY RUN

Hickory Run begins in Hickory Run State Park, much of which has been set aside as a natural area, meaning that you will need to walk. From where it joins the Lehigh River upstream for 1.6 miles, Hickory Run is managed under catch-and-release regulations. The stream begins in the boulder field that is one of the main attractions of the park.

This is a small stream with a lot of canopy, and the well-marked catch-and-release area is easily found. The same section of stream is designated as a wild trout stream and offers a lot of native brook trout and wild browns. Hickory Run seldom exceeds 20 feet in width and is a fine example of a Pennsylvania wild trout stream. This is a beautiful setting, and the park has helped preserve a remnant of the region's virgin hemlock and white pine forests. This little gem flows for only 4 miles, but is well worth the visit.

Hickory is easily fished in hip boots, and light line rods will serve well here, as will drab-colored clothing and a stealthy approach so that rising fish won't see you as you cast. I like this stream because of its natural beauty and its wealth of wild trout, which at times can only be seen as wavering dark shadows on the gravel-strewn bottom.

The park and Hickory Run are easy to find: from I-80 take Exit 41 (Hickory Run State Park), then drive east on SR 534 for 6 miles. From the northeast extension of the Pennsylvania Turnpike (I-476), take Exit 35 and drive west on SR 940 for 3 miles, then turn east on SR 534, which parallels Hickory Run, for 6 miles.

Hickory Run State Park is situated in the western foothills of the Pocono Mountains and covers 15,500 acres. If you don't like small streams, forget this one. But if sneaking up on wild trout in a beautiful setting is your idea of an ideal fishing day, definitely check it out. Hatches and trout numbers are good, and to avoid any crowding, plan a weekday trip.

For information concerning camping in the area and testing all the streams here, contact: Hickory Run State Park, Department of Conservation and Natural Resources, RR 1, Box 81, White Haven, PA 18661-9712; telephone 570-443-0400.

HAYES (BLACK) CREEK

Black Creek, better known locally as Hayes Creek, has recently been designated Class A wild trout water from the mouth, where it joins the Lehigh River, upstream for 3 miles to an area called the Weider Tract. It is nearly 6 miles in total length and is unusual in that its lower reaches have been classified as wild trout rather than the upper section, as is usually the case.

Its source is Mosey Wood Pond, and it flows northwest before turning southwest to enter the Lehigh River below Drifton Junction Station. The stream is accessible from SR 534 in the lower section and close to SR 940 in the midsections. A remote walk-in stream, for the most part, it is full of native brookies and wild brown trout. Although a small stream, it is well worth its weight in gold.

This diminutive water is dotted with nice runs and deep pools. It is important that all trout are returned here. Running under a heavy canopy and secured by Game Lands and Hickory Run State Park, the majority of the stream should remain healthy. But killing fish here is absolutely unnecessary and could be one of the only things capable of destroying this excellent stretch of water. I offer this as a place to find good hatches and a calming environment for those who seek places where wild and native trout still reside in a setting that is suitable to them.

HICKORY RUN AND HAYES CREEK MAJOR HATCHES

Insect	J	F	M	A	M	J	J	A	S	O	N	D
Blue Quill #18				■								
Quill Gordon #14				■								
Hendrickson #14				■								
Gray Fox #12					■							
Tan Caddis #16					■	■	■	■				
March Brown #12					■							
Light Cahill #14					■							
Ants #16–20; Beetles #12–18; Grasshoppers #10–14						■	■	■	■			
Caterpillars # 12, 3X long						■	■	■	■			
Other												
Yellow Adams #16 & 18						■	■	■	■			
Mosquito #12 & 14						■	■	■	■	■		
Terrestrials and caterpillar patterns should always be in your fly box.												

Hickory Run and Mud Run

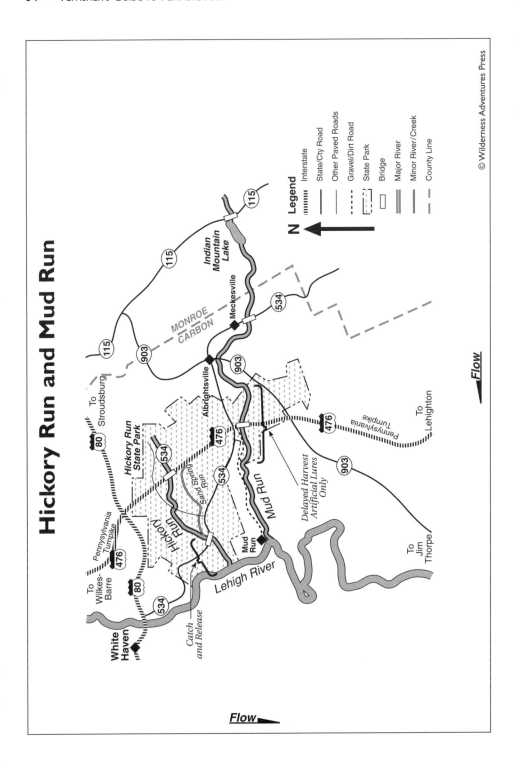

MUD RUN

Mud Run is well worth a visit, not only for flyfishing but for it beautiful setting. The stream is approximately 7 miles long, and during its journey through Hickory Run State Park, is just a perfect trout stream. Where the stream runs through Mud Run Natural Area, which is within the state park, its banks are lined with rhododendron, eastern hemlock, and a mature hardwood forest.

Mud Run's source is located just over the Carbon County line in Monroe County just east of SR 115. It flows through Indian Mountain Lake, Meckesville, and Albrightsville, and then under I-76 (Pennsylvania Turnpike) into Hickory Run State Park.

The Delayed Harvest Artificial Lures Only (DHALO) section is located in the state park and is accessible from SR 534. This section begins as a docile stream but soon starts dropping into deep pools in some of the most rugged and beautiful country anywhere. This area is filled with large boulders that help make a good pool-to-riffle ratio.

To reach the better fishing, plan on hiking in with a daypack and pack rod suitable for a 3-weight line. Because it is next to impossible to wade, I take a rugged pair of hiking boots that I expect to get wet and a dry pair for the hike out. I also take food, water, and a flashlight along, since I am usually in no hurry to leave this spot. Searching patterns, inchworm imitations, and gypsy moth caterpillars work well here. Mud Run does have some excellent hatches, but because they can be unpredictable, take woolly buggers, green weenies, sparse streamers, and anything else that might bring trout to the net so that your hike in won't be wasted.

Although the PFBC stocks the stream heavily, there are enough wild brown and native brook trout to keep the fishing interesting. This is definitely a place to practice catch and release.

The stream enters the Lehigh River at the village of Mud Run, and the lower reaches offer some of the better fishing. From the mouth, access is blocked by private land, so if you want to fish this area, it can be a long hike but, in my opinion, a worthwhile effort. Hickory Run State Park is accessible from SR 534.

MUD RUN MAJOR HATCHES

Insect	J	F	M	A	M	J	J	A	S	O	N	D
Blue Quill #18				▬								
Quill Gordon #14				▬								
Hendrickson #14				▬								
Blue-winged Olive #14					▬							
Tan Caddis #16					▬▬▬▬▬▬▬▬▬							
Sulphur #16					▬							
Light Cahill #14					▬							
March Brown #12					▬							
Midges #20–24 (tan, white, brown, olive)				▬▬▬▬▬▬▬▬▬▬▬▬▬								
Ants #16–20; Beetles #12–18; Grasshoppers #10–14							▬▬▬▬▬▬					
Caterpillars #12, 3X long							▬▬▬▬▬▬					
Inchworm #12, 3X long							▬▬▬▬					
Other												
Floating Nymphs #16–24 (green, yellow, white)					▬▬▬▬▬▬▬▬							
Yellow Adams #16 & 18							▬▬▬▬▬					
Mosquito #12 & 14							▬▬▬▬▬▬					

Terrestrial and caterpillar patterns should always be in your fly box.

FISHING CREEK

In Pennsylvania, it seems that each community named any nearby creek that held fish "Fishing Creek." Or if a stream had trout, it became Trout Run, Trout Brook, Trout Creek, etc. While this naming convention works well within a small area, it becomes problematic when one realizes that it is used throughout the state. Anglers searching for either "Fishing" or "Trout" Creek could be directed almost anywhere in Pennsylvania. Perhaps someday in the future, someone will write a book that locates every "Fishing" or "Trout" Creek in Pennsylvania, but until that time, follow directions carefully. This particular Fishing Creek is located in Columbia County and flows into the Susquehanna River. If someone gives you directions for a Fishing Creek and you find yourself driving across the state on a wild goose chase, I sure don't want to be held responsible.

Wayne Yorks, a former commissioner of the PFBC, showed this Fishing Creek to me with rod in hand. Wayne is an excellent flyfisher and warned me that during the

A typical boulder-filled stream in northeast Pennsylvania.

Fishing Creek

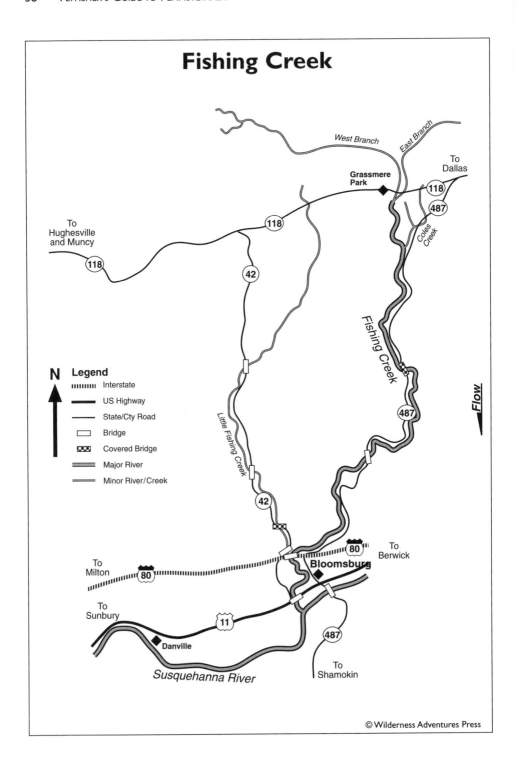

© Wilderness Adventures Press

low flows of early summer, trout would not be easy to take, and he was right. We fished the catch-and-release section that runs for 1.1 miles from the confluence of East and West Branches of Fishing Creek at Grassmere Park downstream to the lower Gary Cook property line. The area is full of fish, stocked by both the area sportsmen's club and the PFBC. It was a sunny but brisk day, and caddis filled the air. As the temperatures warmed up around 10AM, the fish began rising in earnest.

The fish took my grizzly caddis fly one after another, and when I shared the pattern with Wayne, he began enjoying the same success. The number of trout taken doesn't matter, it just proves that fish are found here in good numbers.

This Fishing Creek begins above SR 118 north of Grassmere Park. The East and West Branches join before entering the park, bringing volume and cold water to Fishing Creek, making it possible for upper sections of Fishing Creek to support wild trout.

Fishing Creek is stocked from Coles Creek downstream to Bloomsburg where it enters the Susquehanna River. Be aware, however, that posting is common along the stream, and open water may be closed one year and open the next. It is the policy of the PFBC not to stock water posted against fishing. The West Branch of Fishing Creek is a stocked stream as well, and holds a good number of carryover and wild trout. Closer to its source in Sullivan County, West Fishing Creek turns into a Class A wild trout stream.

As in the case with nearly all freestones, the closer to the source the colder the water and that means better trout fishing. This stream is cold and maintains summer temperatures that would make most freestones blush. It holds a good number of trout from its source downstream for 12 to 13 miles, where warm water reduces their numbers.

Waders are needed to fish the stream, and a 3- to 5-weight outfit will do. I prefer longer rods for this stream, but that is my personal preference.

The stream stretches for 18.5 miles through Columbia County and is extremely easy to find by following SR 487 from Bloomsburg to Benton. North of Benton, take SR 4049 to Grassmere Park.

FISHING CREEK MAJOR HATCHES

Insect	J	F	M	A	M	J	J	A	S	O	N	D
Blue Quill #18				▬								
Quill Gordon #14				▬								
Hendrickson #14			▬									
Blue-winged Olive #14					▬							
Tan Caddis #16					▬▬▬▬▬▬▬							
Sulphur #16					▬							
Light Cahill #14					▬							
March Brown #12				▬								
Blue-winged Olive #20							▬					
Midges #20–24 (tan, white, brown, olive)				▬▬▬▬▬▬▬▬▬▬▬▬▬								
Ants #16–20; Beetles #12–18; Grasshoppers #10–14							▬▬▬▬▬					
Caterpillars #12, 3X long							▬▬▬▬▬					
Other												
Floating Nymphs #16–24 (green, yellow, white)						▬▬▬▬▬▬▬▬						
Yellow Adams #16 & 18							▬▬▬▬					
Mosquito #12 & 14							▬▬▬▬▬					

Terrestrials and caterpillar patterns should always be in your fly box.

MEHOOPANY CREEK

With its mix of good holding water and excellent pools, Mehoopany Creek offers excellent flyfishing, especially for those who like placing a dry fly on slow-moving waters. Temperatures remain within the trout's tolerance level due to the many cold-water tributaries along the creek's path.

Although the water warms up as the creek draws closer to the Susquehanna River, brown trout find their way to coldwater tributaries and springs when this occurs. Here the stream is stocked by the PFBC, but wild trout, carryovers, and native brook trout can be found at the headwaters and throughout the watershed.

Mehoopany begins in Wyoming County north of Shale Pit Road just above the Luzerne County line. It runs north and then northeast through State Game Lands 57 and can be followed north along SR 3001 from Somer Brook to SR 87. It follows SR 87 east to the Susquehanna River at the town of North Mehoopany.

Despite mining practices in and the around the area, this region does have a lot of wild trout, and the many good tributary streams flowing into Mehoopany Creek harbor wild and native trout and act as coldwater sanctuaries for stocked fish, especially brown trout. While it is thought that stocked brook trout are caught too easily to carry over and reproduce, nobody seems to know what happens to rainbows that escape being taken. There are those who believe that their migratory instincts lead them downstream into waters too warm for their existence. This theory may be valid, but in my experience, rainbows simply succumb to the environment even when there are dams on the river with water cold enough to support them. This seems to be true on the Mehoopany.

This creek has a good number of hatches and is enjoyable to fish. During the early season, trout can be brought to hand anywhere along its 10-mile course. I fish closer to the headwaters as the season progresses, where trout seek cooler water. Especially on freestones, I believe a stream thermometer is of more importance than fly selection.

Take waders and a long-sleeved shirt for the cool evenings on Mehoopany. Also, be sure to add attractor patterns to your fly box. When there are no hatches in progress, search the water to find trout and bring them to the surface. A 9-foot rod carrying a 4- or 5-weight line will serve well here.

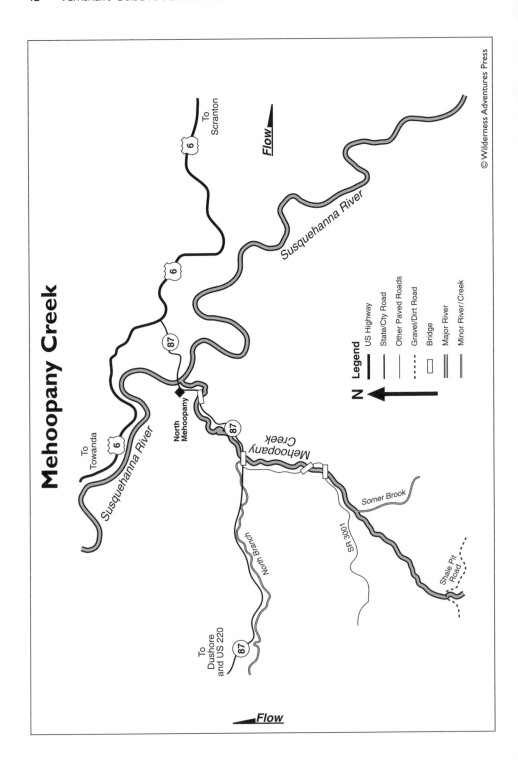

MEHOOPANY CREEK MAJOR HATCHES

Insect	J	F	M	A	M	J	J	A	S	O	N	D
Blue Quill #18				■								
Quill Gordon #14				■								
Hendrickson #14				■								
Blue-winged Olive #14					■							
Tan Caddis #16					■	■	■	■				
Cream Cahill #18					■	■			■			
Light Cahill #14					■	■						
March Brown #12				■	■							
Ants #16–20; Beetles #12–18; Grasshoppers #10–14						■	■	■	■			
Caterpillars #12, 3X long						■	■	■	■			
Other												
Floating Nymphs #16 & 18 (green, yellow, white)					■	■	■	■	■	■		
Yellow Adams #14 & 16						■	■	■	■			
Mosquito #12 & 14						■	■	■	■	■		

Summary of Approved Trout Waters
and Special Regulation Areas for the Northeast

Bradford County	Section / Regulations
Schrader Creek	
Little Schrader Creek	
Seeley Creek	
South Creek	
Sunfish Pond	
Sugar Run	
Wysox Creek	
Tuscarora Creek	
Sugar Creek	East Troy to confluence of south branch of Sugar Creek
Sugar Creek, North Branch	Mouth upstream to Fairgrounds
Towanda Creek	SR 3008 downstream to T- 350 *DHALO:* 1.7 miles, from SR 3001 downstream to T-350

Carbon County	Section / Regulations
Aquashicola Creek	
Big Bear Creek	
Buckwha Creek	
Drakes Creek	
Francis Walters Dam	
Hickory Run	*Catch and Release:* 1.5 miles, from Sand Spring Run downstream to the mouth
Hunter Creek	
Lehigh Canal (Long Run Level)	
Lizzard Creek	
Mahoning Creek	
Mauch Chunk Creek	
Mud Run	*DHALO:* 2.5 miles, in Hickory Run State Park
Pohopoco Creek	
Sand Spring Run	
Stony Creek	

Columbia County	Section / Regulations
Beaver Run	
Briar Creek	
Briar Creek, West Branch	

Briar Creek Lake	
Fishing Creek	Light Street to Grassmere Park *Catch and Release:* 1.1 mile, from the confluence of East and West Branches of Fishing Creek at Grassmere Park downstream to the lower Gary Cook property line
Little Fishing Creek	Mouth upstream to Talmar Road
Mugser Run	
Roaring Creek	
Scotch Run	
West Creek.	

Lackawanna County	Section / Regulations
Aylesworth Creek	
Gardners Creek	
Lackawanna River	
Lehigh River	
Lackawanna Lake	
Lackawanna River	*Trophy Trout Project:* 5.2 miles, from Gilmartin Street Bridge in Archbald downstream to Lackawanna Avenue bridge (SR347) in Olyphant with the exception of 0.7 miles from Deport Street bridge in Jessup downstream to foot bridge in Robert Mellow Park
Merli-Sarnoski Lake	
Panther Creek	*Catch and Release:* 2.5 miles, from the headwaters downstream to the mouth
Roaring Brook	
Roaring Spring	*Catch and Release:* 3.9 miles, from Hollisterville Dam downstream to the Elmhurst Reservoir
Spring Brook	Catch and Release: 2.4 miles, from Watres Reservoir downstream to the Nesbitt Reservoir
Wallenpaupack Creek, West Branch.	
Tunkhannock Creek, South Branch	*DHALO:* 1.0 mile, from US 6 downstream through Keystone College Campus
Luzerne County	
Francis E. Walter Reservoir (Bear Creek Reservoir)	
Harveys Creek	*DHALO:* 1.5 miles, from Pavlick Road (T-497) upstream to Jackson Road (T-812)
Kitchen Creek	
Lake Francis	
Lake Irena	
Lake Lily	

Lackawanna County (cont.)	Section / Regulations
Lake Took-A-While	
Lehigh River	
Moon Lake	
Nescopeck Creek	*DHALO:* 2.4 miles, from the upstream boundary of State Game Lands #187 downstream
Pine Creek	
Sutton Creek (Coray Creek)	
Wapwallopen Creek	
Wrights Creek	

Monroe County	Section / Regulations
Appenzell Creek	
Aquashicola Creek	
Brodhead Creek	First railroad bridge above the mouth upstream
Buchwha Creek	
Bushkill Creek	*DHFFO:* 6.1 miles, off SR 402 on Ressica Falls Scout Reservation property except 200 yards below the falls
Dotters Creek	
Hidden Lake	
Lake Creek	
Lehigh River	
McMichaels Creek	
Pocono Creek	
Princess Run	
Snow Hill Dam	
Tobyhanna Creek	*DHALO:* 1 mile, from the confluence of Still Swamp Run downstream to the PP&L service bridge
Tobyhanna Lake	

Montour County	Section / Regulations
Kase Branch	
Mahoning Creek	
Mauses Creek	

Pike County	Section / Regulations
Bushkill Creek	
Decker Brook	SR 0006 downstream to lower limit of SGL
Dingmans Creek	*DHALO:* 1.5 miles, from the base of Deer Leap Falls downstream to Dingmans Falls
Fairview Lake	
Lackawaxen River	

Lake Loch Lomond	
Lake Minisink	
Little Bushkill Creek	Mouth upstream to lower limit of Charles Peters Estate, lower limit of Lehman Lake Club property to upper limit of Little Bushkill Hunting and Fishing Club property
Little Mud Pond	
Lower Lake in Promised Land State Park	
Mast Hope Creek	
Middle Branch Creek	
Mill Brook (Kellaman Creek)	
Saw Creek	Porter Lake property to Saw Creek Club property
Shohola Creek	SR 0739 to lower limit of SGL 180
Toms Creek	*Catch and Release:* 2.1 miles; from the Delaware Water Gap National recreational Area boundary downstream to the mouth

Sullivan County	**Section / Regulations**
Black Creek	
Double Run	
Elk Creek	
Fishing Creek, West Branch	
Hoagland Branch	Mouth upstream 4 miles
Hunters Lake	
Kings Creek	
Loyalsock Creek	
Mill Creek	
Little Loyalsock Creek	Mouth upstream to SR 87
Mehoopany Creek, North Fork	
Muncy Creek	
Pole Bridge Run	
Rock Run	

Susquehanna County	**Section / Regulations**
Fall Brook	
Gaylord Creek	
Lackawanna River, West Branch	
Lackawanna River	
Martin Creek	
Meshoppen Creek	
Meshoppen Creek, West Branch	
Nine Partners Creek	

Susquehanna County (cont.)	Section / Regulations
Quaker Lake	
Salt Lick Creek	*DHALO:* 1.6 miles, from the downstream boundary of State Game Lands #35 upstream to the bridge on T-638
Silver Creek	
Snake Creek	
Starrucca Creek	
Tunkhannock Creek	
Tunkhannock Creek, East Branch	
Wyalusing Creek, East Branch	
Wyalusing Creek , Middle Branch	
Wyalusing Creek, North Branch.	

Wayne County	Section / Regulations
Butternut Creek	*DHALO:* 2.5 miles, from SR 3002 downstream to mouth
Equiunk Creek	
Dyberry Creek	Honesdale upstream to Tanner's Falls *DHFFO:* 0.8 mile, one mile below Tanner's Falls downstream to Mary Wilcox Bridge, SR 4007
Dyberry Creek, East Branch	
DyberryCreek, West Branch	
Holberts Creek	
Hollister Creek	
Wallenpaupack Creek, West Branch	
Jones Creek	
Lackawanna River	
Lackawaxen River	
Lackawaxen River, West Branch	
Long Pond	
Rose Pond Brook	
Shehawken Creek	
Upper Woods Pond	
Van Auken Creek	
Wallenpaupack Creek, West Branch	*DHALO:* 1.6 miles, from 0.6 mile downstream from the Jones Creek confluence downstream to the SR 3009 bridge

This nice trout was taken from a Pocono area stream.

Wyoming County	Section / Regulations
Bowman Creek	*DHFFO:* 1 mile, from the vicinity of SR 292 downstream to near the confluence with Marsh Creek
Horton Creek	
Lake Winola	
Leonard Creek	
Mehoopany Creek	
Mehoopany Creek, North Fork	
Meshoppen Creek	
Meshoppen Creek, West Branch	
Oxbow Lake	
Riley Creek	
Tunkhannock Creek, South Branch	DHALO: 1.0 mile, from US 6 downstream through Keystone College Campus

Northeast Hub Cities
Honesdale
Population – 5,200

ACCOMMODATIONS
Brookside Country Cabins, RR 191 Box 42100 / 717-253-1038
Deerledge Motel, RR 5 Box 1360 / 570-253-3629
Fife & Drum Motor Inn, 100 Terrace Street / 570-253-1392
Grandview Motel, 160 Grandview Avenue / 570-253-4744
Wayne Hotel, 1202 Main Street / 570-253-3290
Willow Pond Inn, RR 1 Box 1210 / 570-253-3930

CAMPGROUNDS
Hideaway Lakes Camping / 570-253-9940
Ponderosa Pines Camp, Alden Lake Road / 570-253-2080

RESTAURANTS
Bartan's Family Restaurant, Route 652 / 570-253-3186
Bernadette Seafood House, RR 4 Box 940 / 570-729-7945
Coffee Grinder, 526 Main Street / 570-253-2285
Country Corners Restaurant, RR 3 Box 2960 / 570-253-4548

FLY SHOPS
Northeast Flyfishers, 923 Main Street / 570-253-9780
Delaware River Fly Shop, Inc., HC 1 Box 1061 (Starlight) / 570-635-5983
River Essentials, HC 1 Box 1025 (Starlight) / 570-635-5900

CAR RENTAL
Enterprise Rent-A-Car, 401 Park Street / 570-253-3844

AIR SERVICE
See Scranton

MEDICAL
See Scranton

FOR MORE INFORMATION
Chamber of Commerce
303 Commercial Street
Honesdale, PA 18431
570-253-1960

Scranton
Population – 80,000

ACCOMMODATIONS
Days Inn, 4130 Birney Avenue / 570-457-6713
Diskin's Hotel, 2716 Birney Avenue / 570-963-0770
Econo Lodge, 1175 Kane Street / 570-348-1000
Hampton Inn, 22 Montage Mountain Road / 570-342-7002
Hotel Sun, 410 Cedar Avenue / 570-344-4785
Quality Inn, 1946 Scranton Carbondale Hwy / 570-383-9979
Radisson Hotel, 700 Lackawanna Avenue / 570-342-8300
Trotters Motel, 4217 Birney Avenue / 570-457-6732
West Side Hotel, 129 S Main Avenue / 570-961-1978

RESTAURANTS
Glider Diner, 890 Providence Road / 717-343-8036
Cooper's Seafood House, 701 North Washington Avenue / 717-346-6883
Boulevard Café, 1800 Boulevard Avenue / 570-343-4770
Applebee's Neighborhood Grill, 3 Terry Drive #103 / 570-342-2781
Dougherty's Restaurant, 1243 Capouse Avenue / 570-346-8488
La Trattoria Restaurant, 522 Moosic Street / 570-961-1504
Scanlan's, 532 Spruce Street / 570-348-1133

FLY SHOPS
Bob's Flies and More, 2727 Rannsom Road (Clarks Summit) / 570-347-7206

AUTO RENTAL
Budget Rent-A-Car, Route 6 / 717-348-6772
Enterprise Rent-A-Car, 1231 Wyoming Avenue / 570-348-2040
National Car Rental, 4500 Birney Avenue / 570-654-6208
Northern Car & Truck Rental, 626 West Lackawanna Avenue / 570-346-3300
Thrifty Car Rental, 25 Lackawanna Avenue / 717-344-0722

AIR SERVICE
Wilkes-Barre/Scranton Airport, 100 Terminal Road # 221 (Avoca) / 570-457-7371

MEDICAL
Moses Taylor Hospital, 1029 North Main Avenue / 570-969-9378

FOR MORE INFORMATION
Chamber of Commerce
222 Mulberry Street
Scranton, PA 18503
570-342-7711

Stroudsburg
Population – 2,200

ACCOMMODATIONS
American House Hotel, 777 Main Street / 570-421-9746
Colony Motor Lodge, 1863 West Main Street / 570-421-3790
Days Inn, 100 Park Avenue / 570-424-1771
Fox Hill Motel, Route 611 / 570-424-8724
Sheraton, 1220 West Main Street / 570-424-1930
Walter's Motel, 2011 West Main Street / 570-424-1862

CAMPGROUNDS
Arrowhead Campground, Beaver Valley Road / 570-992-7949
Pocono Vacation Park Campgrounds, RR 5 / 570-424-2587

RESTAURANTS
Besecker's Diner, 1427 North 5th Street / 570-421-6193
Ciro's Restaurant, 728 Main Street / 570-476-2476
Country Pheasant, Main & 7th Street / 717-421-2200
Evergreens, 1220 West Main Street / 570-424-1930
Everybody's, 905 Main Street / 570-424-0896
Fallano's at Cherry Valley, Route 191 South / 570-992-5107
Hunt Club Restaurant, 1 Village Circle / 717-420-0400
Key City Diner, 1947 West Main Street / 570-421-5903
Sarah Street Grill, 5th & Sarah Street / 570-424-9120

FLY SHOPS
Windsor's Sport Shop, 348 North 9th Street / 717-424-0938
Dunkelbergers Sports, 585 Main Street at 6th / 717-421-7950
Al Caucci Flyfishing, 38 Chestnut Ridge, Tannersville 717-629-2962

AUTO RENTAL
Enterprise Rent-A-Car, 1232 West Main Street / 570-424-9442

AIRPORTS
Philadelphia International Airport / 215-492-3000

MEDICAL
Pocono Medical Center, 206 East Brown Street (East Stroudsburg) / 570-421-4000

FOR MORE INFORMATION
Chamber of Commerce
556 Main Street
Stroudsburg, PA 18360
570-421-4433

Southeast Pennsylvania

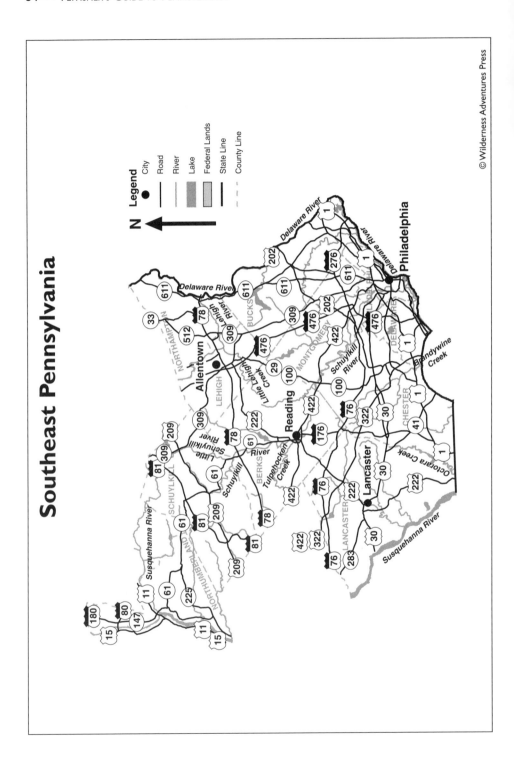

Southeast Pennsylvania

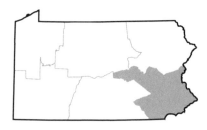

Pennsylvania's southeastern region is a wonderful blend of limestone and freestone streams. Its terrain varies from urban and suburban settings to remnants of rural areas. At first glance, this doesn't seem a likely setting for trout water, or even warmwater, since it can also be tainted by the industries that drive the area's economy. Concentrated urban settings do not generally attract those seeking flyfishing waters.

However, residents of this region have recognized that coldwater and warmwater fisheries are an important asset. Considerable resources have been committed to preserving and enhancing this water resource, and the results have been worth the effort.

In the past, water pollution by Philadelphia's industries had a devastating effect on the area's fisheries, but progress toward recovery is increasing with each passing year. Fish ladders, which allow passageways for anadromous fish, are now in place on both the Delaware and Lehigh Rivers, and residents are demanding more of them. The results have been outstanding, with shad and stripers becoming more abundant than ever in both rivers.

Consider Allentown and Bethlehem, where pledges have been made to make trout fishing better in community parks and money has been allocated to make this pledge a reality. The commitment to clean water and habitat, necessary ingredients for good fishing water, is firmly entrenched in this area of the state. There are many reasons for this commitment, and it seems that a majority of residents want to protect and preserve the uncontaminated resources and to rebuild those that have been damaged.

The challenges of nonpoint pollution from extensive farming, road runoff, and development are not all resolved, and the reclamation and preservation of water will need to be carried on by generations to follow.

There is a trend here that seems apparent in many of the state's sectors where streams have been ruined. Since moving on to greener pastures is not a viable option, it is apparent that residents in areas like Philadelphia and Pittsburgh are extremely appreciative of those quiet little getaways close to home.

Pennsylvanians do not have the free time they once enjoyed. Escaping to the state's northeast and northcentral sectors for a fishing getaway is not as easy as it once was. Today, the need to go elsewhere is diminishing as many southeastern residents find the fishing at home to be as good or better than other places.

With shad, stripers, muskie, smallmouth, largemouth, and trout within a short commute of home, why travel farther? I find it interesting, as I'm sure others do, that flyfishers are coming south to fish the now famous waters of this area. Few of the state's flyfishers have not tested the waters here, and most return time and again...and not only for its historic spring shad runs.

Little Lehigh Creek

Lehigh River

ALLENTOWN

To Bethlehem

To Philadelphia

To Pottstown

To Lehighton

To Hamburg

To Kutztown

Brookside Road

Mill Creek Road

Spring Creek Road

Little Lehigh Creek

Meritztown Road

Centennial Road

LEHIGH
BERKS

Heritage Trout Angling: Flyfishing Only, Barbless Hooks, Catch and Release; Fish Hatchery Road Bridge to 24th Street Bridge

Delayed Harvest Flyfishing Only: T-508 Bridge downstream to T-510 (Millrace Road) Bridge

© Wilderness Adventures Press

Legend

- Interstate
- US Highway
- State/Cty Road
- Other Roads
- River/Creek
- County Line

N

Flow

LITTLE LEHIGH CREEK

Light line and light tippet flyfishers should find this stream to their liking. The Little Lehigh is full of stream-smart trout that will test the mettle of most anglers. While there are days when everything goes just right, this stream should not be considered a pushover.

The stream's water temperatures remain good throughout the season, and it holds both wild trout and fish stocked by the Pennsylvania Fish and Boat Commission (PFBC) as well as Allentown's fish hatchery. The catch-and-release section, a Heritage Trout Water, is a designation given to streams that are steeped in flyfishing tradition, and the Little Lehigh easily qualifies for this. Heritage Trout Angling: 1 mile upstream from the face of Fish Hatchery Road Bridge downstream to near the 24th Street Bridge.

The stream also contains a 1.8-mile stretch regulated under Delayed Harvest Flyfishing Only (DHFFO) water from the downstream face of the bridge on T-508 (Wild Cherry Lane) downstream to the upstream face of the bridge on T-510 (Millrace Road).

Little Lehigh begins near Woodside Avenue in Berks County and falls under the category of Approved Trout Water, meaning that it is stocked by the PFBC. The stream flows for approximately 6 miles before entering Lehigh County, where it flows another 12 miles to join the Lehigh River. From its headwaters, the stream is found just south of Home Road and Hidden Valley Road. After entering Lehigh County, it parallels Mertztown Road and then Spring Creek Road. Taking SR 29 to Fish Hatchery Road will lead you to the park and the Heritage Trout Waters.

Along the river's urban setting, the park provides tranquility and is often shared with bikers and walkers. The stream, which rarely exceeds 50 feet in width, is best fished from the shoreline in hip boots. The Trico hatch here is spectacular, and terrestrial fishing during the summer months is one of my favorite times to fish this stream. I prefer the quiet times, which, as with most highly ranked streams, are best found on summer afternoons.

The Little Lehigh Chapter of Trout Unlimited and the Little Lehigh Flyfishers deserve a lot of credit for their protection and improvement of this river. With a combination of wild browns and stocked fish as well as carryovers, this stream is one of the better streams found within city limits.

LITTLE LEHIGH MAJOR HATCHES

Insect	J	F	M	A	M	J	J	A	S	O	N	D
Blue-winged Olives #10			▦			▦	▦					
Craneflies #18 & 20 (orange)				▦								
Black Stone #16			▦									
Blue Quill #18			▦									
Tan Caddis #16					▦	▦	▦	▦				
Sulphur #16					▦							
Light Cahill #14					▦							
Trico #24							▦	▦	▦			
Yellow Drake #12 & 14					▦							
Slate Drake #12, 3X long						▦						
Midges #20–24 (green, yellow, white, cream)						▦	▦	▦				
Ants #16–20; Beetles #12–18; Grasshoppers #10–14							▦	▦	▦			
Caterpillars #12, 3X long							▦	▦				
Other												
Floating Nymphs #16–24 (green, yellow, white)					▦	▦	▦	▦	▦			
Yellow Adams #16 & 18							▦	▦	▦			

LEHIGH RIVER

The Lehigh River is a precedent-setting river in Pennsylvania. After years of court battles, the river has now been deemed navigable, opening up access to all flyfishers. A navigable river allows anglers to wade anywhere they please or to fish the river by boat or canoe. However, you may not trespass on private property to gain access. Once access is legally gained, the river is yours to fish.

It has been said that the Lehigh River is close to 105 miles in length, and, as the crow flies, I cannot dispute that, nor do I care to. The river's serpentine path is difficult to follow as it winds its way northward from the Delaware River through Northampton, Lehigh, Carbon, Luzerne, Lackawanna, and Wayne Counties. It is said to have its beginning in Pike County. While this may be true for a branch, hours of pouring over maps indicates that the main branch begins in Wayne County.

No matter, the stream is long in length and full of trout. Shad are now finding their way into the reaches of the river as well, which should be good news for everyone who has or ever wanted to fish here. Trout stocking has been continual over the years on this big river. The PFBC stocks the river in Carbon County and the Luzerne County lines. The commission also stocks the stream in Lackawanna and Luzerne Counties.

The Lehigh River Stocking Association stocks the river with browns, brook trout, and rainbows, along with some steelhead. In 1998 alone, they stocked 14,343 adult trout between 11 and 24 inches. In the same year, 14,500 fingerlings from 3 to 5 inches long were also stocked. Some adult trout can weigh up to 14 pounds! In the spring of 1999, the Lehigh River Stocking Association stocked a total of 16,040 adult fish and 10,000 fingerlings.

Without a doubt the stream is going to climb high into the rankings of a premier trout stream within a few years. The court case that has granted river access, the return of the historic shad runs, and both wild and stocked trout as well as carryovers will bring this river into the limelight.

Waders with studded soles and a wading staff should be considered here. The bottom of this stream is treacherous to wade. Rods should measure at least 9 feet in length and 5- and 6-weight lines will help cover the water, which is rarely less than 100 feet wide except for the extreme upper sections.

Hatches are coming back strongly, and heavy hatches as well as a wide variety of hatches can be expected. Nearly every major hatch occurs along the river, including the green and brown drake. But don't be confused by the terminology used in this area—the shad fly is not a green drake here, rather it is the grannom caddis. One can only assume that it was a good fly for shad when the runs were much heavier here. In most regions of the state, shad fly means green drake.

Finding the river is difficult when heading north from Bethlehem into the northern counties, however, I will try to give as much driving information as possible. The sections near the mouth are accessible from SR 78 or 22. Follow SR 940

*The American shad
festival held in
Bethlehem, PA.*

north to find Lehigh Tannery and SR 534 to the stream. SR 2013 parallels much of
the river above the Francis E. Walter Dam. Of course, the river is smaller in the
northern sectors.

When fishing the lower sections of the river, I suggest high floating flies, as the
water is deep and flows rapidly. Sinktips could be used in this river section.

Lehigh River Access Sites

Lehigh County; 16 miles

Kimmet's Lock Access (PFBC); at Allentown; US 22 to Fullerton Avenue exit, go south on Fullerton; left at Tilgham Street to bridge, first left after crossing bridge
- Shallow draft, lightweight fishing boats, canoes, and inflatables
- Boat fishing and recreation
- Surfaced ramp
- Parking available

Canal Park Access; at Allentown; US 22 to 7th Street; take 7th Street to Hamilton Street (center city). Left on Hamilton Street, cross Lehigh River on Hamilton Street Bridge; take next right, follow signs; two access sites
Surfaced river ramp (no water skiing)
- Moderate draft fishing boats, sailboats, and recreational runabout boats
- Boat fishing and recreation
- Parking available
Surfaced canal ramp
- Rowboats, rafts, and canoes only—no motors
- Rentals and parking available

Northampton County; 10 miles

Lehigh River Access; SR 611 in Easton, 250 yards above confluence with Delaware River
- Canoes and other handcarry boats only
- Boat fishing
- Beach-type ramp
- Limited parking

LEHIGH RIVER MAJOR HATCHES

Insect	J	F	M	A	M	J	J	A	S	O	N	D
Grannom #14 & 16				▬								
Quill Gordon #14				▬								
Hendrickson #14				▬								
Blue Quill #18				▬								
Tan Caddis #16					▬▬▬▬▬▬							
Sulphur #16					▬							
Light Cahill #14					▬▬▬							
Gray Fox #12					▬							
Green Drake #12, 3X long (Coffin Fly Spinner)					▬							
Brown Drake #12, 3X long					▬							
Blue-winged Olive #14					▬▬							
Pale Evening Dun #16								▬▬				
Ants #16–20; Beetles #12–18; Grasshoppers #10–14							▬▬▬▬▬▬					
Caterpillars #12, 3X long							▬▬▬▬▬▬					
Other												
Yellow Adams #16 & 18							▬▬▬▬▬					

Comparaduns and 3 hackle dry flies will help locate the fly in fast water and help with flotation.

MONOCACY CREEK

This limestone stream lends to the aura of the Lehigh Valley, and it is found in Northampton County. Nearly 4 miles of the stream has been designated as Class A, wild trout water, which means no stocking. This includes 1.9 miles from the SR 987 bridge downstream to the SR 248 bridge and 1.9 miles from Illick's Mill Dam upstream to and including Gertrude Fox Conservation Center near Route 512 and Bath.

For one reason or another, no stocking means that fewer fishermen come here, even though the latter sector of water is managed as trophy trout, all tackle, and with a minimum size limit of 14 inches. The creel limit is two per day from opening day of trout season until midnight on Labor Day, and from then to the following opening day in April it is no-kill. Why anyone would want to kill wild trout, such a precious commodity here, escapes me, so I will once again repeat my plea not to kill these trout.

The stream averages some 50 feet in width, and its lower reaches as it enters Bethlehem is stocked trout water before entering the Lehigh River. The entire stream offers good fishing, but my personal choice is the 4 miles classified as wild trout water. The stream is fighting urban sprawl, but has been protected and improved by the Monocacy Chapter of Trout Unlimited and the Monocacy Watershed Association, with the cooperation of the City of Bethlehem and the Bethlehem Parks Department.

The proof of their efforts lies in the fact that nearly 4 miles of the creek is a self-sustaining wild trout stream. Although short on hatches, this is a great fishery. The hatches that do happen are often extremely heavy. To fish this stream with consistent success, probe the depths with beadhead nymphs, stonefly nymphs, streamers, and even Green Weenies.

Waders are an excellent choice here, and I like a 9-foot for a 4-weight, but 3- to 5-weights will fill the bill. A lover of leaders 9 feet and longer (7 feet if fishing nymphs), I find 6X and 7X tippets the rule rather than the exception.

The stream is easily accessible by taking SR 512 from US 22.

WHITE CLAY CREEK

The first time I saw the Middle Branch of White Clay Creek, I was director of the Adopt-A-Stream Program for the Pennsylvania Fish and Boat Commission. The stream was aptly named, I remembered thinking, for clay was evident along the eroded banks and on the stream bottom. That was back in 1985, and all that I can say about White Clay is "that you've come a long way, baby."

White Clay and two of its branches, the East and Middle, are all stocked with trout by the PFBC. The Middle Branch is also stocked in October for those flyfishers who prefer a longer season. White Clay Watershed Association, PO Box 10, Landenberg, PA 19350, has completed extensive stream improvements, and although clay will always be part of the White Clay and its branches, this unique stream system is a testimonial to people willing to work together to restore watersheds.

Hatches are becoming better with the passage of time and hard work. The stream does have fairly good canopy in some sections and flows from an urban to rural setting. This is a good trout stream and, despite the clay bottom, will become even better in coming years.

Waders are needed to fish here, since the creek is full of deep holes and structures that have been placed to create a better pool-to-riffle ratio. Since the stream varies in width along its course, I prefer a 9-foot rod that carries a 4-weight line for the majority of fishing.

There is a DHALO section on the Middle Branch spanning 1.7 miles from SR 3009 downstream to its confluence with the East Branch. The East Branch and its delayed harvest area are easily accessible from SR 3009. The stream leaves the state at White Clay Creek Preserve State Park on the Pennsylvania/Delaware border. White Clay Creek Preserve State Park is 1,255 acres with trout fishing on 5.5 miles of White Clay Creek, a 3.5-mile hiking trail, and an 8-mile bridle path.

The East Branch begins just northwest of Avondale off SR 41. The Middle Branch starts at White Horse School Road, just below SR 41. Use the hatch chart for Monocacy Creek.

SAUCON CREEK

This is a little sleeper of a stream that gets lost in the mad rush to find the Lehigh Valley's more popular trout waters. However, all indications point to this stream as being one good little limestoner.

The Pennsylvania Fish and Boat Commission has labeled a sector of this stream Class A wild trout water from its confluence with the Black River downstream to SR 412, a stretch that covers 2.1 miles. This should be a prime indicator of how good a stream this can be.

The headwaters begin at Chestnut Hill along SR 2029 and follow the road north to Saucon Valley Road. From here it heads east into Northampton County on Saucon Valley Road. State Route 412 then follows the stream north to SR 2074 to the creek's mouth at the Lehigh River.

Saucon Creek is an exceptional wild trout stream, containing mostly wild brown trout. The better fishing may be found on the special regulated area within Saucon Park. The stream can be fished from shore with hip boots, and light lines are recommended. Saucon Creek contains a pleasant mixture of wild browns and stocked rainbows, although it covers only 5 miles through Northampton County and some 2 miles in Lehigh.

The stream does have special regulations covering the wild trout section of the stream, 2.1 miles of Selective Harvest Program from the upstream boundary of the City of Bethlehem property downstream to the SR 412 bridge. Use the hatch chart for Monocacy.

CEDAR CREEK

From the SR 1019 bridge downstream to Lake Muhlenberg, a total of 1 .1 miles, Cedar Creek falls under the PFBC's Class A wild trout streams category. From Ott Street down to its junction with the Little Lehigh, the stream is stocked by the PFBC. This is a classy little limestone that holds great numbers of wild browns and requires some thought before fly selection and casting.

At its widest, it is barely 30 feet and long leaders and light lines help here. Hatches are not great in number, but they do bring beautiful wild browns to the surface.

Hip boots are all that is required, and the water is easily reached from SR 222.

This is an excellent stream for terrestrial fishing and for finding Trico hatches (use the hatch chart for Monocacy Creek).

MONOCACY CREEK MAJOR HATCHES

Insect	J	F	M	A	M	J	J	A	S	O	N	D
Blue-winged Olive #20			▓			▓						
Sulphur #16					▓							
Light Cahill #14					▓							
Trico #24								▓				
Tan Caddis #16					▓							
Midges #20–24 (green, yellow, white, cream)						▓						
Ants #16–20; Beetles #12–18; Grasshoppers #10–14								▓				
Caterpillars #12, 3X long								▓				
Other												
Floating Nymphs #16–24 (green, yellow, white)						▓						
Yellow Adams #16–18								▓				

Floating nymphs are widely overlooked but work well on most limestones—always include them in your fly box

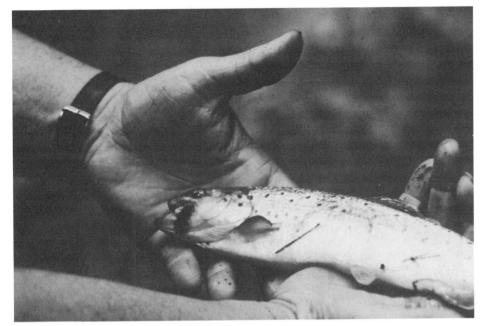

This small brown had a big appetite for the author's
spun deer hair caterpillar imitation.

FRENCH CREEK

French Creek is a stream worth exploring, especially for early season trout fly-fishers and summer bass seekers. The stream is stocked by the PFBC and has a DHFFO section that runs 0.9 miles from the dam at Sleepy Hollow downstream to Hollow Road near SR 100.

Delayed harvest regulations are designed for streams that hold trout well until the water warms. Regulations then allow harvesting 3 trout per day in the belief that they will perish anyway. Like most flyfishers, I release all trout in the hope that it will be a cooler summer than usual or that the trout have the ability to find coldwater refuges, such as underground springs or coldwater tributaries.

Leaving Hopewell Lake in French Creek State Park, French Creek begins its 14-mile eastward journey. After only a few miles in Berks County, it enters Chester County, eventually reaching Phoenixville where it joins the Schuylkill River.

Trout fishing is good in the DHFFO section and above, and the creek is stocked in both spring and fall by the PFBC. As the stream moves closer to Phoenixville, bass become the species of choice. This stream should be considered for early season fishing and again in the fall for trout. Bass flyfishers will find it to their liking all summer.

As a tributary to the Schuylkill, don't be surprised to find everything from muskie to panfish in the lower reaches.

The stream is accessible from SR 100. The Ridley Creek hatch chart works on French Creek, and I fish this stream in waders and rods that carry a 4- to 5-weight line.

RIDLEY CREEK

The Delayed Harvest section of this stream is the better water, since it is set aside for flyfishing only. The area extends 0.6 miles from the falls in Ridley Creek State Park downstream to the mouth of Dismal Run in Delaware County.

Ridley is a stocked trout stream and suffers from thermal pollution. It is believed that some trout do carry over by finding spring seeps and coldwater tributaries. The stream is often crowded during the first few weeks of the season due to its close proximity to Philadelphia. It is stocked by the Pennsylvania Fish and Boat Commission, although sporadically because of posting and private waters. Fishing is best during the early portion of the season and then again in the fall.

Because there are not many waters in this area of interest to flyfishers, this stream is one of the better fisheries. There are a good number of hatches, and the flyfishing can often be excellent, especially during weekdays, making it a natural choice for local flyfishers. The stream can be reached from Sycamore Mills Road. Within the park, a bicycle path leads to the more productive waters.

RIDLEY CREEK MAJOR HATCHES

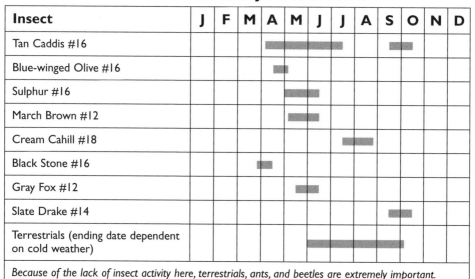

Insect	J	F	M	A	M	J	J	A	S	O	N	D
Tan Caddis #16					█	█	█		█			
Blue-winged Olive #16					█							
Sulphur #16					█	█						
March Brown #12					█							
Cream Cahill #18							█					
Black Stone #16				█								
Gray Fox #12						█						
Slate Drake #14										█		
Terrestrials (ending date dependent on cold weather)							█	█	█	█		

Because of the lack of insect activity here, terrestrials, ants, and beetles are extremely important.

VALLEY CREEK

If there's a trout stream that has been studied extensively, it is Valley Creek. Experiments with species and subspecies have been ongoing for years. Since the discovery of PCBs in the creek, no fish have been harvested from the stream for well over 10 years, which is a blessing of sorts.

Valley Creek is designated a Class A, wild brown trout stream for 7 miles from SR 29 downstream to the mouth where it meets the Schuylkill River. The stream has been under siege for years, but caretakers, including the Valley Forge Chapter of Trout Unlimited and the National Park Service, have been conducting studies and improving the stream as well as limiting undesirable uses of the water.

This is a magnificent stretch of water, with a good portion of it flowing through Valley Forge National Park. The Park has provided valuable information about this stream, and it is one of the better managed streams in the state. Management policies for the stream, such as allowing bait fishing, don't always please flyfishers. However, strict regulations governing the use of bait are posted along the stream.

Valley Creek runs 12 miles through Chester County and is a limestone stream worth exploring. Hatches are getting better as time passes, and wild trout 15 inches and better are not all that uncommon. Twenty-inch browns are taken with regularity without the aid of stocking.

This is an excellent place to work those 1- and 2-weight lines. The stream is easily covered with any rod length since it rarely exceeds 30 feet in width. Wild trout are found throughout the stream's length and in the only branch, Little Valley Creek, although the headwaters are not considered Class A.

I find this stream a delight to fish and always find the studies that are continually being conducted of extreme interest. Stop in the Park Office for information regarding ongoing studies—the wealth of information they hold should be of extreme interest to you.

Valley Creek starts at the intersection of Bacton Hill and Conestoga Roads south of Interstate 76 in East Whiteland Township and flows northeast into the Schuylkill River at Valley Forge National Park. Follow Conestoga Road from the mouth along US 202. The stream is easily accessible from the Pennsylvania Turnpike by following the sign to Valley Forge National Park.

Fishing lasts throughout the year with water temperatures remaining consistently cold enough to support a wild trout population. Bring hip boots and a good selection of flies. This is one of those good terrestrial streams that fishes well throughout the summer.

VALLEY & LITTLE VALLEY CREEKS MAJOR HATCHES

Insect	J	F	M	A	M	J	J	A	S	O	N	D
Blue-winged Olive #14, 16, 20				▆			▆▆	▆				
Craneflies #18 & 20				▆								
Caddis #14 & 16 (grannom, green)				▆▆	▆	▆						
Light Cahill #14					▆							
Tan Caddis #16					▆	▆	▆	▆				
Sulphur #16					▆							
Midges #20–24 (green, yellow, white, cream)					▆	▆	▆	▆	▆			
Ants #16–20; Beetles #12–18; Grasshoppers #10–14						▆	▆	▆	▆			
Caterpillars #12, 3X long						▆	▆	▆	▆			
Other												
Floating Nymphs #16–24 (green, yellow, white)					▆	▆	▆	▆	▆			
Yellow Adams #16 & 18						▆	▆	▆	▆			
Mosquito #12–16							▆	▆	▆	▆		

Floating nymphs are overlooked but work well on most waters—always include them in your fly box.

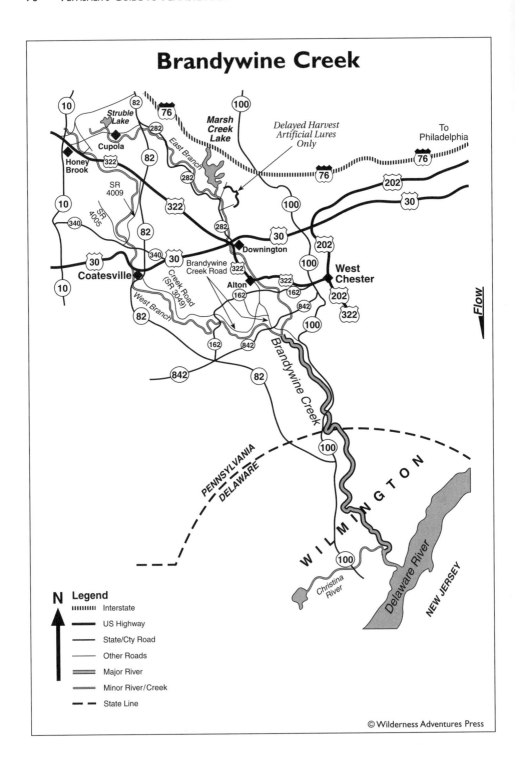

BRANDYWINE CREEK

The late Jim Bashline once penned the outdoor page for a Philadelphia newspaper. A long way from his native Potter County, he was required to live near the paper's offices. Being able to fish often for trout close to home was a necessity, and the stream he chose in the area was the Brandywine, where he and his wife, Sylvia, resided before moving on to the banks of the Yellow Breeches and, finally, Spruce Creek in Centre County.

Brandywine Creek falls 1000 feet over its course of some 60 miles, and adding to its beauty, 15 covered bridges span its flow. It averages less than 4 feet deep and has two main branches, both beginning at the base of the Welsh Mountains. The West Branch flows south through Coatesville, and the East Branch flows south through Downington.

From the source near Honey Brook, follow Pleasant View Road going south to Route 322. Route 322 follows the West Branch southeast to SR 4009 (Hibernia Road), which follows the creek south to SR 340. Here, the creek takes a short jaunt southeast to SR 82 (business route 30 south through Coatesville). South of Coatesville, take SR 3049 to SR 162, where Broad Run Road, Camp Road and SR 3023 wind into the town of Wawaset. Here the East Branch joins in near Brandywine Picnic Park in Lenape to form the main branch. The creek then continues south into the state of Delaware before emptying into the Delaware River.

The East Branch begins only a few miles from the source of the West Branch. Go east on Sulee Road to the town of Cupola, where SR 4031 and SR 4029 take you to SR 282, which follows most of the East Branch south to Downington. From Downington SR 322 proceeds to the town of Alton. Continuing south at Alton, Waltz Road and Brandywine Creek Road lead to the confluence with the West Branch. Brandywine Creek Road becomes SR 100, which parallels the creek to the Delaware border.

The East Branch contains a DHALO stretch that covers a 1.2-mile section from the Dorlans Mill Road downstream to Forge Road. The stream is stocked in both spring and fall by the PFBC from US 30 upstream to SR 282.

Brandywine's West Branch is stocked from SR 4005 downstream to US 30. The main stem is not stocked trout water but does contain a few muskies, bass, and panfish.

Several lakes can be found along the creek's path, including Struble Lake and the lake at Marsh Creek State Park. Struble Lake offers fishing and nonmotorized boating.

The stream flows mostly through meadowland, and fishing here with light weight lines is both easy and enjoyable. A lot of water is posted, so I suggest you give the stocked section a try, since all stocked water is open to public fishing. But the Brandywine has surprising numbers of carryover and wild browns that inhabit its branches.

An excellent brown trout, one to be proud of.

Hatches are not as plentiful as they could be but are enough to keep an angler's interest. I would suggest, however, taking an assortment of beadhead nymphs to fish the stream with consistent success. Waders are needed in some areas, while others are easily fished from the shore.

BRANDYWINE CREEK MAJOR HATCHES

Insect	J	F	M	A	M	J	J	A	S	O	N	D
Blue-winged Olive #20			▆	▆		▆	▆	▆	▆			
Sulphur #16					▆	▆						
Light Cahill #14					▆							
Trico #24								▆	▆			
Tan Caddis #16					▆	▆	▆	▆	▆			
Midges #20–24 (green, yellow, white, cream)						▆	▆	▆	▆	▆	▆	▆
Ants #16–20; Beetles #12–18; Grasshoppers #10–14						▆	▆	▆	▆			
Caterpillars #12, 3x long						▆	▆	▆	▆			
Other												
Floating Nymphs #16–24 (green, yellow, white)												
Yellow Adams #16 & 18						▆	▆	▆	▆			

Floating nymphs are widely overlooked but work well on most limestones—always include them in your fly box.

Octoraro Creek

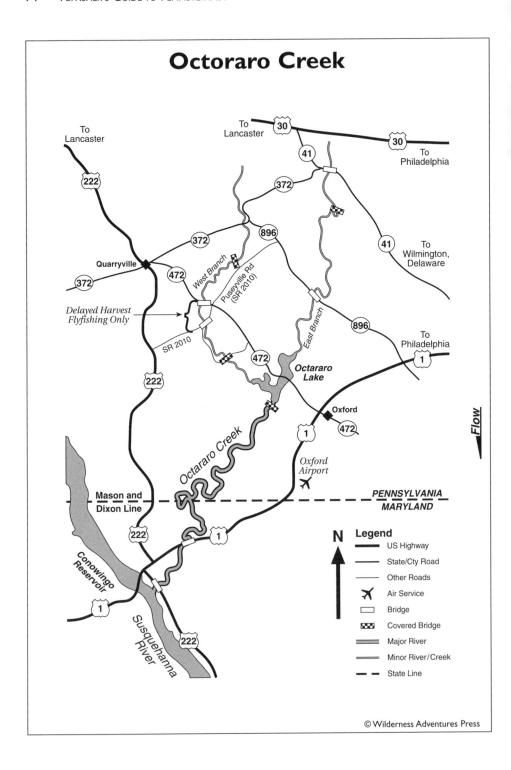

© Wilderness Adventures Press

OCTORARO CREEK AND BRANCHES

The Octoraro and its branches are famed for their trout fishing, particularly within the boundaries of Lancaster County. A heavily farmed section of the state, Lancaster County is not overflowing with great trout waters. It has its share but many have been downgraded because of heavy silt problems.

However, the West Branch of the stream is regulated under DHFFO regulations and is a desirable destination for many flyfishers. The West Branch begins close to Wolf Rock Road and flows approximately 12 miles before reaching Octoraro Lake, a 160-acre impoundment. This is a beautiful stream throughout its length and is stocked by the PFBC.

The special regulations section begins a few hundred yards below SR 472 and extends 1.9 miles to just below SR 2010. The nearly 2-mile stretch of water flows through State Game Lands #136 and offers a very remote setting for flyfishing. Early season hatches are consistent and provide excellent fishing until the waters begin to warm in mid-June or early July. It is a stream with a wealth of trout and hatches and should not be overlooked during the early season.

The East Branch, which begins a few short miles away from the West Branch, is also heavily stocked but does not provide the forested area that the West Branch does. It is more a mixture of farmland and wooded land and warms faster than the West Branch, although it, too, is heavily stocked by the PFBC. Still, both streams are worth a try and both are medium-sized streams, which allows wading and the casting of lines in the 2- to 5-weight range. These streams are good but certainly not the best the state has to offer. Nevertheless, they are streams well worth visiting and offer the solitude that the more popular streams do not.

Both streams are easily reached from SR 472 and SR 896. When fishing the West Branch, especially, bring along some caterpillar patterns.

OCTARARO CREEK MAJOR HATCHES

Insect	J	F	M	A	M	J	J	A	S	O	N	D
Blue Quill #16 & 18			▬									
Hendrickson #14				▬								
Sulphur #16					▬							
March Brown #12					▬							
Light Cahill #14					▬							
Black Stone #16			▬									
Blue-winged Olive #16					▬							
Tan Caddis #16					▬▬							
Yellow Drake #12					▪							
Caterpillar #12, 3X long					▬▬							
Terrestrials (ending date dependent on cold weather)					▬▬							

Because of the lack of insect activity here, terrestrials, ants, beetles, caterpillars, and inchworms are extremely important.

As summer progresses, trout congregate in coldwater sanctuaries,
such as headwaters and springs

Donegal Creek

This is one of my favorite streams in Lancaster County, where extensive farming practices far too often cause streams to be heavily filled with silt. Donegal Creek would be in the same fix if it were not for the stream's caretakers. It should be evident as you scan these pages that in Pennsylvania, trout streams are recognized and treasured, and few streams exist without river keepers. When fishing Donegal Creek, note the stream improvement devices that have been put in place by the Donegal Fish and Conservation Association, a group that monitors the stream and makes continual improvements.

The creek averages slightly more than 20 feet wide and is a fine stream for light lines that can range from 1-weight to 3-weight. However, a light line rod is not necessary to fish here. My 9-foot rod carrying a 4-weight and another carrying a 5-weight have both worked well here. Light lines are fun to fish, can be helpful, and give all of us an excuse to buy another outfit—let's leave it at that.

Donegal is a typical limestone that has an excellent stretch of DHFFO water that regulates 2.4 miles of the 4-mile creek. The fishing here is excellent and hatches are good. Again, as with all limestones, the terrestrial fishing is superb. Water temperatures remain consistently cold enough to support trout throughout the summer months.

The stream begins off Endslow Road at Donegal Springs, and access can be gained from Trout Run Road, SR 772, and SR 23. The stream meets Chickies Creek before entering the Susquehanna at Chickies. This is approved trout water and is stocked by the PFBC.

Special Regulations: Delayed Harvest/Fly Fishing Only for 2.4 miles from 275 yards below SR 772 downstream to T-334.

DONEGAL CREEK MAJOR HATCHES

Insect	J	F	M	A	M	J	J	A	S	O	N	D
Blue-winged Olive #20			▬			▬	▬	▬				
Sulphur #16				▬								
March Brown #12 & 14				▬								
Gray Fox				▬								
Tan Caddis #16					▬	▬	▬	▬				
Caddis #20 (green, black)								▬				
Trico #24							▬	▬	▬			
Midges #20–24 (green, yellow, white, cream)						▬	▬	▬				
Ants #16–20; Beetles #12–18; Grasshoppers #10–14							▬	▬				
Caterpillars #12, 3X long							▬	▬				
Other												
Floating Nymphs #16–24 (green, yellow, white)												
Yellow Adams #16 & 18							▬	▬	▬			

Floating nymphs are widely overlooked but work well on most limestones—always include them in your fly box.

TULPEHOCKEN CREEK

I first visited this stream at the invitation of Bill Fritz, an active member of Trout Unlimited and a nymph fisherman second to none. Bill had been enticing me with the morning Trico hatch and had convinced me that "balls" of spinners would surely descend at 9 am.

Like any good flyfisher, I met Bill on the water early so that I would have time to get acquainted with it. There was also the added advantage that we would be there if the spinnerfall happened earlier than expected that day. Bill handed me two Trico nymphs and suggested I fish them near the bottom. Then, without the aid of a strike indicator, he showed me the proper way to fish the pattern. In doing so, I caught and released 15 nice trout before duns emerged and the spinners arrived just as he claimed they would: "huge balls of glistening white."

Because I had managed to land four or five decent trout and "jag" many more, I was fearful that there would be few fish remaining to rise to our small imitations. However, I should have known better—Bill wasn't the type of fisherman to pound unproductive waters, and he knew this stream well.

At precisely 9 AM, the spinners were beginning to touch the water, and the trout were expecting their arrival. While I usually don't count fish, on a morning like this it would have been impossible. The size and number of fish were generous, and I found this stream to my liking immediately. Stream flows were forgiving and the trout willing, a combination that is hard to find in August. The stream was close at hand and a pleasure to fish, and with the introduction Bill had given me, there was little doubt that I would return time and again.

The stream, located in Berks County, includes a 3.8-mile stretch of Delayed Harvest, artificial lures only section from the first deflector below Blue Marsh Dam downstream to the covered bridge.

In the southeastern sector of the state, anglers expect to find small, meandering limestones or small feeder streams. But here, reaching the far shore in many sectors would require an entire fly line and a lot of backing. The stream is wide with a good ratio of pools and riffles.

Trout have become accustomed to a constant flow of anglers here, and, much like the Yellow Breeches in Cumberland County, a trout may rise so close to you that it seems possible to touch it with your rod tip. The difference is that Tulpehocken fish are more likely to take a properly presented fly.

Most of the better streams in the state have their caretakers and the Tulpehocken is not an exception to this rule. The Tulpehocken Chapter of Trout Unlimited has been working tirelessly on stream improvement work and has had constant cooperation from the Army Corps of Engineers.

The stream has been stocked with fingerling trout for years, which has been supported by Trout Unlimited. The stream would probably be a warmwater fishery without the help of the Corps, which allows coldwater releases from the Blue Marsh and alerts anglers when the releases will occur.

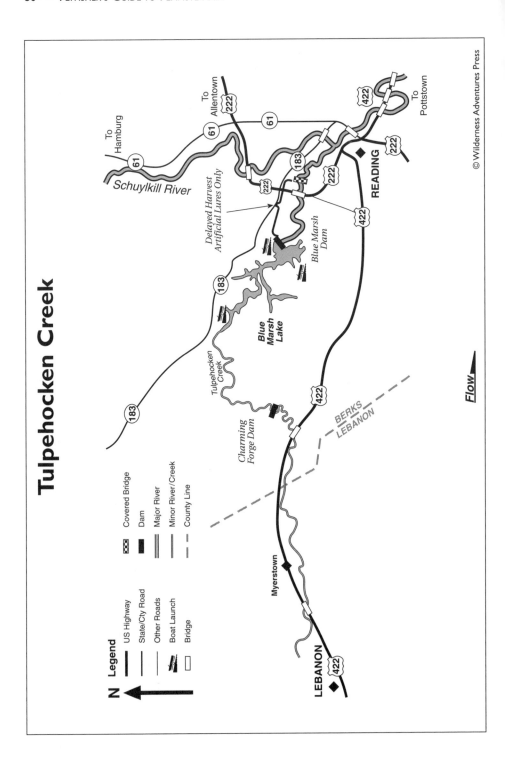

The stream is rich with food, and that is probably due to the water released from the dam. The lake itself provides excellent fishing for anglers (see Blue Marsh Lake). The stream does have its days and weeks of heavy use, but the lake helps distract many a casual angler with the lure of largemouth and other species, allowing the serious trout angler enough elbowroom to make this an excellent stream.

The entire stream is stocked by the PFBC, from one-half mile below Charming Forge Dam upstream to the county line. The stream is easily found by taking SR 183 south from the Pennsylvania Turnpike (Interstate 76; US 22) or from US 422. Excellent fishing may also be found upstream from the dam, however, the better fishing is below the dam, as odd as that may sound for a state that has had problems with dams and spillways that allow top water releases rather than bottom releases.

Because of its close proximity to Reading, the stream draws a lot of folks who want to combine fishing with sightseeing and shopping. For the family looking to vacation, there are a lot of attractions in this sector of the state.

TULPEHOCKEN CREEK MAJOR HATCHES

Insect	J	F	M	A	M	J	J	A	S	O	N	D
Little Black Stone #16				▬								
Blue-winged Olive #20 & 22					▬				▬▬▬			
Tan Caddis #16					▬▬▬▬			▬▬				
Green Caddis #16					▬							
Black Caddis					▬							
Sulphur #16					▬							
Yellow Drake						▬						
Trico #24							▬▬▬					
Cream Cahill									▬			
Terrestrials (ending date dependent on cold weather)						▬▬▬▬▬						

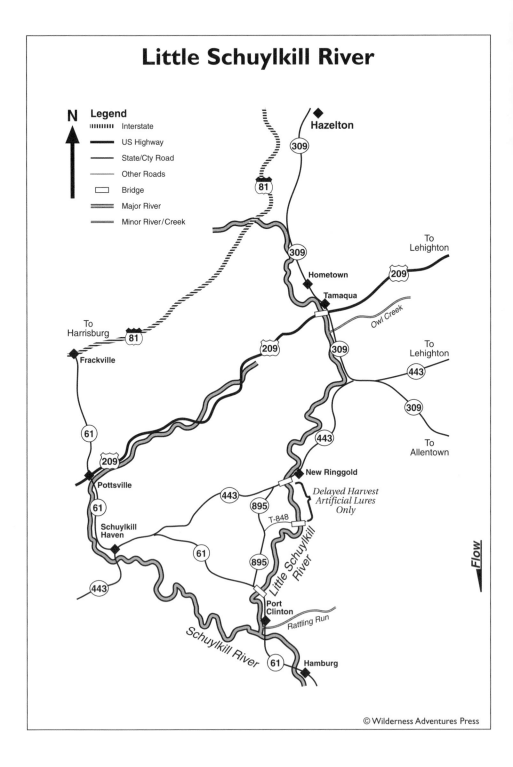

Little Schuylkill River

N

Legend
- |||||||||| Interstate
- US Highway
- State/Cty Road
- Other Roads
- ▭ Bridge
- Major River
- Minor River/Creek

Hazelton

309

81

309

To Lehighton

Hometown

209

Tamaqua

Owl Creek

To Harrisburg

81

Frackville

209

309

To Lehighton

443

61

309

443

To Allentown

209

Pottsville

New Ringgold

Delayed Harvest Artificial Lures Only

443

895

61

T-848

Schuylkill Haven

61

895

Little Schuylkill River

443

Port Clinton

Flow

Schuylkill River

Rattling Run

61

Hamburg

© Wilderness Adventures Press

LITTLE SCHUYLKILL RIVER

Entering the Schuylkill River at Port Clinton, the Little Schuylkill River is a stocked trout stream with a section designated as Delayed Harvest Artificial Lures Only (DHALO) at New Ringgold. This special regulation water is a good choice for trout fishing beginning at the SR 895 bridge and extending downstream to the T-848 bridge.

This 15-mile stream is found within the boundaries of Schuylkill County, beginning above Hazleton near SR 81. This area has long been heavily mined for coal, and the stream is still recovering from severe mine acid drainage that had nearly wiped the stream out. Traces of the pollutants are still present along some of stretches. But the Little Schuylkill is fed by Owl Creek below Tamaqua and Rattling Run near Port Clinton, both of which are Class A wild trout waters. These feeders help the stream tremendously by the addition of cold clean water and by their ability to sustain their own wild trout populations.

While hatches are still sparse, the river is returning slowly. Terrestrial fishing is excellent during the summer months, and tan caddis are often abundant throughout the season. Take an assortment of streamers, nymphs, Glo-bugs, and blue-winged olives for this stream. At this time, a hatch chart is not warranted, but I'm sure it will be in the near future. Waders and a rod that will handle a 4- or 5-weight line are useful here. Fishing can be excellent at the mouths of both Owl Crek and Rattling Run.

The stream is easily reached from state routes 895 and 61.

Flyfishermen and spin fishermen sharing the same water.

Summary of Approved Trout Waters
and Special Regulation Areas for the Southeast

Berks County	Section / Regulations
Angelica Lake	
Antietam Creek	
Antietam Lake	
Furnace Creek	
Little Lehigh Creek	
Little Muddy Creek	
Little Swatara Creek	
Maiden Creek	From Kistler Creek in Kempton downstream to bridge at Blue Rocks
Manatawny Creek	
Mill Creek – tributary to Sacony Creek	
Mill Creek – tributary to Schuylkill River	
Mill Creek – tributary to Little Swatara Creek	
Moslem Creek	
Northkill Creek	
Ontelaunee Creek	SR 4024 downstream to mouth
Perkiomen Creek, Northwest Branch	
Pine Creek – tributary to Maiden Creek	
Sacony Creek	Bowers Road (T-616) downstream to Boro Dam
Scotts Run Lake	
Spring Creek	
Tulpehocken Creek	One-half mile below Charming Forge Dam upstream to county line *DHALO:* 3.8 miles, from the first deflector below Blue March Dam downstream to the covered bridge east of Reading
Wyomissing Creek	SR 222 upstream to headwaters

Bucks County	Section / Regulations
Delaware Canal	
Lake Luxembourg	
Levittown Lake	
Neshaminy Creek	Upstream from Dark Hollow Road
Perkioman Creek, East Branch	Branch Road downstream through Sellersville
Unami Creek	Milford Twp. Park downstream to Trumbauersville Raod

Chester County	Section / Regulations
Beaver Creek (at Downington)	
Beaver Run	
Big Elk Creek	
Birch Run	
Brandywine Creek, East Branch	From Business Route 30 upstream to SR 282 *DHALO:* 1.2-mile section from the Dorlans Mill Road downstream to Forge Road
Brandy Wine Creek, West Branch	From SR 4005 downstream to Business Route 30
Buck Run	
Elk Creek, East Branch	
French Creek	*DHFFO:* 0.9 mile, from the dam at Camp Sleepy Hollow downstream to Hollow Road near SR 100, park off bridge past horse stable
Octoraro Creek, East Branch	
Pickering Creek	
Pocopson Creek	
Valley Creek (at Valley Forge)	*No Kill Zone*
West Valley Creek	*DHALO:* 1.2 miles, from the mouth of Colebrook Run downstream to about 0.25 mile below the railroad tunnel
White Clay Creek	
White Clay Creek, East Branch	
White Clay Creek, Middle Branch	*DHALO:* 1.7 miles, from SR 3009 (Good Hope Road) downstream to the confluence with the East Branch

Delaware County	Section / Regulations
Chester Creek	Downstream to Bridgewater Road
Chester Creek, West Branch	
Ithan Creek	
Little Darby Creek/Darby Creek	Downstream to where SR 1006 crosses Darby Creek below SR 0003
Ridley Creek	*DHFFO:* 0.6 mile, from the falls in Ridley Creek State Park, downstream to the mouth of Dismal Run

Lancaster County	Section / Regulations
Big Bear Creek	
Bowery Run	
Climbers Run/Trout Run	
Conowingo Creek	Spring Valley downstream to 1 mile downstream of T-111, Black Barron Road
Conoy Creek	

Lancaster County (cont.)	Section / Regulations
Donegal Creek	*DHFFO:* 2.4 miles, from 274 yards below SR 0772 downstream to T-334
Eshelman Londonland Runs	
Fishing Creek	
Hammer Creek	
Indian Run	
Little Chickies Creek	SR 4033 downstream of SR 0772
Little Cocalico Creek	County line to Ridge Road
Little Conestoga Creek	From vicinity of SR 722 downstream to Harrisburg Pike, SR 4020
Little Conestoga Creek, West Branch	
Meetinghouse Creek	
Middle Creek	Middle Creeek Waterfowl Project Dam downstream
Muddy Creek - Little	County line to SR 0897)
Muddy Run Lake	
Octoraro Creek, West Branch	*DHFFO:* 1.9 miles, from about 220 yards below SR 0472, downstream to near the second unnamed tributary below SR 2010
Pequea Creek	Mast downstream to SR 0897
Rock Run	County line to the mouth
Swarr Run	T-802 to SR 0741
Tucquan Creek	

Lehigh County	Section / Regulations
Big Trout Creek	
Cedar Creek	From Ott Street downstream to junction with Little Lehigh
Coplay Creek	
Jordan Creek	
Kister Creek	
Little Lehigh Creek	*DHFFO:* 1.8 miles, from the downstream face of the bridge on T-508 (Wild Cherry Lane) downstream to the upstream face of the bridge on T-510 (Millrace Road) *Heritage Trout Angling:* 1 mile, from just above Hatchery Road Bridge downstream to near the 24th Street Bridge
Ontelaunee Creek	
Saucon Creek, South Branch	
Swabia Creek	
Switzer Creek	

Montgomery County	Section / Regulations
Deep Creek Dam	
Loch Alsh Reservoir	
Mill Creek	
Perkiomen Creek	0.5 miles upstream from Tollgate Road downstream to Greenlane County Park boundary
Skippack Creek	
Stony Creek (and unnamed tributary)	
Unami Creek	
Valley Creek	*No Kill Zone:* at Valley Forge
Wissahickon Creek	

Northampton County	Section / Regulations
Bushkill Creek	*Catch and Release:* 1.1 miles, from the dam at Binney and Smith downstream to the 13th Street Bridge in Easton
Hokendauqua Creek	
Indian Creek	
Jacoby Creek	
Lehigh Canal	
Little Bushkill Creek	
Martins Creek	
Monocacy Creek	*Trophy Trout Project:* 1.9 miles, from Illick's Mill Dam upstream to and including Gertrude Fox Conservation Center near SR 512 and Bath
Minsi Lake	Including Martins Creek East Fork within PFBC boundary
Saucon Creek	
Waltz Creek	

Philadelphia County	Section / Regulations
Pennypack Creek	
Wissahickon Creek	

Schuylkill County	Section / Regulations
Bear Creek	*DHALO:* 1.9 miles, from a cable 800 yards above T-662 downstream to T-676
Beaver Creek	
Catawiss Creek (Little)	
Cold Run	
Deep Creek	

Schuylkyll County (cont.)	Section / Regulations
Little Schuylkill River	*DHALO:* 1.7 miles, SR 895 Bridge to the bridge on T-848
Lizard Creek	
Locust Creek	
Lofty Reservoir	
Mahantango Creek	
Mahoning Creek	
Mahonoy Creek (Little)	
Neifert Creek FCR	
Pine Creek–tributary to Schuylkill River	
Pine Creek–tributary to Little Schuylkill River	
Pine Creek–tributary to Mahantango Creek	
Pumping Station Dam	
Rabbit Run Reservoir	
Red Creek	
Swatara Creek (Lower, Little)	
Swatara Creek (Upper, Little)	
Whippoorwill Dam	

Southeast Hub Cities
Allentown
Population – 103,000

There are a large number of hotels and restaurants available in Allentown. The following is only a small sampling.

ACCOMMODATIONS
Allenwood Motel, 1058 Hausman Road / 610-395-3707
Econo Lodge, 2115 Downyflake Lane / 610-797-2200
Hampton Inn, 7471 Keebler Way / 610-391-1500
Holiday Inn, 1715 Plaza Lane / 610-435-7880
Holiday Inn, 3620 Hamilton Boulevard / 610-437-9255
Hotel Traylor, 1444 West Hamilton Street / 610-434-6221
Lehigh Motor Inn, 5828 Memorial Road / 610-395-3331
Sleep Inn, 327 Star Road / 610-395-6603
Tilghman West Motor Inn, 5650 West Tilghman Street / 610-395-2632

RESTAURANTS
Denny's, 2149 Lehigh Street / 610-797-2176
King George Inn, Hamilton and Cedar Crest Boulevards / 610-435-1723
Yocco's, The Hot Dog King, 625 Liberty Street / 610-433-1950
Federal Grill, 536 East Hamilton Street / 610-776-7600
Tailgators Steakhouse, 2035 Downyflake Lane / 610-797-9525
Bull & Bear Inn, 462 Union Boulevard / 610-432-5230

FLY SHOPS
Dale Clemens Custom Tackle, 444 Schantz Spring Road / 610-395-5119
Little Lehigh Fly Shop, Fish Hatchery Road / 610)797-5599
Pro-Am Fishing Shop, 5916 Tilghman Street / 610-395-0885

AUTO RENTAL
Avis Rent-A-Car, A B E International Airport / 610-264-4450
Budget Rent-A-Car, 3311 Airport Road / 610-266-0667
Car Temps U.S.A., 1113 Union Boulevard / 610-770-7788
Enterprise Rent-A-Car, 1896 Catasauqua Road / 610-266-6460
Hertz Rent-A-Car, Lehigh Valley Airport / 610-264-4571

AIR SERVICE
Lehigh Valley International Airport, 3311 Airport Road #4 / 610-266-6000

MEDICAL
Lehigh Valley Hospital, 1200 South Cedar Crest Boulevard / 610-402-8000

FOR MORE INFORMATION
Allentown-Lehigh County Chamber of Commerce
462 West Walnut Street
Allentown, PA 18102
610-437-9661

Lancaster
Population- 52,459

Accommodations
1722 Motor Lodge, 1722 Old Philadelphia Pike / 717-397-4791
Brunswick Hotel, 191 North Queen Street / 717-397-4800
Canadiana Motel, 2390 Lincoln Hwy East / 717-397-6531
Congress Inn Motel, 2316 Lincoln Hwy East / 717-397-3781
Continental Inn, 2285 Lincoln Hwy East / 717-299-0421
Country Living Motor Inn, 2406 Old Philadelphia Pike / 717-295-7295
Econo Lodge, 2165 Lincoln Hwy East / 717-299-6900
Econo Lodge, 2140 Lincoln Hwy East / 717-397-1900
Super 8 Motel, 2129 Lincoln Hwy East / 717-393-8888

Campgrounds
Old Mill Stream Camping Manor, 2249 Rt 30 East / 717-299-2314
Outdoor World Corp., 2111 Millersville Road / 717-872-0929

Restaurants
Lapp's Family Restaurant, 2270 Lincoln Hwy. East / 717-394-1606
Lancaster Malt Brewing Company, Plum Street / 717-391-6258
Alex Austin Steak House, 2481 Old Philadelphia Pike / 717-394-2539
Westside Family Restaurant, 100 South Centerville Road / 717-393-6449

Fly Shops
Trout Run Sports, 438 North Reading Road (Ephrata) / 215-738-2525
Quiet Times Fly Shop, 388 Hess Road (Quarryville) / 717-786-4291
Evening Rise Fly Anglers Shop, 4182 Old Philadelphia Pike (Gordonville) /
717-768-3020

Auto Rental
Car Temps USA, 1339 Fruitville Pike / 717-569-4743
Enterprise Rent-A-Car, 1470 Manheim Pike / 717-391-7080
Hertz Rent-A-Car, 625 East Orange Street / 717-396-0000
National Car Rental, 121 East Liberty Street / 717-394-2158

Airports
Lancaster Airport, 500 Airport Road (Lititz) / 717-569-1221
Also see Harrisburg

Medical
St. Joseph Hospital, 333 North Arch Street / 717-291-0240

For More Information
Lancaster Chamber of Commerce
100 South Queen Street
Lancaster, PA 17603
717-397-3531

Reading
Population-78,380

ACCOMMODATIONS
Dutch Colony Inn & Suites, 4635 Perkiomen Avenue / 610-779-2345
Econo Lodge, 635 Spring Street / 610-378-5105
Freymoyer's Hotel, 2700 Kutztown Road / 610-921-1448
Hampton Inn, 1800 Papermill Road / 610-374-8100
In-Town Motel, 1635 Centre Avenue / 610-376-9744
Penn View Motel, 250 Penn Avenue / 610-376-8011
Ramada Inn, 2545 North 5th Street Hwy / 610-929-4741

RESTAURANTS
Kansas City Steakhouse, 100 North 5th Street / 610-372-3700
Ronie's Home of The Steak Inc, 936 Exeter Street / 610-373-7400
Sahara Restaurant, 334 Penn Street / 610-374-0964
Country Barbeque Corner, North 5th Street Hwy / 610-929-5047
Beverly Hills Tavern, 710 Old Fritztown Road / 610-777-4516
Bistro 614, 614 Penn Avenue / 610-371-9966
Giulio's Italian Eatery, 3227 Perkiomen Avenue / 610-370-9660

FLY SHOPS
Tulpehocken Creek Outfitters, 2229 Penn Avenue (West Lawn) / 610-678-1899
Blue Mountain Outfitters, 2001 Bernville Road, Route 183 / 215-372-6970

AUTO RENTAL
Avis Rent-A-Car, Bernville Road / 610-372-6636 2375
Budget Rent-A-Car, 125 Morgantown Road / 610-775-4888
Enterprise Rent-A-Car, 125 Morgantown Road / 610-376-4722
Hertz Rent-A-Car, RR 9 Box 9416 / 610-374-1448

AIRPORTS
Kutztown Airport, 15130 Kutztown Road (Kutztown) / 610-683-5666
Reading Regional Airport, 2501 Bernville Road / 610-372-4666

MEDICAL
St. Joseph Community Health Center, 145 North 6th Street / 610-478-8704

FOR MORE INFORMATION
Chamber of Commerce
601 Penn Street #101
Reading, PA 19601
610-376-6766

Chamber of Commerce
24 Tewksbury Drive
Reading, PA 19610
610-670-2618

Northcentral Pennsylvania

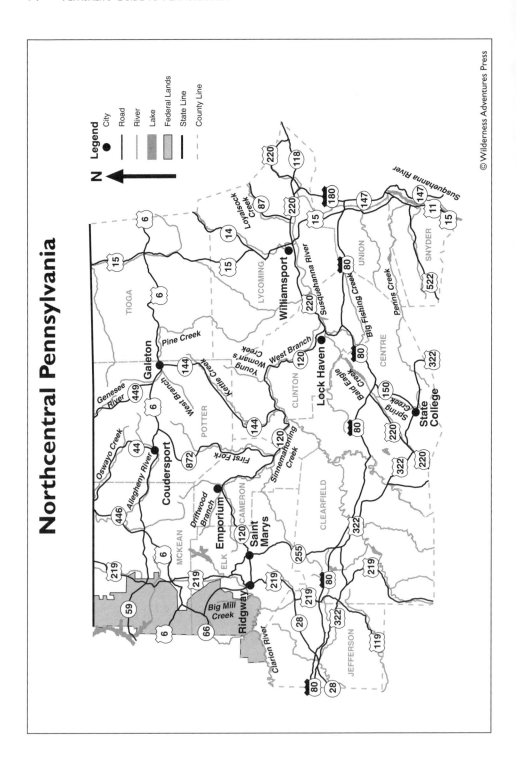

© Wilderness Adventures Press

Northcentral Pennsylvania

The northcentral region of the state has traditionally been a meeting ground for flyfishers.

Here, in this mountainous area of Pennsylvania, a large majority of the land has been purchased by the state. The Bureau of Forestry and the Pennsylvania Game Commission have bought large tracts of land for two reasons: The cost of land is lower since the terrain is generally too mountainous for industrial or residential development; and due to the lack of highways and railways, the shipping and receiving of goods is difficult and expensive.

If there is gold in them thar' hills, it is in the form of trout and small brushy wilderness streams. It is safe to say that the number of trout far exceeds the number of humans that inhabit this area of the state, especially in counties like Potter, Clinton, and Tioga. Timbering is the major industry here, and the resource has been tapped by both state and private landowners.

Early timbering efforts had an adverse impact on the area, and timber was taken in mass cuttings that often left nothing but the stumps behind. Erosion and tannic acid destroyed many streams at the turn of the century, and the booming economy that was based on the timber industry suddenly died out like a flickering light. The rails for transporting timber were yanked up as the companies departed, and many counties came close to becoming ghost towns.

Records indicate that the trout returned along with second growth timber and that some of the residents began poaching trout in good numbers, many sold commercially. The limit then was 25 trout per day, and poachers were able to catch trout in much greater quantities than the limit allowed. The area was truly wild, and when a fish warden was asked to stop a well known poaching ring operating in Potter County in the early 1930s, he requested three months and a deputy force of 25 armed men. His proposal was turned down.

The state and federal government became involved in delivering fish by train that were then stocked in area streams. No one is certain what affect these early stockings had on the region's streams, either positively or negatively.

However, I have heard report after report of large native brook trout taken from Kettle Creek in Potter and Clinton Counties as well as the area's tributary streams. But extensive research indicates that this just isn't true. In the late 1930s and early 1940s, the Pennsylvania State College School of Agriculture conducted studies on the lower section of Kettle Creek and tributaries that included Hammersley Fork. Second growth timber had filled the valley after the majority of virgin timber was removed during a 15-year period that extended from 1895 to 1910. R.L. Watts and noted anglers G.L. Trembley and G.W. Harvey conducted a survey that included a study of water temperatures during that time. Readings on Kettle Creek during the summer

Anglers try their luck on a large northern Pennsylvania freestone.

months soared into the 80s back then, and perhaps more astonishing was that the average brook trout did not exceed 7 inches in length.

Noted then and often ignored now was the importance of feeder streams and that migration into these smaller streams began in late May. Modern day anglers seemingly refuse to accept the fact that many trout, including browns that were delivered via hatchery, first found their way into Kettle around 1920. The trout were not large— brook trout grew at an average rate of less than 1 inch per year. However, migration into the tributaries was commonplace back then and continues to this day.

Modern day anglers argue the merits of stocking and the effect that brown trout have on the food supply of brook trout. Amazingly, a 7-inch limit was suggested for brook trout in the early 1940s in the hope that more would reach sexual maturity. The move from 6 to 7 inches took place a few short years ago, some 50-plus years after it was first suggested.

It may be that high water temperatures have always been a problem on freestone streams, at least in this section of the state, and that we should be taking a closer look at the tributaries that have acted as breeding grounds and an escape from warming waters.

Trout here spawn in the fall of the year, beginning as early as late September, with the majority of brown and brook trout completing their spawning runs by the end of October. When flows are adequate, many of these fish return to the main branch of the stream after spawning.

Anglers visiting this region of the state will find plentiful hatches from April through mid-June. After that, trout are most often found in the deeper pools at the mouths of coldwater tributary streams and in the tributaries themselves. It would seem only prudent for the health of these waters that anglers release the majority of their catch. The Kettle Creek study from the early 1940s voiced concern over angling pressure when a total of 384,231 anglers purchased licenses statewide. Today, there are approximately one million anglers plying their wares on the waters of the Keystone State. That added pressure might be having an adverse effect on all of our trout streams.

The weather in this region of the state is fickle. April can bring snow or 70-degree temperatures, and there are only short spells of summer that do not require a long-sleeved shirt during the evening hours. Besides noting important hatches, anglers must also be aware of rising water temperatures. It is also important to note that a good number of hatches come off during the afternoon hours in April and come off progressively later and later moving into late April, May, and especially June.

But the benefits to fishing this area are many. The wildness that surrounds the streams here is a calling that cannot be ignored. Finding a hatch on the lower reaches of a stream here might result in three weeks of fishing rather than just one or two, as most hatches begin on warmer waters first. Following a hatch upstream rather than waiting on it is always a good option.

This region of the state has all the sights, sounds, and atmosphere of real trout fishing from the small cottage industries that cling to a meager living in exchange for the privilege of living here, to the coyote, white-tailed deer, black bear, and elk that live along the streambanks.

Take warm and cold weather gear, hip-boots and waders, rain gear, insect repellent, polarized sunglasses, a rod that will handle a 4- or 5-weight line, and leaders with tippets from 4X to 8X. Stuff your fly boxes with attractor patterns for the times when fish are not active and leave your urban attitude at home. Here, no one cares what you do for a living—only that you can cast a line and cast it well.

Residents also couldn't care less whether you toss three wets flies or fish a midge fine and far—it's the end result that matters. New patterns come and go, but the staples stay the same. Bigger flies are the rule, and no pattern that catches trout will be scorned. The folks are friendly and never in a hurry. It will take a few hours or a few days to become accustomed to the pace, but that is what most flyfishers are really seeking.

This is trout country, and if you come in pursuit of the bass that are found in many of the lower stream sections, it might be best to keep it to yourself. For the most part, bass are considered somewhere down the list with suckers and carp, and most folks here do not like to hear tales of bass taken from trout waters.

Prices for food and lodging are extremely reasonable, but don't expect any large malls or massage parlors. Soak up the atmosphere in this area and appreciate it for what it is, a truly unique area where wilderness is more important than "improved dirt roads."

Allegheny River

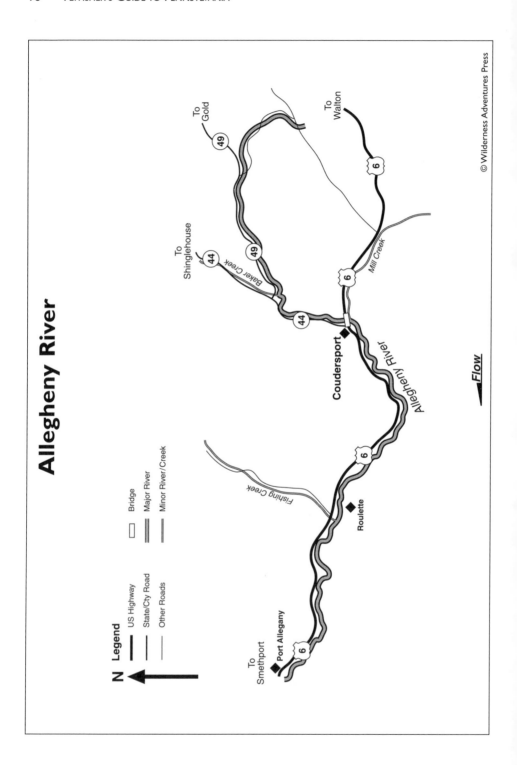

THE ALLEGHENY RIVER

Pennsylvania's western drainage begins in Potter County. The late Jim Bashline wrote of the the Allegheny often, and there is a plaque below the concrete channel honoring him—ironically, the same channel that destroyed some of the better water Jim had fished. Most of his book, *Night Fishing for Trout*, takes place around the Allegheny River.

The river's headwaters can be reached by driving northeast from Coudersport on SR 44 and turning right onto SR 49. Watch carefully for the sign that marks the head-waters of this river, one of Pennsylvania's largest. Admittedly, the headwaters are not very impressive, and the stream is so thin and narrow, it looks more like a pasture stream long forgotten.

However, as it marches past Coleburg toward the county seat, the stream does hold its fair share of brook trout but then turns quickly into brown trout water. The upper water offers beautiful, well-colored brown trout and, although mixed with stocked trout, carryover fish and those born to the stream hold their own. The PFBC stocks approximately 6 miles of water above Coudersport.

The stream has been tinkered with over the years and has changed in character and in its wealth of wild trout. Baker Creek, a small but much-needed tributary because of its cold water, has been the subject of stream improvements conducted by The God's Country Chapter of Trout Unlimited.

The river has a nice Delayed Harvest stretch of 2.7 miles that is well marked along SR 49. The location of the stream, as it appears in the PFBC's summary book-let, gives local names of bridges as landmarks: "From Judge Patterson's Pond Road downstream to ford 0.3 mile downstream of Prosser Hollow Bridge." The judge has long retired and two others have filled his chair since his departure, but that's the nature of Potter County. Head north out of Coudersport and be on the lookout for signs or ask for directions—these are friendly folks. In fact, the entire stream from the headwaters to Coudersport is easily accessible from the roadway.

I have spent many hours on this stream section with Pete Ryan, president of the God's Country Chapter of Trout Unlimited. The stream above the county seat is beautiful water and can be as forgiving as most freestone streams, except for the special regulations areas. Some large trout may be taken above town, but an angler should expect some decently sized brook trout (up to 10 inches) and the average brown in the 12- to 15-inch class. Within the Delayed Harvest area, expect all species of fish, with the average size jumping close to 15 inches with enough browns and rainbows over 20 inches to keep your interest.

In Coudersport, US 6 follows the river to Port Allegany. From the end of the flood control channel that destroyed one of Jim Bashline's favorite fishing holes, the stream changes drastically. With the influence of many tributaries, the stream widens quickly and its pools and riffles deepen. The water here can be unwadable during many parts of the year, and anglers should be sure of their next step at all times.

This angler connects with an early season trout.

However, this portion of the stream is where truly large fish can be taken. Brook trout from nearby Oswayo hatchery find their way into the PFBC's big fish program each year, and the river has given up one state record brook trout after another and will no doubt defeat the current state record in the near future. The PFBC has long accepted stocked fish as state records. This practice is a bit misleading, since only Big Springs is able to produce brook trout of that size within the state that may truly be called wild. However, escaped hatchery fish keep one wondering if even those fish are truly wild natives.

It is well known that a Pennsylvania native brook trout exceeding 15 inches is a trophy of a lifetime. With that in mind, catching and releasing brookies that often exceed 4 pounds is challenging and rewarding when kept in perspective.

But there are no "gimmies" in fishing like there are in golf, and the river here decides when to give up its fish willingly and when to shut down. I have seen red quills and Hendricksons blanket the water and not one trout rose. I have seen a tremendous number of rises when the water was cold and the hatch minimal. The Allegheny, like many trout streams, is like that.

This is also good water to pulsate a marabou streamer through the deeper holes that hold the better fish—good rises are found mostly in the longer and deeper riffles. However, when water temperatures are right and tan caddis, cahills, Hendricksons, or drakes (both brown and eastern green) are hatching, this can be one of the finest streams for large trout to be found anywhere.

As the stream lengthens, it grows in size. By mid-June, most would agree that the trout population gives way to muskie and bass at or near the town of Roulette. By the time it reaches Port Allegany in neighboring McKean County, the bass and muskie are found in good numbers and size. From here the bass fishing can be excellent. It seems that bass are not the favorite fish of those visiting the northcentral sector of the state. However, trout are stocked over the 19 miles that separate Port Allegany and Coudersport, and fishing holds up well between the two towns until mid-June.

In normal years, not like those we have had off and on over the past five, the river provides good water temperatures and oxygen above Coudersport throughout the summer. Although most fishermen dismiss the water below the town, the appearance of large fish in and below the channel occurs each and every summer. If the water temperature heats up below the channel, fish may move out, but the size of fish found there leads me to believe that some of the deeper holes hold trout year-round and that some holes are fed by underground springs.

A host of tributary streams feed the Allegheny, supplying the cooler water it needs. Most of the streams are small and often overlooked. However, Mill Creek is an exceptional wild trout stream, small in most areas and having a wealth of streamside vegetation. It was an excellent wild trout stream when Jim and Silvia Bashline haunted it during their high school sweetheart days and remained one of their all-time favorites. Although Jim claimed it was not the stream it once had been, he said it was an excellent stream when they were fishing it.

Minor tributaries flow into the main stem below Coudersport, and all contribute to forming this large river. Fishing Creek is one of the more notable and is stocked by the PFBC.

The river is then a mixture of both wild trout and stocked, with muskie and bass hanging out on the fringes waiting for the drought years that will bring warmer water temperatures. When that happens, warmwater species move farther up the river to water normally inhabited only by trout. Still, the Allegheny River is a stream that deserves attention. It is an excellent trout stream until mid-June. After that, nature determines how long into the summer trout can be found in good numbers.

The majority of early season hatches appear during the afternoon hours, although I have found the Hendrickson (male, imitated by a red quill) appearing from noon to dusk on some brisk April days. I prefer large imitations downstream from Coudersport, simply because there are some tremendously deep holes there. Weighted nymphs and streamers with bead eyes and even lead eyes are not out of the question. I often use smaller lead eyes for larger nymphs, finding them easier to cast. However, I readily admit that I do not like casting split shot.

My favorite hatches here are sulphurs, tan caddis and green and brown drakes. My favorite streamer is the silver wolf, and my favorite nymphs are hare's ears and large muskrat nymphs. I like comparaduns here to imitate cahills and blue-winged olives. This is good fishing water that only attracts crowds in mid-April, and even then, the stream has so much water to cover that there is always enough room to get lost on your own.

ALLEGHENY RIVER MAJOR HATCHES

Insect	J	F	M	A	M	J	J	A	S	O	N	D
Blue Quill #18 (afternoon)				▬								
Brown Stonefly #12, 3X long				▬								
Quill Gordon #14				▬								
Hendrickson #12 & 14				▬								
Tan Caddis #12–16				▬								
Tan Caddis #16					▬▬▬▬▬▬▬▬							
Grannom #14					▬							
Sulphur #16						▬						
Green Drake #12, 3X long						▬						
Brown Drake Spinner #12, 3X long						▬						
March Brown #12 & 14						▬						
Light Cahill #12						▬						
Blue-winged Olive #16						▬						
Trico #24						▬▬▬▬▬						
Pale Evening Duns #16 & 18									▬▬▬			
Black Ant #16–20						▬▬▬▬▬▬						
Beetles #12–18						▬▬▬▬▬						
Grasshoppers #12 & 14						▬▬▬▬▬						

OSWAYO CREEK

The Oswayo has long been a little known stream, overlooked by many except in the more heavily stocked lower sections. The lower stream sections below Coneville have deep holes and are stocked by the PFBC.

This has always been one of my favorite streams in Potter County, and when a "kiss and tell" outdoor scribe asked me what streams to fish while in the county, I mistakenly trusted him. He and he and his wife were taking a jaunt across the area in search of story material and photos. I told him of the major streams he should visit and then, in a moment of weakness and swearing him to secrecy, told him of the Oswayo, a stream I never wrote about back then. Within a year the stream was written up in a state magazine, coauthored by the writer and his wife.

That experience ingrained within me not to tell fishermen where those few reserved streams of mine remain, and they are very few. That leads me to feel a little like a hypocrite, writing about a stream I had sworn so many others never to divulge. But over the past years, it has appeared in other books and in national magazines, so it seems that one more won't harm this small stream.

The upper portions are above the village of Coneville, where it is small and well guarded with willows and streamside vegetation. Most fishermen are aware that a PFBC hatchery is operated on the stream's uppermost reaches. As with most hatcheries, state or privately owned, some fish escape the confines of the hatchery, and it's not unusual that some of these nice sized trout find their way into Oswayo Creek.

However, the stream's small beginning has its fair share of wild brook trout, and when I first fished there 20 years ago, that is the fish I most often targeted. It is a sweet mix of pastureland with a buffer zone of streamside growth that becomes tunnel-like just upstream of the Coneville Bridge. The fishing here is difficult for casting purposes, and with a wild population of brookies, the meager flow only complicates the problems a flyfisher might encounter.

With the wealth of wild trout in the area, the stream was taken off the stocking list in the early 1980s and was vacated by opening day anglers as soon as the word got out. For the serious fly angler, that did nothing but improve the trout fishing on this unique stretch of water. Its uniqueness comes from the fact that it is a meadow stream in an area of the state where the vast majority of water is surrounded by mountains of hardwood. Meadow streams are often too easily warmed above a trout's tolerance.

Flyfishers come to the area not only for trout but to see the wildlife that gathers near the stream and scenery that is awesome to behold. Meadow streams most often seem to belong to the southern regions of the state.

The upper Oswayo is now considered wild trout waters, and there are many large browns that reside in the deep pools of the S-shaped stream course. The fish of these pools take time, patience, and luck to catch. At times they succumb to a flyfisher that has only the latter, but that is a rare occurrence and one that should not be counted on.

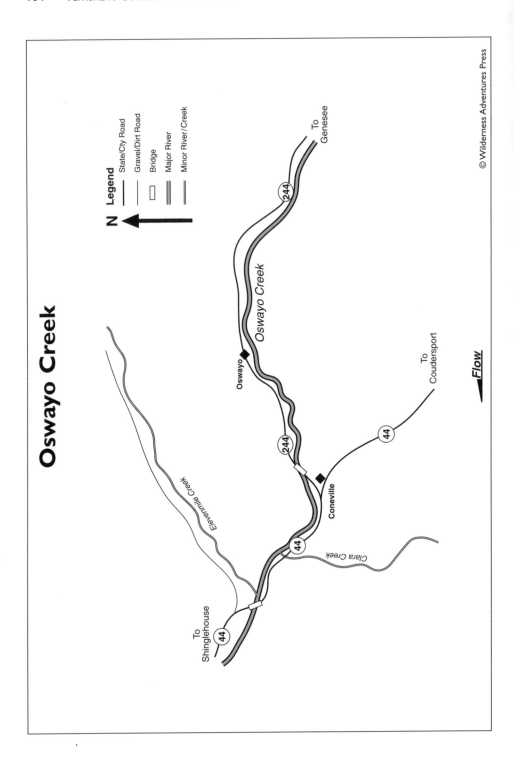

Oswayo Creek

A native brookie takes an Instigator.

This streams is deceptive—while wading in its shallow pools and riffles, the unsuspecting angler can come upon a hole that is 5 to 6 feet deep. It is a rude awakening and, perhaps more importantly, puts truly large trout down for close to a day. Rod choice can be a problem here, and I suggest two rigs, one for the meadow section and one for the section starting a few hundred yards above the Coneville Bridge downstream. My choice for the upper meadow would be a 9-foot, 4-weight, allowing an angler to stay back from the stream bank and deliver longer, delicate casts.

Tippet size should be 6X to 8X, and flies do not need to be as exact here as in many areas of the state. Brook trout often take attractor patterns, not limited to but including the Royal Coachman and my personal favorite, a mosquito pattern in sizes 12 through 16.

Later in the summer, ants, beetles, and hoppers all do well. Trout do not seem to be concerned as much with the pattern as the delivery. Wet flies, streamers, and nymphs are difficult to work in the uppermost sections of this stream, simply because it is important to stay far enough from the bank not to spook the fish. That's why I consider this sector premier dry fly water.

However, the section below the farm lane bridge is better suited for fishing with a 7½-foot rod and carrying a 5- to 6-weight line. Here, a fast action rod allows casting from the brush-crowded shoreline into the deeper pools. I put lead eyes on large muskrat nymphs and tie streamers that might be considered more suited to taking tarpon than trout. A good sign that truly large trout swim in and around the tangled root systems is that they seldom rise to minor hatches in the deeper pools. These trout require heavier tippets to turn flies over, and 4X is often not heavy enough. In this stream, the majority of larger trout will be lost before the battle begins if the tippet is too light.

The deep pools return to shallow riffles above the bridge at Coneville and the fishing returns to beadhead nymphs and small dry flies and more exacting patterns.

Below the Coneville bridge, the state stocks the stream. Be aware that in this section there are deeply cut banks, forming pools that can swallow a fisherman and have him coming up gasping for air. Large trout reside here and stay due to the cool water from tributary streams. Perhaps the most important are Eleven Mile and Clara Creeks, two streams with enough cool water to maintain the water temperature for a wild trout stream and to hold stocked trout.

Oswayo Creek is extremely special and offers the major hatches of the state's northcentral region. The major plus to this stream is that it is full of trout when the Trico hatch appears in July. A prevalent hatch in the northcentral area, it is often lost to warmwaters void of good numbers of trout. On the Oswayo, trout remain throughout the year.

Now that I have written about this wonderful stream, I simply ask that you treat it and its inhabitants with care and respect, so that those who follow will find it in the same condition I did 20-odd years ago.

The stream is found by going 12 miles north of Coudersport on SR 44, then turning right at Coneville onto SR 244 to fish the upper reaches, or stay on SR 44 to fish the larger, deeper water.

OSWAYO CREEK MAJOR HATCHES

Insect	J	F	M	A	M	J	J	A	S	O	N	D
Blue Quill #16				▬								
Hendrickson #14				▬								
Tan Caddis #12–16					▬							
Sulphur #16					▬							
March Brown #12 & 14					▬							
Green Drake #12, 3X long					▬							
Yellow Drake #12 & 14						▬						
Trico #22 & 24							▬					

LYMAN RUN

Lyman Run is a typical brook trout stream. Despite a dirt road parallelling its nearly 6.4 miles, upon leaving your vehicle, a short walk to any stream section will give you an immediate feeling of a wilderness trout stream.

The stream is narrow, about two steps to cross to the other bank, and many sections do not allow much of a backcast. The stream is filled with brook trout, and although it is stocked by the PFBC, it might be better left to fend for itself. There is a lot of canopy in the area, and a good population of native brook trout that measure 5 to 7 inches in length. Because of the stream's small size and clear mountain water, fishing here for wild trout is difficult. The stream does yield some true trophy, native fish that may run up to 12 inches in length. Stocked fish are often caught quickly and rather easily from this small brook during the high waters of spring.

The stream's upper portion is managed under the Commission's Selective Harvest Program, which requires that a legal native brookie must be 9 inches long. This program protects the stream's vast majority of trout in this section that reach sexual maturity at around 5 inches in length. The 4-mile stretch begins at Lyman Lake and extends upstream to Splash Dam Hollow.

Although the lake does remain cold enough to support trout year-round, the Project Water finds rainbow and large browns in the lower sections during many times of the year. The waters of Lyman remain in the 50s and 60s during most years to create a true coldwater resource.

The water below the dam is basically put-and-take since the stream becomes degraded rapidly, and the better fishing concludes in early June. Hatches here are amazing in number, if not quantity, and are much the same as the hatches found on Lyman Lake.

The stream is best fished with a short rod of 7 to 7½ feet carrying a 2- to 4-weight line. Despite a good number of hatches, attractor patterns and terrestrials work well here because the stream's inhabitants are always hungry. The approach and cast are best thought out in great detail before laying a line on this water.

Hip boots are all that is needed to fish this stream. Be forewarned that anglers have encountered more than a few rattlesnakes here during the summer months. The hatch chart will follow Lyman Lake and may be used for both waters.

This stream is located above the lake at Lyman Run State Park off of T396, 7 miles west of Galeton.

LYMAN LAKE

Pennsylvania is not blessed with many true trout lakes. Most are impoundments of older design, built in the name of flood control. Others came into being when the state parks were planned. The plan seemed simple enough: put in a park with places for picnicking and, most recently, rental cabins, then add a lake. However, the need for all to have a lake may have been overkill, and we have lost a lot of trout water because of dam placement on what had been trout streams.

Lyman Run and Lyman Lake

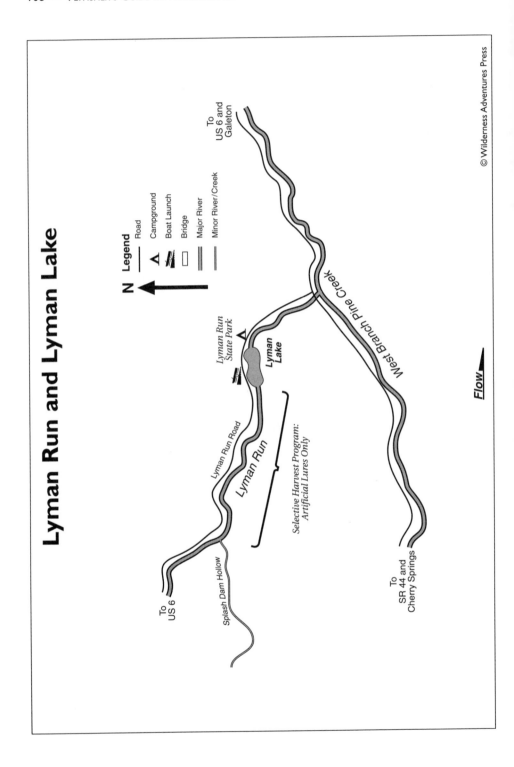

Native brook trout are found throughout Pennsylvania.

We have gained swimming areas and beautiful settings for family outings, and I cannot condemn anyone for that. However, the maintenance of such structures has cost taxpayers dearly and will continue to do so as many need repairs. Lyman Lake, with an old top-water spillway, stopped the coldwater fishery of Lyman Run in its tracks.

Recently, a state park dam was removed and another nixed by legislators as part of a new state park. It seems we have become more educated in what we do. State parks of the future will consider all aspects of the environment—something that has been labeled biodiversity.

I envision parks that stand along a stream filled with wild trout or a warmwater river and a new breed of visitors who appreciate the resource and the value of free flowing streams.

The Army Corps of Engineers, once insistent upon placing dams wherever they could and highly in favor of such structures, has done an about-face. They are now taking a hard stand against the building of new dams within the state. Now, dams must prove their worth and plans must prove that there will be little environmental impact to the waters that they affect. To flyfishers everywhere, this will, in time, help fishing waters, both warm and cold, especially those that are gateways to the sea.

Lyman Lake is significant because it is a true coldwater impoundment. Anglers within the state equate dams with either a warmwater fishery or a put-and-take trout fishery necessitated by the warm water that impoundments create. I believe that most anglers in the state have not learned to fish impoundments that hold trout, simply because there are so few.

When I first visited Potter County in 1972, I was looking for a place to live away from the bureaucracy of larger corporations and the state capital. I have always been thankful that we are not all looking for the same thing in life, or rural Potter County would be far too populous.

My visit was immediately after the 1972 flood, and the area had suffered extreme damage. The trout streams I had come to fish were running over their banks and were chocolate in color. A small country store in Gaines sold hand-tied flies, and I decided to kill a few hours looking through them. Always interested in local patterns that are often unique, I found a nicely tied March brown pattern that was more buggy looking than most. The guard hairs protruded far from the gold tinsel that was wound carefully over the top and around the dubbing. It reminded me of a hare's ear rather than a March brown, and I have always had a strong preference for natural dubbing.

The owner, probably trying to rid herself of a pent-up flyfisher with nowhere to fish, suggested that Lyman Lake might be fishable, and it was ... barely.

Without a boat, I carefully picked my way across the dam breast to find clear water along the opposite shore. Although the lake was filled with silted water, there were some clear water areas littered with woody debris that had gathered 50 feet from the dam breast. I was delighted to find trout rising in the midst of the rubble and within the next two hours took 25 nice firm trout, three topping the 18-inch mark.

The March browns were coming off despite all the havoc Mother Nature had created. The trout were congregated in the clear waters and feeding heavily. Many lake anglers here do not watch for significant fly hatches, and my feeling is that they should, especially spinnerfalls that are even known to deposit their eggs on wet blacktop.

Lyman Lake holds a good population of trout and some carryover fish that may exceed 8 pounds. The lake is best fished from a boat unless you're interested in the stocked fish hanging around the shoreline closest to the park before they become acclimated to the lake and begin to scatter.

Here, a 9-foot rod carrying a 6-weight line is preferable but a 5-weight will do. To fish the lake effectively, carry two reels or an extra spool—one with a floating line and another with a sinktip. Also use small lead eye streamers to probe the deeper water, as well as traditional wet flies to match the hatch in progress. A mosquito pattern is an excellent searching pattern when fishing the shoreline, which is where I catch the majority of trout here.

The great part about Lyman Lake is the fact that it remains cold throughout the summer months. It is rare to find water temperatures here close to 70 degrees, even in August. Anglers should also carry an assortment of large muskrat and stonefly nymph imitations. My favorite nymph here is a muskrat nymph tied on size 6 and 8 streamer hooks.

Lyman Lake is only 40 acres, but it holds large browns, rainbows, and, close to the source, brookies. The lake is located at Lyman Run State Park off T-396, 7 miles west of Galeton.

Regulations on the lake allow electric motors only, and the ramp is a beach type, not suitable for launching large boats. Shallow-draft, lightweight fishing boats, canoes, and inflatables are suggested here. Camping facilities may be found at the park.

The following hatch chart is for both the lake and Lyman Run.

LYMAN LAKE AND RUN MAJOR HATCHES

Insect	J	F	M	A	M	J	J	A	S	O	N	D
Blue Quill #16 & 18				█								
Hendrickson #14				█								
Quill Gordon #14				█								
Black Stone #16				█								
Gray Fox #14					█							
Sulphur #16					█							
March Brown #12					█							
Green Drake #12, 3X long (Coffin Fly Spinner)						█						
Tan Caddis #16					█	█	█		█			
Tan Caddis #12 & 14					█	█						
Cream Cahill #18									█			
Terrestrials (ending date dependent on cold weather)							█	█	█	█		
The Run offers excellent gypsy moth caterpillar fishing.												

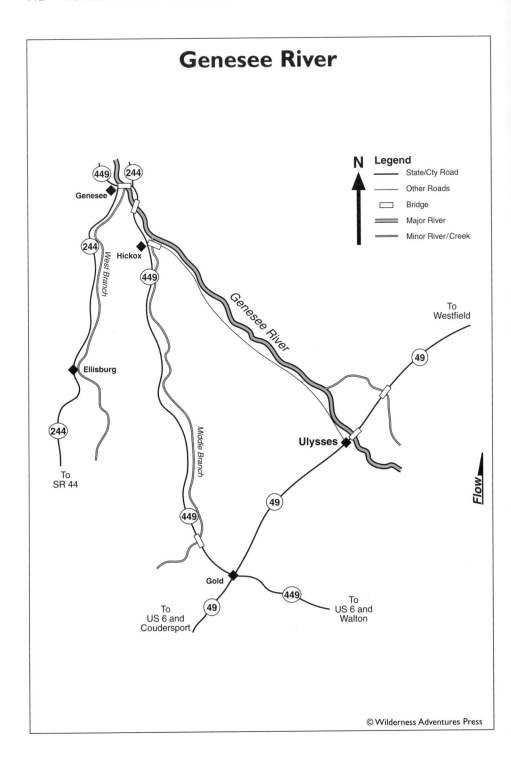

Genesee River

GENESEE RIVER AND BRANCHES

The Genesee River and its branches are all stocked waters—PFBC stocks the main branch and the West Branch. If confusion is a factor here, it lies within the names of the stream and its branches. If you look at the list of "Approved Trout Waters" found in the summary book that accompanies your fishing license, the streams are listed as Genesee River, Middle Branch and West Branch. I don't wish to blame the Commission, they didn't name the river, but the reader should be aware of this.

The fact that this river flows north, rather than south, helps escalate the confusion as well. The river is one of the few in the country that flows north. The Genesee and Middle Branch meet at the town of Hickox, with the Middle Branch paralleling SR 449. The river begins near Ulysses and can be found following SR 1011. The West Branch begins near Rose Valley Lake and can be reached easily from SR 244.

This is a traditional freestone stream—small, with native brookies and carryover browns in the headwaters and stocked with hatchery trout. Unlike many streams here, it does flow through pastureland in places. It is a good early season stream and then begins to falter in early to mid-June. The headwaters and cold tributaries help keep resident trout in the area. This is water worth exploring, even if its northward flow is confusing.

Early season hatches, blue quills, Quill Gordons and Hendricksons, are prevalent here. Hip waders with felt soles are needed near the town of Genesee, while the headwaters may be fished with hip boots.

These streams are not under any special regulations, and Coudersport is the hub city for medical needs and lodging.

PINE CREEK

Until recently Pine Creek had been one of those so-so streams. The main stem warmed too early for good trout fishing, and with the amount of excellent trout water in this part of the state, Pine Creek was virtually ignored.

However, the popularity of Cedar and Slate Runs and Wolfe's Orvis Shop brought the attention of flyfishers across the nation. Because of the size of Slate Run, it can only accommodate so many anglers per day. And with the growing interest and crowds on Cedar, visiting anglers began to test the waters of Pine Creek.

The addition of Delayed Harvest regulations on Little Pine Creek helped the popularity of the stream, and more flyfishers began to find the stream to their liking. The stream is large near Cedar and Slate Runs and reminds many of a Western river. It is large and brawling and does offer some swift current during the spring and deep holes all season long. Nearby Cedar and Slate Runs are on the small size and casting is confined. Here, the angler can cast to his heart's content, making long casts without fear of lurking branches catching backcasts.

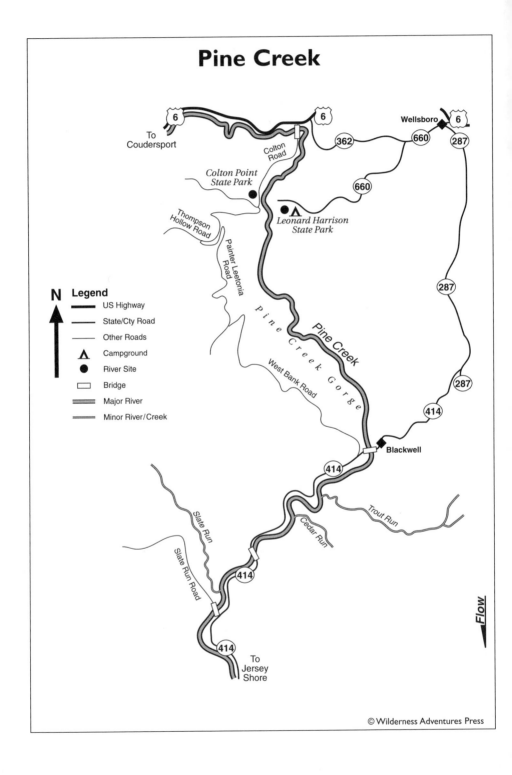

Pine Creek

Riffles, which provide oxygen for trout, are often highly productive.

The stream receives a good amount of stocked fish, some reaching good proportions. Early season angling, April through mid-June, is often excellent but drops off quickly after that. The fishing here is either good or bad, depending mostly on water temperature. Warming water usually means shrinking water, and that equates to less oxygen for trout. Because Pine's riffles can and often do extend for hundreds upon hundreds of yards, as do the pools, riffle fishing a trio of wet flies can last longer than pool fishing and be extremely productive. Fishing a bushy dry fly with a trailing beadhead, stonefly nymph, or caddis larva often produces excellent results. However, as with all streams here, a stream thermometer is extremely important and will dictate when and where to fish.

Although the stream provides decent trout fishing and heavy hatches, the dam in Galeton, located in eastern Potter County, does cause some problems. The dam, a grandiose plan like so many, was built to attract tourists: Galeton would be a town around a recreational body of water. I was there when many well-meaning people were making the plans. Although seldom able to say I was right about something, I was in this instance when I said it would be nothing but a silt catcher. It has also been detrimental to upstream migration of trout and, in turn, has taken with it the excellent trout fishing that was once found on the West Branch. The lake is dredged often to keep some sort of water level trapped within it, and one can only hope that it will be taken out entirely someday in the future.

Pine Creek is a river of many faces, many of them manmade. The canyon section near the town of Wellsboro in Tioga County, is filled with beauty, rafts, and canoes. It offers some excellent fishing in areas if one is patient enough to wait out the steady traffic pattern continuously flowing by. The stream here yields native brookies as well as wild browns. If you really want to fish this section of stream, the best bet is to wait until the water becomes too low for a pleasant canoe or raft trip.

In most years that would require waiting until July or August. Most flyfishermen have given way to the canoes and rafts since they have a right the water, too. Foregoing this section of a river that flows 200 miles is not all that much to give up. Access to good sections of stream that are stocked and carry wild and native trout can be found between Ansonia and Walton off US 6. Pine Creek offers some excellent early season hatches in this area.

The fishing lasts longer into summer than it does in the more popular places near the area where Trout Run, Cedar Run, and Slate Run enter the larger river. The fishing here may be found off SR 44 and then 144 heading north.

As with most large streams of this magnitude, trout migrate in and out of the tributary streams. It has not been scientifically documented to date, but most free-stone flyfishers with enough wading experience to have worn out as many pairs of waders as they have shoes have noted this movement. It has become apparent, in my many years of flyfishing that trout move as the water warms, as I have previously noted. Rainbows tend to turn tail and head downstream, while any native brookie or wild brown, along with stocked browns, looks for underground springs, often found in the deeper pools, or heads up one of the cold tributary streams.

A few miles below Slate Run, the stream turns into stocked trout and bass water. Temperatures here become too high to hold trout except in isolated pockets as late June gives way to early July (see Little Pine Creek).

Pine Creek is an exceptional body of water that tends to fade and then revive with each tributary that it passes. A stream thermometer will lead to the better fishing to be found here, and Pine is a springboard to many of the better tributary streams that enter the large river.

LITTLE PINE CREEK

Little Pine Creek is another DHALO stream located in Lycoming County. The regulated stretch begins 200 yards downstream from Otter Run and ends at the confluence of Schoolhouse Hollow. Although the special regulations apply to only just over a mile, the stream has a mix of wild browns, native brookies, and stocked trout.

The "Little" is used to distinguish this stream from Pine Creek itself, which Little Pine joins a few miles below in the big valley along SR 44. Little Pine Creek is a significant stream in its own right. It is more than 40 feet wide in sections with deceptively swift water and pools that are deeper than they look. Fishing is excellent, but anglers new to the area should be aware of the stream's ever-changing character.

Wild trout streams are often small.

Gravel bars routinely shift positions, and holes "move around" when there is enough winter rain or snowmelt.

The headwaters area is privately owned by a fishing club, but public water runs from just above English Center to the Little Pine Creek Dam, approximately 6½ miles downstream, and there is excellent fishing to found there. From the dam to Waterville, the stream holds mostly stocked fish and warmer water temperatures that make this a put-and-take fishery.

Throughout the open water above the dam, there is a series of nice pools and riffles and a good number of wild browns and native brook trout. Stocking occurs throughout most of its length, and the combination of trout and good water temperatures above the dam provides excellent fishing.

As with all freestones, flows fluctuate routinely according to the amount of rain, which can create problems for some anglers. By wading carefully, extending the leader, and approaching carefully as the season progresses, an angler can experience some wonderful fishing. If a Pennsylvania freestone has good hatches and water temperatures throughout the season, there is little more that can be asked for in a trout stream.

Little Pine is a wonderful freestone stream—one of the better creeks in the region. Follow SR 44 north to Waterville and head east on SR 4001 until the DHALO signs appear.

LITTLE PINE CREEK MAJOR HATCHES

Insect	J	F	M	A	M	J	J	A	S	O	N	D
Blue Quill #16 & 18				■								
Hendrickson #14				■								
Quill Gordon #14				■								
March Brown #12					■							
Sulphurs #16					■							
Gray Fox #12						■						
Blue-winged Olive #16						■						
Green Drake #12, 3X long (Coffin Fly Spinner)						■						
Light Cahill #14						■						
Cream Cahill #16 & 18							■					
Slate Drake #14							■					
Tan Caddis #20 & 24							■					
Blue-winged Olive #18 & 20								■				
Cream Cahill #18									■			
Terrestrials						■	■	■	■			

CEDAR RUN

While living in Potter County and putting my boots on every freestone imaginable, it took a few years and a little coaxing for me to travel to Cedar Run to fish. After that first encounter in the mid-1970s, it didn't take long for me to return. At first, it became a monthly trip, and before long, I found myself going every other week. Cedar Run was and still is a topnotch wild trout fishery.

As is common with all the streams in this area of the state, Cedar Run is paralleled by gravel and dirt roads. Seven and a half miles of the stream is designated as Trophy Trout Water, and many feel the designation does not give the stream enough protection. The 7-mile trophy trout stretch begins at the confluence with Buck Run downstream to the mouth of Pine Creek.

The stream is filled with boulders, and springtime often offers high waters from runoff. However, in recent years, that has not been the case, and the fabulous hatches of April coming off on relatively low, clear water is an experience not to be missed.

It is a small freestone that rarely exceeds 25 feet in width. However, much like Slate Run, which lies only five miles away, it should be treated more like a brook trout stream, where approach and delivery are prime considerations.

Average trout size may have been exaggerated over the years—most run below the 14-inch size limit that trophy regulations call for. But there are large browns that come to the fly year after year. Many of these trout reside in the stream year-round, and many more migrate from Pine Creek beginning in mid-June when the larger stream's water becomes warm and Cedar Run's constant cold flows attract them like humans to an air-conditioner during a heat wave. When these trout first arrive, they are very lethargic and are not in a feeding mood.

If you do convince a trout to take at this time, you will find the fight has gone out of them, and they may even roll over and die from the added stress. I feel strongly that these fish should be left alone long enough to regain the strength they lost fighting the continually warming waters of Pine.

Many of the trout spend some time lying in the cooler flows at the mouth of the tributary before actually entering it. The abundance of food in Pine Creek is hard to pass up since Cedar's food, rich in its own way, does not have the abundance of crayfish, shiners, and aquatic life that the large river has.

When it rains for a few days during the summer months and the small feeder begins to rise, it's time to head for Cedar Run, where large fish have regained their strength and moved farther into the small tributary. This can be the best fishing of the year, as can September when cream cahills and tan caddis arrive.

While a 4-pound trout isn't possible on every visit, they are here in good numbers. In time, a beautiful, streambred brown will be your reward. And don't overlook the state's native jewel, the brook trout, which is a beautiful fish no matter what its size.

SLATE RUN

Slate Run is quickly becoming one of the state's flyfishing hotspots. This small stream can be found by following SR 441 and 114 north along Pine Creek from Waterville. At the bridge, turn left to the Manor Motel and Slate Run Tackle Shop, where there is ample parking. The pools here are beautiful, containing a mix of native brook trout and wild browns. This stream is managed under the PFBC's Heritage Trout Angling Program and is open to flyfishing only, with catch-and-release regulations in effect year-round. The Heritage Trout water is 7 miles in length beginning at the confluence of Cushman and Francis Branch and extending to the mouth.

When I first wandered onto Slate Run back in the 1970s, the stream was of immediate interest to me. Unlike the many brook and wild brown trout streams of Lycoming and Tioga Counties, this stream provided excellent fishing with an opportunity to catch and release fish that seemed far too large for a stream this size.

The lower reaches are easily accessible, which creates rather intense fishing pressure. However, the fish seem to have become accustomed to the parade of anglers and will feed shortly after being put down. I have found the better section to be upstream, where there are only a few paths down the steep mountainside. This is definitely snake country, and rattlesnakes are not that uncommon as early as June and then throughout the summer.

If the steep incline and pathless wilderness do not deter anglers, mentioning venomous snakes helps. I fear the critters as much as the next person, but with water beckoning and the knowledge that some really good fishing is in the offing, I tend to forget snakes until I clamber out of the stream with a dim flashlight in hand. To find the better waters, it is preferable to stay off the beaten path, carry a wading staff to deter snakes, and hum a lot—my friends tell me this warns the snakes that some wader-clad angler is sliding down the steep incline.

Wading is extremely difficult and a staff is helpful in finding your way and getting around the rocks that seem to be everywhere. Keeping in mind that a cautious approach is necessary, fish this stream as you would any wild brook trout stream in the state. This is a stream with a wealth of trout and a great number of hatches, unusual for a small freestone that slides down a steep gradient and often forms near-whitewater rapid conditions. But a series of pools and gentle riffles make the fishing more tolerable than the wading can be.

Patterns used in the upper section remind me of Art Flick and his simple, yet well designed, flies. The wet-fly fisherman of old would do well here with a three wet-fly rig. If the stream doesn't provide a lot of trout on any given day, the scenery of this rather remote and rugged area will make up for it. It is one of those unique streams that requires immense patience and tests one's fishing skills but not in the same manner that a meadow stream does. This is a thin water stream during most of the summer months, and approach is often more important than the pattern.

FRANCIS BRANCH
Tributary to Slate Run

The Francis Branch is a tributary to Slate Run and runs through the same type of terrain found on Slate Run (see Slate Run for hatch chart and equipment). This stream section is managed as Heritage Trout Angling and is managed without stocking. The main feature of this branch is the beauty of the area, the rugged terrain, and the native brook trout that reside here. It is also a coldwater sanctuary, and wild browns appear in this stream section as well.

Heritage Trout Angling regulations begin at the mouth upstream 1.7 miles to Kramer Hollow.

SLATE RUN MAJOR HATCHES

Insect	J	F	M	A	M	J	J	A	S	O	N	D
Little Black Stone #16 & 18			▬									
Hendrickson #14				▬								
Blue Quill # 16 & 18				▬								
Quill Gordon #14				▬								
Tan Caddis #12 & 14					▬							
Tan Caddis #16						▬						
March Brown #12						▬						
Gray Fox #12							▬					
Light Cahill #14							▬					
Green Drake #12, 3X long (Coffin Fly Spinner)							▬					
Sulphur #16							▬					
Blue-winged Olive #16							▬					
Slate Drake #12 & 14							▬					
Trico #24								▬▬				
Terrestrials								▬▬▬				

Terrestrials in the form of caterpillars, elm span worms, and all leaf eating insects are of extreme importance.

One of the area's beautiful freestones.

GRAY'S RUN

Gray's Run, a fairly small stream, falls under the PFBC's Selective Harvest Program, but between Labor Day and opening day in April, it is under catch-and-release regulations and allows both spinning and flyfishing. There are a number of parking areas on the 2.2-mile special regulations section that runs from Gray's Run Hunting Club to the TR 842 concrete bridge. The stream is clearly marked.

Although there is plenty of casting room on most stretches, anglers will also discover spots that require short, accurate casting. Gray's Run does have Class A water below the project area, adding to the possibilities of catching a mix of both wild browns, native brookies, and stocked trout throughout this stream. This section has far too many splits to retain enough cold water to last well into the season.

Gray's Run can be found by following SR 14 through the intersection of SR 15 for three miles to Lower Gray's Run Road. Follow Gray's Run Road to the bridge at the lower limits of the Project Waters. Parking is available from this point upstream to the upper limits.

The complete early spring Gray's fly box contains Matuka streamers in white, black, brown, and green; woolly buggers with yellow, brown, black, and green bodies; Zonkers in green, black, and white; Marabou streamers in white, brown, and black, sizes 6 and 8, 3X long; stonefly nymphs in yellow, black, and brown, sizes 6 to 8, 3X long.

You might find midges during the winter months, and if so, use white, peacock, brown or black bodied flies in sizes 20 to 24. Other flies to consider are green weenies, sizes 8 through 12, 2X and 3X long, and grizzly caddis, dries, size 16 and 18. Also carry a few beadhead nymphs in black, brown, green, and tan, sizes 10 to 16.

My favorite on this water is a Marabou streamer, white with chain eyes to achieve depth and a lot of pearl Flashabou with three strands of green Krystal Flash on top, sizes 6 to 10, 3X long.

Taking a spill is a possibility on any of these streams, making hypothermia a real threat during winter months. It is a good idea to take along a daypack filled with extra clothes (in a plastic bag in case of a dunking) and some high-energy food. The water here is well guarded, and the stream temperature is always cold.

Hatches here are good, having all the standard April through July hatches one would expect to find on a freestone stream this far north. Like all freestones, the water does become thin during the summer months, so expect to be fishing over selective trout with long leaders.

A good mixture of stocked and streambred trout do exist in this stream that is often overlooked as a minor tributary.

GRAY'S RUN MAJOR HATCHES

Insect	J	F	M	A	M	J	J	A	S	O	N	D
Midges #22 & 24 (brown, green, white)	■											
Blue Quill #16 & 18				■								
Hendrickson #14				■								
Quill Gordon #14				■								
Tan Caddis #16					■	■			■			
Gray Fox #12					■							
March Brown #12					■							
Light Cahill #14					■							
Blue-winged Olive #14 & 16					■							
Cream Cahill #16 & 18						■		■				
Terrestrials						■	■	■	■	■		

*An angler tests the
waters of Elk Creek.*

ELK CREEK

Elk Creek is a 16-mile coldwater stream in the truest sense, even though over-shadowed by Penns Creek. However, Elk Creek gives Penns a shot in the arm when it first begins to warm— the expanded All Tackle Trophy Trout water added to Penns is placed strategically below the confluence of Elk Creek.

From the headwaters, 1.5 miles are managed as a native brook trout stream and the remainder as wild brown trout. The stream has very few postings and remains open to the general fishing public. The headwaters are found off Stover Gap Road, and the stream slips into Penns near Coburn.

This small stream holds good numbers of both wild browns and native brookies, and its hatches continue throughout the year. This small limestone stream has many faces and is one of the few streams with wild trout that slips through wooded land and then pasture.

A small stream with all wild trout does not necessarily mean easy fishing, although the hatches and their numbers make it much easier on some days than others. Terrestrial fishing is excellent in the meadow stretches, and the green drake does appear here in fairly good numbers. However, long leaders, a careful approach, and thin tippets will be the order of the day.

Best fished when overcast, the stream challenges and rewards the best flyfishers, and yes, it does have an incredible hatch of sulphurs. To date, the PFBC does little management other than to close these streams before spawning time in order to protect them. Note that no special regulations are placed on this stream and very few other high quality streams in the state.

The lowering of the creel limit from 8 to 5 on all trout water should help, but please release all fish that you take here. Resources like this are too few and far between to take fish from, and with the hatches so prevalent here, it is one of those few food-rich streams that remain loaded with wild trout.

If you do not care for small streams, this stream is not for you. Most sections are less than 15 feet wide, and there are very few as wide as 25 feet.

The stream is easy to locate off SR 45 at Coburn. Access may also be gained off SR 0445 upstream from Millheim. Rods carrying 2- to 4-weight lines work well here, and the stream is easily fished in hip boots.

ELK CREEK MAJOR HATCHES

Insect	J	F	M	A	M	J	J	A	S	O	N	D
Blue Quill #16 & 18					▬		▬					
Tan Caddis #14					▬							
Sulphur #16					▬▬							
March Brown #12					▬							
Green Drake #12, 3X long					▬							
Tan Caddis #16						▬			▬			
Blue-winged Olive #16						▬						
Trico #24								▬▬				
Cream Cahill #18									▬			
Terrestrials (ending date dependent on cold weather)						▬▬▬▬▬						

Ants, beetles, and grasshoppers are extremely important, especially in the meadow section.

MUNCY CREEK

One of my favorite streams in this portion of the state is Muncy Creek. It's small in size and often has clear, low water and can therefore be a challenge. The DHALO section starts a few hundred yards above the TR650 bridge, then continues downstream nearly to the confluence with Big Run at Tivoli. The stream is smaller in size than the Loyalsock, and although there are pools 40 to 50 feet wide, Muncy offers a unique blend of water, from long, slow pools to shallow riffles and small pools with great depth. Heavily stocked, the stream offers excellent fishing amidst a mixture of farmland and mountains.

Fishing the waters deeply and slowly should result in a good number of trout from the deeper pools. During late spring and early summer, the creek's flow becomes thin and the water becomes starkly clear. Hatches are stronger and more intense on some of the larger nearby streams, but Muncy Creek offers the angler a nice mixture of deeper pools and long glides.

The fishing then ranges from casting a fine 15-foot leader over visible fish holding in the thin glides to adding split shot for drifting nymphs through the deeper holes. The fact that the Loyalsock is close at hand usually results in fewer fishermen tromping the banks of Muncy Creek.

Early season hatches are good and this is a prime time to fish here since the stream begins to warm quickly as summer deepens. I would wear waders here, although hip boots are enough to cover many parts of the stream.

There are underground springs seeping into many of the deeper pools, and as summer progresses, a stream thermometer is a necessary item to take along. Thin glides can warm the water above the trout's tolerance level by the end of June and especially into July. However, this is when trout move on to the cooler waters of deeper holes. Some may be taken with surface imitations, but many will need to be brought from the depths of these pools that can be at least waist deep.

Crayfish patterns, beadhead nymphs, and thinly tied streamers usually do the trick. Green weenies with rubberlegs work extremely well. The last time I visited here, the only things that took fish with great regularity were green weenies, elm span worms, and sulphurs during an evening hatch.

This is a challenging stream that allows fishing longer than is possible on most freestones. Many anglers are not aware of the opportunities that exist on Muncy beyond the mid-June to July fishing when other freestones begin to falter.

Access is readily available off SR 220—watch for the Delayed Harvest signs if you want to fish the project area that contains some excellent fishing. As with all freestones, the upper reaches are where colder waters are found and thus wild and native trout as well as a chance to fish longer. The upper portion is near Sonesville in Sullivan County, and the lower reaches are found around Muncy before the stream enters the Susquehanna River.

Early season fishing may be found throughout the stream's length. Good hatches prevail, but as a rule, it's best to proceed upstream as the season progresses for the best fishing.

The Yellow Adams in sizes 12 to 16 is a must here, as it imitates many insects found in this stream, from cahills to yellow drakes and even sulphur spinners.

MUNCY CREEK MAJOR HATCHES

Insect	J	F	M	A	M	J	J	A	S	O	N	D
Blue Quill #16 & 18				■	■							
Hendrickson #14				■								
Quill Gordon #14				■								
Gray Fox #14					■							
Sulphur #16					■							
Tan Caddis #16					■	■	■	■	■			
Slate Drake #14					■							
Light Cahill #14					■							
Yellow Drake #12 & 14							■					
Cream Cahill #18									■			
Blue-winged Olive #18 & 20				■								
Terrestrials (ending date dependent on cold weather						■	■	■	■			

Loyalsock Creek

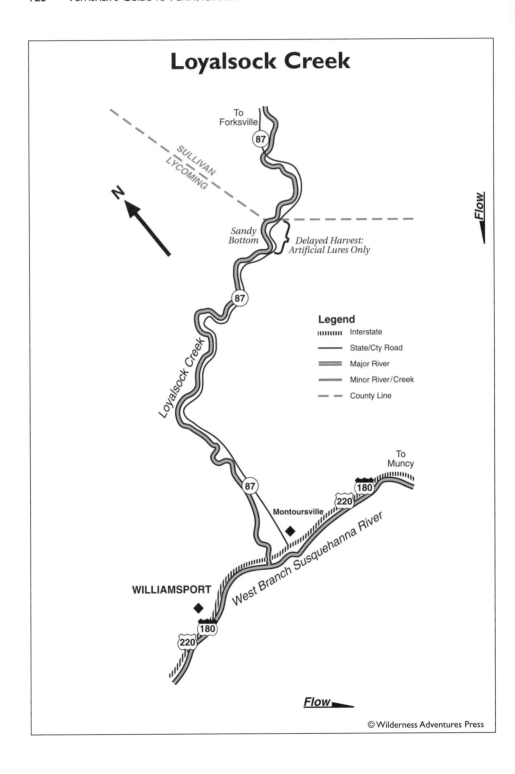

To
Forksville

87

SULLIVAN
LYCOMING

N

Flow

*Sandy
Bottom*

*Delayed Harvest:
Artificial Lures Only*

87

Loyalsock Creek

Legend

⁓⁓⁓⁓	Interstate
⎯⎯	State/Cty Road
▭▭▭	Major River
⎯⎯	Minor River/Creek
⎯ ⎯	County Line

To
Muncy

87

180

220

Montoursville

West Branch Susquehanna River

WILLIAMSPORT

180

220

Flow

© Wilderness Adventures Press

LOYALSOCK CREEK

The section of the 'Sock from the Lycoming County line downstream to Sandy Bottom should rightfully be labeled a river. It is steeped in history and bold in character. The flow may be up at any given time of the year, and a good pool-to-riffle ratio is to be found on the 1.4-mile stretch of DHALO designated water. The larger pools are more than a single cast across, and the depth, when flows are up, makes wading the width of this stream dangerous if not impossible. It is a brawling river with white-capped riffles and deep, silent pools, true symbols of a freestone river.

This creek should be waded with care because of its flow capabilities and boulder-strewn bottom that can make a slip into the chilly currents a stark reality. It is wise to dress warmly and carry an extra set of clothing—a good idea wherever you happen to wander during the early season.

This section of the Loyalsock is open to all forms of artificial lures and flies. During the early portion of the year, the fly angler will need to probe the depths with a wide variety of streamers and large nymphs. Green weenies take fish here as they do all over the state, and I would not take off for an early-season stream without large muskrat nymphs and a variety of stonefly nymphs tied in sizes 6 and 8 with 3X long hooks. Of course, the woolly bugger in a variety of colors and sizes is a must for early-season fishing.

The Loyalsock is found in a beautiful setting and is a favorite destination for many anglers. It is found by following SR 87 north from Williamsport. Access is easily available along the well-marked Delayed Harvest Artificial Lures Only (DHALO) stretch.

The water here reminds me of Western rivers during spring. There are deep holes that make wading difficult most of the year, and a wading staff is highly recommended as are felt-soled waders, something that everyone should have when wading in a freestone stream.

Even when the water recedes during the summer months, deep holes remain and enough coldwater tributaries enter this stream to allow for extended angling. During thin water times, trout find the main current that moves back and forth throughout the flow. One small section of stream may require wading the slippery bottom to the far side in order to cast to the far bank where trout are rising.

The 'Sock is not without its problems, however, since mining in the area continues. It is beautiful country, but trout fishing here on the Loyalsock is poor. Many of the feeder streams are either filled with mine acid runoff or silt from logging operations. Many of the better feeder streams flow through private property. The fishing really does not pick up to any degree before the Little Loyalsock joins forces with the its larger relative to dance some 15 miles downstream. Below the Project Water, the stream begins to warm rather quickly, and trout fishing declines on the way downstream to Montoursville where it enters the Susquehanna River.

The stream is rich with aquatic life, and the green drake hatch is back in good numbers, enough to allow excellent dry-fly fishing. Because of my love for dry-fly

Waders are essential on many Pennsylvania streams and rivers.

fishing and larger rivers, the Loyalsock fills that bill nicely. In the past, the stream held few fish throughout the summer, but the carryover rate and amount of good feeder streams seems to be helping it retain fish over a longer period of time. For those without the time to explore this stream, I would begin fishing in the Special Regulation Waters and work upstream.

Be aware that there are a good number of posted waters along the stream but enough open water to make this a good stream and well worth a visit. For those who like long casts and rising trout, this stream could be a favorite. The better fishing ends sometime in late June into July.

LOYALSOCK CREEK MAJOR HATCHES

Insect	J	F	M	A	M	J	J	A	S	O	N	D
Blue Quill #16 & 18				█	█	█						
Hendrickson #14				█								
Quill Gordon #14				█								
Brown Stone Fly # 12 & 14				█								
Gray Fox #14					█							
Sulphur #16					█							
March Brown #12					█							
Green Drake #12, 3X long (Coffin Fly Spinner)						█						
Tan Caddis #16					█	█	█		█			
Slate Drake #14					█	█						
Cream Cahill #18						█	█		█			
Trico #24 (spotty)							█	█				
Terrestrials (ending date dependent on cold weather)						█	█	█	█	█		

This is a forested area, so be sure to carry a good supply of ants, beetles, hoppers, and elm spanworms as well as other leaf eating insects.

WHITE DEER CREEK

White Deer Creek is not a nationally known stream. It may be due to its size and the fact that the DHFFO area is located in a rather remote area. For the most part, fly-fishers like open water that allows longer casts than White Deer. But because of special regulations placed on the stream, attention has been drawn to this stream. However, this short stretch (3.1 miles) of designated water gives anglers only a small taste of what the stream has to offer.

White Deer Creek begins near the town of Livonia in Centre County and flows a short four miles before entering Union County. The stream then flows 17 miles through Union before reaching the West Branch of the Susquehanna River near the town of White Deer.

This small stream that is only two jumps wide intimidates many would-be fly-fishers. It is difficult water to fish, but there is a good supply of wild trout and native brookies, as well as PFBC stocked trout. Hatches are excellent, and although the waters are clear and low the better part of the year, water temperatures remain surprisingly cold. There are numerous riffles as this stream flows over and around many ankle-twisting boulders. The older method of wet-fly fishing is probably the best bet here, and the broken water is ideal for sweeping wet flies through the clear, low waters.

Streamers can be downright deadly, but the approach to this stream should be like that of a native brook trout stream. Although hatches are fairly abundant, getting the fly to the trout remains much more challenging than finding the hatches and subsequent rising trout.

Both fishing from the bank and wading can be done here—a good pair of felt-soled hip boots will suffice. Rods are a matter of choice: The smaller 7 to 7 ½ -footers, carrying 3- to 4-weight lines or lighter, work well on streams like this. The 9-foot rod works well when one can find room along the shoreline to shoot line into the riffles with a sidearm cast. Light lines and long leaders should help, and since I am a strong believer in light tippets, I find this stream to my liking.

White Deer's characteristics will keep many anglers at bay simply because of its size and complexity. I find that to my liking, as well. However, if you like native brook trout streams, you will like White Deer Creek. The difference is in the size and variety of fish that you land.

The entire stream follows I-80, and lodging choice depends on which section of stream is being fished. The State College Area is a good choice (see Spring Creek) because restaurants and lodging are easily found at any one of the exits that lead from I-80.

WHITE DEER CREEK MAJOR HATCHES

Insect	J	F	M	A	M	J	J	A	S	O	N	D
Blue Quill #18				▬								
Hendrickson #14				▬								
Caddis #14 & 16 (grannom, olive & gray, brown & tan)				▬	▬							
Light Cahill #14					▬	▬						
Tan Caddis #16					▬	▬	▬	▬				
Quill Gordon #14				▬								
March Brown #12					▬	▬						
Green Drake #12, 3X long (Coffin Fly Spinner)						▬						
Sulphur #16						▬						
Blue-winged Olive #14 & 16						▬						
Cream Cahill #16 & 18									▬	▬		
Ants #16–20; Beetles #12–18; Grasshoppers #10–14)							▬	▬	▬			
Caterpillars #12, 3X long						▬	▬					
Other												
Mosquito #12–16						▬	▬	▬				
Streamers			▬	▬	▬	▬	▬	▬	▬	▬		

Young Woman's Creek

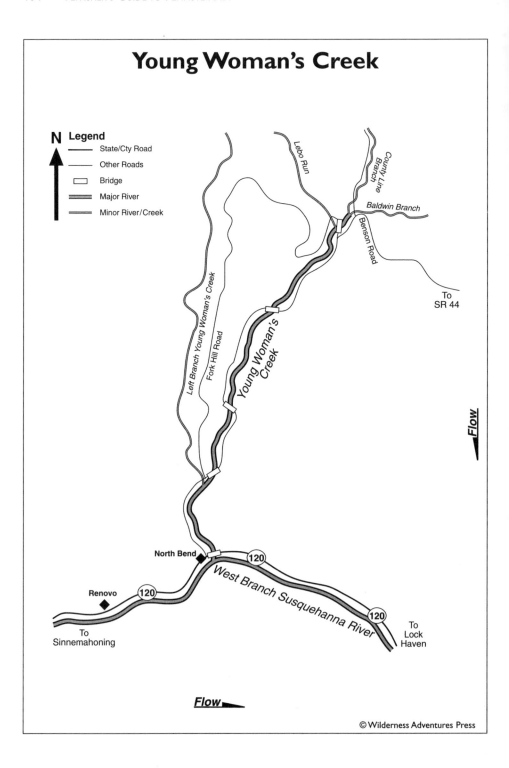

YOUNG WOMAN'S CREEK

My grandfather touted the merits of Young Woman's Creek when I was young. I would listen to him and Charlie Wetzel talk about the virtues of this wonderful stream with two branches. That was in the late 1950s, and when I moved to this area, one of the streams on my hit list was Young Woman's Creek.

I found it easy to reach from SR 120 and stopped for a few hours of fishing while on a trip to the southern limestones. Located near the town of Hyner between Renovo and Lock Haven, I was quite frankly disappointed with what I found.

I was anxious to find the stream in some semblance of its former glory, and after discussions with flyfishing cronies, a group of us set out to explore the waters more thoroughly. None of us wanted to dismiss this water, and I admitted that I had fished there in late June when most of the major hatches had passed.

I had been fishing the Left Branch when it was still under catch-and-release regulations, and although I did find a good number of stocked fish, the area did not measure up to most other waters in the state with the same regulations. During our group trip, we found that the fishing was better and more productive. Even though we found no truly large fish, we did take our fair share of both native and streambred fish.

Because the scenery that surrounds a fishing excursion has always been an important element for all of us, we returned again and again. In time, we found this stream to be one of beauty that held trout in good numbers and, when flows were good, some excellent hatches.

Both branches are stocked by the PFBC, despite the fact that this stream makes one feel like it should be a stream capable of taking care of itself without stocked trout.

We found that the better fish in terms of size were stocked fish and a few carryovers. The heads of wild trout that we found were, for the most part, smaller in size, and the stream did lack an abundance of good holding water. Once again, this stream presents the flyfishing writer's dilemma of whether to write about a stream or not. This is a remote stream that has found help through local sportsmen's groups and Trout Unlimited. A remote stream is often sacrificed simply because it does not attract enough attention to warrant concern in many flyfishers' minds. On the other hand, extreme fishing pressure can send a stream into decline. Because this is a rather remote area, it is not fished as heavily as many other streams in the state and can use the exposure.

The stream is a typical smaller freestone—water temperatures remain good throughout the summer months, and the farther up either of the branches, the better the fishing. Hatches are prolific and a Selective Harvest Area is now found on the Right Branch of the stream from the state forest property line upstream to Beechwood Trail.

The size limit imposed is a minimum of 12 inches for brown trout and 9 inches for brookies, rainbows, and palominos. This is a rather new program, and many anglers fall on one side of the proverbial fence or the other: either they like it or they don't. The limit is two per day, except from midnight Labor Day until opening day in mid-April.

The author lands a good rainbow.

When hatches are excellent, this stream can be a great place to fish. Sporting a lot of canopy, anglers should be aware that leaf-eating insects are in abundance. My favorite hatch is the sulphur, and it appears here in good numbers. However, give me a blue quill hatch in April, and I will be one happy flyfisherman.

Young Woman's Creek offers both. And, although I find fishing during the sulphur hatch extremely rewarding and admittedly my favorite, especially the spinnerfall, allow me to add that the blue quill is the hatch I most anxiously await. It means fish rising in abundance—something that does not occur on that many streams in April.

I highly recommend a trip here, especially during April and May. The stream is accessible from SR 120 at a very small town called North Bend. But use Hyner as a reference point, since you may go through North Bend and never see it. The stream is marked as it passes beneath SR 120 before reaching the West Branch of the Susquehanna, and signs posted on the dirt road lead to the Left Branch. Turn onto the only hard road in town to find the Right Branch.

PENNS CREEK

Penns Creek is one of, if not the most, famous streams found in northcentral Pennsylvania. The stream earned its reputation many years ago when flyfishers flocked here when the "shad fly" was on the water. Perhaps it was Charlie Wetzel's book, the first on entomology in Pennsylvania, that identified the correct name as the green drake.

This is a beautiful river, with a good pool-to-riffle ratio. It holds trout over from the town of Weikert upstream and from below the mouth of Cherry Run upstream. There is no stocking of trout in the Special Regulations Area. It is the stream that has always attracted interest, especially the interest of flyfishers, and is indeed good fly-fishing water.

The green drake hatch has been its calling card for so long that it would seem that the fly was invented here. And when any words are penned concerning the stream, there is a loud outcry of protest from the regulars who have fished there "since dirt."

I have been fishing this stream for nearly as long, beginning at the age of six. We were fortunate to have a cabin in Poe Valley that was just 3 miles from the old rail-road bridge just above the catch-and-release area beginning 650 yards downstream of Swift Run and extending to 500 yards below Cherry Run. This 3.9 miles of water is managed as Flyfishing Only and does get overcrowded during the green drake hatch. I highly suggest that if you want to experience the hatch, choose another stream section to fish.

The crowding and popularity of this remote stream has necessitated additional regulations. Recently, another 7-mile stretch from the confluence of Elk Creek in Centre County downstream to the Catch and Release section has been designated as All Tackle Trophy Trout. The significance of this stream is stated in the stricter regulations placed over an 11-mile stretch of water.

The stream begins at Penns Cave and, under private management, offers excellent fishing for a fee from the lake below the cave downstream. Here, even at the headwaters, the stream is 30 feet wide not far from its source. Native brook trout may be found in this headwater section, but the land is posted against trespass. Below SR 45 near the town of Coburn, the stream gains size and volume. Within the confines of Centre County, the creek runs 13 miles, much of it overlooked except by the early season trout angler.

The stream widens to one-half mile above Weikert, and the fishing is great due to the cold water of Elk Run entering the stream. It's an unbeatable situation when combined with the rising mountains, the boulder-strewn bottom, and no homes crowding the banks. The fishing and hatches are superb, and stocked fingerling trout took hold and filled the gaps where natural reproduction of trout allowed.

However, be forewarned that the stream, like many in the state's northern region, has been plagued by drought in recent years. As of this writing (1999), this year's drought may be the most significant in 40 years. The warm waters are moving

Penns Creek

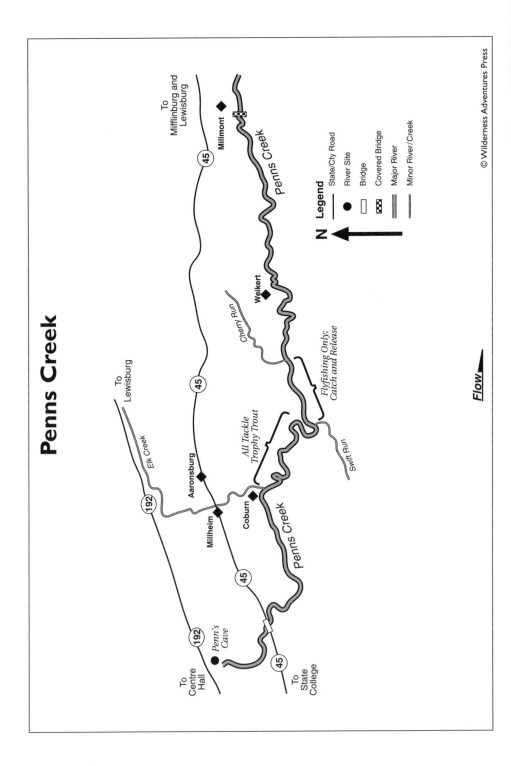

© Wilderness Adventures Press

A beautiful wild brown trout.

upstream and have already had their effect on water below Weikert. Streams the size of Penns need coldwater influences in the way of tributary streams, and as these shrivel and warm up, the main stem suffers dramatically.

The fishing may wane a bit this year, and it may take some time to recoup from its loss of continual cold running waters. And the hatches? No one knows for certain, but many will survive in fewer numbers and then take time to rebuild. Upon reaching the project areas, the stream flows into Mifflin and Union Counties as it snakes its way southward. Only 3 miles are found in Mifflin, and the remaining 26 miles flow through Union. That is a total of 42 miles of stream that changes its faces and moods often and holds a wide variety of fish.

In this section of the creek, we will cover the trout water that is most likely to be of interest to flyfishers. Here, hatches are prolific and pools and riffles require long casts to reach the opposite shoreline. In some areas, the far shore is more than a cast away.

From the source to Weikert, the primary fish are brown trout. On my last visit to Penns, I fished the large pool in front of Station 22, a PFBC holding near the midsection of the Catch and Release waters. This is a deep and productive pool more than 50 yards in length. However, trout are often difficult to entice here, and rises may be few and far between. Enjoying the opportunity to get away from civilization, I waited for the fish to rise, even though I knew that probing the water here with a good crayfish pattern would more than likely take a few trout.

I didn't have much time to settle in on that mid-May day before two trout began rising against the far shore. The rises became rhythmic while I was trying to decide exactly what insects the fish were targeting. I waited patiently and scanned the water for any duns or caddis that might float by. I saw a few tan caddis and, that being one of my favorite patterns, I promptly tied a size 16 to the end of a 7X tippet.

As is usually the case, even with wild fish, the larger trout were feeding closer to the bank. The trout were only five feet apart, and the closest fish was rising three feet below the one nearest to the bank. I slipped into the water carefully because the flow was so calm that expanding rings from wading could have easily put these fish down. When the ringlets of water expanded to and over the trout, it was apparent that it had not bothered them.

I measured the cast and dropped the caddis imitation three feet above the closest fish. It took immediately and without hesitation, and I tried to pull it to my left so that the fight could be contained below what I thought was a larger fish. But the rod bent deeply, the line was slipping through my fingers, and I could tell that this was a hefty fish—this could be the bigger fish of the two.

When it came to hand, I was shocked to see a heavy brown between 18 and 19 inches—a beautifully colored fish with a red adipose fin and fins feathered in white. Still, I was certain that the fish that was still rising was larger and would probably be more difficult to take. But it took on the first cast as well, and its first leap proved that it was less than an inch larger than the one I had just released.

Two large wild trout rising that close together is unusual here, and after releasing the second fish, I reeled in and drove the Jeep down the dirt road in the direction of home. I didn't want to keep fishing on this perfectly good day in fear of ruining it.

The scenery here is beautiful, and you may cast as far as your equipment allows. There are few cabins crowding the shores. Could one ask for more? Yes, a few less anglers and trout that rise every day to every hatch. But that would be asking far too much, wouldn't it?

This section of stream can be reached by following the signs off SR 322 to Poe Valley, then taking SR 144 from Potter's Mill one mile north, and turn right to Poe Valley. Turn left at Glen Iron off SR 235 to find the secondary road that leads to Weikert.

Cherry Run

Cherry Run is a beautiful, native brook trout stream found upstream on Penns Creek from Weikert. The stream is exactly what you would expect from such waters. It is lined with rhododendron and mountain laurel, and consists of a series of shallow pools and riffles with an abundance of native brook trout and a good number of wild browns.

The stream is 5 miles in length, with 2.7 miles regulated under the PFBC Selective Trout Program. An important tributary to Penns Creek, this stream provides

The swift, tricky waters of Cherry Run.

cold water and a sanctuary for Penns Creek's wild trout population when Penns' water warms up. It is undoubtedly a spawning ground as well.

This is a precious and much needed resource. Anglers should release trout they capture here and tread lightly on surrounding lands. Small fly rods, 7 feet in length, and 3- to 4-weight lines are ideal for this stream. Attractor patterns work well if one keeps a low profile and delivers the fly with pinpoint accuracy. I really like fishing floating caterpillar patterns here, and mosquito dries work well as an attractor pattern.

However, the wet-fly fisherman, using soft hackled flies, is not to be dismissed. Because of the crowded shoreline and a stream draped with vegetation, fishing is difficult for those not used to casting in tight quarters. Allowing a tandem of wet flies to drift downstream into the tunnels of streamside growth is as effective as any other form of fishing here.

The stream runs from 20 to 30 feet wide in places to a mere jump across closer to the headwaters. However, this is a stream to experience, a place to get away and catch native and wild trout—some of good size, others no more than 5 to 6 inches. The mix of cold water and the scent of rhododendron and mountain laurel permeating the air is enough for many of us to return time and again.

PENNS CREEK MAJOR HATCHES

Insect	J	F	M	A	M	J	J	A	S	O	N	D
Blue Quill #16 & 18				▆								
Hendrickson #14				▆								
Quill Gordon #14				▆								
Brown Stone Fly #12 & 14				▆								
Gray Fox #14					▆							
Sulphur #16					▆							
Light Cahill #14					▆							
Green Drake #12, 3X long (Coffin Fly Spinner)					▆							
Tan Caddis #16					▆	▆		▆				
Slate Drake #14					▆	▆		▆	▆			
Cream Cahill #18						▆		▆				
Trico #24 (spotty)							▆	▆				
Caddis, Grannom #12				▆								
Tan & Green Caddis #14 & 16*				▆	▆	▆	▆	▆	▆	▆		
Terrestrials (ending date dependent on cold weather)						▆	▆	▆	▆			

Caddis are extremely important here and should be carried in brown, green, yellow, and black at all times.

Fishing Creek

This stream has something for almost anyone. A Trophy Trout Water, billed as a wild trout fishery, there is little doubt in my mind that some stocked fish appear in these waters from time to time. They come from the main stem and from hatchery escapees. However, stocked fish are few and far between; this stream is loaded with large wild fish.

Despite the fact that trout are large and the fishing pressure heavy at times, these trout are willing fish if they are approached correctly and cast to properly. The stream's gradient is steep and allows for many pockets of water and a good amount of broken water. That means that even educated trout don't have a lot of time to decide on whether or not to take your imitation.

The drawback is that one needs to mend line properly and proficiently and, in some areas, cast a good amount of line accurately. Although the stream is not that wide in many areas, there are pools that require casting nearly all your line in order not to disturb the fish.

Getting into proper position can often be difficult. A steep bank guards the road-side of the stream and then drops steeply to the stream with large boulders—not a casting platform that allows drag-free floats and good presentations. Trout seem to know that anglers visit here and lie contentedly in waist-deep water as the angler casts well beyond them.

Hatches are fairly constant, and searching patterns are not ignored by these fish. The stream is one that may test your patience, but remember that on this stream, casting to the water is productive even when fish are not rising, which is a blessing. Because of the cahills, sulphurs, and caddis that dance over the flow here, I like a size 16 yellow Adams as a searching pattern. I have been scoffed at and dismissed for using it until the leader stretches tight time and again throughout much of the season. It has proven its worth on almost all water fished throughout this state and others. So the naysayers may be wrong in their disdain for this fly. As they say, "the proof is in the pudding."

Terrestrial fishing here is outstanding during the summer months up until the first frost of fall. With an outbreak of gypsy moth, elm span, and other leaf-eating insects, the fishing can be great. It seems that most anglers overlook this important food source when, in fact, they have become one of the more important in the food chain. Perhaps labeling them terrestrial is incorrect; a better term may be mast insects to coincide with the mast crop many of the infested trees provide. But for the sake of simplicity, the inchworm has always been an important food source, despite our failure to match it correctly in a floating form.

Certainly green weenies are taken mistakenly for caddis larvae, but I'm sure they are also taken for leaf-eating insects that includes the inchworm. Be certain to carry enough terrestrials here to cover the summer months.

There is little doubt that the best section of this stream is within the Trophy Trout section, located from the Tylersville Fish Hatchery downstream to Flemmings Bridge

Fishing Creek

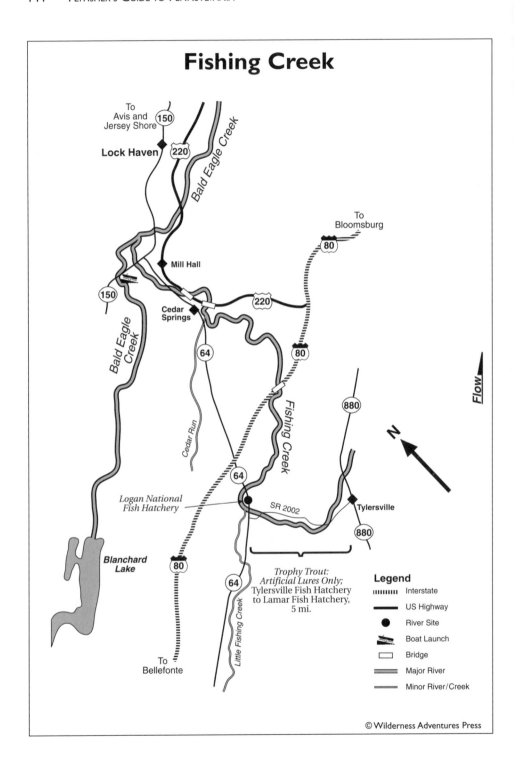

To Avis and Jersey Shore (150)

Lock Haven (220)

Bald Eagle Creek

To Bloomsburg

(80)

Mill Hall

(150)

(220)

Bald Eagle Creek

Cedar Springs

(64)

(80)

Cedar Run

Fishing Creek

(880)

Flow

N

(64)

Logan National Fish Hatchery

SR 2002

Tylersville

(880)

Blanchard Lake

(80)

(64)

Little Fishing Creek

Trophy Trout: Artificial Lures Only; Tylersville Fish Hatchery to Lamar Fish Hatchery, 5 mi.

To Bellefonte

Legend

||||||||| Interstate

———— US Highway

● River Site

Boat Launch

▭ Bridge

━━━ Major River

——— Minor River/Creek

© Wilderness Adventures Press

Wild brown trout are an important resource in the state.

at the Lamar Fish Hatchery. This is exceptional water and fishing above this section can often be excellent.

The 5-mile stretch of trophy water attracts the most anglers, although the entire stream provides cool water and plenty of trout. When the green drake hatch appears, you may want to try other stream sections, from near Logansville over the some 16 miles it flows until reaching the West Branch Susquehanna River near Lock Haven. The stream is heavily stocked from Cedar Run downstream to below Mill Hall and receives less pressure than the Trophy Trout Area. This section of stream is often nearly void of anglers when major hatches occur. This stream is large over most of its length, allowing any one angler nearly a lifetime of exploring.

The stream is easily accessible from SR 80 at the Lamar exit. The special regulations area may be found by following signs to the Lamar fish hatchery found on SR 64.

FISHING CREEK MAJOR HATCHES

Insect	J	F	M	A	M	J	J	A	S	O	N	D
Blue Quill #16 & 18				▬								
Hendrickson #14				▬								
Blue Dun #20 & 22				▬		▬▬▬▬						
Quill Gordon #14				▬								
Tan Caddis #12 & 16					▬▬▬▬▬▬▬▬							
March Brown #12 & 14					▬							
Sulphur #16					▬▬▬							
Green Drake #12, 3X long (Coffin Fly Spinner)						▬						
Slate Drake #14						▬						
Green Caddis #14 & 16						▬						
Light Cahill #14						▬						
Blue-winged Olive #14							▬					
Blue-winged Olive #20 & 22							▬▬▬▬					
Terrestrials					▬▬▬▬▬▬							

SPRING CREEK

It was here, at the ripe old age of 6, that I took my first trout on a fly. Then it was called Fisherman's Paradise and rightfully so. It was heavily stocked by the PFBC from the hatchery that stood on the far shore. There was a pass to get in, and anglers came in numbers that overflowed the banks. Back then, there was a women's only area on the far side of the hatchery, and the main stream was open to everyone.

The limit was managed under "one trout and done" regulations, and when I promptly killed a trout only minutes after the opening hour, I was relegated to watch my grandparents catch and release fish throughout the remainder of the day.

I recall the fish, a 17½-inch rainbow, and the imitation, one of Paul Berger's honey bugs that he sold along the bank. I recall that when sales slowed, which was seldom, Paul would take a honey bug and promptly catch enough trout to bring customers back to his table.

The following year I was determined to fish the entire day. It was a cold, blustery day, and in spite of the overcast sky and the intermittent rain, I was able to take a few fish, not as many as were normally to be expected at Fisherman's Paradise, but enough to keep my interest. During the late afternoon hours with my grandfather at my side, I hooked and somehow landed a brown trout that exceeded 32 inches. My grandfather did not allow me to decide if this fish was worth keeping, as he promptly killed it before I was able to pull it from the landing net.

It's a bit of a shame, for I can recall only the length of the fish, despite the fact that it was weighed as required at the Fish Commission's weigh in station. It may well have been the heaviest fish I have taken in Pennsylvania. I do know that my photo appeared in the local paper, but that has since disappeared as well.

Since that time, Fisherman's Paradise has gone through a lot of changes. Now managed as wild trout water with no-kill regulations, trout numbers from the days of old have shrunk considerably, and the Project Water has been improved to the point that much of the good holding water is gone.

The change came when Myrex and Kepone were found in the water, forcing the Pennsylvania Fish and Boat Commission to stop stocking the stream and to put an advisory in place against eating any fish from the stream. The deadly blow was a blessing in disguise.

Trout came back in large numbers, and the number of anglers visiting the Catch and Release waters shrank dramatically. I revisited the waters after my grandfather had passed away during the mid 1970s. It was to be a trip in remembrance of him—a tribute.

I was pleasantly surprised when trout began rising to a hatch and then a subsequent spinnerfall of sulphurs. Toward evening, I was able to land a large brown that may well have been the second largest fish I have taken in the state. I know that it took a polywing spinner attached to 7X, but I did not measure the fish or attempt to weigh it. I realized that this trout, taken only yards upstream from where I had taken the 32-inch fish some 20-years earlier, was a fish to be released. My catch-and-release conviction may have well begun here with that 17½-inch rainbow and the

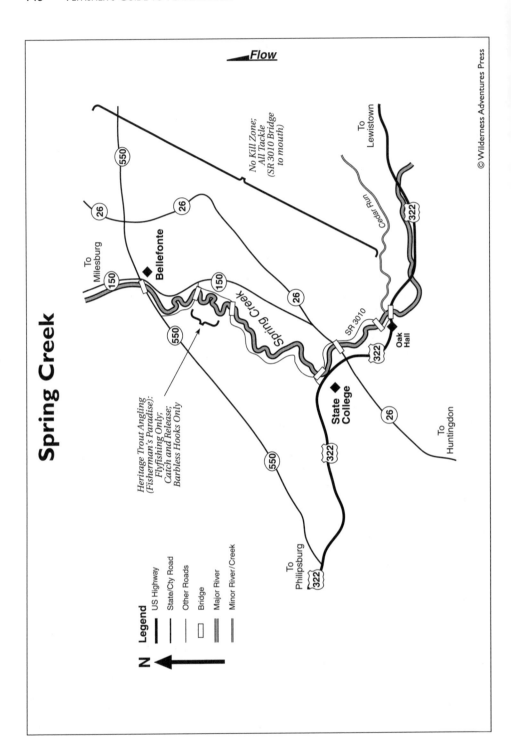

Spring Creek

Flow

No Kill Zone;
All Tackle
(SR 3010 Bridge
to mouth)

To
Lewistown

Bellefonte

To
Milesburg

Cedar Run

Heritage Trout Angling
(Fisherman's Paradise):
Flyfishing Only;
Catch and Release;
Barbless Hooks Only

Spring Creek

SR 3010

Oak
Hall

State
College

To
Huntingdon

To
Philipsburg

Legend

US Highway
State/Cty Road
Other Roads
Bridge
Major River
Minor River/Creek

N

© Wilderness Adventures Press

A brown trout ready to be released.

one trout rule, which meant you had to stop fishing after you harvested one trout. It just shows how much things remain the same and how much they change.

The large stocked fish are gone, but because of its former poisoning, Spring Creek has become one of the best wild trout streams in the state. The entire stream, despite its designation, is now under no-kill regulations. The 1-mile stretch from the lower boundary of the Spring Creek Fish Culture Station to a well-marked point below the Stackhouse School pistol range is managed as Heritage Trout Water. From the SR 3010 bridge to the mouth, it is regulated as no-kill, all tackle.

Much of the former Paradise stretch and the upstream portion of water above it has been ignored for the better water and hatches that occur from the bridge downstream. The banks that were once shoulder-to-shoulder now greet fewer anglers than any other stream section, but the trout are still there in sufficient numbers. It was only a few years ago that a large brown came from beneath the walk bridge abutment, directly in front of the PFBC's training school.

I nearly duped an outlandish brown there with a grasshopper pattern on a hot August afternoon. The large fish came out of nowhere, using its large snout to actually bump a Dave's hopper. But something did not feel right, and the large fish sulked in the depth of the pool. I recast and jerked the popper before him. He came back to it and again actually bumped it with his snout three times, as attested by onlookers from the bridge. The trout then disappeared in a hurry and could not be coaxed back into view.

The stream is dripping with trout, mostly wild, and the hatches are returning. Most consider this the best wild trout fishery in the state for truly large fish. Beadhead nymphs work well when a hatch is not in progress. And, as usual, I love the terrestrial fishing on this stream.

Patterns need to be exacting to take many of these fish, but like all trout streams, they may take just about anything when the conditions are right. The famous green drake hatch is a memory here, but it might return in time as the stream mends. However, fishing here is good if the water is covered properly, and fish 16 to 20 inches are commonplace. Larger trout are not uncommon nor unexpected.

Every flyfisher has a preferred spot on this stream, all different. It will take a little exploring to find the water that you like best. The stream is accessible from SR 550 between State College and Bellefonte. To find Fisherman's Paradise, follow the signs leading off SR 550. At the bottom of the hill, turn left to find Paradise or left to find the SR 3010 bridge. To fish below Bellefonte, follow SR 550 and 150.

SPRING CREEK MAJOR HATCHES

Insect	J	F	M	A	M	J	J	A	S	O	N	D
Blue Quill #16 & 18				▬								
Blue-winged Olive #20 & 22				▬								
Tan Caddis #16					▬▬▬▬							
Green Caddis #14					▬							
Sulphur #16					▬							
Light Cahill #14					▬							
Blue-winged Olive #14						▬						
Trico #24							▬▬					
Cream Cahill #22 & 24								▬▬				
Caenis #24 & 26								▬▬				
Cranefly #14 & 16							▬▬					
Blue-winged Olive #18 & 22								▬▬				
Black Midge									▬			
Cream Cahill #18										▬▬		
Terrestrials						▬▬▬▬▬						

LICK RUN

Lick Run is regulated as Trophy Trout Water and deservingly so. The stream's entire length, 2.5 miles from the headwaters to the mouth at Foster Joseph Sayer Lake, has been placed under these regulations. This is wild brown trout water and depends on natural reproduction to maintain the fishery.

Because it is only 2.5 miles in length and is a small stream in width, I hesitate to list it here. The stream is fragile, as most small wild trout streams are, and all trout need to be released to preserve this fishery. The Trophy Trout regulations here help, but they are not enough, in my opinion. So, please release all of your fish immediately.

The stream may be fished in its entirety in hip boots. Light lines, 3- to 4-weight, and a long leader are good choices for successfully fishing this water. Use your favorite small stream fly rod.

The stream may be found off SR 26 near the town of Howard. Use the hatch chart for Spring Creek.

SPRUCE CREEK

Spruce Creek is one of the most noted waters in the state—President Jimmy Carter fished here! Before Carter fished Spruce Creek, it was a stream loaded with a population of wild trout that was difficult to beat. Private landowners along the stream had their own hatcheries or bought large trout to embellish the stocks of fish that existed here.

There was and is what is called the "College Stretch," a section of water that was studied extensively to discover the movement and feeding behavior of wild brown trout. The study was long and painstaking and exposed myths about trout behavior. However, the study was nearly dismissed because it was conducted on a small section of water that experts claimed was not large enough to dispel popular beliefs. Still, the study raised doubts and questions, and in time may prove its worth, as many of the discoveries are now backed by additional studies.

Because of the small amount of access to the stream due to the number of private and club properties that have cropped up on its banks, only a handful of anglers bother to even try the stream these days. The College Stretch (Pennsylvania State Experimental Fisheries Area) is under Catch and Release Regulations and is 0.5 miles in length. This stream section may be found 0.6 miles above the village of Spruce Creek.

There are few, if any, well-known anglers who have not fished this storied water over the years. When Carter told the Pennsylvania Fish Commission he wanted to fish in Pennsylvania, the agency made arrangements for the President and First Lady to fish Spruce Creek. The fact that the Commission could have chosen any stream in the state and that Carter was so impressed with the fishing there that he wrote about it in national flyfishing magazines should be an indicator of how good Spruce Creek is.

I was fortunate enough to be on the environmental committee of Trout Unlimited and, during a weekend meeting, was asked if I wanted to fish Spruce Creek. That was back in the mid-1970s, and I had heard enough about the stream to

A flyfisherman stalks a trout on Spruce Creek.

jump at the chance. From that time forth, I have been fortunate to fish the waters on an annual basis. Last year I fished the stream again through arrangement with Spruce Creek Outfitters.

Alan Bright, the owner of Spruce Creek Outfitters, proved to be a gracious host, providing access for Harry Redline and me on private water. As we approached the stream I had fished many times over the years, I could feel the tradition of flyfishing that pervaded the area. The water around the strategically-placed boulders and the pool-to-riffle ratio were ideal. In just a few short hours, Harry and I had taken more than 50 trout, and I had hooked a colorful holdover brown in the 4-pound range that came to my caddis dry. Harry took a rainbow around 6 pounds, although the average-sized fish measured around the 14-inch mark, with a generous amount of browns, rainbows, and brookies that exceeded 16 inches... a good afternoon of fishing anywhere.

Spruce Creek holds an incredible amount of fish and an abundance of hatches. Yes, even a beginner should catch fish here, but with added skill and the right imitation, a decent angler will have an unforgettable day on Spruce Creek. You deserve to give it a try and follow the advice of a seasoned guide for the flies you will need to match the ever-changing hatches. From blue-winged olives to Tricos, you will find large trout willing to take even the smallest of imitations, in fact, they are often required, along with a 7X tippet.

Spruce Creek is in the truest sense a taste of tradition comparable to the chalk streams of England. A pure limestone, Spruce Creek is everything it has been promoted to be and more.

Harry Redline considers Spruce and the surrounding streams to be a limestone belt that compares with the streams of Cumberland County. Harry should know—he's been fishing and guiding in this area for over 20 years.

Spruce Creek is composed primarily of posted waters and well patrolled. Access to the stream is affordable, and you will more than likely be fishing with a guide. Guides here are extremely knowledgeable, and I have found most of them to have years of experience under their belt. That means they know the water and flies and will not be fishing when you are. Guides that fish over "your" fish should be considered unacceptable.

Locate the town of Spruce Creek northwest of Huntingdon off SR 22 and 435. This is the hub for premier flyfishing waters. Spruce Creek may also be reached via SR 45 west from State College.

SPRUCE CREEK MAJOR HATCHES

Insect	J	F	M	A	M	J	J	A	S	O	N	D
Black & Gray Midge #20 & 22			▬									
Blue Quill #18				▬								
Blue Dun #20				▬								
Blue-winged Olive #18 & 20				▬								
Hendrickson #14				▬								
Grannom Caddis #12 & 14				▬								
Sulphur #16					▬▬▬							
Slate Drake #12 & 14					▬▬▬▬▬▬							
Blue-winged Olive #14					▬▬							
Light Cahill #14						▬						
Blue-winged Olive #16–20							▬▬					
Tan Caddis #16							▬▬					
Trico #24								▬▬				
White Fly #16										▬▬		
Blue-winged Olive #20 & 22											▬▬	
Terestrials						▬▬▬▬▬▬▬						

Note: The stream has many more hatches than listed—call Spruce Creek Outfitters for additional information. Terrestrial patterns are a must.

Cross Fork Creek and Kettle Creek

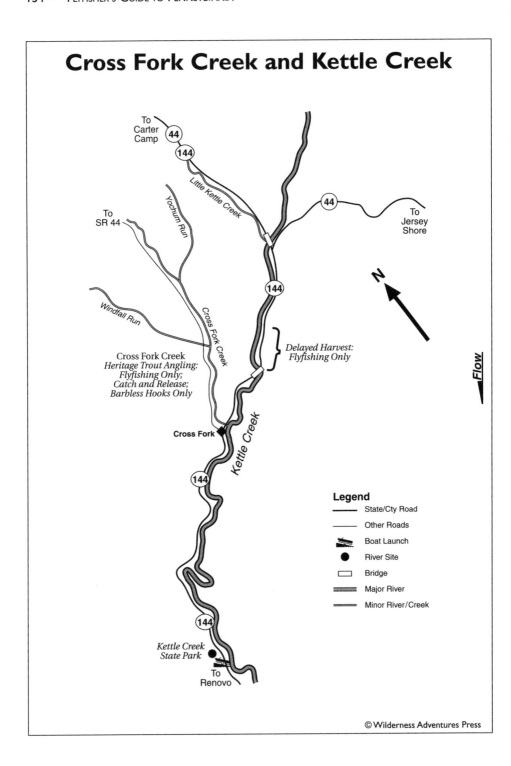

To Carter Camp

44
144

Little Kettle Creek

Yochum Run

To SR 44

44

To Jersey Shore

144

N

Windfall Run

Cross Fork Creek

Flow

Delayed Harvest: Flyfishing Only

Cross Fork Creek
Heritage Trout Angling:
Flyfishing Only;
Catch and Release;
Barbless Hooks Only

Cross Fork

Kettle Creek

144

Legend
State/Cty Road
Other Roads
Boat Launch
River Site
Bridge
Major River
Minor River/Creek

144

Kettle Creek
State Park

To Renovo

© Wilderness Adventures Press

CROSS FORK CREEK

Once a heavily stocked stream, Cross Fork Creek is now maintained as a Heritage Trout Water, a designation reserved for wild trout water that requires no stocking of fish. Cross Fork Sportsmen, realizing that the creek deserved to be recognized as such a water, led the effort to stop stocking the stream.

Today, the special regulations cover 5.4 miles with easy access to the lower reaches. However, there are sections of the stream that require a walk in, and despite the fact that it rarely requires a walk over 400 yards, these sections of stream are not fished heavily. The stream is easily accessible from a dirt road that parallels the creek. The drive from Cross Fork is less than a mile.

Cross Fork Creek is nearly 20 miles long and has a good number of tributary streams that have excellent brook trout fishing and contribute the cold water that makes Cross Fork fishable throughout the season.

The creek holds an excellent population of native brook trout and a good amount of wild browns, occasionally giving up a large trout. Most fish are small, typically in the brook trout size. Fishing pressure isn't heavy, consisting mostly of locals who enjoy a taste of the traditional fishing of the past. But with its catch-and-release and flyfishing only regulations, Cross Fork is a stream that should be visited.

It rarely exceeds 40 feet across in the lower section before it enters Kettle Creek a few hundred yards below the village of Cross Fork. This is excellent water and is seldom mentioned to visiting anglers. However, an angler can expect to catch a lot of natives in the 6- to 9-inch range, and an occasional brookie that could exceed 12 inches in length. It is not trophy trout water by any stretch of the imagination, although it does see some excellent hatches.

As one moves upstream from SR 144, the stream narrows and offers an isolated setting where one might find anything from a black bear to a rattlesnake. A few summer cabins border the stream, but they take nothing away from the beauty of this babbling brook. There are sections of water that require nothing more than a very short cast, and there is an excellent pool-to-riffle ratio.

Cross Fork Creek is not one of those streams where a flyfisher can wade deep pools and cast carelessly. These are wild fish in relatively small water, and along with being wild, they have had the educational experience that comes with catch and release—quite evident in the easily accessible pools.

These fish see their share of anglers in a given year and even brook trout, not known to be selective, can be here at times. They have been elevated above the many brook trout waters of Potter and Clinton Counties under the Heritage Trout Program, where they are protected under catch-and-release and no-kill regulations.

Perhaps above all else, Cross Fork Creek exemplifies exactly what has attracted anglers for decades to Potter and Clinton Counties: the essence of fishing for native brook trout and wild browns. The PFBC, in recognition of the area and its many freestones, has rightfully set Cross Fork Creek aside. They have given it the proper designation and have let it stand as a symbol of something unique and with a taste of wildness.

*Cross Fork Creek
in Potter County.*

There are a host of native brook trout streams that enter Kettle Creek. Hammersley Fork is a prime example. These are jump-across streams and most offer excellent fishing for native brook trout. You will also find browns migrating into these smaller feeder streams.

Pennsylvania struggles to maintain wild trout populations in most streams throughout the state, trying to determine what streams can be fished without harm to the resource. On many of these streams, the water can be unfishable for those fishing an hour or so after a previous angler. Too many anglers wading these waters may be detrimental to nymphs and caddis larvae in streams where the food supply is already extremely scarce.

These are not secret places, and nearly any visiting angler can find out about them by visiting Phil at Kettle Creek Tackle or Mike at the Cross Fork Fly Shop. Both are full service shops with flies, boots, rods, lines, and fly tying material. And they will both supply you the information you need to find the smaller streams—the lifeblood of the large trout waters found within this book.

The importance of fishing to this area can easily be calculated in the fact that there are two fly shops within 5 minutes of one another, and both have survived and prospered over the past 20 years. That alone should be enough to indicate the amount of water and fishing opportunities available.

CROSS FORK CREEK MAJOR HATCHES

Insect	J	F	M	A	M	J	J	A	S	O	N	D
Little Black Stone #16 & 18			▓									
Blue Quills #16				▓								
Quill Gordon #14				▓								
Red Quill, Hendrickson #14					▓							
Tan Caddis #12–16				▓	▓	▓	▓	▓				
Blue-winged Olive #16				▓	▓							
Green Drake #12, 3X long						▓						
Brown Drake #12, 3X long						▓						
Sulphur #16						▓						
Cahill #14						▓						
Trico #24							▓	▓				
Pale Evening Dun #16 & 18							▓	▓	▓			
Cream Cahill									▓			
Ants #16–24; Beetles #12–24									▓			
Grasshoppers #12, 3X long					▓	▓	▓	▓	▓			

KETTLE CREEK

Kettle Creek is one Pennsylvania's historic streams that attracts anglers throughout the state and country. Most flyfishermen have made, at the least, a maiden voyage to these waters.

As is the case with many trout streams throughout the state, Kettle's once famed "Catch and Release Area" had been the main attraction. The PFBC has recently claimed that the stream is not suitable to carry a significant amount of trout year-round. The decision erupted into a yearlong battle with the Project Water changed first to Delayed Harvest, allowing lures and flies, and finally, Delayed Harvest, Flies Only.

The Kettle Creek Watershed Association was formed to address the problems that this stream has faced for years. Thermal pollution has been detrimental to the stream and the trout that reside there. Three years of drought conditions resulted in poor fishing within the Project Waters from mid-June to September. Delayed Harvest allows keeping trout at the rate of 3 per day, 9 inches or more in length. The stream remains an excellent early season trout stream and rebounds again in September when stocking is conducted by local sportsmen's organizations, the state, and local businesses.

The Kettle Creek Project Water enticed this angler.

Kettle Creek, one of the many freestones in the north-central region of the state, is now being scrutinized to find out why this nationally known stream is suffering. It would seem that it is not a stream to be dismissed, and it is far from dead and gone.

The history of Kettle is steeped in tradition. Nearly all the famous names in the flyfishing world have fished here, from the late Charlie Wetzel to Joe Brooks. They did not gather here without reason. Fishing on Kettle was and still is world-renowned. The stream's popularity has brought attention to the woes it has experienced in recent years. Money has poured in from all over the country. It would seem apparent that the concern is sufficient to bring the stream back to its former status—perhaps beyond. However, nature will have to cooperate as well. Simply put, for streams in this area to supply excellent fishing throughout the summer months, the droughts must end.

The stream is nice-sized, measuring 40 to 60 feet across in most areas, and tributary mouths and the headwaters do hold fish year-round. Kettle remains a good fishery until mid-June and rebounds again in the fall.

The most popular hatch is the eastern green drake, with a good hatch of sulphurs a close second. Important early season hatches include: Quill Gordons (#14), blue quills (#16), March browns (#12), and a wide variety of caddis (#12 to 16), best imitated with a green and tan body, topped with deer or elk hair wing.

The often forgotten picket pin and zug bug are great wet flies here. Hare's ear, muskrat and cahill nymphs, or beadheads in black, gray, brown, green, yellow, and tan have become a "must" on all streams in this area of Pennsylvania. They have grown in popularity simply because they are effective and allow flyfishers to carry far fewer flies than in the past. Beadheads imitate caddis larva, mayfly nymphs, and even the smaller and most common stoneflies found in our streams.

Fishing resumes in earnest in September when pale evening duns appear along with a good number of caddis. Cooler waters return and migrating fish can be found throughout the project area. Early season fishing is available throughout the entire Kettle Creek run from above Ole Bull State Park downstream to Alvin Bush Dam. The dam provides excellent fishing for smallmouth bass and pickerel throughout the summer as well as a wide variety of sunfish. Coldwater tributaries and underground springs maintain some good fishing throughout the summer months, as well. And throughout the drought-plagued years, bass have moved as far upstream as the Project Water and beyond. The lake holds smallmouth that exceed 20 inches, while the stream usually offers up smaller bass in the 10- to 18-inch range. Flyfishers will do well on leech, crayfish, streamers, and popping bugs when fishing for bass.

For information on smallmouth, including flies, leaders, and tactics, refer to the chapter on the Susquehanna River, with little argument, the best smallmouth water available to the flyfisher in the state.

Cross Fork is a sleepy little town, and finding food after fishing hours in a rural area is difficult. The closest and most convenient is Deb's Place. The food is great and they cater to fishermen—nothing fancy, just excellent food at a reasonable price and a friendly atmosphere. The place adds flavor to the backcountry setting of this area.

Lodging is sparse in this part of the state, although campgrounds at the dam and at Ole Bull offer very reasonable camping facilities.

With the help of the Kettle Creek Watershed Association, local sportsmen, state agencies, and a concerned cottage industry, Kettle is predicted to come back stronger than ever. Trout streams in the area are important to residents and are treated like the treasured waters they are.

The special regulation sections of Kettle are easily accessible, and a parking lot lies 500 yards upstream from the project's lower reaches next to the SR 144 bridge. The project encompasses a stretch of 1.7 miles upstream and is well marked.

KETTLE CREEK MAJOR HATCHES

Insect	J	F	M	A	M	J	J	A	S	O	N	D
Black Stone #16 & 18			▬									
Blue Quill #16				▪								
Red Quill, Hendrickson #14				▬								
Tan Caddis #16					▬▬▬▬▬▬▬							
Gray Fox #12 & 14					▬							
March Brown #12					▪							
Blue-winged Olive #14 & 16						▪						
Green Drake #12, 3X long						▬						
Brown Drake #12, 3X long						▬						
Sulphur #16						▬						
Cahill #14						▬						
Pale Evening Dun								▬				
Ants & Beetles #14–24; Grasshoppers #12, 3X long-16; Elm Span Worms & Gypsy Moth Caterpillars #12, 3X long							▬▬▬					

Note that water flows dictate summer hatches and quality of fishing.

FIRST FORK OF SINNEMAHONING CREEK

The First Fork of the Sinnemahoning was my home stream for more than 12 years, and a vast majority of the trout I have taken came from these waters. The stream parallels SR 872 for nearly 17 miles before reaching the town of Costello. From Costello it meanders off route 872 and follows SR 3003 north to Prouty Run. Here, the Borie Branch and Prouty Run join to form the First Fork's headwaters, and most consider this junction the extreme headwaters of the Fork.

This water is one of my personal favorites, probably because at one point in my life I had the opportunity to flyfish the waters an average of five days a week. The First Fork is a typical northcentral freestone stream, its water levels rising and dropping with each passing shower. In its lower reaches, water temperatures increase above the trout's tolerance by late summer.

The First Fork offers a variety of trout: native brook trout, wild and carryover browns, and a large dose of stocked rainbows, browns, and brookies. The stream is 10 to 15 feet wide at the headwaters, and from there to the town of Costello, wild browns and native brook trout are the mainstay trout in this area. The PFBC electroshocked stream sections immediately above Moore's Run and found that over 90 percent of the trout there were wild brown trout.

An angler working the upper reaches of the First Fork.

First Fork Sinnemahoning Creek

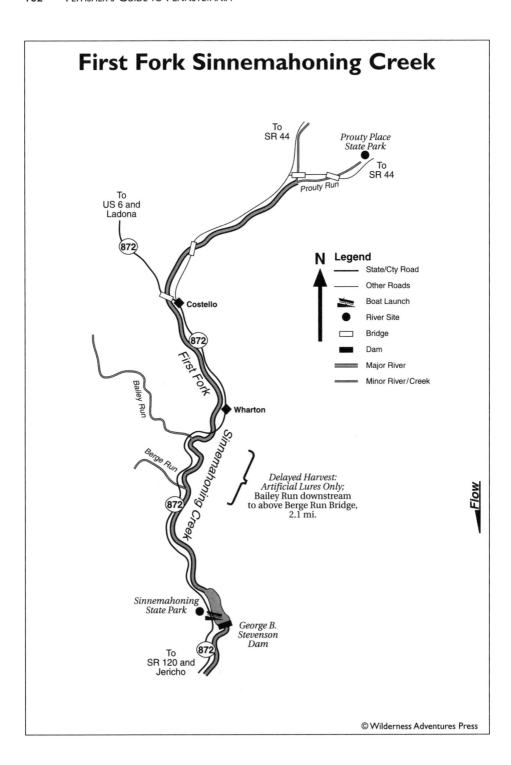

To
SR 44

*Prouty Place
State Park*

To
SR 44

Prouty Run

To
US 6 and
Ladona

872

N Legend

——— State/Cty Road

——— Other Roads

Boat Launch

● River Site

▢ Bridge

▪ Dam

Major River

Minor River/Creek

◆ Costello

872

First Fork

Bailey Run

◆ Wharton

Sinnemahoning Creek

Berge Run

872

*Delayed Harvest:
Artificial Lures Only;*
Bailey Run downstream
to above Berge Run Bridge,
2.1 mi.

Flow

*Sinnemahoning
State Park* ●

*George B.
Stevenson
Dam*

To
SR 120 and
Jericho

872

© Wilderness Adventures Press

From Costello to Wharton, easily accessible from route 872, the stream widens (40 to 60 feet) and is surrounded by the beautiful hardwoods of sparsely populated Potter County. Below the town of Wharton, the First Fork widens up to 60 to 90 feet and becomes one of the larger freestones capable of harboring trout.

Although the stream warms up by mid-June, there are a large number of cold tributary streams that allow trout to escape the often lethal waters of its lower portions, where temperatures rise into the upper 70s and even 80s by July. Fishing on northern freestones offers solitude and brawling, boulder-strewn rivers with large numbers and sizes of mayflies.

From the village of Wharton to George B. Stevenson Dam, the water becomes marginal for trout, with fishing normally lasting into July and then coming back in the fall. Below the dam, downstream to the Driftwood Branch of the Sinnemahoning, the water is better suited for bass, although some early season fishing for stocked trout does exist.

At the mouth of Bailey Run, situated nearly 3 miles below Wharton, a Delayed Harvest Artificial Lures Only area stretches downstream to the bend above Berge Run Bridge. The 2.1-mile Project Water draws more than its fair share of anglers and is easily accessible from SR 872.

Although the Project Water is primarily stocked with trout from the Pennsylvania Fish & Boat Commission, the East Fork Sportsmen and the Potter County Anglers Club, a number of wild trout and carryover browns do exist, something I contribute to the coldwater influence of Bailey Run.

The stream is easily fished with a 4- or 5-weight line and a rod of 7 ½ to 9 feet. Early season anglers may prefer a rod carrying a 6-weight line during the early season's swollen waters, and late season flyfishers often carry the lighter 2- and 3-weight rods, but they are more of a personal preference than a necessity. Leaders as short as 7 ½ feet may be used during April and early May and 9- to 10-footers from May on. Depending on the fly size being used, most anglers begin the season with 5X tippets dropping to 7X as the season progresses. Waders with felt soles are essential on most of the stream, and it is a good idea even on the extreme headwaters.

Warm clothing during the early season, including insulated undergarments, is almost necessary. April has iced many a fly rod guide, and snowflakes are not unusual and are a possibility into early May. Even during the summer months, no one should be caught without a sweater or warm shirt as evening hours often find air temperatures dropping into the low 60s and even 50s. I personally carry a chamois shirt in the back of my vest when fishing until dark, something that is usually necessary once the sun goes down.

Trout season on open water that is not under special regulations begins statewide the first Saturday after April 11. Anglers visiting the Fork during the opening weeks may find afternoon hatches of blue quills (#16), black stones (#16), quill Gordons (#14), Hendricksons (#14), and one of the most prolific and long lasting of hatches, the tan caddis (#14). Although anglers may find these hatches throughout the afternoon and evening hours, water temperatures often dictate afternoon hatches.

The First Fork's Special Regulation section.

I prefer to be on the water in mid-April from 12:30 to 3:30 PM. In my experience, I have found that most of the hatches begin when the water temperature crawls into the mid-50s, which most often occurs during the afternoon.

Opening Day and the following weeks leading into the first week of May might require a lot more subsurface fishing depending on water flow and clarity. I have witnessed the Fork during April with low, clear waters and balmy 70-degree days. I have also seen the streambank full and water temperatures in the 40s and air temperatures to match. It is not unusual for the air temperature to drop below freezing after dark.

When streams are high, dry-fly fishing is often limited to slower pools and back eddies, with the majority of anglers fishing weighted nymphs and exploring the deeper pools with streamers. The woolly bugger (# 8, 3X long), instigator (#8, 3X long), and large stonefly imitations, such as the Montana, and oversized muskrat nymphs in size 8 often do the trick. Here, traditional wet flies work well. The blue dun (#12), picket pin (#12), red quill (#12), and Hendrickson (#12) do well. Anglers should also carry caddis emerger patterns (#14) and soft hackle flies in size 14. A variety of caddis larvae should also be included in an angler's fly box.

Because of the large number of hatches through the first three months of the season, my box always includes a large variety of nymphs to match the hatch as well as beadheads with gray, brown, green, and tan bodies in sizes 12 through 16. I also carry a good supply of hare's ear nymphs and muskrat nymphs in large numbers and sizes 12 to 18. These two patterns cover a lot of species and have proven deadly here.

Although many fishermen look forward to early season, dry-fly action, those looking for such action should fish the lower reaches above the Stevenson Dam. The larger water is more subject to the warming sun, and hatches occur off the lower reaches and then slowly begin hatching upstream. If you can catch a particular hatch below Wharton and drive approximately 1 mile upstream the next evening, then continue to repeat the process, it is not unusual to be fishing the height of any particular hatch for a period of three weeks or more.

Perhaps one of the lures of northcentral freestone waters is the average size of the fly. Although most southern streams have rather prolific hatches, the northcentral section of the state has the traditional hatches most often matched by #14 and larger. For the avid flyfisher, the better fishing is from the second week of May through the second week of June. There are times when hatches overlap one another, which can often make fly choice difficult.

For example, the following hatches can be occurring at the same time: gray fox (#12), March brown (#12), light cahill (#14), brown drakes (#12, 3X long), green drakes (#12, 3X long), sulphurs (#16 to #18), blue-winged olives (#14), tan caddis and grannoms (#14), and slate drakes. You can imagine the plight of the visiting angler. Hardly a complaint is whispered on the stream, however, because when water temperatures move into the upper 60s, trout get active and can be found rising throughout the day.

Evening spinnerfalls of drakes and sulphurs draw the most attention, and the green drake brings traveling anglers to the area. Anglers gather from the southern regions of the state and from out-of-state to find the hatch they have not found at home.

Morning caddis and blue-winged olive hatches and evening gray fox, sulphurs, and cahills are the most prevalent hatches. But when green drakes come toward the end of May, anglers ignore most others. Many have called the eastern green drake overrated, but most would agree that some of the largest browns of the year might be taken on the dun and the coffin fly spinner.

I would rate the brown drake spinnerfall as the most incredible of all mayflies and most likely to bring fish to the surface. I have taken my best trout during this amazing spinnerfall at dusk. The most overlooked mayfly would be the sulphur and the sulphur spinner (#16), which often overlaps the drake. Trout find a spinner with a poly-wing design and an orange egg sack irresistible, even when green drakes are on the water.

The Fork was a sleeper of a stream until the addition of the Delayed Harvest Area below Bailey Run. This special regulations area is open year-round and has brought a lot more attention to the stream. But the better water is above the project from Wharton to the upper reaches. A good mixture of wild browns and native brook trout are best found from Costello upstream to Prouty Run. Many a 20-inch trout has come from these waters. Native brookies average 6 to 8 inches, and stocked trout of all three species average 10 to 12 inches, with an occasional breeder exceeding the 20-inch mark.

After these magnificent hatches are but a memory, trout hunting on this freestone will test your mettle, although a few Tricos can be found during the morning hours and sparse spinnerfalls in the evening, mostly rusty spinners (#12, 3x long). I prefer searching the waters with a mosquito pattern in size 14 and a grizzly caddis in size16. Trout begin to move as the water wanes, and finding them is a pleasure in itself. Many trout find the cooling waters of tributary streams, while others find spring seeps and underground springs. Here, fish rise freely during the evening hours.

Late summer fishing requires a selection of ants, beetles, elm span worms, caterpillars, grasshoppers, and inchworms. Considering the hardwoods that surround these areas and the recent infestations of gypsy moths and elm span worm, elm span and caterpillars become effective and necessary patterns for fishermen visiting this area.

Be aware that although trout can be seen stacked like cordwood at the mouths of many tributaries at times during the summer months, they are extremely lethargic and severely stressed. They should be left alone as they seldom feed in this condition and the extra exertion of fighting a hook could cause a fish to die. Taking fish in this condition is not sporting and could affect the next year's fishing. While survival from year to year has not been documented, carryover fish do exist on the Fork.

Fall brings minor late afternoon hatches of pale evening duns (#18) and caddis (#12-16). I have spent some extremely pleasurable hours on the upper reaches of the First Fork, taking fish as the water cools. At these times, the stream is isolated and trout are not yet spawning. Most spawning occurs here in late October into November, and the conscientious angler leaves the headwaters to go downstream to stocked waters, so as not to interfere with the natural reproduction process. Wild trout are a precious commodity and are best left alone to produce future generations of their own for coming years.

The state's northcentral freestones have felt the effects of drought in recent years, perhaps due to global warming. This condition has not gone unnoticed, and The God's Country Chapter of Trout Unlimited and the Kettle Creek Watershed Association are busy monitoring Kettle Creek, only one valley removed from the Fork. The studies being conducting should help find and rectify the problems of many of our larger freestones.

However, the Fork, with its beautiful surroundings, is one of those streams you do not want to overlook. It is seldom that a visiting angler doesn't experience the sighting of white-tailed deer, black bear, turkey, or even the possibility of an elk when fishing the area's waters— something that adds immeasurably to the experience.

Coudersport serves as the hub city for the Fork. As with the rest of the northern counties, the pace is slower here and there are no four-lane highways or traffic jams. The county of nearly 1,300 square miles, with a population of 18,000 people, is 40 percent state-owned, allowing for many isolated, unposted waters. Consider that Potter County holds 800 miles of trout water alone—it would take a lifetime to fish all of them.

Although Coudersport is the hub city, I have also added some of the more rural areas where one can find lodging, some decent fly shops, and be closer to the streams. Coudersport is 19 miles north of this area on SR 872.

FIRST FORK MAJOR HATCHES

Insect	J	F	M	A	M	J	J	A	S	O	N	D
Black Stone #18				▬								
Blue Quill #16				▬								
Red Quill, Hendrickson #14				▬▬								
Quill Gordon #14				▬								
March Brown #12					▬							
Blue-winged Olive #14–16					▬							
Cahills #14						▮						
Green Drakes #12, 3X long (Coffin Fly Spinner)						▮						
Brown Drake #12, 3X long						▮						
Sulphur #16						▮						
Tricos #24 (spotty)							▬	▬				
Cream Cahill #18										▬▬		
Caddis #14 & 16 (grannom, tan)					▬▬▬▬▬							
Ants #14–22; Beetles #16–24; Gypsy Moth Caterpillars #12, 3X long)							▬▬▬▬					

Driftwood Branch Sinnemahoning Creek

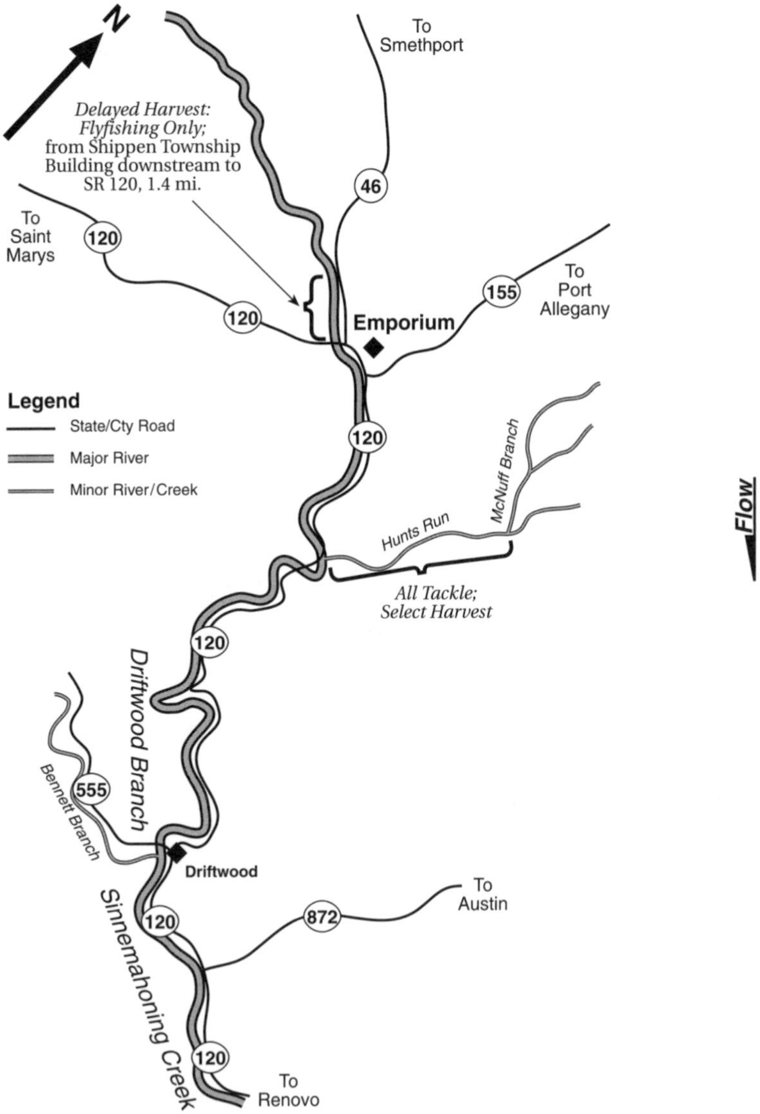

To Smethport

Delayed Harvest:
Flyfishing Only;
from Shippen Township
Building downstream to
SR 120, 1.4 mi.

46

To
Saint
Marys

120

120

155

To
Port
Allegany

Emporium

Legend

State/Cty Road

Major River

Minor River/Creek

120

McNuff Branch

Flow

Hunts Run

All Tackle;
Select Harvest

120

Driftwood Branch

Bennett Branch

555

Driftwood

To
Austin

120

872

Sinnemahoning Creek

120

To
Renovo

© Wilderness Adventures Press

DRIFTWOOD BRANCH SINNEMAHONING CREEK

It was a cold rainy day in April, and the rain was intense, to say the least. Norm Brooks and I were on a mission to find some decent trout fishing. We had thought the rain might stop, but it hadn't. We had chosen the lower sections of the Driftwood Branch simply because we felt like fishing bigger water. However, the rain was bringing the stream up quickly, and we decided smaller water might be more desirable.

We found ourselves in the Delayed Harvest Section of the Driftwood Branch, where large puddles of rainwater were expanding as the rain pounded on the roof of the Jeep. We had taken the day off to fish, and although not easily discouraged, the weather was becoming severe.

I cracked the thermos and we shared the hot black coffee inside. We sat and swapped stories, not as good as fishing itself, but close, on this day that simply didn't want us to stay in the water. But my eyes remained on the flow, and though difficult to tell raindrops from rising fish, I could have sworn that I had witnessed a few sipping rises.

We talked hopefully about the white sky in the distance that was coming our way and would turn off the rain, but black clouds smothered any semblance of white from the sky. The rain came even harder than before, and the sheets of water made it difficult to see the ever-rising flow that began to turn milky. Norm turned to me and

*Good afternoon hatches of blue quills and small blue-winged olives
occur in mid-April.*

Trees line many of Pennsylvania's streams.

shrugged his shoulders—we had both forgotten rain gear, and all hope of fishing was fading fast. I was about to give in when one last glance at the water revealed a slip of a rise and then another and another.

I stunned Norm by walking out of the Jeep and jointing my rod, which had a blue quill already attached to the 6X leader. I was drenched by the cold rain before I entered the stream, but rising fish will block out the effects of nature, for me, at least. The first cast brought one hefty brown to hand, one that measured a good 15 inches. The second cast brought another nice brown, and a few more casts brought yet another fish to be released. Norm had been watching from the comfort of the Jeep, but three trout had been enough to bring him to the water, and I heard him laugh in delight before I saw him.

It wasn't long before we had taken close to 30 trout as the hatch of blue quills kept the fish rising. The hatch was not over with, but we had not noticed how wet and chilled we had become. My hands stung and were swollen and red. Norm and I thought it would be best if we retreated after a few last casts. In the warmth of the Jeep's heater, we sat shivering and watching rising fish, and found that the heater was not chasing the chill away.

The next day I called Norm while fashioning more blue quills at the vise. I found his wife Martha to be more than a little disturbed when she blurted out something about men that were too stupid to come in out of the rain. She then conveyed that Norm was in the hospital, a victim of hypothermia. I went to visit him that night, and Martha stormed off to bed when I handed Norm some freshly tied blue quills and we planned our next trip.

The Driftwood Branch is a good trout stream in the reaches above Emporium, and the Project Water and waters upstream are considered the best. From Emporium downstream, the water turns quickly to bass water, a stream so thick with small smallmouths that it is almost impossible not to catch them (see northcentral warmwater).

But the trout water above town is good and does have its share of wild browns and carryover browns as well. The stream fishes best from late March through mid-June, but the uppermost reaches may be fished throughout the season.

This Delayed Harvest stretch is excellent water until early July when fish begin to migrate out of the area. The green drake hatch here is fabulous, as is the sulphur and blue quill.

The project area begins at the Shippen Township Building and extends downstream to near SR 120 west of Emporium and covers 1.4 miles of stream.

The stream begins in Elk County and flows for 3 miles before entering Cameron County, where 33 miles of stream may be found. Stocking takes place above and below the town of Emporium. The PFBC stocks close to 25 miles of the stream with legal-sized fish. The Delayed Harvest Flyfishing Only area is easily found off SR 120.

HUNTS RUN

Hunts Run is a small tributary stream that bleeds into the Driftwood Branch of the Sinnemahoning below Emporium. The stream is, of course, a mountain stream and has been deemed as Class A water by the Pennsylvania Fish and Boat Commission. The stream is classified as a wild brown trout fishery and is managed under the Commission's All Tackle Select Harvest Program.

The regulated section ranges from the confluence with the McNuff Branch downstream to the mouth. This 4.7-miles section of water is an important coldwater influence to the reaches of the Driftwood Branch below Emporium and serves as a coldwater sanctuary and spawning area for browns from the main stem. The McNuff Branch is even smaller and is classified as a Class A wild brown and native brook trout fishery.

It is important when fishing this stream to keep in mind the importance of smaller wild and native trout streams within the state and the need to release fish in these waters. I share these waters with you in expectation that they remain as they are found. Those who appreciate smaller streams for their wild nature and fish are also responsible for protecting them.

Both streams are small enough to be fished with hip boots. The brush-lined banks call for a smaller rod carrying a 4-weight line. Most prefer 7- to 7½ -foot rods for small streams, while I cling to the theory that I can work the water more easily with a 9-foot. The choice of tackle is yours.

DRIFTWOOD BRANCH SINNEMAHONING RIVER MAJOR HATCHES

Insect	J	F	M	A	M	J	J	A	S	O	N	D
Blue Quill #16 & 18				■								
Hendrickson #14				■								
Sulphur #16					■	■						
March Brown #12					■							
Quill Gordon #14				■								
Black Stone #16				■								
Blue-winged Olive #16					■	■						
Tan Caddis #14					■							
Tan Caddis #16						■	■	■	■			
Gray Fox #14					■							
Green Drake #12, 3X long (Coffin Fly Spinner)					■							
Brown Drake #12, 3X long						■						
Light Cahill #14					■							
Cream Cahill #16 & 18					■	■				■		
Terrestrials (ending date dependent on cold weather)						■	■	■	■	■		

Terrestrials—ants, beetles, caterpillars, and inchworms—are extremely important.

BIG MILL CREEK

Elk County is one of those places where fishing is often forgotten due to the popularity of the elk herd found here, the only area of the state that has held elk in their natural habitat for nearly a century. Currently, the Pennsylvania Game Commission is hard at work in an effort to expand the elk range, but this is still THE place to come.

Big Mill Creek is 10 miles in length and blessed with a Delayed Harvest Artificial Lures Only section from its confluence with Rocky Run downstream to just above the SR 1461 bridge. Big Mill Creek flows to the town of Ridgway, where a dam has been placed to hold water for use as Ridgway's water supply.

At the edge of Allegheny National Forest, the stream lies in a beautiful area of the state and has plentiful hatches. It begins as a small stream and widens as it approaches Ridgway.

A native brook trout comes to hand.

Big Mill Creek

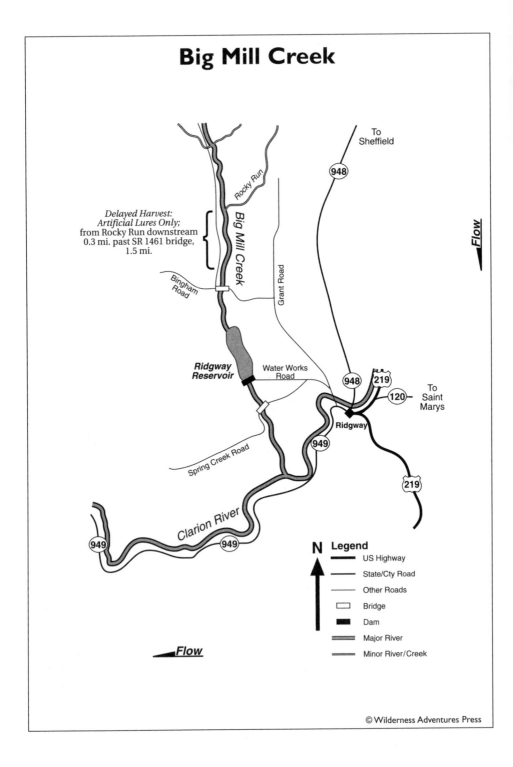

To
Sheffield

948

*Delayed Harvest:
Artificial Lures Only;
from Rocky Run downstream
0.3 mi. past SR 1461 bridge,
1.5 mi.*

Rocky Run

Big Mill Creek

Bingham
Road

Grant Road

**Ridgway
Reservoir**

Water Works
Road

948 219

120

To
Saint
Marys

Ridgway

949

Spring Creek Road

Flow

Clarion River

949

949

219

N

Legend

———— US Highway

———— State/Cty Road

———— Other Roads

▭ Bridge

▮ Dam

▬▬ Major River

▬▬ Minor River/Creek

Flow

© Wilderness Adventures Press

Hatches are plentiful throughout its course and the pool-to-riffle ratio is good. Access to this stream is difficult, but it can be reached off SR 1004 northwest of Ridgway.

This stream, as I stated earlier, lies on the edge of the Allegheny National Forest, which holds miles upon miles of native brook trout and native brown trout streams, all worth exploring. The PFBC stocks Big Mill Creek, and there are a fair number of wild browns and native brookies close to the headwaters.

Take waders with felt soles or hip boots for the upper reaches. My favorite rod is a 9–foot with a 5-weight.

BIG MILL CREEK MAJOR HATCHES

Insect	J	F	M	A	M	J	J	A	S	O	N	D
Blue Quill #18				■								
Hendrickson #14				■								
Caddis #14 & 16 (grannom, olive & gray, brown & tan)				■	■	■						
Quill Gordon #14				■								
Tan Caddis #16					■	■	■	■				
Light Cahill #14						■						
Green Drake #12, 3X long (Coffin Fly Spinner)						■						
Sulphur #16						■						
Blue-winged Olive #14 & 16						■						
Pale Evening Dun #18								■				
Ants #16–20; Beetles #12–18; Grasshoppers $10–14)							■	■	■			
Caterpillars #12, 3X long						■	■	■	■			
Other												
Yellow Adams #14–16					■	■	■	■	■			
Mosquito #12–16					■	■	■	■	■			

Clarion River

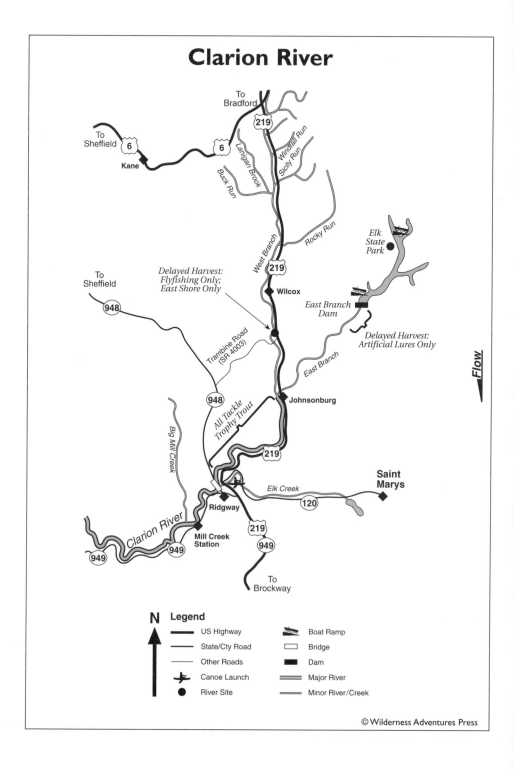

To Bradford

To Sheffield

219

6

6

Kane

Lanigan Brook

Windfall Run

Sicly Run

Buck Run

Rocky Run

West Branch

219

Elk State Park

Delayed Harvest: Flyfishing Only; East Shore Only

Wilcox

East Branch Dam

To Sheffield

948

Trambine Road (SR 4003)

Delayed Harvest: Artificial Lures Only

East Branch

Flow

948

All Tackle Trophy Trout

Johnsonburg

Big Mill Creek

219

Saint Marys

Elk Creek

120

Ridgway

Clarion River

219

949

Mill Creek Station

949

949

To Brockway

N Legend

— US Highway
— State/Cty Road
— Other Roads
— Canoe Launch
● River Site

◢ Boat Ramp
▢ Bridge
■ Dam
═ Major River
— Minor River/Creek

© Wilderness Adventures Press

CLARION RIVER

The Clarion River and its branches are slowly returning from the ravages of man and, at some future point, may return to their former glory. There are a lot of reasons for its demise, but it is difficult to determine what exactly has caused so many problems on this river.

However, it is a beautiful river, short on good hatches, but with reports of large trout being captured. Those with the desire to nymph fish on large water will find this stream to their liking. The main stem that forms at the juncture of the East and West Branch near the town of Johnsonburg may be easily reached from SR 219.

Special regulations here (All Tackle Trophy Trout) govern 8.5 miles of the main stem from the confluence of the East and West Branches downstream to the polluted confluence of Elk Creek. The Clarion's total length is 25 miles, although the better trout water is found in the north-central area of the state before the stream enters the northwestern region.

The East Branch has a Delayed Harvest, Artificial Lures Only section and is maintained primarily with stocked trout. The DHAO is l.15 miles from 110 yards downstream of the outflow of East Branch to Clarion River Lake. This section lies along T358, accessible from SR1001. The East Branch is 10 miles in length.

The West Branch also has special regulations. A 0.5-mile Delayed Harvest Fly-Fishing Only section begins at the intersection of SR 219 and SR 4003 and goes upstream to Texas Gulf Sulphur property. Fishing is permitted from the east bank only.

Because of the apparent lack of good hatches, this area is ignored by most. It takes some hunting to find trout, but fingerling stockings by the PFBC have helped, and some extremely large carryover browns have been taken and continue to be taken from the main branch. The East and West Branches are more suitable for those who want to fish for well educated stocked trout in the special regulation waters.

The stream remains a mystery, and it is not a prime destination for those wanting to do a lot of dry-fly fishing. Despite the drawbacks, the tan caddis, one of my favorites, does bring enough trout to the surface from mid-May on to keep my interest. And terrestrial fishing can be good during the summer months.

If the Clarion has its advantages, it comes in the form of a large river with long glides and trout in sufficient numbers to challenge the best of flyfishers. Caddis flies are more prevalent than mayflies, and emergers and beadhead nymphs, as well as large stonefly nymphs, take the bulk of the larger fish.

The river seems nearly lifeless in certain sections and abundant in others. Finding the large fish can be a real puzzle and, when they are found, they seem to be in pods. It is a combination of hunting and fishing that makes this stream an interesting one—one that I would not pass over.

You will need waders and a wading staff is helpful. I prefer a 9-foot rod here, carrying a 5-weight line and leaders tapered to 6X for the majority of my fishing—9-foot leaders for dries and 7 feet for nymphs.

There are few, if any, guides serving this stream, but Smith's Sport Shop is a full Orvis dealer and may be instrumental in suggesting flies and times of hatches. The West Branch offers approximately 42 miles of wilderness canoeing. Ideal canoeing is from March through June, and rentals are available at Cook Forest and Ridgway. Suggest trips include: Ridgway to Hallton (a nice one-day trip); Ridgway to Clear Creek (2 days); and down to Cook Forest for a 3-day trip. Secondary roads follow the Clarion nearly its entire length with hand launching available at many locations for shorter trips.

CLARION RIVER MAJOR HATCHES

Insect	J	F	M	A	M	J	J	A	S	O	N	D
Blue Quill #18				▬								
Hendrickson #14				▬								
Caddis #14 & 16 (grannom, olive & gray, brown & tan)				▬▬▬▬								
Light Cahill #14					▬▬							
Tan Caddis #16					▬▬▬▬▬							
Ants #16–20; Beetles #12–18; Grasshoppers #10–14							▬▬▬▬					
Other												
Mosquito #12–16					▬▬▬▬							
Streamers				▬▬▬▬▬▬▬▬▬								

Summary of Approved Trout Waters
and Special Regulation Areas for Northcentral Pennsylvania

Cameron County	Section / Regulations
Brooks Run	
Clear Creek	
Driftwood Branch	*DHFFO:* 1.4 miles from the Shippen Township Building downstream to SR 0120 west of Emporium
George B. Stevenson Reservoir	
Hick's Run East Branch	
Hick's Run West Branch	
Hunts Run	*All Tackle Selective Harvest:* 4.7 miles from the confluence with McNuff Branch downstream to the mouth
Jerry Run Upper	
Mix Run	
North Creek	
Portage Creek	
Sinnemahoning Creek, First Fork	
Sinnemahoning Creek, East Fork	
West Creek	
Wykoff Run	

Centre County	Section / Regulations
Bald Eagle Creek	
Beech Creek, South Fork	
Black Bear Run	
Black Moshannon Creek	*DHALO:* 1.3 miles from Dry Hollow downstream to 0.3 miles downstream of Huckleberry Road Bridge
Cold Stream Run	
Dicks Run	
Eddylick Run	
Little Fishing Creek	
Laurel Run (Flat Rock Creek)	
Marsh Creek	
Mountain Branch	
Penns Creek	*No Kill Zone:* 7 miles from the confluence with Elk Creek downstream tot he Catch and Release area. Trout: 14-inch minimum size limit, creel limit 2 per day during the period from opening day of regular season to midnight Labor Day
Poe Creek	

Centre County (cont.)	Section / Regulations
Poe Lake	
Seven Mountains Boy Scout Dam	
Sinking Creek	
Six Mile Run	
Spring Creek (Fisherman's Paradise)	*Heritage Trout Angling:* 1 mile, lower boundary of Spring Creek Hatchery Grounds to a point adjacent to the Stackhouse School Pistol Range *Special Regulations:* 1 mile from SR 3010 Bridge at Oak Hall above the HRI Quarry, formerly Neidig Brother's Limestone Co., to the mouth
Wallace Run	
White Deer Creek	
Wolf Run	

Clearfield County	Section / Regulations
Anderson Creek	
Beaver Run	
Beech Run	
Bennetts Branch South Branch	
Chest Creek	
Little Clearfield Creek	*DHALO:* 1.1 miles from 0.2 mile upstream of LR 17038 (Turkey Hill Bridge) upstream 1.1 miles
Curry Run	
Cush Creek	
Gazzam Run	
Gifford Run	
Goss Run Dam	
Hockenberry Run	
Jack Dent Branch	
Little Muddy Run	
Laborde Branch	
Janesville Dam	
Laurel Run	
Medix Run	
Moose Run	
North Witmer Run	
Parker Lake	
Sawmill Run	
Sinnemahoning Creek, Bennetts Branch	
South Witmer Run	

Tannery Dam	
Wilson Run	

Clinton County	**Section / Regulations**
Baker Run	
Hyner Run	
Cooks Run	
Fishing Creek	From Cedar Run downstream to mouth *Trophy Trout Project:* 5 miles, from the bridge at Tylersville Fish Hatchery downstream to Fleming's Bridge (SR 2004) at Lamar Hatchery
Kettle Creek	
Kettle Creek Lake	
Hyner Run, Left Branch	
Hyner Run, Right Branch	
Little Fishing Creek	
Long Run	Confluence of Pepper and Washburn Runs downstream to SR 2009 in Rote
Paddy Run	Forestry Road near Austin Hollow downstream to Hensel Fork
Rauchtown Creek	Dam breast at Ravensburg State Park downstream to SR 2010
Young Woman's Creek, Left Branch	
Young Woman's Creek, Right Branch	*Selective Harvest:* 5.5 miles, from State Forest property line upstream to Beechwood Trail

Elk County	**Section / Regulations**
Bear Creek	
Bear Run	
Belmouth Run	
Big Mill Creek	*DHALO:* 1.5-mile section from the confluence with Rocky Run downstream to 0.3 miles downstream of the SR 1461 Bridge
Big Run	
Boggy Run	
Byrnes Run	
Clarion River, East Branch	*DHALO:* 1.15-mile section from 100 yards downstream of the outflow of the East Branch Clarion River Lake downstream for a distance of 1.15 miles
Clarion River, West Branch	*DHFFO:* 0.5 miles, from intersection of SR 219 and SR 4003 upstream to Texas Gulf Sulphur property (fishing permitted from east shore only)
Crooked Creek	

Elk County (cont.)	Section / Regulations
Hicks Run	
Hicks Run, East Branch	
Hicks Run, West Branch	
Hoffman Run	
Laurel Run Reservoir	
Little Toby Creek	
Maxwell Run	
Medix Run	
Middle Fork	
Big Mill Creek	
Millstone Creek	
Millstone Creek, East Branch	
Mix Run	
Powers Run	
Ridgeway Reservoir	
Rocky Run	
Spring Creek	
Spring Creek East Branch	
Spring Run	
Twin Lakes	
West Creek	
Wilson Run	
Wolf Lick Run	
Wolf Run	

Jefferson County	Section / Regulations
Big Run – tributary of Mahoning Creek	
Big Run – tributary of Little Sandy Creek	
Callen Run	
Cathers Run	
Clear Creek	
Clear Run	
Cloe Dam	
Five Mile Run	
Horm Run	
Laurel Run	
Little Sandy Creek	
Little Toby Creek	
Little Mill Creek	

Mill Creek–tributary to Sandy Lick Creek

Mill Creek–tributary to Clarion River

Mahoning Creek, East Branch

Pekin Run

Rattlesnake Creek

Rattlesnake Run

Red Bank Creek

Red Bank Creek, North Fork	*DHFFO:* 1.9 miles, from SR 0322 in Brookville upstream

Sandy Lick Creek

Walburn Run

Wolf Run

Lycoming County	**Section / Regulations**
Black Hole Creek	
Blockhouse Creek	
Cedar Run	*Trophy Trout Project:* 7.2 miles, from the confluence with Buck Run downstream to mouth
Gray's Run	*Selective Harvest:* 2.2 miles, from Gray's Run Hunting Club property line downstream to concrete bridge (T-842) at old CCC camp
Hoagland Run	
Larry's Creek	
Little Bear Creek	
Little Muncy Creek	From West Branch downstream to Big Run
Little Pine Creek	*DHALO:* 1.0 mile, from 200 yards downstream of Otter Run to the confluence of Schoolhouse Hollow
Little Pine Lake	
Loyalsock Creek	Route 973 upstream to county line *DHALO:* 1.4 miles, from Lycoming County line downstream to Sandy Bottom
Lycoming Creek	Cogan Station upstream to county line
Mill Creek	SR 2039 below Warrenville upstream 6 miles
Muncy Creek	Mouth of Little Muncy Creek upstream to county line *DHALO:* 1.1 miles, from $. Sullivan property 600 yards upstream of T-650 bridge downstream to vicinity of confluence of Big Run at Tivoli
Pine Creek	Waterville on SR 0044 to Blackwell on SR 0414
Pleasant Stream	
Roaring Brook Rock Run–tributary to Muncy Creek	
Rock Run–tributary to Lycoming Creek	

Lycoming County (cont.)	Section / Regulations
Spring Creek	
Upper Pine Bottom Run	
Wallis Run	

McKean County	Section / Regulations
Allegheny-Portage Creek	Bridge at coal tipple to headwaters
Allegheny River	SR 0155 bridge east of Port Allegany upstream to county line
Bell Run	
Bradford Reservoir 3 (Marilla Brook Reservoir)	
Brewer Run	
Chappel Fork	
Clarion River, West Branch	
Cole Creek	
Cole Creek, South Branch	
Colegrove Brook	
Combs Creek	
Hamlin Lake	
Havens Run	
Kinzua Creek	*DHALO:* 2.3 miles, from SR 219 at Tallyho downstream to Camp Run, north of US 6 about 6 miles
Kinzua Creek, South Branch	
Marvin Creek	*DHFFO:* 1.1 mile, from 3 miles south of Smethport downstream
Potato Creek, West Branch	
Potato Creek	Marvin Creek upstream to confluence of East Branch Potato Creek and Havens Run
Red Mill Brook	
Seven Mile Run	
Skinner Creek	
Sugar Run	
Sugar Run, North Branch	
Tionesta Creek, East Branch	
Tunungwant Creek, East Branch	*Trophy Trout Project:* 3.0 miles, from the confluence with Pigeon Run downstream to the Main Street Bridge in Lewis Run
Tunungwant Creek, West Branch	*DHALO:* 1.2 miles, from T-499 bridge downstream to pipeline crosing near confluence of Gates Hollow
Two Mile Run	
Willow Creek	

Northumberland County	Section / Regulations
Little Shamokin Creek	
Mahantango Creek	
Roaring Creek, South Branch	
Schwaben Creek	
Zerbe Township Rod and Gun Club Pond	

Potter County	Section / Regulations
Allegheny River	*DHALO:* 2.7 miles, from Judge Paterson's Pond Road downstream to Ford 0.3 mile downstream of Prosser Hollow Bridge
Bailey Run	
Cowanesque River	
Cowley Run, East Branch	
Cowley Run, West Branch	
Cross Fork Creek	*Heritage Trout Angling:* 5.4 miles, from Bear Trap Lodge downstream to Weed property
Eleven Mile Creek	
Fishing Creek	
Fishing Creek, East Branch	
Fishing Creek, West Branch	
Freeman Run	
Genessee River	
Genessee River, Middle Branch	
Genessee River, West Branch	
Kettle Creek	*DHFFO:* 1.7 miles, from 500 feet downstream of SR 144 Bridge upstream 1.7 miles
Little Kettle Creek	
Lyman Lake	
Lyman Run	*Selective Harvest:* 4 miles, Lyman Run Lake upstream to Splash Dam Hollow
Oswayo Creek	
Oswayo Creek, South Branch	
Pine Creek	
Pine Creek, West Branch	
Sartwell Creek	
Sinnemahoning Creek, East Fork	*All Tackle Selective Harvest:* 2.9 miles, from the confluence with Wild Boy Run downstream to confluence with Camp Run
Sinnemahoning Creek, First Fork	*DHALO:* 2.1 miles, from teh mouth of Bailey Run downstream to a bend above Berge Run Bridge
South Woods Branch	

Snyder County	Section / Regulations
Kern Run	
Mahantango Creek North Branch	
Mahantango Creek West Branch	
Middle Creek North Branch	
Middle Creek South Branch	
Middle Creek	
Swift Run	

Tioga County	Section / Regulations
Asaph Run	
Asaph Run, Left Branch	
Beechwood Lake	
Blacks Creek	
Cedar Run	*Trophy Trout Project:* 7.2 miles, from the confluence with Buck Run downstream to the mouth
Cowanesque River	From Troups Creek upstream to the Potter County line
Francis Branch, Slate Run	*Heritage Trout Angling:* 2 miles, from the mouth upstream to Kramer Hollow
Lake Hamilton	
Long Run–tributary to Pine Creek	
Marsh Creek	Mouth upstream to the mouth of Straight Run
Mill Creek	
Pine Creek	
Roaring Brook	
Seeley Creek	
Slate Run	*Heritage Trout Angling:* .5 mile, from the confluence of Cushman and Francis Branch to the mouth
Stony Fork Creek	
Stony Fork Creek, East Branch	
Tioga River	From Fall Brook upstream to county line
West Mill Creek	

Union County	Section / Regulations
Buffalo Creek	Cowan Bridge upstream to T-366
Buffalo Creek, North Branch	
Cherry Run	*All Tackle Selective Harvest:* 2.7 miles, from the mouth upstream
Halfway Lake	
Laurel Run	

Penns Creek	Glen Iron is downstream limit *Catch and Release:* 3.9 miles, from approximately 650 yards downstream from Swift Run downstream to 550 yards below Cherry Run
Rapid Run	
Spring Creek	
Spruce Run	
White Deer Creek	*DHFFO:* 3.1 miles, from Cooper Mill Road upstream to Union/Centre County line

Northcentral Hub Cities
Coudersport and Galeton
Population-3,000

ACCOMMODATIONS
Laurelwood Inn, 3 miles east of US 6 (Coudersport) / 814-274-9220
Paul's Motel, 513 East 2nd Street (Coudersport) / 814-274-8700
Potato City Motor Inn, US 6 East (Coudersport) / 814-274-7133
Rustic Cottages, US 6 East (Coudersport) / 814-274-8589
S & S Whispering Pines, RR 1 Box 183 (Coudersport) / 814-274-0820
Sweden Valley Motel, RR 1 Box 348 (Coudersport) / 814-274-8770
Westgate Inn, 341 1/2 Port Allegany Road (Coudersport) / 814-274-0400
J T's Motel, US 6 (Galeton) / 814-435-6787
Nob-Hill Motel & Cabins, US 6 East (Galeton) / 814-435-6738
West Pike Motor Lodge, West Pike (Galeton) / 814-435-6552

RESTAURANTS
Laurelwood Inn, US 6 East (Coudersport)
Potato City Country Inn, US 6 East (Coudersport)
In-Between Restaurant, Road 3 US 6 West (Coudersport) / 814-274-3663
Jack's Steak & Seafood, 478 East 2nd Street (Coudersport) / 814-274-0805
Jim's & Hilda's Restaurant, 127 North Main Street (Coudersport) / 814-274-8390
Mosch's Tavern, 762 North Main Street (Coudersport) / 814-274-9932
Sweden Valley Inn, RR 1 (Coudersport) / 814-274-7057
Gelton Diner, 23 West Street (Galeton) / 814-435-6534
Waldheim, RR 1 (Galeton) / 814-435-8815
Wonder Bar & Grill, 22 Union Street (Galeton) / 814-435-3485

FLY SHOPS
Hollern's Hardware & Sporting Goods, 201 North Main Street (Coudersport) / Hollern's does have a few flies and other essentials but is not a full-service fly shop
Northern Tier Outfitter, 15 Fairview Avenue (Galeton) / 814-435-6324

AIRPORTS
Bradford Airport, McKean County / Approximately 1½ hours from Coudersport

MEDICAL
Charles Cole Memorial Hospital, RR #1 Box 205 (Coudersport) / 814-274-9300

FOR MORE INFORMATION
Chamber of Commerce
9 North Main Street
Coudersport PA 16915
814-274-8165

Lock Haven
Population – 9,230

ACCOMMODATIONS
Best Western Inn, 101 East Walnut Street / 570-748-3297
Fallon House, 131 East Water Street / 570-748-7477
Keystone Motel, 430 Woodward Avenue / 570-748-8017
Partnership House B&B, Baird Lane & Island Route / 570-748-1990
Victorian Inn B&B, 402 East Water Street / 570-748-8688

CAMPGROUNDS
Little Place Camping Area / 570-769-6359
Sunrise Campgrounds, HC 75 Box 43d / 570-769-7154

RESTAURANTS
Assante Hotel, 218 Bellefonte Avenue / 570-748-9811
Clinton Hotel, 375 East Clinton Street / 570-748-2880
Darla's Country Kitchen, 225 East Main Street / 570-748-2234
Dutch Haven Restaurant, 201 East Bald Eagle Street / 570-748-7444
Kathy's Kitchen, 201 Logan Avenue / 570-748-7977
Mangy Moose, RR 1 Box 457a / 570-769-6400
Mountain Top Inn, HC 75 Box 54 / 570-769-6238
Packer's Restaurant, Island Route / 570-769-7275
Rocky Point Lodge, RR 2 Box 170c / 570-748-1818

FLY SHOPS
Kettle Creek Tackle Shop, HCR 62, Box 140 Rt. 44 (Renovo Hammersley Fork) /
     717-523-1416
Fred Reese Trout Shop, 220 Thompson Street, Box 698 (Jersey Shore) / 717-398-
     3016
Slate Run Tackle Shop, Rt. 414 (Slate Run) / 717-753-8551

AUTO RENTAL
Rent-A-Wreck, 288 Hogan Boulevard / 570-748-9336

AIRPORTS
Piper Memorial Airport, 340 Proctor Street / 570-748-5123

MEDICAL
Lock Haven Hospital & ECU, 24 Cree Drive / 570-893-5000

FOR MORE INFORMATION
Clinton County Chamber of Commerce
151 Susquehanna Avenue
Lock Haven, PA 17745
570-748-5782

Ridgway

Population – 5,500

ACCOMMODATIONS

Royal Motel, Boot Jack Road / 814-773-3153
Summit Manor Motel, Boot Jack Road / 814-776-2311
Towers Victorian Inn, 330 South Street / 814-772-7657
The Post House B&B, 130 South Street / 814-772-2441

RESTAURANTS

Ling Ling, 201 Main Street / 814-772-9591
Original Italian Pizza, 163 Main Street / 814-772-7576
Pennsy Restaurant, 157 North Broad Street / 814-772-9935
Royal Drive-In, Boot Jack Road / 814-772-2044
Susan's Family Restaurant, 102 Main Street / 814-776-6064
Tasta Pizza, 149 Main Street / 814-772-2285

FLY SHOPS

Smith's Sport Shop, 10 Erie Avenue (St. Mary's) / 814-834-3701

AIRPORTS

See Erie or Pittsburgh

MEDICAL

Elk County Regional Medical Center, 94 Hospital Street / 814-776-6111

FOR MORE INFORMATION

Ridgway-Elk County Chamber of Commerce
231 Main Street
Ridgway, PA 15853
814-776-1424

State College
Population – 38,981

Accommodations
Brewmeisters B&B, Cato Avenue / 814-238-0015 2070
Hotel State College, 100 West College Avenue / 814-237-4350
Imperial Motor Inn, 118 South Atherton Street / 814-237-7686
Nittany Budget Motel, 240 South Pugh Street / 814-237-7638
Northland Motel, 1521 Martin Street / 814-237-1400
Ramada Inn, 1450 South Atherton Street / 814-238-3001
Residence Inn, 1555 University Drive / 814-235-6960
Rodeway Inn, 1040 North Atherton Street / 814-238-6783
Shaner Hotel Group, 303 Science Park Road / 814-234-4460
Sleep Inn, 111 Village Drive / 814-235-1020
South Ridge Motor Inn, 1830 South Atherton Street / 814-238-0571
Stevens Motel, 1275 North Atherton Street / 814-238-2438

Restaurants
Allen Street Grill, 100 West College Avenue / 814-231-4745
American Ale House & Grill, 821 Cricklewood Drive / 814-237-9701
Hoss's Steak & Sea House, 1450 North Atherton Street / 814-234-4009
Ruby Tuesday, 1550 South Atherton Street / 814-234-6256
Seoul Garden, 129 Locust Lane / 814-237-7444
Tavern Restaurant, 220 East College Avenue / 814-238-6116

Fly Shops
Flyfisher's Paradise, 2603 East College Avenue. / 814-234-4189

Auto Rental
Budget Rent-A-Car, 1450 South Atherton #105 / 814-238-5196
Enterprise Rent-A-Car, 218 West Clinton Avenue / 814-238-4450
Hertz Rent-A-Car, 2493 Fox Hill Road / 814-237-1728
National Car Rental, 2493 Fox Hill Road / 814-237-1771
Rent-A-Wreck, 1500 North Atherton Street Rear / 814-234-2817

Airports
University Park Airport, 2535 Fox Hill Road / 814-865-5511

Medical
Centre Community Hospital, 1800 East Park Avenue / 814-231-7000

For More Information
Centre County Convention and Visitors Bureau
1402 South Atherton Street
State College, PA 16801
814-231-1400

Williamsport
Population – 30,000

ACCOMMODATIONS
The Long Reach Plantation, 2887 South Reach Road / 570-326-9396
Bing's Motel, 2961 Lycoming Creek Road / 570-494-0601
City View Inn, Route 15, RD #4 Box 550 / 570-326-2601
Colonial Motor Lodge, 1959 East Third Street / 570-322-6161
Econo Lodge, 2401 East Third Street / 570-326-1501
Hampton Inn, 140 Via Bella / 570-323-6190
Quality Inn Williamsport, 234 Montgomery Pike / 570-323-9801
Sheraton Inn Williamsport, 100 Pine Street / 570-327-8231

RESTAURANTS:
Court Grill, 320 Court Street / 570-326-3611
Mulberry Street Cafe, 166 Mulberry Street / 570-322-9423
DiSalvo's Restaurant, 341 East Fourth Street / 570-327-1200
Kansas City Steakhouse, 100 Pine Street / 570-322-2957
Peg & Bill's Diner, 312 West Fourth Street / 570-326-1059
Bullfrog Brewery, 231 West Fourth Street / 570-326-4700

FLY SHOPS
E. Hille Angler's, 2303 Lycoming Creek Road / 800-326-6612
Wheary's Country Store and Fly Shop, Route 44 (Waterville) / 570-753-82

AUTO RENTAL
Enterprise Rent-A-Car, 716 Washington Boulevard / 570-326-9669
Ugly Duckling Rent-A-Car, 3575 West 4th Street / 570-326-2121

AIRPORT
Williamsport Regional Airport, contact the Airport Office at 368-2444, Monday
through Friday, 9AM to 5PM, for more information

MEDICAL
Divine Providence Hospital, 1100 Grapion Boulevard / 570-326-8175

FOR MORE INFORMATION
Williamsport/Lycoming Chamber of Commerce
454 Pine Street
Williamsport, PA 17701
570-326-1971

Southcentral Pennsylvania

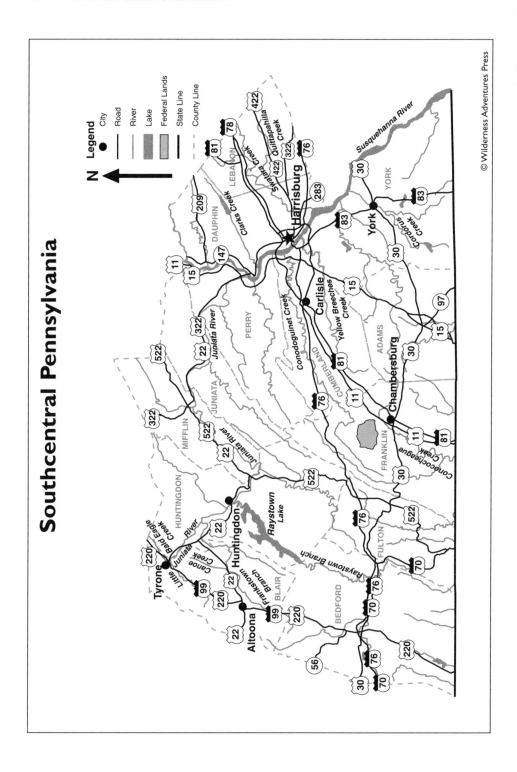

Southcentral Pennsylvania

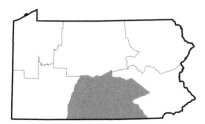

Southcentral Pennsylvania is a hub for flyfishing opportunities. Unlike the mountainous areas to the north, most of the land here is rolling farmland. But a limestone belt runs through the area, and many more limestone streams begin their flows here than in the north.

The exception would be found in Huntingdon and Centre Counties, where limestones are common despite the steep mountains that surround the area. The rule is that trout grow larger in limestones than in freestones. The reason for this is that water flows and temperatures remain more constant, staying cooler in the summer and warmer in the winter. This means that many of the streams here are not affected by thermal pollution or bottom ice.

Fertile limestones usually contain enough elodea and watercress to support shrimp and cress bugs, and the often-overlooked crayfish. Because the food supply is more abundant, trout are often more difficult to entice.

But streams in this portion of the state are not without problems. Streams here are often found around or near heavily populated areas. Housing and commercial buildings, as well as a strong farming community, cause heavy silting that retards natural reproduction.

While these streams have remained fishable in spite of the pressures of civilization, every trout stream and warmwater needs a friend. Few streams throughout the state do not have a Trout Unlimited chapter, watershed association, or local sportsmen's group nursing them back to health or conducting studies to determine a stream's condition.

For the most part, the well-known hatches of northern streams do not exist here. The eastern green drake, for example, is sorely missing. Yes, transplants of the mayfly have been tried, but they failed.

With the introduction of more special regulation waters in the north, anglers found that trout caught and released several times became wary. But, my personal fly box, which once included thousands of patterns, has shrunk considerably and I have found that under many circumstances, exacting patterns are not needed. However, emergers, floating nymphs, and beadheads have replaced many of my discarded fly patterns.

Southcentral hatches begin later than in the north. While northern trout fishermen are covering rising fish with little black stones and blue quills, the limestone flyfisher is impatiently awaiting the first full-blown hatch. But the northern streams' better hatches are often over by mid-June. The better southcentral streams are experiencing incredible hatches that last through the summer months.

It is highly unfair to compare one area of the state to another; however, it is helpful to know the differences, strengths, and drawbacks that exist from one area

*Anglers lined up
on a southcentral
trout stream.*

to another. There are, of course, exceptions to the rules since I have painted the regions with a broad brush.

My solution is simple: I fish the north country during the months of April, May, and into mid-June, then I head south and fish the limestones throughout the summer months. Since I am a dry-fly fanatic and love terrestrial fishing, this schedule allows me to fish each area during prime conditions throughout the entire year. I do know that I might be missing something on a cool feeder stream in the north, but I accept the loss since no one can be everywhere at once. Fishing for trout anywhere at any time is a pleasure that is hard to rival, and I seldom pass up a fishing trip no matter where the stream is located.

The southcentral region fishes best from mid-May on, for anglers interested in hatches. For a more in-depth discussion of flies and patterns as well as how and when to fish them, refer to the "Coldwater Fly Box" section of this book. When in doubt, a good rule of thumb here is to go one size smaller. If trout are rising to a size 14 blue-winged olive but aren't taking the fly, switch to size 16—that alone often makes a difference.

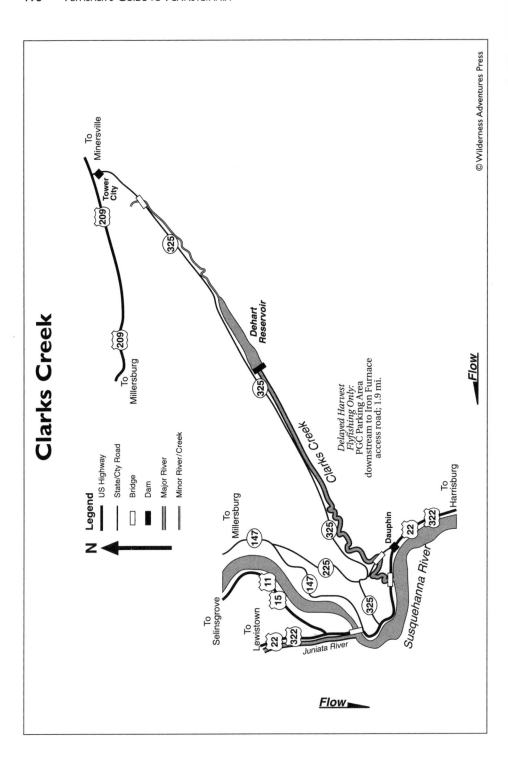

Clarks Creek

N

Legend
US Highway
State/Cty Road
Bridge
Dam
Major River
Minor River/Creek

To Minersville

Tower City

209

209

To Millersburg

325

Dehart Reservoir

325

Clarks Creek

Delayed Harvest
Flyfishing Only:
PGC Parking Area
downstream to Iron Furnace
access road; 1.9 mi.

To Millersburg

147

147

225

325

Dauphin

22

322

To Harrisburg

To Selinsgrove

11

15

To Lewistown

22

322

Juniata River

Susquehanna River

Flow

Flow

© Wilderness Adventures Press

CLARKS CREEK

Clarks Creek is located only 20 minutes from the state capitol. It would seem like the poor cousin of trout streams, being surrounded by the giants of limestone waters, with such names as the Letort, Yellow Breeches, and Big Spring. But this small freestone takes the city dweller from asphalt into the remnants of virgin hemlock that guard, cool, and protect the gin-clear waters and selective trout that reside here.

Clarks is always fishable, even when the area's major streams become clouded from recent rains. The stream has drawn its share of regulars from the masses who reside in or visit the capitol city. It is a divine getaway from the congestion of a four-lane highway to a curved and isolated black-top with gravel parking lots and trails to the waters that wash the city from memory in a matter of minutes.

Although Clarks averages only 30 to 40 feet in width below the DeHart Reservoir, 10 miles above its confluence with the Susquehanna River, the small impoundment provides cool water temperatures throughout the summer months. The stream is heavily guarded by hemlock, pine, and hardwood forests throughout the Delayed Harvest Flyfishing Only area. While many freestones are warming up, the shade provided by the forest canopy not only helps keep the water cool here but also provides surprisingly cool air temperatures.

The stream is fishable year-round on the 1.9-mile Flyfishing Only stretch, beginning at the Pennsylvania Game Commission (PGC) parking lot downstream to the PGC access road at the Iron Furnace. The stream is paralleled by SR 325, and the special regulations area is well marked with posted signs.

Browns, brookies, and rainbow are heavily stocked from late winter into fall, and carryovers as well as some natural reproduction does occur. Fish average 12 to 14 inches, although there are enough 18- to 20-inch plus browns to make it interesting. Flyfishermen with a keen eye and a few years of experience under their belts should consider a 12- to 15-fish day a decent one. I have had 30-plus fish days, but I would consider those outings exceptional.

Although most of the stream may be fished in hip boots, the steep terrain on both banks may require stream crossings. I prefer waders because I have had only rare occasions when I have not waded in over the tops of my hip boots. Felt soles are a must.

The stream originates near Tower City and flows some 20 miles before entering the Susquehanna River above the town of Dauphin. The river is well protected by streamside vegetation, and a fly angler should be adept at roll casting or making long casts through a shoot of overhanging trees. Long leaders measuring 10 to 12 feet in length are required, and low water conditions make light tippets, 6X through 8X, a must. The ability to make pinpoint, delicate casts and complete, drag-free floats are often necessary. Clarks is a boulder-strewn gravel stream that runs thin and gin clear and attracts enough catch-and-release anglers to produce fussy trout.

This angler is working a brushy section of Clarks Creek.

Early season anglers can expect hatches of black stoneflies (#16), brown stone-flies (#12), and blue-winged olives (#20). The most important early season hatch is the Hendricksons (#14), and area anglers flood the stream when the hatch begins. Blue quills (#18) are also present during the early season as are black quills (#14). Most early season anglers carry a 7- to 9-foot rod with a 4- to 5-weight line. Despite the wide variety of fly sizes required for fishing during the early season, the lighter the tippet the more success is possible.

Because of the clear, thin waters, many anglers consider Clarks to be a premier dry-fly stream, and although anglers cast dries in the early season, good nymph and streamer fishermen also do well during this time. The majority of hatches are not prolific, and it requires keen observation to decide exactly what trout are eating— something that can change without notice.

As the season progresses into mid-June, the creek becomes a terrestrial fisher's delight. Because of the overhanging vegetation, terrestrials become as dense as hatches, and although tan caddis (#16) are present during the majority of the season, trout here seem much more willing to take an inchworm, gypsy moth caterpillar, elm span worm , ant, or beetle than all other available food.

Many anglers now throw light lines, 1- to 3-weights, and lengthen their leaders to 12 feet. Lighter tippets also become part of the angler's arsenal, along with good sunglasses. Even with larger imitations, anything above a 7X tippet decreases an angler's success. Flyfishermen here do well with a dry fly and a nymph as a dropper. Although an observant angler should be able to see the fish take a nymph in the crystal clear waters, fishing both gives trout a choice and usually results in more hookups.

The stream does have a good riffle-to-pool ratio, due in large part to the work of the Dauphin County Anglers, who placed stream improvement structures throughout much of the stream's length up to DeHart Reservoir. During the summer months, trout are most often found within the deeper pools and are easily visible to an angler walking carefully along the bank. Feeding fish are usually at the head as well as the tails of pools.

Ideally, it is best to fish from shore, keeping a low profile, but the embankments are three feet higher than the stream with very little room to cast. Anglers should wade as slowly as possible into the water and wait for fish to settle before casting. After a hookup, it is often necessary to "rest" the pool before casting again. This may be accomplished by leaving the water to work another pool or retreating to the shore and waiting for trout to begin rising again.

Fall fishing is a test of trout hunting and matching the hatch. A variety of small midges—I prefer the pheasant tail (#24) and pale evening duns (#16) as well as tan caddis (#16)—will take fish that may have moved out of the warmer waters of late summer. Many flyfishermen catch their fair share of fish on woolly buggers (#8-12) and green weenies (#12), although muskrat nymphs (#18-20) and pheasant tail nymphs (#16) do take trout. The fish are well scattered and fewer in number by this time, and so are the anglers, who catch trout well into November, although it requires some walking and stalking.

Access to the river is easily found, and there are parking lots and pulloffs along its length. There is open water governed by statewide regulations above and below the Project Waters. These areas offer fishing in secluded woodland and open meadows, and there is a children-only area located next to the Dauphin County Anglers Club near the mouth. Above DeHart Reservoir, the stream narrows and is extremely brushy. This section is full of fish but a challenge for anyone not used to fishing Pennsylvania's small native brook trout streams. The trout are less fussy about the imitation used, but bow and arrow casts are needed (bending the rod and slinging the line through narrow openings). Fishing an old-fashioned wet fly by feeding line downstream crawling along the banks is a good method here.

One hazard that anglers should be aware of is that Clarks has a healthy copperhead population and that encounters with this poisonous snake are possible. Always look first before taking a step, or if crawling, where you place your hand, and you shouldn't have any trouble.

Access is easily found along the entire length of Clarks. Game Commission parking lots are scattered throughout the Delayed Harvest Flyfishing Only area, and well-defined pulloffs can be found along the length of the creek.

Lodging and food are available in the hub city of Harrisburg, and there is a Hardee's restaurant in the town of Dauphin along SR 322.

Clarks Creek is small in reputation when compared to many of the area's more popular limestones, but it offers solitude in a genuine freestone setting only a short way from the capitol city. Add a large number of trout and you have a stream worth visiting. It's my guess that you will come back, time and again.

CLARKS CREEK MAJOR HATCHES

Insect	J	F	M	A	M	J	J	A	S	O	N	D
Black Stone #16			■									
Brown Stone #12				■								
Blue Quill #16				■								
Blue-winged Olive #18 & 20				■								
Hendrickson #14				■								
Sulphur #16					■							
March Brown #12 & 14					■							
Blue-winged Olive #14 & 16					■							
Light Cahill #14					■							
Slate Drake #14, 3X long					■							
Tan Caddis #16					■	■	■	■				
Yellow Stone #14 & 16							■					
Green Stone #16 & 18						■						
Cream Cahill #18								■				
Terrestrials					■	■	■	■	■			

Note: Inchworms and caterpillar patterns are extremely important here. If in doubt when choosing a pattern, go one size smaller.

STONY CREEK

Stony Creek begins near Lickdale in Lebanon County. Its upper reaches are in an area that was heavily mined for coal, and this beautiful stream has suffered tremendously because of it.

The three miles of water in Lebanon County are miniscule in size and distance. After entering Dauphin County, it treks 16 miles through some of the most beautiful pieces of unpopulated land surrounding the Harrisburg area. The upper reaches are not heavily fished, although brook trout do dart about the small, crystal clear waters.

Rausch Run has polluted the stream with mine acid and destroyed the native trout populations below it. Trout Unlimited, in cooperation with the PFBC, put limestone wells in the area, and the stream is on the rebound.

Game Commission land borders one side of the stream and Fort Indiantown Gap, a military base, the other until it nears the Susquehanna River. The upper portion of the stream is tough fishing and is not stocked. But, for those willing to run into the occasional copperhead and/or rattlesnake, the fishing here is hard to beat. An old railroad grade parallels the majority of the stream, and walk-in fishing provides all the solitude anyone could want. The stream's lower section is heavily stocked by the Commission and is extremely popular during the early part of the season.

Better fishing is found by following the first road to the right after exiting SR 322 at the town of Dauphin. The paved road turns into dirt, and parking is available at road's end. From this point on upstream is where to find better fishing. Hip boots will do for this area, but downstream, waders are needed to cast to the stocked trout found here.

See Clarks Creek for a hatch chart.

SHERMANS CREEK

Shermans Creek is a trout stream of some note in its upper reaches. It flows nearly 49 miles through Perry County, beginning near Big Spring State Park, before entering the Susquehanna River south of Duncannon, where it is bass water of some character. Shermans Creek is stocked with trout by the PFBC from Cisna Run upstream to the mouth of Hemlock Run.

I have a friend who claims this is his favorite stream for flyfishing and who has taken many large trout and excellent smallmouth to prove it. However, silt accumulation in its lower reaches causes the stream to warm up early in the season, making it a better smallmouth fishery than trout fishery.

The stream does produce some excellent fishing, however, and sports some shaded and mountainous areas along its course. Its coldwater influences produce some carryover trout as well as a few brookies nearer the headwaters.

As with so many streams that enter the Susquehanna, the whitefly is the mainstay for bass and trout that survive into late July and early August. If you want to test all of the water, waders are needed. Once again, I want to emphasize that bass like mayflies and caddis flies as well as trout, making this is a good stream to take bass on dries and crayfish imitations that also take trout in good numbers. Trout fishing is better early in the season, while bass fishing kicks into high gear during mid-June.

There is a lot of water to be explored, and fishing can be excellent for trout and even better for bass. This is a good example of what kind of bass fishing may be found beyond the larger streams and rivers of the state.

The stream's stocked section is accessible from SR 274, and the lower reaches from SR 850. Shermans is really two streams in one, flowing from a mountainous region into a valley floor, offering the best of both worlds.

SHERMANS CREEK MAJOR HATCHES

Insect	J	F	M	A	M	J	J	A	S	O	N	D
Blue Quill #18				■								
Hendrickson #14				■								
Caddis #14 & 16 (grannom, tan)				■	■							
Quill Gordon #14				■								
Tan Caddis #16					■	■						
Light Cahill #14					■							
Sulphur #16					■							
Cream Cahill #18					■				■			
Blue-winged Olive #14 & 16					■							
Ants #16–20; Beetles #12–18; Grasshoppers #10–14						■	■	■				
Caterpillars #12, 3X long						■	■	■				
Other												
Yellow Adams #16							■	■				
Mosquito #12–16							■	■	■			

YELLOW BREECHES CREEK

The popularity of Yellow Breeches Creek in Cumberland County cannot be over-stated. Despite the famed waters that surround it, this creek, particularly the 1-mile stretch of Catch-and-Release water from the "Run" downstream to the lower limits of the Allenberry property, is probably the most fished water in the state if not the most famous.

A past manager of the Yellow Breeches Fly Shop, located in Boiling Springs, told me that visiting anglers coming to the area wanted directions to the Letort immediately upon their arrival. The same anglers would return within a day or less and then ask where they could catch fish. The answer, of course, was the Yellow Breeches.

Being fortunate to live on the stream for over five years and fishing it for 30 years, I have found that the stream has changed little in that time. For some unexplainable reason, Yellow Breeches trout seem more interested in surface feeding than chasing nymphs, emergers, or streamers, although they can and do take all three.

Dry-fly fishermen from all over the world come to this famed creek. There are few months out of the year that fish do not rise here, and the Breeches' top asset is its rising fish. I find it an amazingly interesting stream, one that has enough fussy feed-ers that 7X and 8X tippets are often a necessity. But for some odd reason, there are always enough uneducated fish to take almost any fly, within reason, thrown their way. But hold on before you start tying a bunch of Royal Wulff and Humpies and take off for the stream, these fish are not that much of a pushover.

The Yellow Breeches is a stream where tippets and drag-free floats are prime con-siderations. If you get a drag-free float over these fish (by drag free, I mean to a much greater degree than required on most streams), then success is almost a guarantee. Remember that the fly pattern is important but not as important as presentation.

For example, during the afternoon hours beginning in early June through late September, I fish a spun-deer hair beetle almost exclusively here. I tie the pattern in sizes 12 through 20 and "make" the trout take the fly. I find the challenge fascinating to say the least. Unlike anglers who continually change flies throughout the day, I stay with my chosen pattern until the fish is either put down or ceases to feed. I care-fully monitor each cast, move into a position that I feel will allow a better presenta-tion than the last, and try my best to have the fly arrive before the leader. This often requires a down and across stream cast rather than an upstream or quartering upstream cast that is often used for dry-fly fishing. Knowing how to mend line prop-erly also helps delivery. It may take 20 to 30 casts to get the proper drift, but when you do, a take is almost a certainty.

Trout here are almost always rising, and I have found the best approach on this stream is to simply walk the streamside and keep a sharp eye out for rising fish. Take note of the fact that larger trout most often make a slip of a rise, while splashing rises are often those of juvenile trout.

The stream here is an exceptional fishery, from the small stream called the "Run," beginning at the spillway of Children's Lake, downstream to the main stem of Yellow

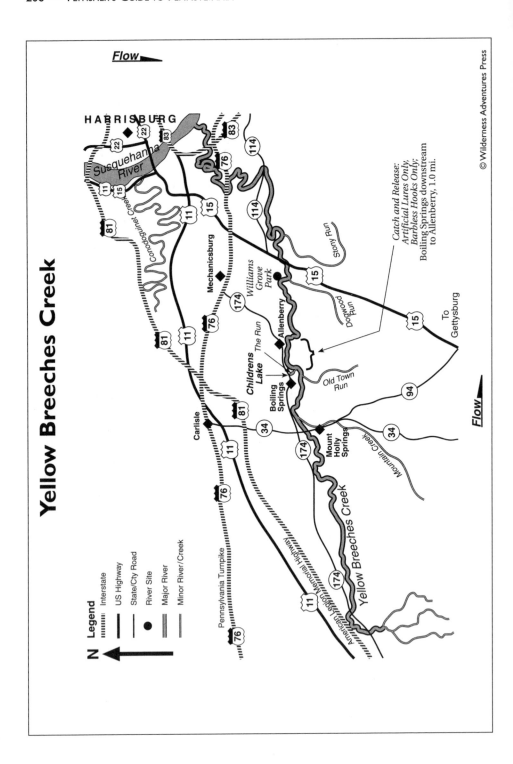

The "Run" on the Yellow Breeches is a short stretch of Class A wild trout water, although not listed as such.

Breeches Creek. The parking lot located here has confused many visiting anglers, with many mistaking the "Run" for the Yellow Breeches.

The "Run" is a feeder stream that is of extreme importance to the system's overall health. Here, the lake's cold waters spill into a stream not more than 20 feet wide, and even narrower at some places. This stream section is a healthy Class A fishery and serves as a spawning ground for fish that migrate here from Yellow Breeches Creek. The water is clear and often thin, and the pools are waist deep for the most part. The "Run" is the heart and soul of the Yellow Breeches. Without it, the main stem would not qualify for Catch-and-Release regulations, and fishing would become dependent almost entirely on stocked fish.

The clarity of the water has both advantages and disadvantages. Nymph fishermen, who need to visually track their offering in order to set the hook at the right time, benefit the most from the water's clarity. Dry-fly fishermen find themselves at

The Yellow Breeches.

a disadvantage, because even fine tippets look like thick rope on such clear water. The stream's tricky currents are also a problem for dry-fly fishers.

The stream holds a good mixture of wild, stocked, and carryover fish, with browns being the most prevalent wild and carryover fish and brook trout a close second. The amount of large rainbows that appear here, especially during late fall when they make and protect spawning redds, might lead many to believe that an excellent population of wild rainbows is present. This is rarely the case, although small rainbows that I have taken here lead me to believe that there is some natural reproduction, although limited. However, the amount of rainbows that do carry over is amazing. Large rainbows, well over 20 inches and weighing 5 pounds or better, are not unusual. And brown trout in the same size range exist here as well. Brook trout, as expected, are much smaller in size, except for stocked fish that can exceed 20 inches.

*Good fishing is available
in the fall on the
Yellow Breeches "Run."*

Most fishing is easily accomplished from the streambank, however, below the walk bridge at the Iron Furnace parking lot, the streambank gets considerably steeper. Anglers wishing to fish some of the pools in this section will need to get in the water to fish it correctly. Hip boots will work for both situations, since the pools get too deep to venture very far out in them. Wading should be restricted to as close to the streambank as possible, since wading midstream will more than likely spook fish and put them down.

Fishing Yellow Breeches Creek is entirely different in complexity and character than many other streams. At the Junction, the catch-and-release section extends upstream 50 yards and offers excellent fishing during the early part of the season. However, without the cold water of the "Run," this stream section falls into the marginal water category quickly.

The Junction is most often used for stream crossing rather than fishing. It's important that all fishing takes place from the far streambank at this point. The Run's cold water stays close to the streamside from which it enters, and the difference in water temperature can be as much as 10 degrees from the one bank to the other. This means that, to find trout, the stream must be crossed and then fished from that side to the streamside in which the run enters. A well-defined path parallels the far bank downstream to the limits of the 1-mile stretch.

The variety of water here will please almost any angler. The downstream section begins with moving water—a set of riffles that expands for nearly a hundred yards. Water clarity is rarely crystal clear and runs somewhat off-colored throughout the length of the riffles.

Here, fish can be found in a waist deep cut that flows through the middle portion of this stream section, and early season flyfishers will find an abundance of trout here by drifting pheasant-tail and muskrat nymphs. Large fish, however, cling to the far bank, where the water has greater clarity. It is also so thin that one expects to see adipose fins protruding from it, and when fish are raiding the shallows, the fins do protrude.

The angler must be able to present the fly tight against the far bank and then achieve a drag-free float as the main current separates the angler from the fly. This is not an easy task for many. If achieved, however, the fly might not be as exact as on other waters, and trout will take something in size 16 with amazing consistency. Although anglers need to pay close attention to any hatch in progress, trout will often take a well-presented caddis imitation or a terrestrial, ant, or beetle.

Below the riffles is a deep, slow-moving glide. The current can be tricky here, and trout are more selective than in the riffles. However, rising fish cruise right beneath the surface and are plainly visible to the angler. Presentation of the fly is again important, but even between rises, it's possible to place a fly two to three feet above the trout.

When a fish is visible, it is easier to present the fly at the precise time that a fish would take a natural. Since the fish can head downward or backward, visibility becomes extremely helpful. Anglers should also know that these trout often follow a fly with their nose nearly touching the fly for 6 to 10 feet. It is apparent that they are not only inspecting the offering closely, they are also waiting for any form of drag whatsoever. This sector of water is appealing to those who like the challenge of difficult trout that are willing to take a dry fly.

The Breeches continues downstream past the beautiful Allenberry Resort and Playhouse. Anglers will find designated and well marked parking here. The area below the falls is full of larger fish, and nymph fishermen shine here. The stream then changes, and fishing is most productive against the far bank. Trout might be found hugging the streambank or taking refuge in the series of pools created by anglers many years ago.

To fish most of the main stem, an angler needs waders since much of the water in the slower sections is at least waist deep. A long-sleeved shirt and long underwear

Anglers lined up on the Yellow Breeches awaiting the evening white fly hatch.

are recommended, especially during evening hours. The stream here measures 50 to 60 feet across in most areas here.

This section is difficult to beat for excellent flyfishing, and dry-fly action is found throughout much of the year. Add to that the charm of the village of Boiling Springs, and it is easy to understand why the stream is one of the most productive and most visited in the state.

Trout fishing extends upstream to the headwaters near Lees Cross Roads and downstream to the town of New Cumberland. The stream parallels SR 174 and then Creek Road on the lower sections until it meets up with 174 once more.

The upper sections of the stream do hold some excellent Trico hatches in August, but the stream becomes marginal quickly after leaving the immediate headwater area. Posted land here also hinders fishing. There is also the fact that fishing starts as a Class A stream and falls to a Class C on a single mile of catch-and-release water.

One of the largest springs east of the Mississippi is found near the town square of Boiling Springs and quickly forms Children's Lake. Also near here, water from the Run rarely exceeds 65 degrees, turning the Yellow Breeches into a coldwater resource that has attracted flyfishers for so many years. This area serves as the hub of the limestone belt.

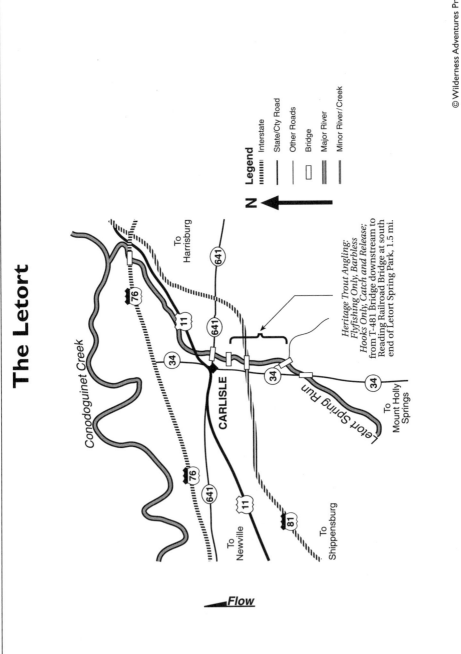

The Letort

Conodoguinet Creek

To Harrisburg

CARLISLE

Letort Spring Run

To Newville

To Shippensburg

To Mount Holly Springs

Heritage Trout Angling: Flyfishing Only, Barbless Hooks Only, Catch and Release; from T-481 Bridge downstream to Reading Railroad Bridge at south end of Letort Spring Park, 1.5 mi.

N

Flow

Legend

|||||| Interstate
—— State/Cty Road
— Other Roads
▭ Bridge
━ Major River
— Minor River/Creek

© Wilderness Adventures Press

THE LETORT

The Letort is a limestone like few others. Charlie Fox was considered "the dean of the Letort," and Vince Marinaro brought the stream to national attention with his book, In the *Ring of the Rise*. The Letort's legend and lure brought famed anglers from all parts of the world, and Charlie Fox, a gracious man, became a gracious host.

Fox's book, *This Wonderful World of Trout*, mentioned the Letort frequently. But the team of Fox and Marinaro, who both wrote such wonderful articles, brought anglers from around the nation who were enchanted with chalk streams. Marinaro visited the famed Test in England in order to make comparisons. A ceremony was held when a vial of water from the English stream was poured into the waters of the Letort as a symbol of the two waters' marriage.

Few have worked so feverishly and yet so graciously on a small sector of limestone stream without monetary reward. There had been a ritual gathering of Letort Regulars, a group without dues, at the small farmer's market restaurant on the outskirts of Carlisle. To become a Letort Regular, the only requirement was that you fished the stream and showed up occasionally for Sunday breakfast.

Of course, there was Vince's meadow to add to the charm and Charlie Fox's famed bench, where one could watch the fabled waters and fish to the rise of a single trout. It was here in front of that bench that Charlie poured clean gravel suitable for spawning into the waters. He also built dividers so that trout could spawn side by side.

A few hundred yards away, Charlie constructed a house, because "he wanted to live on a trout stream." The Cumberland County Chapter of Trout Unlimited became involved with the stream as well, and a shrine to Vince Marinaro was erected in his meadow. The group decided long ago that this stream would be open to all flyfishers, and they accomplished that task through writing and stream monitoring.

When the stream was polluted by a cress farm and large fish rolled up in great numbers, one would have thought that a national disaster had occurred, and perhaps it did. Fox and Marinaro were on hand as the Pennsylvania Fish and Boat Commission electroshocked the stream and found that it had lost a large majority of its wild trout. The Commission offered to help by stocking the stream, an offer declined immediately by both Fox and Marinaro. They would wait, they proclaimed, until the wild stock replenished itself and, as they had predicted, it did.

The Letort was to be a dry-fly stream, and dragging nymphs through the water was unheard of. The reality that there were few hatches of mayflies present did not dash the group's hope. Mayflies were transplanted from Penns Creek and other northern streams but didn't take.

Today, freshwater shrimp patterns and cress bug imitations are more common than the blue-winged olive and sulphur hatches that occur there. Sawyer's book on nymphs brought the pheasant tail nymph to the waters of this hallowed stream. I have also read of one angler who broke tradition entirely when he wrote an article on fishing woolly buggers on the Letort throughout the winter months. The Letort regulars were appalled by the piece.

The Letort River on the outskirts of Carlisle.

The Letort has its traditions and place in history. It also has a good number of wild brown trout that grow large and very selective in waters filled with crayfish, freshwater shrimp, and cress bugs. As I talked to Charlie Fox a month before his death, he shared his concerns for the stream that he loved so much. It was still on the mend, and although fish were present in good numbers, the loss of watercress was disturbing him. He knew that it was the main food source for the stream and that, without it, the stream would never be the same.

The stream and its players are changing—less tonkin cane and more graphite and boron mixes are showing up along the stream that flows through the city of Carlisle. The upper portion from 300 yards upstream (above the bridge on Twp. Route 481) downstream to the southern edge of Letort Spring Park, has been designated Heritage Trout Angling, restricted to catch-and-release fishing and flies only.

The Letort is an extremely difficult stream to fish, with the most productive water filled with tricky currents and midstream pocket, surrounded primarily by water-cress. Wading is nearly impossible due to the silt on the bottom, and drag-free floats are tough.

However, it is a stream for anglers who have great patience, and if it is any consolation, I asked Charlie Fox in a final interview how many fish would constitute a good evening of fishing. He paused and pondered, and then smiled, "I would say five trout would be a great evening. A good one would be the taking of one or two."

If you need a measuring stick for success, you now have it.

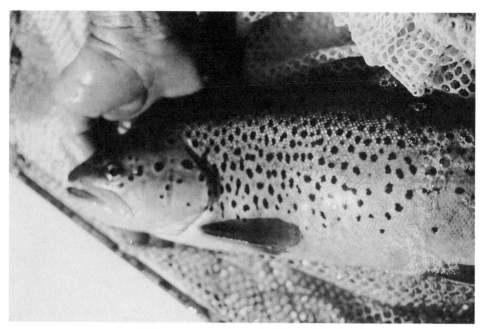

A brown trout from the Letort River.

LETORT RIVER MAJOR HATCHES

Insect	J	F	M	A	M	J	J	A	S	O	N	D
Blue-winged Olive				▬								
Sulphur #16					▬▬▬							
Trico #24						▬▬▬▬						
Cress Bugs #14–18					▬▬▬▬▬▬							
Scuds #16–20					▬▬▬▬▬▬							
Ants #16–20; Beetles #12–18; Grasshoppers #10–14						▬▬▬▬						
Caterpillars #12, 3X long						▬▬▬▬						

Terrestrial and caterpillar patterns should always be in your fly box.

Big Spring and Green Spring Creeks

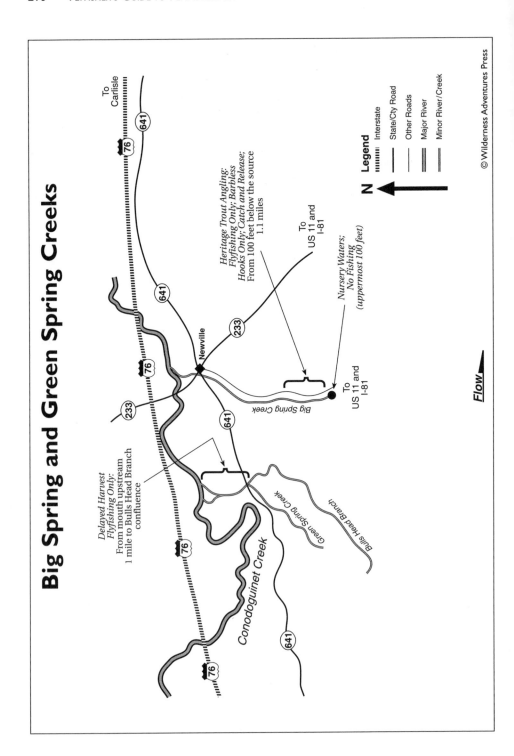

To Carlisle

641

76

Heritage Trout Angling:
Flyfishing Only; Barbless
Hooks Only; Catch and Release;
From 100 feet below the source
1.1 miles

To
US 11 and
I-81

Nursery Waters;
No Fishing
(uppermost 100 feet)

641

233

Newville

76

233

641

To
US 11 and
I-81

Big Spring Creek

Delayed Harvest
Flyfishing Only:
From mouth upstream
1 mile to Bulls Head Branch
confluence

Green Spring Creek

Bulls Head Branch

76

Conodoguinet Creek

76

641

N

Legend
▬▬▬ Interstate
——— State/Cty Road
——— Other Roads
▬▬▬ Major River
——— Minor River/Creek

© Wilderness Adventures Press

Flow

BIG SPRING CREEK

Big Spring Creek is often overshadowed by the Yellow Breeches and the Letort, perhaps because it is near the small town of Newville, and while it is a first-class lime-stone, it is a difficult stream to fish. Unlike the Letort, it did not have famous flyfish-ers writing about the stream's ability to produce extremely large trout that many anglers could not catch with a great deal of regularity.

Big Spring has been ignored by many, perhaps due to the stream's management, which had been Trophy Trout Regulations allowing two trout per day over 15 inches in length. This being a region filled with staunch advocates and practitioners of catch and release only might alone have kept flyfishers off this stream, which may, in turn, have created the perception that the stream had problems.

However, there are a great number of flyfishermen in this area of the state who quietly, yet effectively, pressured for change. They are a conservative lot with deep pockets when it comes to protecting a resource and have gone to such lengths as hir-ing lawyers and biologists to further their cause. Big Spring, like the Letort, is now under the Heritage Trout Program, allowing no killing of fish, flyfishing only, and a year-round season.

In the creek's midsection, loss of aquatic vegetation has been detrimental to fish populations, and effluent discharges from the hatchery located on the headwaters have been targeted as the culprit. Whatever the reason, fishing has dropped off con-siderably in the lower sections of the special regulations area, which begins 100 yards below Big Spring hatchery downstream to the Nearly Road Bridge.

The uppermost 100 feet is closed to fishing and has been set aside as nursery water to protect spawning fish. Although large browns as well as rainbow are present, the opportunity to catch extremely large, wild brook trout is Big Spring's real attrac-tion. Brook trout up to 5 pounds have been taken and released here, with 3- and 4-pounders not uncommon.

Despite the fact that the stream has had problems, you can be certain that groups like the Cumberland County Chapter of Trout Unlimited will continue its efforts to resolve them.

Big Spring Creek begins as a narrow trough that widens quickly. It is extremely difficult to fish, but not any more so than the Letort. Tactics must be changed, as freshwater shrimp, scud bugs, and cress bugs are the order of the day. Hatches are minimal, making approach and presentation on this water extremely important. Use 1-, 2-, and 3-weight lines with 8X tippets.

With its abundance of aquatic vegetation and large trout, you will find this stream as challenging as any in the state. The first obstacle is finding a trout that is willing to take, and then landing it on light tackle from the spider web of cress. This is not a forgiving stream, and it is filled with selective trout. Dry-fly fishermen may not love this stretch of water, but it delivers rewards in the largest brook trout found in the Commonwealth.

Big Spring is easily reached from US 11 by taking the Newville exit. Hip boots are all that is needed to fish the water.

BIG SPRING CREEK MAJOR HATCHES

Insect	J	F	M	A	M	J	J	A	S	O	N	D
Blue-winged Olive #20				▄								
Tan Caddis #16				▄▄								
Sulphur #16					▄							
Trico #24							▄▄					
Ants & Beetles #14–24						▄▄▄▄▄▄▄						
Scud bugs and cress bugs are extremely important here.												

GREEN SPRING CREEK

Green Spring Creek is a small meadow stream near the town of Newville that is overlooked due to the number of limestone giants in this area. The stream is only 3 miles in length but does have a DHFFO area from the mouth upstream for 1 mile to near the confluence of Bulls Head Branch.

The stream is stocked within the project area and has excellent hatches, very similar to those on Big Spring. It is a delightful stream that can be fished with a 1- to 3-weight line and a rod of your choosing. I find this stream offers excellent terrestrial fishing.

Green Spring is found off SR 4004 near the town of Green Spring. This is a good stream but, because of its length and tendency to warm up near the mouth, has slipped from view behind Big Spring and others. See the Big Spring Hatch Chart for hatches.

CODORUS CREEK

Codorus Creek, a look-like limestone, is a freestone stream in southern York County. The stream has excellent water, good pool-to-riffle ratio, and in its narrow width, resembles a small limestone stream.

The area is now regulated as Selective Harvest water, and my favorite hatch and spinnerfall, sulphurs, appear here in abundance. With the help of coldwater bottom releases from Lake Marburg, this stream is a year-round fishery. The entire stream length, 8.5 miles, is stocked with trout from the PFBC. The project area is open all year.

Fishing here is for those who like chilly waters and rising fish, although there are times that a good selection of beadheads will save your bacon. Pools are full of weeds, and scud bug and freshwater shrimp patterns work well here.

Except for local anglers, the stream is mostly unknown and is often uncrowded during weekdays. Hatches can be profuse, and I find the terrestrial fishing to be

Angler with a trout caught on a freestone stream.

Codorus Creek

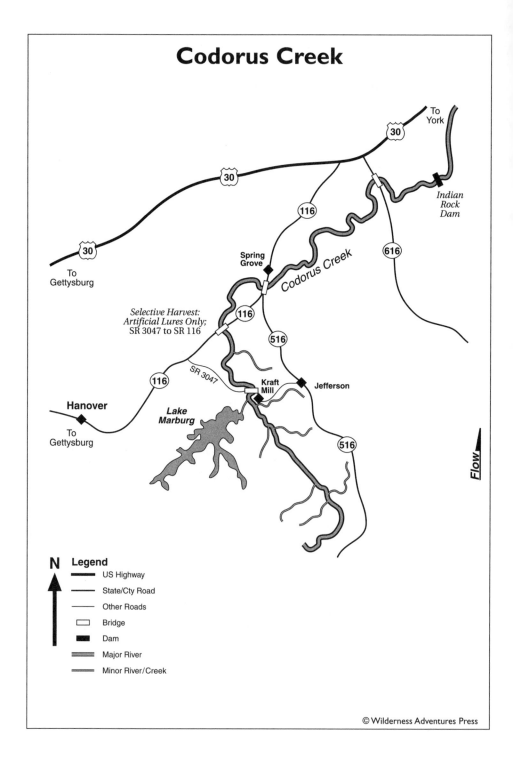

Legend
US Highway
State/Cty Road
Other Roads
Bridge
Dam
Major River
Minor River/Creek

© Wilderness Adventures Press

excellent. This stream is a sleeper, and even though small in size, it will become known as one of the better trout streams in the state in years to come as tailwater fishing grows in popularity.

Food passed down through the dam makes this a fishery with carryovers, which can grow to a good size. All anglers are encouraged to release every fish they take, as Selective Harvest allows the taking of browns at 12 inches and brook and rainbows at 9 inches—taking fish this size will not enhance the fishing that Codorus Creek could offer in the future.

Because of the deep pools found here, you may want to wear waders, especially for stream crossing. However, hip boots will suffice for the majority of fishing. Because of the stream's size, rods carrying line weights 3 through 5 are suggested.

The Selective Harvest Area extends from SR 3047 at Kraft Mill downstream to SR 116. Access to the stream is easily obtained from either route. The project area is 3.3 miles in length.

CODORUS CREEK MAJOR HATCHES

Insect	J	F	M	A	M	J	J	A	S	O	N	D
Tan Caddis #16					▓	▓	▓		▓			
Black Stone #16			▓									
Sulphur #16					▓	▓						
March Brown #12					▓	▓						
Cream Cahill #18						▓			▓	▓		
Black Stone #16				▓								
Blue-winged Olive #16					▓	▓						
Light Cahill #14						▓						
Gray Fox #14						▓						
Trico #24							▓	▓	▓			
Terrestrials (ending date dependent on cold weather)							▓	▓	▓	▓		

MUDDY CREEK

Muddy Creek received its name quite honestly—it is often muddy. Due to the urban sprawl encroaching on the stream, it becomes swollen quickly after even a minor rain and becomes off-colored. However, the stream does offer some excellent fishing when it's not raining.

The majority of this water, nearly 14 miles, is stocked. The Delayed Harvest section extends 2 miles from 300 yards above the SR 2032 bridge in Bridgeton to 300 yards from Bruce. This stream can provide excellent fishing and then turn off quickly when discolored. Found in York County near the town of Muddy Creeks Fork, all branches north and south are also stocked with trout.

This stream is definitely an early season trout stream with some good hatches. It warms quickly in the summer (around July), when it often becomes marginal trout water. The stream has potential, and with a little help, could be a good trout stream.

The main attraction of this stream is during the early season when fishing pressure is low. This, alone, makes it worth traveling to Southern York County, not far from the Maryland state line. Muddy Forks can be found on SR 2004.

MUDDY CREEK MAJOR HATCHES

Insect	J	F	M	A	M	J	J	A	S	O	N	D
Green Caddis #14					▪							
Gray Fox #14					▬							
Sulphur #16					▬▬							
March Brown #12					▬▬							
Blue-winged Olive #14					▬▬							
Tan Caddis #16						▬						
Trico #24 (sparse)								▬▬				
Terrestrials (ending date dependent on cold weather)							▬▬▬▬▬▬▬▬▬					

Because of the lack of insect activity here, terrestrial ants, beetles, caterpillars, and inchworms are extremely important.

CONEWAGO CREEK

Flowing through some 35 miles of Adams County and containing a mixture of trout, bass, panfish, and suckers, it is evident that Conewago Creek holds both cold water and warm water. It probably leans more to the warmwater side, and its bass are not all that large. That doesn't mean that it's a throwaway stream—its beauty is really something to behold, especially on the DHFFO stretch near Biglerville. However, trout fishing is pretty much dependent on stocked fish, and the PFBC stocks the stream from SR 234 downstream to SR 3011.

The delayed harvest section is also stocked before and during the regular trout season and again in the fall. This means a good number of trout are available to anglers throughout much of the year. The regulated area covers only 1.1 miles from T-340 downstream to SR 34.

It is relatively large water and should be fished with waders in most sections. Hatches are good early and late in the season, but midsummer fishing slows down as the water warms up. This is a good stream to try smaller weight lines and rod lengths of your choice. The countryside is beautiful, and the creek provides some good fishing into early June, and then again in the fall as stocked fish are placed into the cooling waters.

*A rainbow comes
to the net.*

I prefer waders here because far too often, I've waded over the top of my hip boots. Felt soles are also a good idea since the stream does have a rocky bottom in many areas. Spring and fall offer the best fishing here for stocked browns and rainbows.

While this is not a highly ranked stream, it has given me some exciting angling, and I'm sure it will do the same for you.

CONEWAGO CREEK MAJOR HATCHES

Insect	J	F	M	A	M	J	J	A	S	O	N	D
Blue Quill #18				▬								
Hendrickson #14				▬								
Caddis #14 & 16 (grannom, tan)				▬	▬	▬						
Quill Gordon #14				▬								
Tan Caddis #16					▬	▬	▬	▬				
Light Cahill #14						▬						
Sulphur #16						▬						
Cream Cahill #18						▬				▬		
Blue-winged Olive #14 & 16						▬						
Ants #16–20; Beetles #12–18; Grasshoppers #10–14							▬	▬	▬	▬		
Caterpillars #12, 3X long							▬	▬	▬	▬		
Other												
Yellow Adams #16							▬	▬	▬			
Mosquito #12–16							▬	▬	▬	▬		

FALLING SPRINGS BRANCH CREEK

At the tail end of the limestone belt is Falling Springs, which may be the last, but not the least significant, of all the limestone streams in this area. Falling Springs Branch Creek is a stream that is recovering rather than deteriorating due to the efforts of concerned flyfishers in both Pennsylvania and Maryland.

Falling Springs Branch Creek is a premier limestone and native trout stream located southeast of Chambersburg in Franklin County. It flows through a rural section of the county that is experiencing rapid residential growth.

Known for its tremendous, nearly blizzard-like Trico hatch throughout the summer months, it also had some blue-winged olives and a few sulphurs. But suddenly, the bottom seemed to drop out of the stream. Anglers realized that a stream with a Trico hatch of the magnitude one found here could not be lost, and stream improvement quickly became a priority.

Recovery plans started with streamside fencing, then cattle crossings, and then streambank stabilization. At the quarterly meeting of the PFBC in the spring of 1999, acquisition of land on Falling Springs was made a priority. The property to be acquired was owned by the Falling Spring Greenway Association, a nonprofit conservation group actively involved in the protection and restoration of the Falling Spring corridor. The association also actively promotes angling and responsible use of natural resources.

A Falling Springs rainbow.

Falling Springs Branch Creek

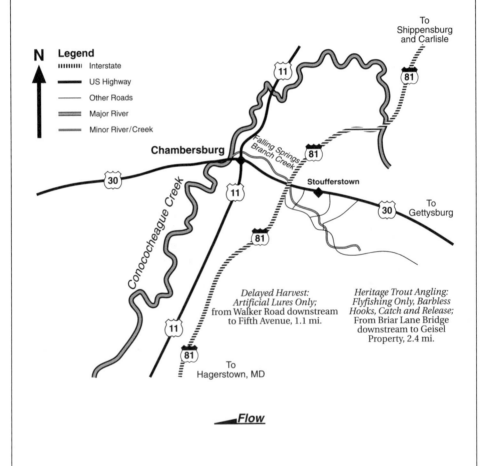

The Association had recently acquired two parcels of property along the Falling Springs Branch Creek and offered to sell these properties to the Commission at a cost less than the appraised value. The two parcels contained a total of approximately 3.2 acres with 640 feet of frontage along Falling Springs. The group offered to convey this land to the Commission for a fee of $15,600, which includes the purchase of the land and also title insurance for the properties at the time of closing.

It is the intention of the Association to use the proceeds of the sale as matching funds to secure additional federal grant money. The grant funds will be used to enhance and improve the habitat within and along Falling Springs Branch Creek. The Association has also expressed an interest in cooperating in management of the subject property. The meadow limestone is now in good hands and is improving with each and every passing year.

Hip boots will suffice on this meadow stream that, like most limestones, can be very productive on some days and not at all on others. Hatches are good and are improving each year. Two sections are governed under special regulations: 2.4 miles of Heritage Trout Angling from Briar Lane Bridge downstream to a fence crossing the Thomas L. Geisel property; and a Delayed Harvest Artificial Lures Only section of 1.1 miles from Walker Road to the 5th avenue Bridge in Chambersburg.

FALLING SPRINGS BRANCH CREEK MAJOR HATCHES

Insect	J	F	M	A	M	J	J	A	S	O	N	D
Blue-winged Olive #16–20				▆								
Tan Caddis #16					▆	▆	▆					
Black Caddis #16				▆								
Sulphur #16						▆						
Light Cahill #14						▆						
Trico #24							▆	▆	▆	▆		
Ants #16–24; Beetles #12–20; Grasshoppers #12, 3X long; Letort Cricket #14–18							▆	▆	▆	▆	▆	

Trout can become fussy here, try new and more innovative patterns as the hatch or season progresses.

Little Juniata River

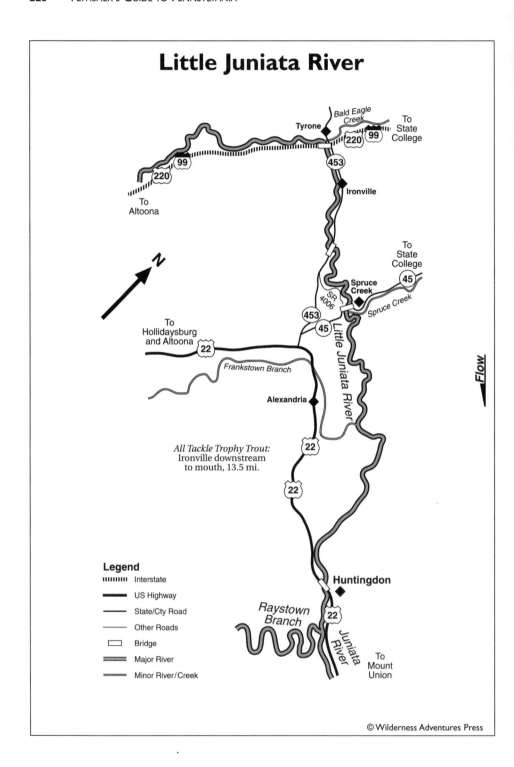

To
Altoona

Bald Eagle
Creek

Tyrone

To
State
College

220 99

453

Ironville

To
State
College

Spruce
Creek

45

SR
4006

Spruce Creek

453

45

Little Juniata River

To
Hollidaysburg
and Altoona

22

Frankstown Branch

Alexandria

Flow

All Tackle Trophy Trout:
Ironville downstream
to mouth, 13.5 mi.

22

22

Legend

Interstate

US Highway

State/Cty Road

Other Roads

Bridge

Major River

Minor River/Creek

Huntingdon

Raystown
Branch

22

Juniata
River

To
Mount
Union

© Wilderness Adventures Press

East Branch Antietam Creek

East Branch Antietam Creek is a nice limestone stream found in the very southern sector of Franklin County. Close to a mile of the stream is under DHFFO from SR 16 downstream to T-365. Although only 7 miles in length, the stream does produce some decent carryover fish and is stocked in the spring and fall by the PFBC.

The West Branch joins the East Branch close to SR 316 near the Maryland border. Both branches are stocked by the PFBC and both have a tendency to warm up during the summer months. But there is cold water from feeder streams and at the headwaters, where trout find refuge.

This stream is often overlooked in favor of the more popular and thus more populated streams in the state. Hatches are not great in number, but trout are willing to rise to all hatches that occur here, and terrestrial fishing can be, and often is, extremely rewarding.

The East Branch is the better of the two, but they are so close together that both are worth a visit. Light lines and rods varying in length from 7 feet to 9 feet are suitable here.

Both are easily accessible from state routes 316 or 997. See the hatch chart for Falling Springs.

Little Juniata River

There is little doubt that fishing in the Raystown area is among the best in the East—make that the country. The Little Juniata is a prime example. These storied waters allow public fishing for nearly 14 miles. The town of Spruce Creek, northwest of Huntingdon off state routes 22 and 435, is located in the center of premier flyfishing waters.

Except for a mile stretch from the Junction Pool, where Spruce Creek joins the Little "J" downstream for a mile, easy access is available along the stream's entire length. While it's true that this wonderful river has had its difficulties, it is on the mend. The last time I visited here in August, Harry Redline, a well-known local fisherman and guide, showed me trout in good numbers lining the bank just upstream from Spruce Creek. He also took a good number of terrestrial-sipping trout on a long line and fine tippet. The fish in that area were healthy and rising constantly.

The Little Juniata has been maintained with PFBC stocked fingerlings. Special Regulations cover 13.5 miles of the stream from the railroad bridge at the east border of Ironville downstream to the mouth. Trout here might as well be considered wild trout once they reach legal size, which is 14 inches or larger, and can be fished from opening day to the day after Labor Day. The limit is two per day during that period, with no-kill regulations the remainder of the year. All tackle is allowed. Despite the two-trout limit, anglers are encouraged to release fish.

The river is large and allows the long casts that Pennsylvania fishermen are rarely able to practice. The added attractions of beautiful scenery, profuse hatches, and seasoned trout willing to take a properly presented fly complete a flyfisher's dreams.

*A nice rainbow
to be released on
the Little Juniata.*

A brightly colored trout that has spent nearly its entire life in the river makes this fly-fishing at its best. These fish are challenging and can be as selective as any trout, but most anglers are able to take more than their fair share.

In spite of its problems, the Little Juniata remains one of the finest streams in the state, and there are plenty of concerned anglers in and out of the area who are determined to keep it that way. With a river full of willing trout larger than many anglers catch in a lifetime and plenty of elbowroom, can anyone with a fly rod ask for much more?

The stream begins as marginal at best, and the Special Regulations waters are considered the finer for fishing the Little "J". The stream actually begins as a freestone, but with all the limestone tributaries feeding into it, it is a full-blown limestone stream before it reaches the village of Spruce Creek.

Anglers can easily follow the stream's course along SR 453 in the upper reaches and then by picking up SR 4006. From here downstream to the Juniata River, the stream can be located off Water Street in Huntingdon.

At Spruce Creek, there is a section of private water beginning at the mouth of Spruce Creek. Many anglers in the area believe that the Little "J" should be navigable water as stated in laws dating back to the 1800s. If that argument were accepted, it would mean the stream could not fall under private ownership and would be open to the general public.

However, at the time of publication, arrangements to fish the Little "J" in the water below the Spruce Creek juncture must still be made through the Orvis Shop in Spruce Creek. The remainder of the stream remains open to public fishing.

The varying waters of the Little "J" make it one of the more popular streams in the state. Overall, fish are large, many from fingerling stock. The profuse hatches and the limestone character make this a year-round trout fishery.

Waders are a must, and a wading staff is a good idea. The lower reaches of this stream are far too deep to wade in many areas, so flyfishers should practice extreme caution. A choice rod for this river would be 9 feet in length and carrying a 5- or 6- weight line.

LITTLE JUNIATA RIVER MAJOR HATCHES

Insect	J	F	M	A	M	J	J	A	S	O	N	D
Black & Gray Midge #20 & 22			▬									
Blue Quill #18				▬								
Blue Dun #20				▬								
Blue-winged Olive #18 & 20				▬								
Hendrickson #14				▬								
Grannom Caddis #12 & 14				▬								
Sulphur #16					▬▬							
Slate Drake #12 & 14					▬▬▬▬▬▬							
Blue-winged Olive #14					▬▬							
Light Cahill #14						▬						
Blue-winged Olive #16–20							▬▬					
Tan Caddis #16							▬▬					
Trico #24								▬▬				
White Fly #16									▬▬			
Blue-winged Olive #20 & 22									▬			

Note: The stream has many more hatches than listed. Call Spruce Creek Outfitters for additional information. Terrestrial patterns are a must.

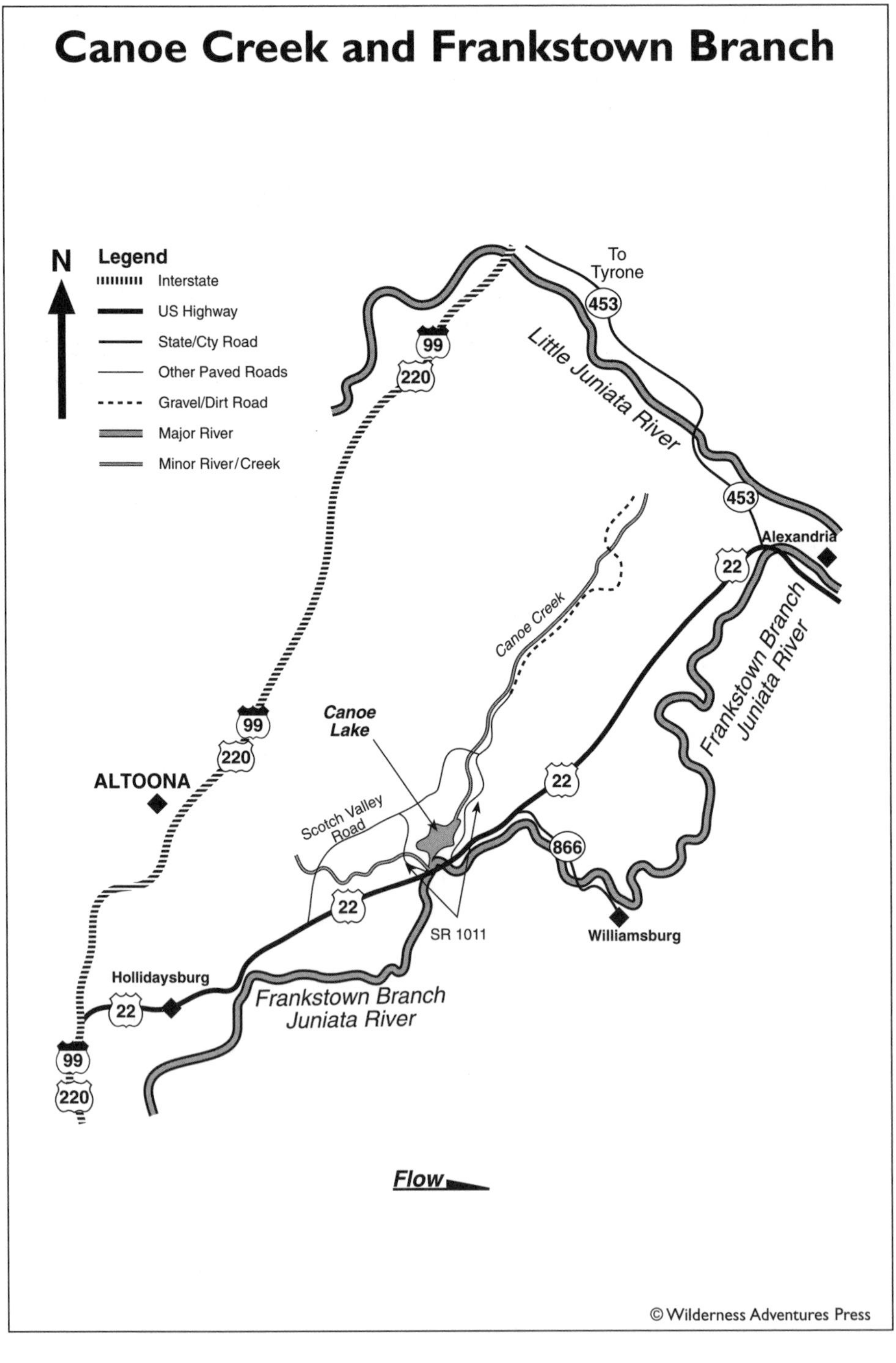

Canoe Creek and Frankstown Branch

N

Legend

IIIIIIII	Interstate
	US Highway
	State/Cty Road
	Other Paved Roads
- - - -	Gravel/Dirt Road
	Major River
	Minor River/Creek

To Tyrone

453

99

220

Little Juniata River

453

Alexandria

22

Canoe Creek

Frankstown Branch Juniata River

99

220

Canoe Lake

ALTOONA

22

Scotch Valley Road

866

22

SR 1011

Williamsburg

Hollidaysburg

22

99

220

Frankstown Branch Juniata River

Flow

© Wilderness Adventures Press

CANOE CREEK

Mention of a green drake hatch in Pennsylvania can cause hordes of anglers to flock to such streams as Penns Creek, Kettle Creek, the First Fork, and the Allegheny, which is both a blessing and a curse to such waters. This hatch, which was once so anticipated, now causes such overcrowding on some streams that many anglers stay away. Any more, I rarely, if ever, chase a green drake hatch, preferring sulphurs and my favorite spinnerfall, brown drakes.

Green drake hatches happen on lesser-known streams, and many anglers now seek these out as an alternative to the better known but overcrowded waters. Although the green drake hatch on Canoe Creek is not as dramatic as on other streams, it occurs in sufficient numbers to bring trout to the surface. However, a single hatch, no matter how highly heralded, does not, in itself, make a great trout stream. Canoe Creek has decent hatches throughout most of the year, and fishing here is often rewarding.

The creek flows 7.5 miles through Blair County before entering the Frankstown Branch. Better fishing is found above Canoe Creek Lake and is accessible from Scotch Valley Road. The remainder of the upper portion can be reached by turning onto SR 1011 from SR 22 northeast of Altoona. The stream runs through Canoe Creek State Park, and both the stream and lake are stocked trout waters.

The author works his favorite terrestrials on midsummer's thin waters.

Canoe Creek is a good trout stream that does deserve some regulated waters. At this time, it is open to statewide regulations and draws early season crowds. However, the crowds do not last long and the hatches, although not profuse, make for some interesting fishing on this stream.

Take waders to fish the entire stretch and a 9-foot rod with a 4- or 5-weight is a good selection here. As the season progresses, lightening the tippet and lengthening the leader will result in more success. Below the dam, the water does warm up, but there are coldwater influences to take advantage of. Stream improvement devices have been placed in many areas by the Blair County Chapter of Trout Unlimited.

The stream allows easy casting with a longer rod. If fishing the headwaters, a shorter rod is needed and a much more cautious approach. Some wild trout can be found here as well as a fair amount of native brook trout. On the larger section of stream, anglers will find primarily stocked trout with a few good carryover browns that often come as a welcome surprise. I also like the terrestrial fishing on Canoe Creek, which is a stream worth fishing beyond the early days of the season when it gets the bulk of its attention.

CANOE CREEK MAJOR HATCHES

Insect	J	F	M	A	M	J	J	A	S	O	N	D
Tan Caddis #16						▄			▄			
Hendrickson #14				▄								
Sulphur #16					▄							
March Brown #12					▄							
Cream Cahill #18						▄			▄			
Green Drake #12, 3x long (Coffin Fly Spinner)					▄							
Blue-winged Olive #16 (spotty)					▄	▄						
Trico #24 (spotty)						▄	▄					
Terrestrials (ending date dependent on cold weather						▄	▄	▄	▄			
Other												
Yellow Adams #16						▄	▄	▄	▄			
Mosquito #14						▄	▄	▄	▄			

Because of the lack of insect activity here, terrestrial ants, beetles, caterpillars, and inchworms are extremely important.

FRANKSTOWN BRANCH JUNIATA RIVER

The Frankstown Branch is a real sleeper of a stream. Recent surveys conducted by the Pennsylvania Fish and Boat Commission revealed a good number of wild trout along its length. This stream has both length and potential and is, once again, a good-sized body of water that most Pennsylvanians don't associate with trout, much less wild trout. I am mostly impressed with this river because of the incredible amount of access available via Rails to Trails—11 miles of stream access from Williamsburg in Blair County to Alexandria in Huntingdon County. The trail is readily accessible from SR 22 and from a number of small, winding blacktop roads. I would suggest getting a copy of the Rails to Trails map from the Raystown Country Visitors Bureau or by writing Rails-To-Trails of Blair County, Inc., P.O. Box 592, Hollidaysburg, PA 16648-0592.

The charm of the Frankstown Branch is that many knowledgeable anglers never considered the Frankstown Branch worth fishing for anything other than bass. But the truth is, with a little exploration, wild trout are found in abundance. This is still virgin territory for flyfishermen willing to hoof the trail that is open to all but motorized vehicles.

Small limestone tributaries enter the river at various points, most holding browns and native brook trout, and the Rails to Trails path provides access without landowner intervention. As a fledgling wild trout fishery, the Frankstown Branch is still under statewide regulations for trout and susceptible to overfishing. Because this fragile stream has an abundance of access, wild trout, and even smallmouth bass, it should be enjoyed as a catch-and-release fishery.

Feeder streams offer excellent flyfishing as well. Perhaps it's the explorer in me or the knowledge that pinpointing certain areas could be harmful to a fishery that causes me to only touch on this stream and its tributaries. But let me whisper this: For those so inclined and those willing to explore, wild trout that are measured in pounds can be found here. But finding them will be up to you—take your bike, a horse, or simply hike the river and explore its waters.

Hatches in the area vary from caddis to green drakes, with brown and slate drakes thrown in as well as whiteflies and blue-winged olives. Of course cahills, March browns and gray fox may also be found, and the terrestrial fishing can be superb.

The usual assortment of beadhead nymphs have proven their worth, as well as the old standbys, such as woolly buggers, and a good streamer selection. The stream is a beautiful stretch of water and has superb pools and ledges that offer some spectacular wild trout, mostly browns with a sprinkling of brook trout.

The water here is cool rather than cold, and it may be a mystery to unlock. Good numbers of smallmouth bass can be taken on crayfish patterns, leeches, and topwater popping bugs. Bugs of cork are beautifully produced by the Gaines Company and can be found in the better sporting goods stores throughout the state. The newer closed cell foam bugs that have been producing superb results on many waters are a little harder to come by, although they are beginning to appear in the marketplace.

Limestone water.

Topwater fishing is by far my favorite form of flyfishing and a stream like the Frankstown Branch is made to order.

It is remote enough not be overcrowded, and I am able to fish for bass and wild trout in the same stream sectors. Fishing is usually best accomplished with a 9-foot rod that carries a 6-weight line. Take a selection of leaders that are designed to turn over 6-pound tippets and roll over 2-pound test.

Some call it a full-blown trout stream and others call it a bass fishery. Presently, it's a fine combination of both. Sometime in the future it might become warmer or colder, either of which will determine what kind of fishery it is then. For now, it is one of the very few that offers both trout and bass fishing. Dyed-in-the-wool trout anglers might not like it, but for the time being I find the mixture a pleasant one.

Take waders to fish this branch and a willingness to carry them in.

FRANKSTOWN BRANCH MAJOR HATCHES

Insect	J	F	M	A	M	J	J	A	S	O	N	D
Black Stone #16			▆									
Green Caddis #14				▆								
Grannom Caddis #14				▆								
Tan Caddis #16					▆▆▆▆▆▆▆▆▆							
Blue Quill #18				▆								
Sulphur #16					▆							
Cahill #14					▆							
Green Drake #12, 3X long (sparse hatch)					▆							
Gray Fox #12 & 14					▆							
March Browns #12					▆							
Slate Drake #12 & 14					▆▆							
Blue-winged Olive #16					▆							
White Fly #14 & 16								▆				
Terrestrials					▆▆▆▆▆▆▆							

Bald Eagle Creek

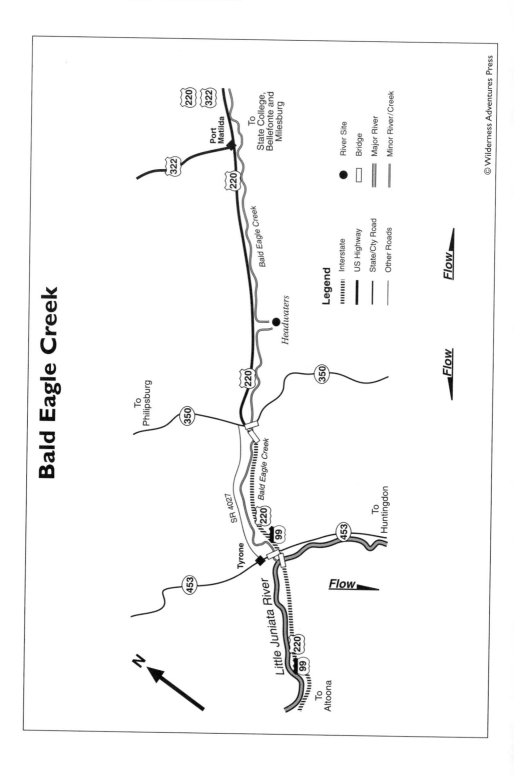

Legend

Interstate
US Highway
State/Cty Road
Other Roads

River Site
Bridge
Major River
Minor River/Creek

© Wilderness Adventures Press

Bald Eagle Creek

Chasing trout is often confusing and difficult: choosing what fly patterns to take; whether to take waders or hip boots; and choosing rod lengths and line weights. And that doesn't include the fact that there can be multiple streams with the same name. Trying to find the correct one on a map can be quite a chore.

In the process of writing this book, I found so many streams with the same name that, even though I have fished this Bald Eagle Creek and one other Bald Eagle, I needed the help of a map to determine which one I fished on what day. There are at least three Bald Eagle Creeks within the state, two of which are found nearly side-by-side at the headwaters in Blair County. There is yet another in York County.

The better of the Bald Eagle Creeks, in my opinion, starts on State Game Lands #278 and flows toward Tyron before joining the Little Juniata River. Coldwater influences keep this stream filled with a good supply of native brookies as well as wild and carryover brown trout.

Both Bald Eagle Creeks starting in Blair County are approved trout streams without special regulations, which means there are opening day crowds; both are heavily fished during the early season. The streams provide plenty of good flyfishing after the crowds thin out. Both streams are pleasant to fish and are not difficult to wade. You might want to break out your lightweight lines here as summer approaches and flows decrease.

A typical opening day. To avoid the crowds, fish prior to the statewide opening day on special regulation waters that are open year-round or late in the season.

The stream that flows northeast through Milesburg is an entirely different stream than the one that flows southeast toward Tyrone. The 6.5-mile section toward Milesburg comes close to being a Class A trout stream. The upper section of Bald Eagle flowing toward Tyrone could also qualify with a good amount of carryover browns and native brookies in the headwaters. Stocking supplements the wild fish found here.

Despite the scorn many anglers have for stocked trout, browns that are stocked here result in a good number of carryover trout, which can reach good size if catch and release is practiced. It seems to me that special regulations on a stretch of both streams would help tremendously.

Flyfishers discovered long ago that, despite public perception, plenty of trout remain after the stocking truck leaves. Of course, the water needs to remain cold and have enough oxygen to keep trout throughout the season—fortunately, the two Bald Eagle Creeks have both.

Hatches are plentiful, including the ever-popular green drake and my favorite, the sulphur, and of course, the blue quill, that wonderful mid-April hatch that spells the beginning of a new flyfishing season most freestones in the state. There is also the terrestrial fishing that extends fishing into the afternoon, when many anglers are off chasing warmwater species or waiting for a late evening hatch. The southeast flowing Bald Eagle runs near SR 220 as it approaches Tyrone. The upper sections can be found off SR 4027, and SR 150 follows the other Bald Eagle to near Lock Haven, where it empties into the West Branch of the Susquehanna River.

BALD EAGLE CREEK MAJOR HATCHES

Insect	J	F	M	A	M	J	J	A	S	O	N	D
Blue Quill #18				▬								
Hendrickson #14				▬								
Caddis #14 & 16 (grannom, tan)				▬	▬	▬						
Quill Gordon #14				▬								
Tan Caddis #16					▬	▬	▬	▬				
Light Cahill #14						▬						
Green Drake #12, 3X long (Coffin Fly Spinner)						▬						
Sulphur #16					▬							
Yellow Drake #12						▬						
Cream Cahill #18						▬		▬				
Ants #16–20; Beetles #12–18; Grasshoppers #10–14						▬	▬	▬	▬	▬		
Caterpillars #12, 3X long						▬	▬	▬	▬			
Other												
Yellow Adams #16							▬	▬	▬	▬		
Mosquito #12–16						▬	▬	▬	▬			

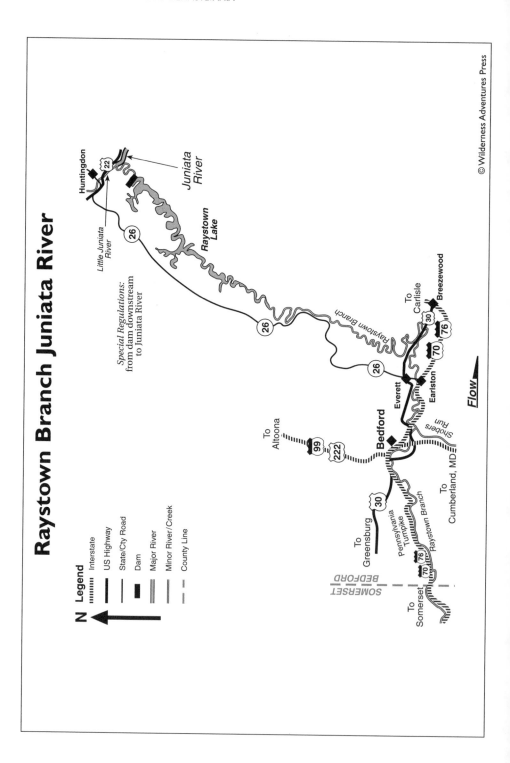

Raystown Branch Juniata River

N

Legend
- Interstate
- US Highway
- State/Cty Road
- Dam
- Major River
- Minor River/Creek
- County Line

Little Juniata River

Special Regulations: from dam downstream to Juniata River

Huntingdon

Juniata River

Raystown Lake

Raystown Branch

To Carlisle

Breezewood

To Altoona

Bedford

Everett

Earlston

Shobers Run

To Cumberland, MD

To Greensburg

Pennsylvania Turnpike

Raystown Branch

To Somerset

SOMERSET

BEDFORD

Flow

© Wilderness Adventures Press

RAYSTOWN BRANCH JUNIATA RIVER

The Raystown Branch of the Juniata River begins in Somerset County, where the Pennsylvania Fish and Boat Commission releases stocked trout. Stocking continues into Bedford County all the way to Shobers Run near Bedford.

This large river runs in serpentine fashion to Raystown Lake in Huntingdon County. The better trout fishing, in my opinion, is found from Bedford upstream to just over the Somerset County line. The river averages over 100 feet wide and hosts anglers chasing both warm and coldwater species.

Trout fishing begins yielding to warmwater bass, muskie, pickerel, and panfish as it winds toward Everett on the Breezewood, all easily found off marked exits of the Pennsylvania Turnpike.

Starting with the coldwater fishing, Raystown Branch attracts those who like large water and plentiful early season hatches, as well as those who are willing to carry a stream thermometer for finding cold water as spring gives way to summer.

With its mix of trout and bass, Raystown Branch is well suited to a rod of 9 feet that will carry a 6-weight line. Long casts are often the rule rather than the exception, and heavier line allows casting of both trout flies and weighted and wind resistant bass flies on the same outfit. Waders are necessary, and a small shallow draft boat is a good idea in the warmwater sections closer to Raystown.

Like the Susquehanna River, Raystown Branch hosts hatches of white flies. The pure white mayfly is an incredible hatch on any water and has to be ranked at least as high as the green drake, even though it is found on a size 16. The hatch seems to occur more often on warmwater streams, although it is prevalent on the Yellow Breeches and other tributaries of the Susquehanna and Juniata Rivers.

The whitefly brings bass to the surface in the same manner as it does trout, and if you like smallmouth bass rising to a dry fly, nothing can be more welcome than the whitefly. As anglers have expanded their horizons beyond trout flyfishing, they have found that a fly rod and bass go together very well.

They also find that smallmouth like the mayfly hatches as well as trout do and, when conditions are right, are more than willing to rise to hatches and spinnerfalls. Depending on which stretch of the river being fished, the white fly can be found from the third week in July on. As with most hatches, this one begins on the lower sectors of the stream first and then moves upstream and into the coldwater tributaries. Start by catching the hatch on warm water while fishing for bass and then follow it to coldwater for trout, and it's possible to fish this hatch for three weeks or longer—I call it hatch chasing.

Generally, the closer to the Branch's headwaters in Somerset County the more holdover trout are available, but there are exceptions to every rule. The Raystown Branch, simply because of its length, has a lot of coldwater tributaries. Some excellent fishing is found at the mouths of all these tributaries. Anglers often fish the coldwater side and catch trout, then turn to cast to the opposite shoreline to take bass, pickerel, and even muskie.

An excellent example of holding water for trout.

Those looking for a combination trip that includes trout, bass, and muskie, will find this stream extremely attractive. Most of the river can be fished with a floating, weight-forward line, but if chasing bass and muskie, it's a good idea to carry a sink-tip line as well.

When planning a trip for both species, I would carry a 9-foot with a 5-weight for trout and a 9-foot with an 8-weight for bass. This river deserves a lifetime of exploring, but with so many rivers in the state to choose from, that would be impossible. As with all rivers of this size, a guide is recommended. Good guides and advice from local fly shops give all anglers the needed information to find and fish a river properly.

If you want to fish for large muskie, a 9- or 10-weight line might be a good idea. However, most fish can be handled on an 8-weight, especially when exploring sections downstream of the dam by boat. Be sure to use shock tippets for muskie. Obviously, you can't fish for all species at one time, but whenever I am fishing where muskies might be found, I have my 9-foot for a 10-weight rigged with a fly attached to a shock tippet. Muskies in Pennsylvania are an elusive fish—you might only have time for a cast or two when they are feeding on top.

The PFBC stocks tiger muskie with regularity in the Raystown Branch, so the odds of hooking into one are excellent. For trout fishing, get on the stream near the town of Bedford along US 220. Heading toward Somerset County, use SR 31 to keep close to the stream. For warmwater fishing, follow SR 26 for access to the stream.

Raystown Branch River Access

Bedford County

Warriors Path State Park (DER); located above Raystown Lake, two miles south of Saxton Borough
- Picnicking
- Canoes, inflatables, and small rowboats
- Shallow draft, lightweight fishing boats, canoes, and inflatables
- Boat fishing and recreation
- Surfaced ramp
- Parking available

Shawnee Lake (DER); 451 acres; located in Shawnee State Park. Ramp located off Rt. 96 between Schellsburg and Mann's Choice
- Electric motors only
- Shallow draft, lightweight fishing boats, canoes and inflatables
- Boat fishing and recreation
- Surfaced ramp
- Parking available

Somerset County: no access

Huntingdon County; 5 miles
Species: Bass, Muskie, Panfish, Pickerel, Walleye

Raystown Branch Access (PFBC); located below Raystown Dam
- Canoes, other handcarry boats, and small outboards only
- Boat fishing and float trips
- Beach-type ramp

RAYSTOWN BRANCH JUNIATA RIVER MAJOR HATCHES

Insect	J	F	M	A	M	J	J	A	S	O	N	D
Blue Quill #16 & 18				■								
Quill Gordon #14				■								
Caddis #14 & 16 (grannom, olive, gray, brown, tan)				■	■							
Light Cahill #14					■							
Tan Caddis #16					■	■	■	■				
Blue-winged Olive #14					■	■						
White Fly #14 (depending on river section)								■				
Brown Drake #12, 3X long						■						
Cream Cahills #16						■	■	■				
Gray Fox #14					■							
Ants #16–20; Beetles #12–18; Grasshoppers #10–14							■	■	■			
Caterpillars #12, 3X long							■	■	■			
Other												
Yellow Adams #16					■	■						
Streamers				■	■	■	■	■	■	■		
Mosquito #12–16					■	■	■	■				
Consult the Warmwater Fly Box for bass and muskie patterns.												

TUSCARORA CREEK

This is the kind of beautiful stream I like. In the setting of Tuscarora State Forest, this should be a native brook and wild brown trout stream only, but despite the setting, it isn't.

Tuscarora begins above Blairs Mills in Huntingdon County and proceeds 6 miles until it enters Juniata County, where is proceeds until it enters the Juniata River on the outskirts of Port Royal. The stream is stocked in Huntingdon County and again in Juniata from East Waterford to the county line.

Within the state forest, the stream remains cool and holds carryover brown trout and a few native brook trout. As expected in such a setting, it is a rather small water in this section. Fish it like native brook trout water, and you will find it to your liking.

The forested setting should also hold some white-tailed deer, turkey, and perhaps a black bear or two. As the creek approaches the Juniata, it begins to warm, so smallmouth bass along with muskie and panfish become available.

This is one of those streams that will take you away from it all. Again, the white-fly will appear here in the lower reaches and, when it does, the bass fishing can be superb.

The creek is paralleled by SR 2009 for much of its length.

A brook trout ready for release.

TUSCARORA CREEK MAJOR HATCHES

Insect	J	F	M	A	M	J	J	A	S	O	N	D
Blue Quill #18				▰								
Hendrickson #14				▰								
Caddis #14 & 16 (grannom, tan)				▰▰▰▰								
Quill Gordon #14				▰								
Tan Caddis #16					▰▰▰▰▰▰							
Light Cahill #14					▰							
Sulphur #16					▰							
Cream Cahill #18					▰			▰				
Blue-winged Olive #14 & 16					▰▰							
Ants #16–20; Beetles #12–18; Grasshoppers #10–14						▰▰▰▰▰						
Caterpillars #12, 3X long						▰▰▰▰▰						
Other												
Yellow Adams #16						▰▰▰▰						
Mosquito #12–16						▰▰▰▰						

HONEY CREEK

I was fortunate enough to find this stream through a friend, when I was invited to his cabin during buck season. Although the hunting was poor, I did notice the shadows of darting brook trout as I crossed this tiny stream on my way to the mountains.

When I was invited back for a spring fishing trip, I jumped at the opportunity. Fishing for native brook trout on the headwaters, which is not stocked, I enjoyed the peaceful setting amidst the hemlocks and hardwoods lining the banks. A size 16 blue quill took dozens upon dozens of fish, all small but beautiful native trout.

This is the type of stream I seek on opening day, when multitudes of anglers flock to the more popular streams. While big fish are definitely fun to catch and I expect to land my share in any given year, fish size is not always the most important ingredient in a good fishing day. I doubt that my memories of opening day on Honey Creek would be nearly as vivid if I had been catching stale-looking, freshly stocked fish that came in a monotonous 9-inch package. And if I had joined the

*Spring runoff
on Honey Creek.*

crowds in elbow-to-elbow warfare on the more popular streams, it might have been a fun social event but not a really memorable experience.

There were a few good-sized fish in the deeper pools that were few and far between on this step-across stream, but overall, this creek offered what I believe is the real essence of flyfishing: a beautiful stream meandering through a leaf-covered forest floor and offering wild trout.

Honey Creek is 13.5 miles in length and begins as a wild brook trout stream in a small valley just off Knob Ridge Road. Stocking takes place from the confluence of Treaster Run upstream along SR 1002 at Reeds Gap.

The headwaters contain a fairly good number of wild trout in the form of native brookies and wild browns. However, the section from Alexander Caverns downstream to the mouth is also good, due to the wealth of feeder streams in the area, and is a Class A water.

Hatches are returning from a decline in water quality that occurred years ago, and it can still have problems. But the stream is on the mend, and the section of Class A water is producing wild trout over 20 inches. Wild browns are found here, and hatches are improving each and every year. Please return all fish that are caught here, especially those found in the Wild Trout Area. The PFBC has not deemed it necessary to put special regulations on this stretch of water.

From SR 322, take SR 1002, which parallels the creek for most of its length.

HONEY CREEK MAJOR HATCHES

Insect	J	F	M	A	M	J	J	A	S	O	N	D
Blue Quill #16 & 18				▬					▬			
Hendrickson #14				▬								
Sulphur #16					▬▬							
March Brown #12					▬							
Cream Cahill #18						▬			▬▬			
Black Stone #16			▬									
Blue-winged Olive #16					▬▬							
Tan Caddis #16					▬▬▬				▬▬			
Gray Fox #14						▬						
Green Drake #12, 3X long (sparse) (Coffin Fly Spinner)						▬						
Terrestrials (ending date dependent on cold weather)							▬▬▬▬▬▬					

MANADA CREEK

Manada Creek is an important trout stream near Hershey, home of the chocolate bars, the Hershey Bears hockey team, and an amusement park. The arena and stadium hosts concerts with singing stars from all over the world.

Because of the amount of activity in the area, a flyfisher with family in tow might be able to find a few hours to fish this stream while the rest of the family enjoys other activities. The stream has character and is heavily stocked by the PFBC. It is not a fertile stream and does need some help in the way of stream improvements that would enhance the amount of holding water for trout.

The stream's blessing is a good head of trout until mid-July, and its drawbacks are few, such as thin water in some parts. Clarity is not as much of a problem, but there are far too many riffles that run too thin to keep trout. A few excellent pools seem to hold the majority of trout.

I did a television show here once, when footage for a show in mid-April was needed. Putting a half-hour weekly show together is not an easy task, and footage of six or more trout is necessary to put it all together. The stream had recently been added to the list of Delayed Harvest Waters, and I was attempting to produce shows featuring streams close to home and open to the public.

That day the sun cooperated, and I chose to fish the first pool I found, knotting a silver wolf to 5X tippet. I was in for a pleasant surprise—before I reached the pool's

Early fall can be a great time to take large fish.

end, I had taken and released a good dozen fish in a little over 45 minutes. We did the intro and exit and were gone within a total of two hours. It was difficult to dismiss the caddis that were bringing fish to the surface near midday and tear myself from the stream to the editing studio.

This stream has a lot of potential and a scattering of wild brookies, but it fishes best until the end of June and then again in September and October. Gear for this stream includes hip boots and a 5-weight rod or lighter. Manada holds primarily stocked trout, and the better section is the well-marked Delayed Harvest Area. This section covers 0.2 miles, from Fogarty Road downstream to Furnace Road. It is easily accessible from I-81 north by taking the Manada Hill exit or by taking SR 39 from the Hershey Park parking area.

MANADA CREEK MAJOR HATCHES

Insect	J	F	M	A	M	J	J	A	S	O	N	D
Tan Caddis #16				■	■	■			■			
Hendrickson #14				■								
Sulphur #16				■	■							
March Brown #12				■								
Cream Cahill #18					■				■	■		
Black Stone #16			■									
Blue-winged Olive #16					■	■						
Terrestrials (ending date dependent on cold weather)						■	■	■	■			

Because of the lack of insect activity here, terrestrial ants, beetles, caterpillars, and inchworms are extremely important

QUITTAPAHILLA CREEK (AND SNITZ CREEK)

Quittapahilla Creek had been on its deathbed since the 1950s, its once-rich water poisoned by arsenic. It wasn't only the water that died: trout, mayflies, caddis, and crayfish floated downstream as lifeless as the water that carried them. Few people mourned their passing, and few knew that arsenic had entered the stream. It was a time of economic prosperity, and almost no one gave more than a passing thought to the Quittapahilla.

Today, though, the "Quitty" is back. After the arsenic plant closed in the mid-1980s, this limestone-influenced Lebanon County stream began to attract attention from anglers, community organizations, and government water quality improvement programs. A watershed association is now in place, and extensive scientific studies on the tributary streams have pinpointed pollutants and their sources.

Wengert's Dairy, a large landowner along Snitz Creek, has implemented a streambank facing project with the help of the Department of Environmental Protection that will keep dairy cattle out of the water and away from the banks. Now the Quitty flows cleaner than it has in decades, and the excellent trout fishing available there is proof.

"Trout stocked in the early '80s rolled over and died," says PFBC fisheries manager Larry Jackson. "Today, the Commission considers the Quitty a good put-and-take trout fishery."

Some of the best fishing on the Quitty is from the Spruce Street bridge at the eastern end of Annville (where the Delayed Harvest Artificial Lures Only project begins) downstream to the lower end of Quittie Nature Park. The Special Regulation section ends at SR 934. Snitz Creek, a coldwater limestone, enters just above the special regulation section and improves the fishing below its influence. Snitz Creek itself is stocked by PFBC and the Palmyra Sportsmen's Association.

The green weenie is an early season favorite, and the sulphur hatch is outstanding. Also look for blue-winged olives, cahills, Hendricksons, and even a few whiteflies that apparently find their way upstream from the Susquehanna River. Terrestrial fishing during the summer months is superb, with beetles, ants, and grasshoppers heading the list. Of course, streamers, such as the Zonker pattern, work well throughout the stream's entire length.

Downstream from the SR 934 bridge, the Quitty is open water for approximately 8 miles before entering Swatara Creek near Valley Glen in North Londonderry Township, Lebanon County. The PFBC and the Palmyra Sportsmen's Association also stock the lower portion of the stream. After leaving Annville, the stream takes on the characteristics of a limestone as it weaves through meadow grasses.

Fishing here is excellent: browns, brookies, and rainbows are liberally stocked, as well as a sprinkling of palominos. Trout over 20 inches are becoming commonplace. It takes something over 24 inches to draw genuine interest from frequent Quitty anglers.

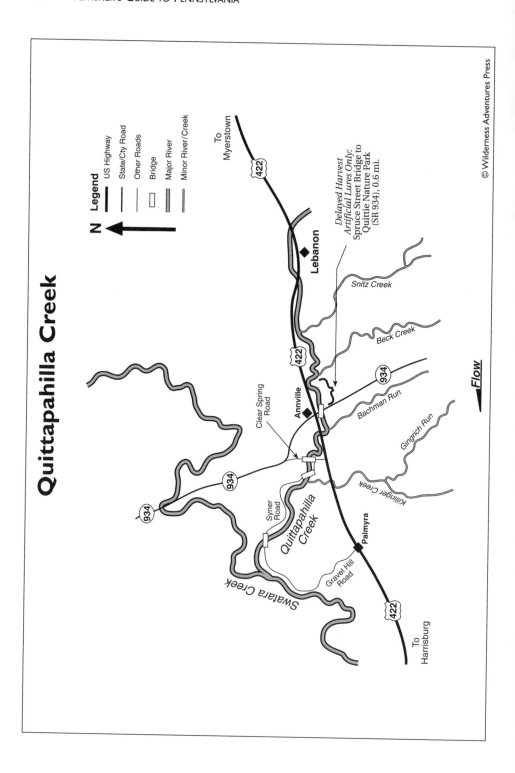

Quittapahilla Creek

The lower reaches of the Quittapahilla in Lebanon County.

The stream winds north of the towns of Annville and Palmyra and can be found by taking any road north from SR 422 between those points. Best access to this stretch is on Syner Road, which branches off from Clear Spring Road just north of 422. The lower end, near the confluence with Swatara Creek, is best reached via Gravel Hill Road. There are only short sections of posted water along this section, and public access is widely available throughout its length.

The Quitty's comeback has mostly gone unnoticed, situated only 45 minutes from such famous Cumberland Valley limestone creeks as the Yellow Breeches and Letort. As a result, the stream is rarely crowded except on opening day and a few weekends after that. The Quitty could then be considered a sleeper. Many area anglers are under the mistaken impression that the stream is still dead. But this stream is not only carrying stocked fish throughout the season, it is now carrying them over from year to year. And despite the assessment of PFBC biologists, some anglers swear a limited amount of natural reproduction is taking place.

I spent the majority of last trout season getting to know the Quitty with Jim Yurejefcic as my guide and companion. I kept no records, but 15- to 20-trout outings were not unusual, nor were trout that exceeded 20 inches. We caught many 17- to 18-inchers. Naturally, we began with nymphs in the early part of the season, switching to Hendricksons and then blue quills as spring progressed.

The fishing improved as terrestrials became available during the early summer months; at about the same time, one of the largest sulphur hatches I've ever seen hit the waters. The hatch was so thick that I could hardly breathe. Then the cahills came, as well as pale evening and pale morning duns, and the sulphurs seemed to last for months on end. Summer flyfishers had to lengthen their leaders and drop to 7X tippets to fool the educated trout in the Delayed Harvest Area.

Caddis were present throughout the year, and trout were usually willing to take them. As we trudged into fall, various caddis patterns and pale evening duns continued to produce good fish, and fishing pressure became nearly nonexistent on the lower stretches of the stream.

The fishing remained superb through a warm December, when deer hunting sidetracked me, but the reports of large fish came pouring in, taken on green weenies, streamers and woolly buggers, and giving proof that the Quitty is a year-round trout fishery. And because of its limestone influences, the stream seldom freezes.

Of course, there are tricky currents to deal with, and the Quitty can be as fickle a trout stream as any. But the important point is that chances for success have nothing to do with stocking schedules. This stream has earned the right to give up its trout grudgingly—it has been through a lot.

QUITTAPAHILLA CREEK MAJOR HATCHES

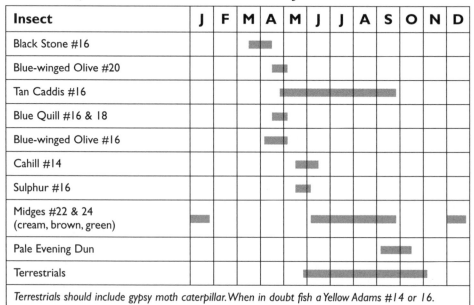

Insect	J	F	M	A	M	J	J	A	S	O	N	D
Black Stone #16			▬									
Blue-winged Olive #20				▬								
Tan Caddis #16					▬▬▬▬▬▬▬▬							
Blue Quill #16 & 18				▬								
Blue-winged Olive #16				▬								
Cahill #14					▬							
Sulphur #16					▬							
Midges #22 & 24 (cream, brown, green)	▬						▬▬▬▬▬					▬
Pale Evening Dun										▬▬		
Terrestrials						▬▬▬▬▬▬▬▬						

Terrestrials should include gypsy moth caterpillar. When in doubt fish a Yellow Adams #14 or 16.

Summary of Approved Trout Waters
and Special Regulation Areas for Southcentral Pennsylvania

Adams County	Section / Regulations
Antietam Creek, East Branch	
Bermudian Creek	
Carbaugh Run	
Conococheague Creek	
Conewago Creek	From SR 234 downstream to SR 3011 DHFFO: 1.1 mile, from 0.1 mile below SR 340 downstream to SR 34
Latimore Creek	
Little March Creek	
Marsh Creek	SR 30 upstream to SR 3011
Middle Creek	
Opossum Creek	
Toms Creek	T-300 bridge downstream to SR 0116
Waynesboro Water Company Reservoir	

Bedford County	Section / Regulations
Beaver Creek	
Beaverdam Creek	
Beaver Run Rod & Gun Dam	
Bobs Creek	
Cove Creek	
Evitts Creek	
Gladdens Run	
Imlertown Run	
Juniata River	Raystown Branch (mouth of Shobers Run upstream to county line)Little Wills Creek
Little Wills Creek	
Maple Run	
Potter Creek	
Sherman Valley Run	
Shobers Run	
Three Spring Creek	
Wills Creek	From B&O Railroad Bridge about one mile below Hyndman upstream to county line
Yellow Creek	DHFFO: 1.25 miles, from mouth of Maple Jacks Run by the sawmill upstream to cable near Red Bank Mill

Blair County	Section / Regulations
Bald Eagle Creek	
Beaverdam Creek	
Bells Gap Run	
Blair Gap Run	
Bobs Creek	
Canoe Creek	
Canoe Lake	
Clover Creek	SR 2005 at Henrietta to SR 7009 near Larke
Juniata River, Frankstown Branch	Mouth of Pine Run near Claysburg downstream to Brooks Mill near East Freedom
Little Juniata River	From mouth of Bald Eagle Creek (near Tyrone) downstream 2.1 miles to the railroad bridge at the east (downstream) border of Ironville. No closed season on trout; daily limit opening day of regular season to Labor Day, 8 trout; day after Labor to succeeding opening day of trout season, 3 trout. All other species, Inland Regulations apply.
Poplar Run	
Riggle's Gap Run	
Smokey Run Rod & Gun Club Pond	
South Poplar Run	
Vanscoyoc Run	

Cumberland County	Section / Regulations
Big Spring Creek	Heritage Trout Angling: 1.1 miles, from 100 feet below the source (Big Spring) downstream to the Nearly Road Bridge
Boiling Springs Lake (Childrens Lake)	
Doubling Gap Lake	
Fuller Lake	
Green Spring Creek	DHFFO: 1 mile, on former C.F. property, near SR 641 from the mouth upstream to near confluence with Bulls Head Branch
Laurel Lake	
Letort Spring Run	Heritage Trout Angling: 1.5 miles, from 300 yards above the bridge on T-481 downstream to Reading Railroad Bridge at the southern edge of Letort Spring Park
Middle Spring Creek	
Mountain Creek	
Old Town Run	
Opossum Creek Lake	

Yellow Breeches Creek	Catch and Release: 1 mile, from Boiling Spring, in the middle of town, just past the dam and the pond downstream to vicinity of Allenberry

Dauphin County	Section / Regulations
Armstrong Creek	
Clarks Creek	DHFFO: 1.9 miles, PGC parking area on SR 325 downstream to PGC access road at the Iron Furnace
Manada Creek	DHALO: 1.8 miles, from Fogarty Road downstream to Furnace Road (T-616)
Middletown Reservoir	
Pine Creek	
Powell Creek	
Powell Creek, South Fork	
Rattling Creek	
Rattling Creek, East Branch	
Rattling Creek, West Branch	
Stony Creek	
Wiconisco Creek	

Franklin County	Section / Regulations
Antietam Creek, East Branch	DHFFO: 1 mile, from SR 0016 downstream to T-364
Antietam Creek, West Branch	
Buck Run (Dickeys Run)	
Campbell Run	
Carbaugh Run	
Conococheague Creek	From SR 56 at Boyer Mill to headwaters
Conococheague Creek, West Branch	From SR 0030 at Fort Loudon to SR 4005 at Amberson
Conodoguinet Creek	SR 0433 upstream to mouth of Bear Valley Run
Dennis Creek	
Falling Springs Branch	Heritage Trout Angling: 2.4 miles, from Briar Lane Bridge near T-544 downstream to a wire fence crossing the Robert L. Geisler Farm (near I-81) DHALO: 1.1 miles, from Walker Road downstream to Fifth Avenue
Five Forks Creek	
Letterkenny Reservoir	
Little Cove Creek	
Muddy Run	Mouth upstream to Browns Mills
Rowe Run	

Fulton County	Section / Regulations
Barnetts Run	
Brush Creek	
Cove Creek	DHALO: 1-mile section from 200 yards downstream of the SR 0928 bridge downstream to the lower Buchanan State Forest boundary
Cowan's Gap Lake	
Laurel Fork Creek	
Licking Creek	
Little Aughwick Creek	
Little Aughwick Creek, North Branch	
Little Aughwick Creek, South Branch	
Little Brush Creek	
Little Tonoloway Creek	Downstream to SR 0655
Oregon Creek	
Roaring Run – tributary to Cove Creek)	
Sideling Hill Creek	From SR 4013 and SR 0913 upstream to SR 915, confluence of Organ Creek and Laurel Fork
Spring Run	
Wooden Bridge Creek	

Huntingdon County	Section / Regulations
Blacklog Creek	
Garner Run	
Globe Run	
Great Trough Creek	
Greenwood Lake	
Hares Valley Creek	
Laurel Run	
Little Aughwick Creek, North Branch	(Nine Mile Creek)
Little Juniata River	All Tackle Selective Harvest: 13.5 miles, from the Railroad Bridge at the east downstream border of Ironville downstream to the mouth
North Spring Branch	
Raystown Lake/Raystown Branch	Special Regulations: From dam downstream to Juniata River; no closed season; 5 per day during regular season; 3 per day after Labor Day
Saddler Creek	
Shade Creek	
Shaver Creek	From DeArmills Mill upstream to University Dam

Spruce Creek	Catch and Release: 0.5 miles, Penn State Experimental Fisheries Area (about 0.6 miles above Spruce Creek Village)
Standing Stone Creek, East Branch	Black Bridge on SR 0026 upstream to county line
Stone Valley Creek	
Three Springs Creek	
Tuscarora Creek	
West Licking Creek	
Whipple Lake	

Juniata County	**Section / Regulations**
Big Run	
Blacklog Creek	
Cocolamus Creek	
Delaware Creek	
East Licking Creek	DHALO: 4-mile section from the Texas Eastern gas pipeline crossing downstream to the upstream boundary of the Carl B. Guss State Forest picnic area
Horning Run	
Horse Valley Run	
Laurel Run (Liberty Valley Run)	
Lost Creek	From SR 0035 at Oakland Mills downstream to mouth
Tuscarora Creek	East Waterford upstream to the county line

Lebanon County	**Section / Regulations**
Bachman Run	
Conewago Creek	
Hammer Creek	
Lions Lake	
Marquette Lake	
Mill Creek	
Quittapahilla Creek	DHALO: 0.6 mile, from Spruce Street Bridge on T-398 downstream to the lower boundary of Quittie Nature Park
Snitz Creek	
Stony Creek	
Stovers Creek	
Trout Run	
Tulpehocken Creek	

Mifflin County
Section / Regulations

Havice Creek	
Honey Creek	Confluence of Treaster Run upstream to SR 1002 at Dean Gap
Kishacoquillas Creek	
Licking Creek, East	DHALO: 4-mile section from the Texas Eastern gas pipeline crossing downstream to the upstream boundary of the Karl B. Guss State Forest picnic area
Licking Creek, West	
Meadow Creek	
Musser Run	
Penns Creek	Catch and Release: 3.9 miles, from approximately 650 yards downstream fo Swift Run downstream to approximately 550 yards downstream of Cherry Run
Strodes Run	
Town Run	
Treaster Run	

Perry County
Section / Regulations

Bixler Run	
Buffalo Creek	SR 0849 at Walnut Grove upstream to T-326
Bull Run	
Fishing Creek	
Fowler Hollow Run	
Horse Valley Run	
Laurel Run (Liberty Valley Run)	
Little Buffalo Creek	From Park entrance road bridge upstream to SR 4003 (Cold Storage Road) and from dam breast downstream to Juniata River
Little Juniata Creek	
McCabe Run	
Montour Creek	
Panther Creek	
Raccoon Creek	
Shaeffer Run	
Sherman Creek	From Cisna Run at SR 3008 upstream to mouth of Hemlock Run
Shultz Creek (Browns Run)	

York County
Section / Regulations

Bald Eagle Creek	
Beaver Creek	

Blymire Hollow Run	
Fishing Creek – tributary to	
	Susquehanna River (Craley)
Codorus Creek	Selective Harvest: 3.3 miles, from SR 3047 at Kraft Mill downstream to SR 116
Codorus Creek, East Branch	
Codorus Creek, South Branch	
Deer Creek	
Fishing Creek (Goldsboro)	
Furnace Run	
Leibes Creek	
Muddy Creek	From confluence of North and South Fork branches downstream 1.6 miles of SR 0425 in Woodbine DHFFO: 2 miles, from cable 300 yards above SR 2032 bridge in Bridgeton up to the cable 300 yards downstream from Bruce
Muddy Creek, South Branch	
Otter Creek	
Saw Mill Run	
Shepherd-Myers Dam	
	(Hanover Water Dam)
Toms Run	
Yellow Breeches Creek	

Southcentral Hub Cities
Carlisle
Population – 20,000

ACCOMMODATIONS
Appalachian Trail Inn, 1825 Harrisburg Pike / 717-245-2242
Carlisle Motel, 1075 Harrisburg Pike / 717-249-4563
Days Inn, 101 Alexander Spring Road / 717-258-4147
Hampton Inn, 1164 Harrisburg Pike / 717-240-0200
Harvon Motel, 851 North Hanover Street / 717-243-3113
Pike Motel, 1121 Harrisburg Pike / 717-249-3120
Rodeway Inn, 1239 Harrisburg Pike / 717-249-2800
Stardust Motel, 1502 Holly Pike / 717-243-6058
Super 8 Motel, 100 Alexander Spring Road / 717-245-9898

CAMPGROUNDS
Carlisle Campground, 1075 Harrisburg Pike / 717-249-4563

RESTAURANTS
Back Door Café, 156 West High Street / 717-249-4310
California Café, 38 West Pomfret Street / 717-249-2028
Hamilton Restaurant, 55 West High Street / 717-249-4410
Hoss's Steak & Sea House, 1151 Harrisburg Pike / 717-258-4468
Longhorn Steak Buffet, 1188 Spring Road / 717-243-6968
Ricky's Open Pit Barbecue, 40 Harmony Hall Drive / 717-243-4899

FLY SHOPS
Cold Springs Anglers, 419 East High Street. Suite A / 717-245-2646
Angling Adventures, 328 Zion Road (Mt. Holly Springs) / 717-486-7438
Green Spring Fly Shop, 202 Steelestown Road (Newville) / 717-768-3020
Jim Chestney Co., 817 Nesbit Drive / 717-249-0709
Yellow Breeches Outfitters, 2 First Street / 717-258-6752

AUTO RENTAL
Carlisle Rent-A-Wreck, 519 South Hanover Street / 717-243-3512
Enterprise Rent-A-Car, 800 North Hanover Street / 717-258-4495
Thrifty Car Rental, 1702 Harrisburg Pike / 717-243-1505

AIRPORTS
Carlisle Airport, Petersburg Road / 717-243-2133
Also see Harrisburg

MEDICAL
Hospital & Healthsystem of Pennsylvania, 4750 Lindle Road / 717-564-9200

FOR MORE INFORMATION

Carlisle Chamber of Commerce
212 North Hanover Street
Carlisle, PA 17013
717-243-4515

Chambersburg
Population – 16,846

ACCOMMODATIONS
Carson's Motel, 414 West Loudon Street / 717-264-5188
Comfort Inn, 3301 Black Gap Road / 717-263-6655
Econo Lodge, 1110 Sheller Avenue / 717-264-8005
Fairfield Inn, 1122 Wayne Avenue / 717-264-1200
Rodeway Inn, 217 Hedgerow Drive / 717-264-4108
Roselawn Motel, 2347 Molly Pitcher Hwy / 717-264-5019
Super 8 Motel, 3648 Olde Scotland Road / 717-264-6288

CAMPGROUNDS
Twin Bridge Meadow Campground, 1345 Twin Bridge Road / 717-369-2216

RESTAURANTS
Chris's Country Kitchen, 1329 Lincoln Way East / 717-263-6088
Hoss's Steak and Seafood House, 1740 Lincoln Way East / 717-263-0264
Lighthouse Restaurant, 4301 Philadelphia Avenue / 717-263-4878
Perkins Family Restaurant, 1324 Lincoln Way East / 717-263-1112

FLY SHOPS
Falling Spring Outfitters, Inc., 3813 Old Main Street (Scotland) / 717-263-7811
Mike Heck's Trout Guides, 532 Bracken Drive / 717-261-0070

AUTO RENTAL
Enterprise Rent-A-Car, 1404 Lincoln Way East / 717-267-0674

AIR SERVICE
See Harrisburg

MEDICAL
Chambersburg Health Service, 260 North 7th Street / 717-267-2668

FOR MORE INFORMATION
Chamber of Commerce
75 South 2nd Street
Chambersburg, PA 17201
717-264-7101

Harrisburg
Population – 52,376

Harrisburg is the state capital and has a wide range of facilities. The following is just a small sampling.

ACCOMMODATIONS
Best Western Inn, 300 North Mountain Road / 717-652-7180
Blue Star Motel, 7500 Allentown Boulevard / 717-652-0101
Capital Inn, 1450 North 7th Street / 717-234-5931
Comfort Inn, 4021 Union Deposit Road / 717-561-8100
Fairview Inn, 1350 Eisenhower Boulevard / 717-939-9531
Greenlawn Motel, 7490 Allentown Boulevard / 717-652-1530
Harrisburg Inn, 5680 Allentown Boulevard / 717-652-3811
Marriott Hotels & Resorts, 4650 Lindle Road / 717-564-5511
Ramada Inn, 23 South 2nd Street / 717-234-5021
Reese's Motel, 6290 Allentown Boulevard / 717-545-8241
Super 8 Motel, 4125 North Front Street / 717-233-5891
Tall Timber Motel, 7600 Allentown Boulevard / 717-652-0200

CAMPGROUNDS
Harrisburg East Campgrounds, 1134 Highspire Road / 717-939-4331

RESTAURANTS
Doc Holliday's Steakhouse, 469 Eisenhower Boulevard / 717-564-4448
Glass Lounge Restaurant, 4745 North Front Street / 717-255-9919
Mr G's Place, 3745 North 6th Street / 717-233-0456
Philadelphia Steak & Sub Co, 23 North 4th Street #23 / 717-236-6082
Camp Curtin Bar-B-Que Station, 2504 North 6th Street / 717-232-1080
Alva Hotel & Restaurant, 19 South 4th Street / 717-238-7553
Casablanca Cafe & Restaurant, 1415 North 3rd Street / 717-236-8592
Cassady's Restaurant & Lounge, 4301 Linglestown Road / 717-545-3956
Gabriella Italian Restaurant, 3907 Jonestown Road / 717-540-0040
Olive Garden, 5102 Jonestown Road / 717-540-9904
Sbarro, 407 Strawberry Square / 717-233-8893

FLY SHOPS
Clouser's Fly Shop, 101 Ulrich Street (Middletown) / 717-944-6541

AUTO RENTAL
Avis Rent-A-Car, 601 South Cameron Street / 717-236-8097
Enterprise Rent-A-Car, 479 Eisenhower Boulevard / 717-441-1788
Enterprise Rent-A-Car, 1100 South 29th Street / 717-564-9444
Enterprise Rent-A-Car, 107 North Arlene Street / 717-671-8455

AIRPORTS
Harrisburg International Airport, 513 Airport Drive (Middletown) / 717-948-3905

MEDICAL
Harrisburg State Hospital, 2101 North Cameron Street / 717-772-7555

FOR MORE INFORMATION

Chamber of Commerce
3211 North Front Street #201
Harrisburg, PA 17110
717-232-4121

Chamber of Commerce
417 Walnut Street
Harrisburg, PA 17101
717-255-3252

Huntingdon
Population – 6,843

ACCOMMODATIONS
Days Inn, 22 South 4th Street / 814-643-3934
Valley Motel, South 10th Street & US 22 / 814-643-0736
Vista Vu Motel, Route 22 East / 814-643-2544

CAMPGROUNDS
Lake Raystown Family Resort (Piney Ridge) / 814-643-5778

RESTAURANTS
Bogey's, US 22 / 814-641-7227
Boxer's Cafe, 410 Penn Street / 814-643-5013
Hoss's Steak & Sea House, US 22 / 814-643-6939
Kelly's Korner, 1430 Pennsylvania Avenue / 814-643-4900
K's Family Restaurant, US 22 / 814-641-9668
Top's Diner, US 22 / 814-643-4169
Walt's Café, 422 Washington Street / 814-643-5551

FLY SHOPS
Spruce Creek Outfitters, SR 45 (Spruce Creek) / 814-632-3071

AUTO RENTAL
Enterprise Rent-A-Car, US 22 / 814-643-5778

AIRPORTS
See State College or Harrisburg

FOR MORE INFORMATION
Chamber of Commerce
530 Washington Street
Huntingdon, PA 16652
814-643-1110

Northwest Pennsylvania

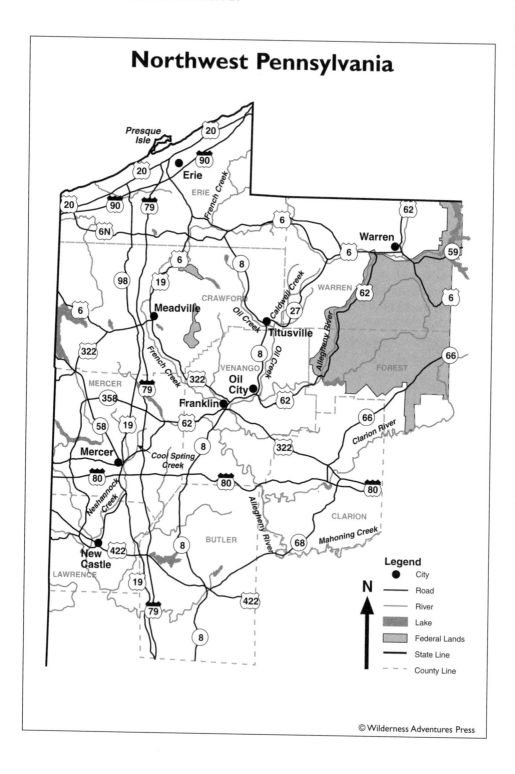

Northwest Pennsylvania

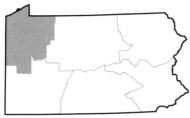

Most regions of the state have something unique to offer. If I had to choose one from the northwest, it would be steelhead and coho in the Lake Erie tributaries. This is a tremendous and unique opportunity to capture truly large Pacific salmon that can't be found anywhere else in the state.

Pennsylvania's diversity has been taken for granted, when one considers the natural resources of our state. This area has as much diversity as any I know. Anglers have the opportunity to take a tiny mountain brook trout, muskie, or northern pike on a fly in everything from tumbling brooks to the mighty Allegheny River. The northwest corner of the state has become home to many state records, from the expected steelhead, coho, and chinook salmon to such unexpected fish as northern pike, muskie, lake and palomino trout, and white bass. Many expect the next state record smallmouth to come from Lake Erie, but only time will tell.

This region has so much to offer, and although some areas are heavily fished, few have tested their flyfishing skills on the Great Lake or even Kinzua Dam. As interest in warmwater fishing picks up, I suspect this region will see more flyfishers on its waters.

The area is not heavily populated and there are miles of cold, cool, and warmwater fishing to be enjoyed here. Its major watershed, the Allegheny River, should find an influx of native fish returning as the river becomes cleaner, and fishing will improve throughout the entire area.

I have noted the presence of more warmwater fishermen on the region's lakes, and with the explosion of saltwater flyfishing popularity, it will not be long before saltwater tactics will be practiced on lakes and deeper running rivers. Flyfishing has always been linked to trout, but flyfishers in this area are finding that they don't need to bind themselves to a single fish species. And with the fly rods and lines available today, there is no reason to fish trout only.

While there are plenty of trout here to attract flyfishers, there is a wide variety of species that have been pursued only by spin and bait casters, who will be sharing that pursuit with flyfishers in increasing numbers over the next few years. That could make this one of the premier flyfishing destinations in the state, because more and more flyfishers are discovering the joy of diversity.

Oil Creek

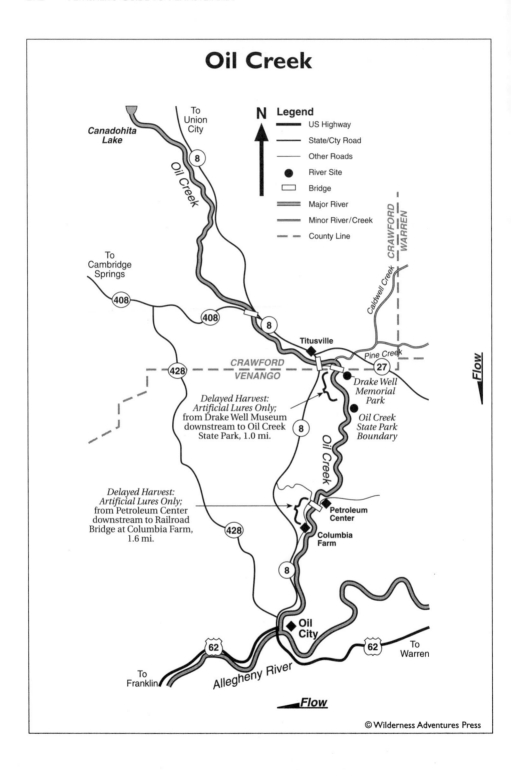

Legend

▬▬	US Highway
—	State/Cty Road
—	Other Roads
●	River Site
▭	Bridge
▬▬	Major River
—	Minor River/Creek
– –	County Line

To Union City

Canadohita Lake

Oil Creek

8

To Cambridge Springs

408

408

8

Titusville

CRAWFORD
VENANGO

Caldwell Creek

CRAWFORD
WARREN

Pine Creek

27

Drake Well
Memorial
Park

Oil Creek
State Park
Boundary

Delayed Harvest:
Artificial Lures Only;
from Drake Well Museum
downstream to Oil Creek
State Park, 1.0 mi.

8

Oil Creek

Delayed Harvest:
Artificial Lures Only;
from Petroleum Center
downstream to Railroad
Bridge at Columbia Farm,
1.6 mi.

428

428

Petroleum
Center

Columbia
Farm

8

Oil
City

62

62

To
Warren

To
Franklin

Allegheny River

Flow

Flow

© Wilderness Adventures Press

OIL CREEK

A few years ago, as I was on my way to teach a beginner's flyfishing class on Oil Creek for the northwest division of Pennsylvania's wildlife federation, I was concerned that I had had no time to check on stream conditions or hatches prior to the class. However, as I drove along Oil Creek late at night the day before the class, my windshield was spattered with tremendous hatches of mayflies and caddis. The two hatches were so heavy that there was no need to worry about the success of students who chose to linger after the class.

Due to the efforts of the Oil Creek Chapter of Trout Unlimited, this stream is now enjoying greater popularity due to its improved conditions. This chapter has worked diligently to protect and promote Oil Creek, and they have been extremely successful.

Over the years, the group has lobbied for two DHALO sections on the creek, which are now in place on 2.6 miles of Oil Creek. The first section to be approved for DHALO starts 1 mile from the Drake Well Museum and proceeds downstream to Oil Creek State Park. The other runs 1.6 miles from Petroleum Center downstream to a railroad bridge at Columbia Farm.

The stream is wide enough to allow easy casting with waders throughout its length, which is quite long—some 25 miles through Crawford and Venango Counties. The stream begins at Canadohita Lake north of Lincolnville. Except for a few areas, SR 8 rarely leaves the stream, following it to Oil City where it joins the Allegheny River. Petroleum Center Road, off SR 8, allows access to the special regulations area at the southern end of the state park. South of Titusville SR 2024 leads to the upstream special regulations area.

This stream has long glides and offers a good mix of boulders, gravel, and deep pools. The Trout Unlimited chapter is working to achieve a better pool-to-riffle ratio. Hatches are plentiful and there are a lot of trout stocked in the stream. The catch-and-release sections in Venango County are stocked in the spring and fall. In the upper section that falls within Crawford County, there is a spring stocking. Some carryover and wild browns have been reported within the park and above it.

There are few days that trout are not working the surface here, and caddis are a big ticket item. The stream does tend to warm up in summer, and a stream thermometer helps to find cooler water. Within the park, it is necessary to walk or bike to many sections of stream, and there is enough water to find solitude. The major hatches here are the brown caddis, March brown and sulphur. However, within the special regulation areas, midges and floating nymphs are often needed to bring trout to the surface. This stream is expected to get better with each passing year. Vestiges of the oil boom days still exist in the park, but the stream is rebounding quickly. An abundance of hemlock and broadleaf forest borders much of the stream.

For equipment, take waders and a rod with a 4- or 5-weight line, although a 6-weight will do. For more information contact: Department of Conservation and Natural Resources, Oil Creek State Park, RD 1, Box 207, Oil City, PA 16301; telephone 814-6765915. Oil Creek State Park consists of 7,026 acres in Crawford and Venango Counties.

An angler casts on Oil Creek in Venango County.

Oil Creek Access Sites

Drake Well Access (DER); Oil Creek State Park off East Bloss Street, Titusville
- Canoes and other hand-carry boats only
- Beach-type ramp
- Parking available

Petroleum Centre Access (DER); in Oil Creek State Park off SR 1007 at Petroleum Centre
- Canoes and other hand carry boats only
- Beach-type ramp
- Parking Available

Rynd Farm Access (DER); in Oil Creek State Park of SR 8, 4 miles north of Oil City
- Canoes and other hand carry boats only
- Beach-type ramp
- Parking Available

OIL CREEK MAJOR HATCHES

Insect	J	F	M	A	M	J	J	A	S	O	N	D
Blue Quill #18				▬								
Quill Gordon #14				▬								
Hendrickson #14				▬								
Brown Caddis #14					▬							
Tan Caddis #16					▬▬▬▬▬							
Gray Fox #12					▬							
Light Cahill #14					▬							
March Brown #12					▬							
Sulphur #16					▬▬							
Ants #16–20; Beetles #12–18; Grasshoppers #10–14						▬▬▬▬						
Caterpillars #12, 3X long						▬▬▬▬						
Other												
Floating Nymphs #16 & 18 (green, yellow, white)					▬▬▬▬▬							
Yellow Adams #14 & 16						▬▬▬▬						
Mosquito #12 & 14						▬▬▬▬						

Terrestrial and caterpillar patterns should always be in your fly box.

Caldwell Creek and West Branch

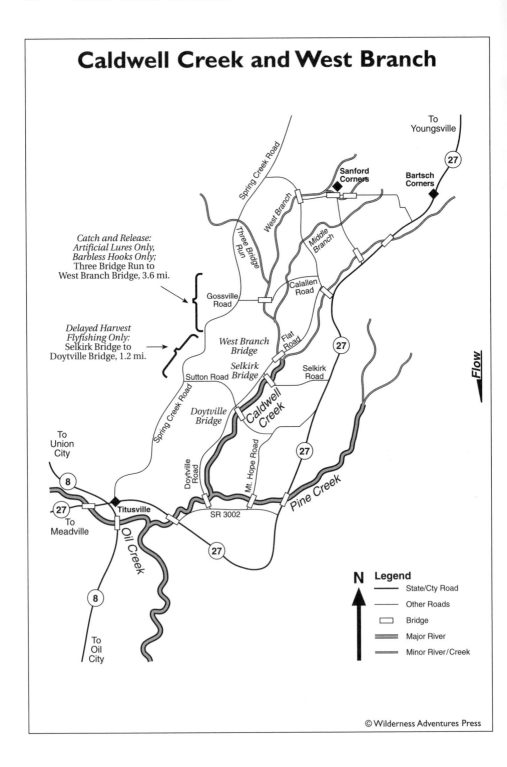

To Youngsville

Sanford Corners

Bartsch Corners

Spring Creek Road

West Branch

Three Bridge Run

Middle Branch

Catch and Release: Artificial Lures Only, Barbless Hooks Only; Three Bridge Run to West Branch Bridge, 3.6 mi.

Calallen Road

Gossville Road

Delayed Harvest Flyfishing Only: Selkirk Bridge to Doytville Bridge, 1.2 mi.

West Branch Bridge

Flat Road

Selkirk Bridge

Sutton Road

Selkirk Road

Doytville Bridge

Caldwell Creek

To Union City

Spring Creek Road

Doytville Road

Mt. Hope Road

Pine Creek

8

27

Titusville

SR 3002

To Meadville

Oil Creek

8

To Oil City

27

Flow

N

Legend

State/Cty Road
Other Roads
Bridge
Major River
Minor River/Creek

© Wilderness Adventures Press

CALDWELL CREEK

Caldwell Creek has a 1.4-mile stretch of its 10-mile length protected by DHFFO regulations. The stream is moderately sized, and wading allows casting into the better pools and riffles. Caldwell Creek is stocked in both spring and fall by the PFBC, and hatches are abundant here. Caldwell Creek, especially in the upper reaches, has a plentiful supply of wild browns and a sprinkling of brookies. At this time, it is safe to say that many sections of Caldwell border on a Class A wild trout designation.

Good hatches bring heavy trout to the surface, and the better fishing lies within the special regulation area of the stream. The stream finds its source just below Bartsch Corners and follows SR 27 downstream to Grand Valley. From there, take Flat Road to Dotyville Road to reach the lower part of the special regulation area where it enters Pine Creek. Dotyville Road is also found off SR 27.

The special regulation area extends from the Selkirk Road Bridge along Flat Rock Road downstream to just above the Dotyville Bridge. The regulated area is less than a mile from the entrance of the West Branch. Because of the abundance of wild and carryover trout this stream holds, it would make a lot of sense to keep the resource more stringently protected by catch-and-release regulations on this section.

Take waders and be sure to have imitations of gypsy moth caterpillars and inchworms in your vest. The stream is not all that big, and a small stream rod will work, as will a 4-weight and fine tippets.

A nice brook trout.

CALDWELL CREEK MAJOR HATCHES

Insect	J	F	M	A	M	J	J	A	S	O	N	D
Blue Quill #18				▪								
Hendrickson #14				▪								
March Brown #12				▪								
Gray Fox #12					▪							
Tan Caddis #16					▬▬▬▬							
Cream Cahill #18									▬▬			
Light Cahill #14					▪							
Green Drake, 3X long #12 (Coffin Fly Spinner)					▪							
Trico #24							▬▬					
Ants #16–20; Beetles #12–18; Grasshoppers #10–14						▬▬▬▬						
Caterpillars #12, 3X long						▬▬▬						
Other												
Floating Nymphs #16 & 18 (green, yellow, white)					▬▬▬▬▬							
Yellow Adams #14 & 16						▬▬▬						
Mosquito #12 & 14						▬▬▬▬						

Terrestrial and caterpillar patterns should always be in your fly box.

WEST BRANCH CALDWELL CREEK

The West Branch of Caldwell deserves its rightful spot in this book. This creek has climbed the ladder into Class A, wild trout status. Catch-and-release regulations are already in place, and I would like to see the remainder of the stream falling into the same category.

This is a beautiful stretch of water with a heavy canopy that helps hold water temperatures down throughout the year. In turn, anglers are blessed with an abundance of wild brown trout and a good amount of native brookies.

This valuable resource calls for releasing all trout taken here. We need to recognize and protect all fisheries in this manner. While poor access does help protect the stream to some degree, anglers practicing catch and release on the entire stream and its tributaries would be the greatest help of all. For now, catch-and-release regulations begin at the West Branch Run and continue downstream for 3.6 miles to the West Branch Bridge.

The stream's source is near Sanford Corners and runs through some incredibly beautiful country before hooking up to the main branch of Caldwell Creek northeast of the town of Selkirk. The upper reaches can be reached via road T-381 from Sanford Corners. Gossville Road and Calallen Road allow access to the upper reaches of the project water, and Flat Rock Road allows access by hiking in.

This is small stream fishing, so take a small stream rod and expect good hatches and hefty trout. There are good pools and tumbling riffles, and it can be fished in hip boots. Bring some warmer clothing for morning and evening fishing even in the height of summer.

Use the hatch chart for Caldwell Creek.

LITTLE SANDY CREEK

Little Sandy Creek begins in Mercer County, north of Wades Corner. Savannah Valley Road (SR 3024) follows the stream into Venango County where it flows into Sandy Creek at the town of Polk.

From SR 3024 at the town of Polk upstream for 1.3 miles to the Polk Center Pump Station, the stream is regulated as a DHFFO area. The stream is 5.5 miles in length and is a good coldwater tributary to the larger Sandy Creek, which is also stocked but warms up quickly during the summer and carries no special regulations. However, if you visit the area, you might want to give both of them a try, especially in the spring.

Little Sandy is full of aquatic life, despite the fact that it is a small stream flowing through a heavily wooded area of the state. The streambred and carryover trout are found throughout its length, and the majority of the stream is stocked in the spring and again in the fall.

Most flyfishers will like the Flyfishing Only area. Little Sandy can be fished in hip boots, although you may want to take waders to enjoy both the Little Sandy and Sandy Creek. For wild trout, however, stick to the upper portion of Little Sandy, which is narrow but produces some awfully nice trout.

LITTLE SANDY CREEK MAJOR HATCHES

Insect	J	F	M	A	M	J	J	A	S	O	N	D
Blue Quill #18				▬								
Quill Gordon #14				▬								
Hendrickson #14				▬								
Blue-winged Olive #14					▬							
Tan Caddis #16					▬▬▬▬▬▬							
Cream Cahill #18					▬				▬▬			
Light Cahill #14					▬							
March Brown #12				▬▬								
Green Drake #12, 3X long (Coffin Fly Spinner)						▬						
Gray Fox #12						▬						
Ants #16–20; Beetles #12–18; Grasshoppers #10–14							▬▬▬▬					
Caterpillars #12, 3X long							▬▬▬▬					
Other												
Floating Nymphs #16 & 18 (green, yellow, white)						▬▬▬▬▬▬						
Yellow Adams #14 & 16							▬▬▬▬					
Mosquito #12 & 14							▬▬▬▬					

Terrestrial and caterpillar patterns should always be in your fly box.

NESHANNOCK CREEK

Neshannock Creek is one of those lengthy streams that offers excellent trout fishing in the upper reaches but offers less and less trout as the water warms on its journey of 19 miles to the Shenango River in New Castle. The stream is a worthy stream for two reasons: it has an excellent offering of hatches and has special regulation waters. It is safe to say that the majority of flyfishers are split on their preference for wild trout waters and special regulation areas.

I have noted, in my travels, that streams with special regulations are fished harder and longer than the 'open waters.' Wild trout streams are finding their niche, and many flyfishers search desperately to find these streams. However, wild and native streams in this region are, for the most part, small and brush-lined, something many anglers do not find to their liking. This stream is somewhere in the middle. It is wide enough, with some wild trout and DHALO regulations to allow fishing to be extended over a longer period of time.

Neshannock Creek is heavily stocked in the spring and early summer in Mercer County, and in the spring and fall in Lawrence County. The stream begins north of Springfield Falls, located on US 19. Here, Beaver Run, Otter Creek, and Mill Run join forces to begin the stream. Follow Creek Road off US 19 to Volant for access to the uppermost areas of the stream. From Volant downstream, access becomes difficult, but can be found off SR 168 until it intersects with SR 956, which parallels the stream until it takes a southerly dip south of Mayville. From there, Falls Roads leads to Lakewood Park on the outskirts of New Castle.

This would have to be considered a medium-sized freestone, and from here to New Castle, the stream warms considerably. The better fishing is from Volant and above.

Special regulation water begins at the base of the Mill Dam in Volant and runs downstream 2.7 miles to the covered bridge. Despite the fact that this stream does not measure much more than 45 feet wide, I would still take waders and a rod suitable for a 4- to 5-weight line.

There have been confirmed reports of brown drakes found on this stream, and if the hatch and spinnerfall is as good as it is on my home waters on the First Fork in Potter County, expect good fishing, especially during the spinnerfall.

Brown drakes have been misidentified for years. I first found them on the Fork back in the 1970s when the crowds had dispersed. The hatch often begins in warmer waters first and then proceeds upstream. Following the hatch is becoming more popular with each passing year.

Neshannock and Cool Spring Creeks

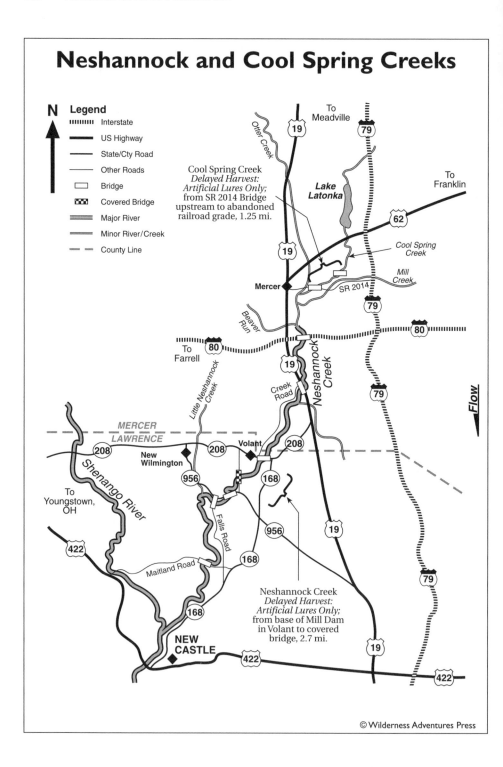

Legend
- ⅢⅢⅢ Interstate
- ▬▬ US Highway
- ▬ State/Cty Road
- — Other Roads
- ▭ Bridge
- ▦ Covered Bridge
- ▬▬ Major River
- ▬▬ Minor River/Creek
- – – County Line

Cool Spring Creek
Delayed Harvest:
Artificial Lures Only;
from SR 2014 Bridge
upstream to abandoned
railroad grade, 1.25 mi.

To Meadville

To Franklin

Lake Latonka

Otter Creek

Cool Spring Creek

Mill Creek

Mercer

SR 2014

Beaver Run

To Farrell

Little Neshannock Creek

Creek Road

Neshannock Creek

Flow

MERCER
LAWRENCE

New Wilmington

Volant

Shenango River

To Youngstown, OH

Falls Road

Maitland Road

Neshannock Creek
Delayed Harvest:
Artificial Lures Only;
from base of Mill Dam
in Volant to covered
bridge, 2.7 mi.

NEW CASTLE

© Wilderness Adventures Press

NESHANNOCK CREEK MAJOR HATCHES

Insect	J	F	M	A	M	J	J	A	S	O	N	D
Brown Drake #12, 3X long					X							
Quill Gordon #14				X								
Hendrickson #14				X								
Blue-winged Olive #14					X							
Tan Caddis #16					X	X	X	X				
Cream Cahill #18					X				X			
Light Cahill #14					X							
March Brown #12					X							
Green Drake #12, 3X long (Coffin Fly Spinner)					X							
Sulphur #16					X							
Ants #16–20; Beetles #12–18; Grasshoppers #10–14						X	X	X	X			
Caterpillars #12, 3X long						X	X	X	X			
Other												
Floating Nymphs #16 & 18 (green, yellow, white)					X	X	X	X	X			
Yellow Adams #14 & 16							X	X	X			
Mosquito #12 & 14						X	X	X	X			

Floating nymphs and emerger patterns work well here on the special regulations area.

COOL SPRING CREEK

A tributary to Neshannock Creek, Cool Spring is smaller in size, but not stature, than the larger stream it feeds. It is a short creek, covering only 5 miles, but it does have the special regulation waters that stretch for 1.2 miles.

Regulated as a DHALO area, this stream is of better water quality than the Neshannock, although its water does warm up—the reason for delayed harvest regulations. However, the stream is stocked heavily by the PFBC and does receive trout in both spring and fall.

Fall fish stockings usually take place in early October, although flyfishers haven't taken advantage of the extended angling opportunities that this allows. No-kill regulations are in place once again in the fall, offering trout the opportunity to carry over to the next year and perhaps becoming the wild trout of the future.

An example of good overhead canopy.

Far too many anglers look upon these areas as early season streams only, rather than taking the view that it is a "half full glass." This is a great stream to fish in the fall, and almost all area streams have a hatch of caddis, pale evening duns, or cream cahills during October. Terrestrials are often plentiful as well, until the first frost.

This stream can be fished in hip boots, but with the other good streams close at hand, I personally wear waders far more often, especially now that they have been designed to roll down to the waist. A rod of your favorite length, carrying a 3- to 5-weight line will serve well here.

The stream begins approximately 1 mile below Five Points, where it can be followed along Airport Road to Cool Spring Road. Then a series of secondary roads lead to Mercer, found off US 19 and SR 58 from the north or SR 258 or 158 off Interstate 80 from the south.

On the eastern edge of Mercer, SR 2014 is the beginning of the special regulations area, which extends upstream for 1.25 miles. At Mercer, the stream joins Otter Creek.

Use the hatch chart for Neshannock Creek.

STEELHEAD
Lake Erie Tributaries

Lake Erie's tributaries host a mixture of lake-run rainbows and steelhead, although many anglers cannot tell the difference. In my opinion, true steelhead make better fishing than lake-run rainbows. Most of those who fish these streams from September through April find these trout-like fish fascinating, to say the least. Sight-fishing is the predominant method, and the adrenaline rush caused by seeing quantities of large fish crowded into these small tributaries can cause some fishermen to exhibit poor fishing etiquette.

We are fortunate that snagging was never permitted within the Keystone State, despite efforts to make it legal, which arose when New York allowed snagging. Some Pennsylvania anglers were upset that the same rule did not apply here. New York, thankfully, now enforces a stringent no-snagging law that was put into effect over a five-year period of time. Now both states are on equal and ethical footing.

Lake Erie's tributary streams were once known for chinook and coho, but plantings of these fish did not yield many returns to the tributaries. No one is certain why this is so, but a reasonable assumption is that Lake Erie tributaries are simply too small to host continual numbers of these large fish.

Many mourned the passing of substantial runs of these Pacific salmon, but steelhead filled the void quickly and effectively. However, it became apparent quite quickly that the majority of anglers had more difficulty catching these new fish than the steelies had adjusting to their new home.

When chinook and steelhead arrived in the small, slate-bottomed tributaries in October, flyfishers used rods carrying 8- to 10-weight lines. Their reasoning was sound, since no one wants to break off a chinook in a stream at low flow and barely 40 feet wide.

Steelhead from a Lake Erie tributary.

My first encounter with a steelhead here was in early October. The first cold rains of the year came steadily, and I was fortunate enough to have Walnut Creek to myself. The stream was off-colored, and despite the fact that it ran less than three feet deep in most places, I could not see the bottom. I did, however, find some pocket water and a chunk of slate that created a small piece of holding water.

I dead-drifted a size 6, two-egg sperm fly imitation through the milky waters and allowed it to drift over the slate and into the small holding water. I was using a 9-foot rod and an 8-weight line. Without moving an inch, I landed 8 steelhead and lost 4 others as the chilly rain continued and the stream rose. I used no weight other than the lead eyes I had incorporated into the pattern. All of the fish were 8 pounds or better.

Returning the next morning, I was greeted by a stream too off-colored to fish, filled with leaves floating toward the lake. My steelhead fishing was finished for a few days.

Of course, as with any new introduction of fish, the steelhead books written for large waters in Michigan, New York, and Pacific coastal streams, simply do not work here, although some of the patterns do. If there is a problem here, it is because steelhead that manage to get into the streams often act in trout-like fashion.

Author with a Lake Erie steelhead.

The debate over equipment and tactics continue, with one contingent opting for light tackle and nymph fishing in the same manner they use for trout, and others using heavier lines and larger flies. In my opinion, conditions dictate what equipment and flies will work best.

Take warm clothing and waders and a rod of 8½ to 9 feet with a 6- or 7-weight line. These streams are too shallow for sinktips, so floating lines are all that is needed. Leader length depends on stream conditions. I like longer leaders when flows are low and shorter leaders when streams are high. Leaders with tippets testing 6 pounds seem to be the preference of most flyfishers on these tributaries.

Many incorporate the use of strike indicators, which can be helpful when fish are not visible. However, I have found sight fishing to be the most rewarding way to fish steelhead—finding a steelhead, stalking into the proper position in order to float a fly to the fish, and then watching the take.

While steelhead fishing on Lake Erie's tributary streams has much to offer, there are drawbacks to consider: overcrowding and small streams with slate bottoms that must have sufficient rainfall to maintain their volume. But these problems seem minor when a steelhead leaps in a pool above you, and you are hoping that the

Anglers gather along the shore of Lake Erie.

stream's tangle of grapevines, slate, boulders, and woody debris do not put a quick end to the fight.

Access to many streams is limited because of the few flyfishermen who have abused their privileges on private land. Be sure to get landowner permission, and then treat the land with respect and do not litter. Regulations that close many streams from 10pm to 5am have helped reduce these problems, as has enforcement of the no-snag law, which is easier to accomplish with stream closure during the night. And most flyfishermen would rather pursue steelhead during daylight hours anyway.

Take waders and more clothing than you think you will need—snowstorms in November and December due to the lake effect are not uncommon. A wading staff is a great idea for stream crossing.

Considering the record fish taken from Lake Erie over the years should indicate what the tributaries have to offer. And with most steelhead anglers practicing catch and release, these tributaries have more than likely yielded some large fish that have gone unrecorded.

State Records
- Steelhead, 19 lb. 2 oz., 1992
- Lake Trout, 27 lb. 13 oz. 1996
- Palomino Trout, 11 lb. 10 oz. 1986
- Pink Salmon, 4 lb. 8 oz. Elk Creek, 1995
- Coho Salmon, 15 lb. 5 oz. 1985
- Chinook Salmon, 28 lb. 15 oz. 1990

STEELHEAD STREAMS WEST SIDE

Please consult the Summary Book that is issued with a fishing license—changes occur frequently.

Walnut Creek
The birthplace of salmon fishing in northwestern Pennsylvania, Walnut Creek is 8 miles in length, has a shale-like bottom, and is a popular stream with excellent runs of steelhead as well as the occasional chinook or coho. This stream can be an excellent fishery depending on crowds and water flow. This is one of the larger streams in the area and fishes well over its entire length. Walnut Creek is accessible from SR 5 by taking Manchester Road. Access can also be made from US 20, SR 832, and I-79. Stream levels fluctuate with each passing storm, and in general, the better fishing is found in November and December. South of SR 5, the stream is closed to fishing from 10PM to 5AM.

Nearby Trout Run and Godfrey Run are nursery waters closed to fishing.

Elk Creek
Elk Creek is one of the larger streams here and one that seems capable of carrying large fish. It runs 18 miles through Erie County. The stream's mouth is accessible from SR 5. It crosses beneath West Lake Road (part of SR 5) and then parallels North Creek Road. Access is available from US 20, SR 98, and I-79. The state record pink salmon, weighing 4 pounds, 8 ounces, came from this stream in 1995. Ironically, the state record for rock bass also came from this stream, weighing 3 pounds, 2 ounces. Elk Creek is closed to fishing from 10PM to 5AM south of SR 5.

Crooked Creek
Crooked Creek is smaller than Elk and is filled with plenty of streamside growth. Found near the Ohio state line, the best fishing is from SR 5 to the mouth. Crooked

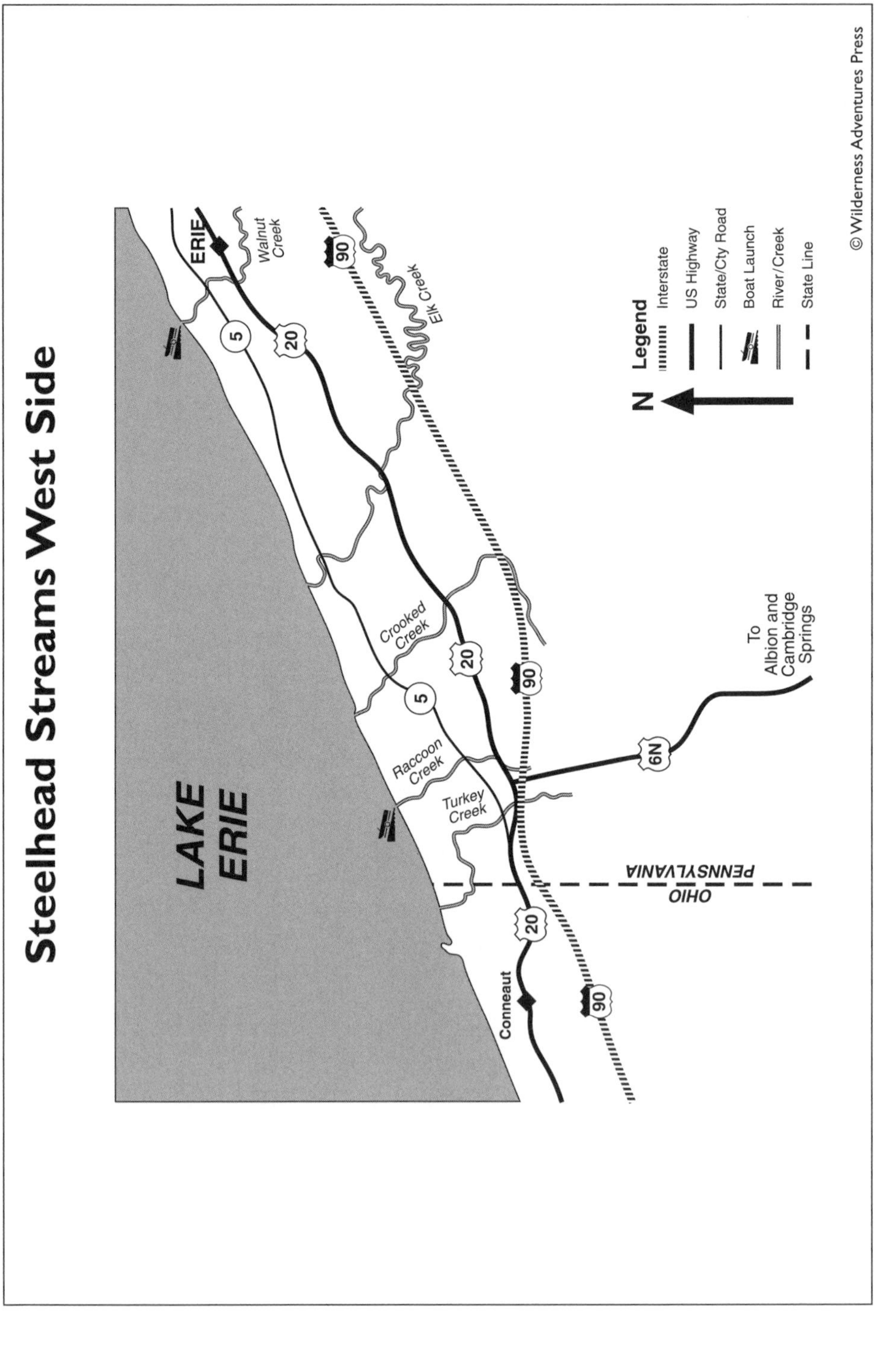

Steelhead Streams West Side

LAKE ERIE

ERIE

Walnut Creek

Elk Creek

Crooked Creek

Raccoon Creek

Turkey Creek

Conneaut

To Albion and Cambridge Springs

OHIO
PENNSYLVANIA

Legend

Interstate	
US Highway	
State/Cty Road	
Boat Launch	
River/Creek	
State Line	

N

© Wilderness Adventures Press

Creek is 6 miles in length and has become a favorite of many. It is closed to fishing from 10PM to 5AM south of SR 5.

Raccoon Creek

Found in a remote and wooded area, Raccoon Creek does have steelhead runs in spite of its small size. This creek offers some unexpectedly large fish, and while a few local fishermen know this, the stream is mostly uncrowded.

Take Elmwood Road toward the lake from SR 5 to find the best fishing. South of SR 5, it is closed to fishing from 10PM to 5AM.

Turkey Creek

While this is an extremely small stream, it does get steelhead runs and is mostly uncrowded. Fish will need to be hunted here, and a cautious approach is necessary. Since Turkey Creek flows into Ohio on its way to Lake Erie, it is best to go no farther that State Game Lands #314 unless you have an Ohio fishing license. From SR 5/US 20, take Rudd Road and Childs Road to get on the creek.

Conneaut Creek and Branches

Conneaut Creek is a larger tributary stream that travels 25 miles through Crawford County before entering Erie County, where it flows some 18 miles before entering Ohio. Flyfishers should be warned that Pennsylvania has no reciprocal license agreement with either Ohio or New York, and anglers having only Pennsylvania licenses need to be very careful not to cross the state line.

The stream is accessible along Clover Road and/or Griffey Road to the Ohio state line, and on US 6N heading south. From US 6N, take Barney Road heading north or take SR 2013 from SR 215 to follow the main stem to the town of Albion, where the East Branch enters the main stem. Meadeville road parallels the East Branch through most of the county. Bessemer Road parallels the creek to Conneautville in Crawford County.

This large stream and its branches take some scouting in order to find fish, but it is well worth the effort.

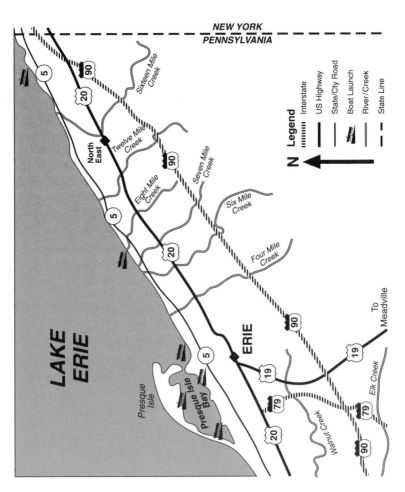

Steelhead Streams East Side

© Wilderness Adventures Press

STEELHEAD STREAMS EAST SIDE

Fishing is closed from 10PM to 5AM unless indicated otherwise.

Four Mile Creek

This small stream has a shale bottom structure and does receive some decent runs of fish.

Seven Mile Creek

The fishable portion of the stream is very small, extending from the falls below SR 5 to the lake. It is open to walk-in only and cannot handle many anglers on any given day.

Eight Mile and Twelve Mile Creeks

As with Four Mile and Seven Mile, these streams are small but loaded with fish. The shale bottom and thin water pose some problems, but they can be overcome. The best conditions are when there are few fishermen and fresh run fish. These creeks are worth trying, and sight fishing is usually possible. A quick look at these streams is enough to determine whether to stay or move on. Both are accessible from SR 5.

Sixteen Mile Creek

Sixteen Mile flows 8 miles through Erie County. However, a waterfall above SR 5 keeps steelhead from migrating any farther upstream. The stream has a shale bottom and runs thin most of the year. Wherever significant falls or a dam is found, steelhead will be stacked like cordwood depending on conditions. Such pools are usually lined with anglers, and the fish are more difficult to catch. However, there are exceptions to all rules, and over the years, Sixteen Mile has been kind to me. Again, the stream can be reached from SR 5.

Twenty Mile Creek

This is a medium-sized stream in comparison with other Lake Erie tributaries, but it turns to a small, brushy stream very quickly. This creek is a favorite of many fly-fishers because of its large runs, however water levels on this slate-bottom stream can and do become extremely low at times.

As with all the Lake Erie tributaries, it too is found along SR 5, and I have spent as much time driving the route and checking for fish as I have fishing. Twenty Mile can be full of fish one day and nearly empty the next.

Lake Erie

Shore fishing along the mouths of most streams may save your bacon when tributary streams are too low (see regulations governing shore fishing—it is illegal to fish near the mouths of Trout and Godfrey Creeks.) Fish are often rolling close to the shoreline, staging to go into the tributaries.

On the east side, especially, wading is rather easy and reaching fish is not all that difficult. Streamers work well here, as do all patterns. You may want to carry a sink-tip line and split shot for this type of fishing and a 9-foot or longer rod carrying an 8-weight line to reach fish and to cast flies. Make sure that you are not trespassing on private land while fishing the tributaries. If you do not find fish in the tributaries, check the lake near the mouths if you can—it might save the trip!

The Steelheader's Fly Box

- Two-egg sperm fly, #6 through #12, streamer hooks. Red, Orange.
- Egg clusters, #8-10, short shank.
- Woolly bugger, #6 through #12, streamer hooks. Red, orange, white, olive, black, brown & white.
- Glo-bugs, #8 through #14, shot shank, wide gap. Chartreuse, yellow, pink, orange, red. Add pearl Flashabou, it helps.
- Wolf's streamer, #8 through #12.
- Wiggle nymphs, #8 through #12 tied on streamer hooks, favorite patterns. Hare's Ear, Muskrat.
- Sucker spawn, #8 through 16. Wide Gap, short shank. Red, yellow, blue, orange, peach & white.
- Boss: Streamer, #6 through #12. Orange, red, and yellow.
- Skyomish sunrise, #6 through 12. Red, Orange.

I prefer to use Mustad 36890 salmon hooks in low water conditions for nymphs and streamers and their 9321 for egg patterns. I prefer the extra strength of the hooks and the added weight the latter stainless steel allows.

During winter months, some steelhead flyfishers go down as far as size 20, and some use strike indicators, while others do not. Many claim they need nothing more than their trout streamers and nymphs, and I am sure they are right. This steelhead fishery is still new, and flyfishers are adjusting to these conditions just as the fish are.

Steelhead are more than welcome, and their future, unlike that of coho and chinook, seems extremely bright. A steelhead flyfisher can only pray for rain—not too much of it—and being on the water when it does rain.

Guide Services

Ken Wenzel
Erie Experience
831 Pittsburgh Street
Springdale, PA 15144
724-274-5471

Mark DeCarlo
Fly Fisher's Edge
4864 Lucerne Road
Indiana, PA 15701
724-349-8742

John Nagy
Steelhead Guide Service
606 Crysler Street
Pittsburgh, PA 15226-1305
412-531-5819

John Bondar
Fish Man Guide Services
118 Shippen Drive
Coraopolis, PA 15108
412-269-1285

Neshannock Creek Fly Shop
Main Street
Volant, PA 16156
724-533-3212

Karl N. Weixlman
The Steelhead Connection
3911 Canterbury Drive
Eria, PA 16506
814-836-8013

Joe McMahon
21 Cherry Street
Pittsburgh, PA 15223
412-781-4373

Prowler Charters
Captain Brian Selai
1220 Williamsport Road
Pittsburgh, PA 15037
1-888-ONPROWL

Eric Lyle
3022 Hidden Lane
Erie, PA 16506
814-838-9512

Summary of Approved Trout Waters
and Special Regulations Areas for the Northwest

Butler County	Section / Regulations
Bear Creek	
Buffalo Creek	
Conoquenessing Creek	
Glade Run Lake	
Harbor Acres Lake	
Little Buffalo Run	
Little Conoquenessing Creek	
McMurray Run	
Silver Creek	
Slippery Rock Creek	
Slippery Rock Creek, North Branch	
Thorn Creek	

Clarion County	Section / Regulations
Beaver Creek	
Canoe Creek	
Cathers Run	
East Sandy Creek	
Leatherwood Creek	
Mill Creek	
Piney Creek	
Richey Run	
Toms Run	
Turkey Run	

Crawford County	Section / Regulations
Caldwell Creek	
Conneaut Creek	Dicksonburg downstream to Beaver Street (T-855) in Springsboro
Five Mile Creek	
Little Sugar Creek	
McLaughlin Creek	Mouth upstream 3 miles
Muddy Creek	SR 1033 upstream
Oil Creek	Confluence of Mosey Run near Lincolnville downstream to SR 0027 just upstream from Titusville
Oil Creek, East Branch	Centerville upstream to Spartansburg
Pine Creek	

Sugar Creek	SR 0027 upstream to township road on State Game Lands #69
Thompson Creek	SR 3031 to mouth
Woodcock Creek	

Erie County	**Section / Regulations**
Conneautte Creek	
French Creek, South Branch	Upper gravel pit
Lake Pleasant	

See "Steelhead" for streams and regulations governing them.

Forest County	**Section / Regulations**
Beaver Run	
Big Coon Creek	
Bluejay Creek	
East Hickory Creek	*DHALO:* 1.7 miles, from Queen Creek Bridge downstream to Otter Creek Bridge, SR 666 to East Hickory Road
Little Coon Creek	
Little Hickory Run	
Maple Creek	
Millstone Creek, West Branch	
Queen Creek	
Ross Run	
Salmon Creek	
Spring Creek	
The Branch	
Tionesta Creek	County line downstream to Kellettsville
Tionesta Creek, South Branch	
Toms Run	
Wards Ranch Pond	
West Hickory Creek	

Lawrence County	**Section / Regulations**
Bessemer Lake	
Deer Creek	
Hickory Run	
Honey Run	
Little Beaver River, North Fork	
Neshannock Creek	*DHALO:* 2.7 miles, from the base of the Mill Dam in Volant downstream to teh covered bridge on T-476

Lawrence County (cont.)	Section / Regulations
Slippery Rock Creek	From 0.25 mile below Armstrong Bridge (SR 2022) upstream to county line *DHFFO:* 0.5 mile, from Heinz Camp property downstream to .25 mile below SR 2022 bridge

Mercer County	Section / Regulations
Cool Spring Creek	*DHALO:* 1.25 miles, from SR 2014 bridge upstream to the abandoned railroad grade, east of Fredonia and SR 19
Little Neshannock Creek, West Branch	
Little Shenango River	
Mill Creek – tributary to French Creek)	
Mill Creek – tributary to Cool Spring Creek	
Neshannock Creek	SR 58 at Mercer downstream to Lawrence County line
North Deer Creek	
Sandy Creek	Mouth to first bridge below Lake Wilhelm
Shenango River	Tailrace of dam downstream to Walnut Street Bridge
Wolfe Creek, North Branch	

Venango County	Section / Regulations
East Sandy Creek	
Hemlock Creek	
Horse Creek	
Justus Lake	
Little Sandy Creek	*DHFFO:* 1.3 miles, from SR 3024 at Polk upstream to old bridge at Polk Center pumphouse
Little Scrubgrass Creek	
Mill Creek	
Oil Creek	From SR 8 upstream *DHALO:* 1.6 miles, from the bridge at Petroleum Center downstream to railroad bridge at Columbia Farm *DHALO:* 1-mile section from the two green posts near the Drake Well Museum downstream to the Oil Creek State Park hiking trail bridge
Pine Run	
Pithole Creek	
Prather Creek	
Sandy Creek	
Sugar Creek	
Sugar Creek, East Branch	

Two Mile Run, Lower	
Two Mile Run, Upper	From Justus Lake downstream to the confluence with the Allegheny River
West Pithole Creek	

Warren County	**Section / Regulations**
Akeley Run	
Blue Eye Run	
Brokenstraw Creek	
Browns Run	
Caldwell Creek	*DHFFO:* 1.4 miles, from Selkirk highway bridge downstream to near the Dotyville bridge
Caldwell Creek, West Branch	*Catch and Release:* 3.6 miles, West Branch bridge upstream to Three Bridge Run
Chapman Lake	
Coffee Creek	
Farnsworth Branch	
Fourmile Run	
Hemlock Run	
Hickory Creek East	
Hickory Creek West	
Jackson Run	
Little Brokenstraw Creek	
Perry McGee Run	
Pine Creek	
Queen Creek	
Six Mile Run	
Six Mile Run, North Fork	
Spring Creek	
Spring Creek, East Branch	
Thompson Run	
Tidioute Creek	
Tionesta Creek	
Tionesta Creek, East Branch	
Tionesta Creek, South Branch	
Tionesta Creek, West Branch	
Whitney Run (Spring Creek, Northwest Branch)	

Northwest Hub Cities
Erie
Population – 150,000

Erie is a large town with a wide variety of facilities available. The following is just a small sampling.

ACCOMMODATIONS
Avalon Hotel, 16 West 10th Street / 814-459-2220
Best Western Inn, 7820 East Perry Highway / 800-528-1234
Econolodge, 8050 Peach Street / 814-866-5544
Lake Erie Lodge, 1015 Peninsula Drive / 800-835-3493
Vernondale Motel, 5422 West Lake Road / 814-838-2372
Swanson's Resort Cottages, 161 Kelso Drive / 814-838-6243
Presque Isle Cottages, 320 Peninsula Drive / 814-833-4956

CAMPGROUNDS
Note: No camping is allowed in Presque Isle State Park
Erie KOA Campground, 6645 West Road (McKean) / 814-476-7706
Sara's Beachcomber Campground, 50 Peninsula Drive / 814-833-4560

RESTAURANTS
There are a host of restaurants in and around Erie, from fast food to fine dining.
La Bella Bistro, 556 West 4th Street / 814-454-3616 / Midrange prices and eclectic fare
Pie in the Sky Cafe, 463 West 8th Street / 814-459-8638 / Good food at cafe prices
Hoppers Brewpub, 123 West 14th Street / 814-452-2787
The Stonehouse Inn, 4753 West Lake Road / 814-838-9296 / Definitely upscale and reservations are required

FLY SHOPS
Lakes, Ponds, Streams & FlyFishing, 8236 Perry Highway / 814-864-3269
Erie Sport Store, 3702 Liberty Plaza / 814-868-0948
Erie Sport Store, 701 State Street / 814-459-2289

AUTO RENTAL
Avis Rent-A-Car, Erie International Airport / 814-833-9879
Enterprise Rent-A-Car, 1925 State Street / 814-459-8239
Budget Rent-A-Car, 4411 West 12th Street / 814-838-4502

AIR SERVICE
Erie International Airport, 4411 West 12th Street, / 814-833-4258

MEDICAL
Hamot Medical Center, 201 State Street / 814-877-6000

FOR MORE INFORMATION
Erie Area Chamber of Commerce
109 Boston Store Place
Erie, PA 16501
814-454-7191
Website: www.erie.net

Meadville
Population – 14,318

Accommodations
Days Inn, 18360 Conneaut Lake Road / 814-337-4264
Holiday Inn Express, 18240 Conneaut Lake Road / 814-724-6012
Motel 6, 11237 Shaw Avenue / 814-724-6366
Super 8 Motel, 17259 Conneaut Lake Road / 814-333-8883
Towne & Country Motel, 15760 Conneaut Lake Road / 814-724-6082

Campgrounds
Brookdale Family Campground, 25060 State Hwy 27 / 814-789-3251

Restaurants
Hoss's Steak & Seafood House, 18817 Smock Highway, / 814-333-4333
Deerhead Inn, 412 North Street / 814-724-1863
Hunter's Inn, 25594 State Hwy 27 / 814-789-2755
Kafferlin's, 17137 Cussewago Road / 814-337-5292
Mike's Place Tavern & Restaurant, 136 Lincoln Avenue / 814-336-2007
Perkins Family Restaurant, 18276 Conneaut Lake Road / 814-336-6000

Fly Shops
The Fly Fisherman's Shop, Monroe Valley Road #1 Box 263 (Fredricksburg) /
    717-865-5712
Conneaut Lake Tackle, Conneaut Lake / 814-382-6095

Auto Rental
Enterprise Rent-A-Car, 16285 Conneaut Lake Road #101 / 814-337-7626
Snappy Car Rental, 1623 Conneaut Road / 814-337-5858

Medical
Meadville Medical Center, 751 Liberty Street / 814-333-5000

For More Information
Meadville Chamber of Commerce
211 Chestnut Street
Meadville, PA 16335
814-337-8030

Warren

Population – 15,000

ACCOMMODATIONS
Holiday Inn, 210 Ludlow Street / 814-726-3000
Penn Laurel Inn, 706 Pennsylvania Avenue West / 814-723-8300
Super 8 Motel, 204 Struthers Street / 814-723-8881
Warren Motel, 2240 Pennsylvania Avenue West / 814-723-5550

RESTAURANTS
Docksiders Café, Route 59 / 814-726-9645
Draft House, 707 Pennsylvania Avenue East / 814-723-9818
Gilbert's Italian Dining, 1413 Pennsylvania Avenue West / 814-723-4040
Liberty Street Café, 211 Liberty Street / 814-726-3082
Penn Glade Restaurant, 2043 Pennsylvania Avenue East / 814-723-1608

AUTO RENTAL
Enterprise Rent-A-Car, 6 Market Street / 814-726-2600
National Car Rental, 315 Pennsylvania Avenue East / 814-723-7191

AIRPORTS
See Erie

MEDICAL
Warren General Hospital, 2 Crescent Park (West Warren) / 814-723-3300

FOR MORE INFORMATION
Warren County Chamber of Commerce
315 2nd Avenue, Room 409
Warren, PA 16365
814-723-3050

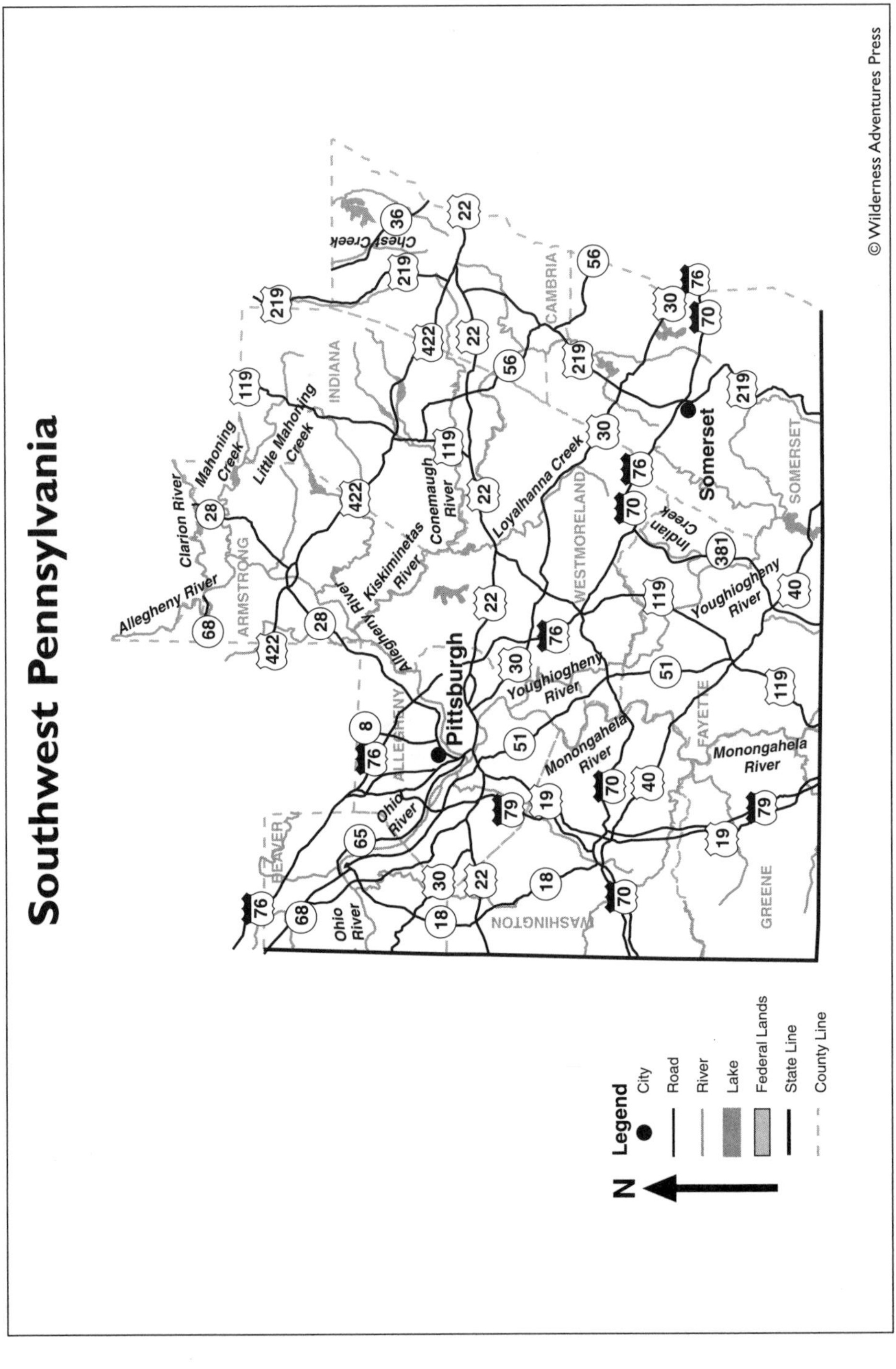

Southwest Pennsylvania

© Wilderness Adventures Press

Chest Creek

CAMBRIA

Clarion River

Mahoning Creek

Little Mahoning Creek

Allegheny River

INDIANA

Conemaugh River

Kiskiminetas River

Loyalhanna Creek

WESTMORELAND

Indian Creek

SOMERSET

Somerset

Youghiogheny River

ARMSTRONG

Allegheny River

Youghiogheny River

FAYETTE

Monongahela River

Monongahela River

Pittsburgh

Ohio River

BEAVER

Ohio River

WASHINGTON

GREENE

Legend

● City

Road

River

Lake

Federal Lands

State Line

County Line

N

Southwest Pennsylvania

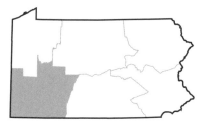

Pennsylvania's southwest offers the visiting angler a great deal of variety: bustling cities and quiet, uncrowded countryside; large rivers and small brooks; mountains and gently rolling hills. The region has always been a manufacturing hub, and its three major rivers, the Allegheny, Monongahela, and Ohio, still bustle with water traffic. Two cities typify the contrasts found in the southwest: Pittsburgh and Somerset. Only a 2½-hour drive apart, these two places are as different as night and day. If I sound like a choirboy singing the region's praises, it is only because there is so much to enjoy.

With everything from white bass hybrids to wild trout and brooks barely as deep as your ankle to huge river highways, your choices are just about limitless. For those who enjoy professional sports, Pittsburgh is home to the Penguins, Pirates, and Steelers, making it possible to end a wonderful day of fishing with an evening game.

The southwest attracts anglers from bordering states and across the country. Fishing is an important pastime here. Area newspapers feature weekly fishing reports, and fly shops contain all the gear any flyfisher could want along with knowledgeable staff.

Warmwater species can be found in abundance here, and good trout water is found in the southern parts of the region. There are waters that will test an angler's powers of observation in determining what trout are eating and skill in keeping a drag-free float. And then there are streams, lined with evergreens, where wild brook trout snap up anything thrown their way. Large rivers require a fast action rod, sometimes with a sinking line, and long casts to reach the depths where anything from a muskie to a fish the locals call Kentucky bass might run off with a Clouser's minnow. And while others raft the Youghiogheny River, anglers probe the back eddies until the water runs smooth with long pools and mild rapids.

Due to the amount of industry in and around Pittsburgh, water resources have suffered. But as have most of the Commonwealth's cities, the "Steel City" has implemented new water standards and is monitoring the progress being made. Less-polluting businesses are filling the gaps as factories have closed.

The past few years of drought have shown that clean water is important for more than good fishing. While anglers have long been proponents of cleaner water, the specter of a dwindling supply of drinking water has served as a wake-up call to everyone. And for those who love to cast a fly to healthy fish, that is certainly good news.

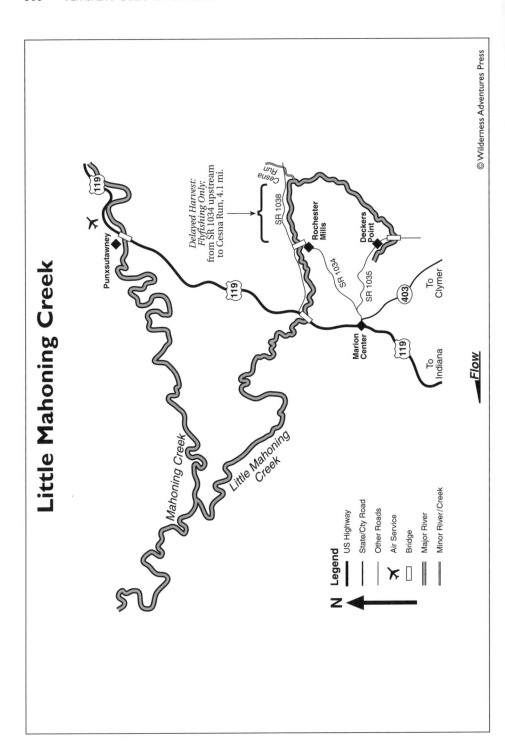

Little Mahoning Creek

Punxsutawney

119

*Delayed Harvest:
Flyfishing Only;
from SR 1034 upstream
to Cesna Run, 4.1 mi.*

Cesna Run

SR 1038

Rochester
Mills

SR 1034

Deckers
Point

SR 1035

119

Marion
Center

403

To
Clymer

119

To
Indiana

Flow

Mahoning Creek

Little Mahoning
Creek

Legend

—— US Highway

— State/Cty Road

| Other Roads

✈ Air Service

▯ Bridge

▌▌ Major River

|| Minor River/Creek

N

© Wilderness Adventures Press

LITTLE MAHONING CREEK

Little Mahoning Creek, running 31 miles within Indiana County, is one that fly-fishers return to time and again. Beginning just northwest of Deckers Point on road T555 and entering Mahoning Creek near Smicksburg, it averages 10 to 25 feet wide and is loaded with woody debris, which makes it tough to flyfish. Beginning in pastureland, it winds through woodland and offers a complex variety of flyfishing situations. Streamside growth helps stabilize the banks, prevents excessive accumulation of silt, and keeps the water cooler.

Adding to this creek's attractions is an unusually long 4.1-mile flyfishing only section, which starts at Rochester Mills and runs upstream into rugged, mountainous terrain that keeps this stretch from being overrun with anglers. Hiking into this section is rewarded with excellent fishing. The combination of large boulders, gravel-strewn bottom, plenty of deep undercuts, and cool water throughout the summer make this a perfect trout haven and an excellent terrestrial fishery. It also has a good pool-to-riffle ratio.

There are two options to reach the start of the DHFFO section at Rochester Mills. From US 119 just north of Hamill, take SR 1038 to Rochester Mills or take SR 1034 from Marion Center, which lies on US 119 and SR 403.

Some streams require a hike to find better water.

Waders with felt soles are my choice for this creek, and a rod carrying a 4-weight floating line should be all that is needed to fish here. And don't forget to put a dozen or so gypsy moth caterpillars in your vest before hiking in.

Ken Sink, who was instrumental in developing Trout Unlimited in Pennsylvania, would be proud of the Ken Sink Chapter's accomplishments on Little Mahoning. This chapter's concern for preserving and enhancing this coldwater resource are evident in the stream improvement devices that have been placed on the stream throughout its length. In Pennsylvania, fisheries such as the Little Mahoning exist due to the efforts of those who love trout streams.

LITTLE MAHONING CREEK MAJOR HATCHES

Insect	J	F	M	A	M	J	J	A	S	O	N	D
Black Stone #16			▉									
Quill Gordon #14				▉								
Hendrickson #14				▉								
Blue Quill #18				▉					▉			
Tan Caddis #16					▉	▉	▉	▉				
Sulphur #16					▉							
Light Cahill #14					▉							
March Brown #12					▉							
Green Drake #12, 3X long (very sparse hatch)					▉							
Midges #20–24 (green, yellow, white, cream)						▉	▉	▉	▉			
Ants #16–20; Beetles #12–18; Grasshoppers #10–14							▉	▉	▉			
Caterpillars #12, 3X long							▉	▉	▉			
Other												
Floating Nymphs #16–24						▉	▉	▉	▉	▉		
Yellow Adams #16 & 18							▉	▉	▉			

Terrestrial and caterpillar patterns should always be in your fly box.

CHEST CREEK

Chest Creek's headwaters are located in Cambria County near Winterset, which is just west of Loretto. From US 219, local roads provide access to the creek's upper reaches. From Carrolltown, take SR 4015 to Patton, where SR 36 parallels the creek into Clearfield County and to its confluence with the West Branch Susquehanna River. The Delayed Harvest Artificial Lures Only section is accessible from SR 36. Chest Creek runs approximately 12 miles in each county.

The creek warms up quickly as it nears the West Branch Susquehanna, however trout fishing usually holds into mid-June. Better fishing is found in Cambria County, above, within, and below the project area. Chest Creek hasn't attracted a lot of attention; in fact, few have heard of it. But it does provide some excellent trout fishing as well as some marginal bass fishing in its lower reaches.

The 1.8 miles of DHALO-regulated water is the section most often visited, but, as with most freestones, the headwaters offer good fishing, as well. Little Chest Creek joins Chest Creek in Patton, which is where the special regulations area begins. Primarily a stocked trout stream, the creek does have a few good early season hatches and shouldn't be overlooked since crowds thin out considerably after opening day.

An angler probing a freestone stream.

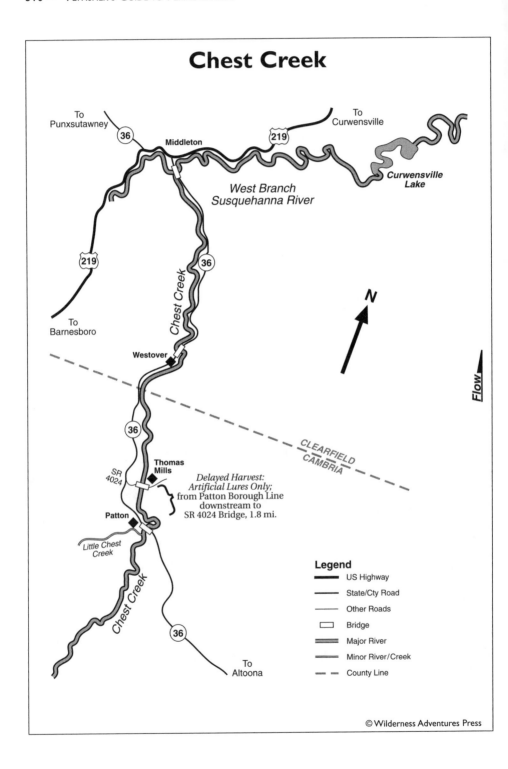

Chest Creek

To Punxsutawney

To Curwensville

36

219

Middleton

West Branch Susquehanna River

Curwensville Lake

219

36

To Barnesboro

Chest Creek

N

Westover

Flow

36

CLEARFIELD
CAMBRIA

Thomas Mills

SR 4024

Delayed Harvest: Artificial Lures Only; from Patton Borough Line downstream to SR 4024 Bridge, 1.8 mi.

Patton

Little Chest Creek

Chest Creek

Legend
━━━ US Highway
─── State/Cty Road
── Other Roads
▭ Bridge
▬▬ Major River
═══ Minor River/Creek
‑ ‑ County Line

36

To Altoona

© Wilderness Adventures Press

Chest Creek averages 18 to 20 feet wide and runs through forested and meadow areas. It is a typical freestone with a mix of boulders and gravel-strewn bottom. Drought conditions for the last few years has been hard on it, but it has escaped some of the degradation from coal mining that other streams in the area have suffered.

Take waders, a 4-weight line, and a variety of streamers and attractor patterns. Chest Creek continues to have good fishing into the summer if water levels remain high enough. To find better fishing as the season progresses, look for underground springs and areas where there is good canopy. There can also be good fishing where gypsy moth caterpillars are found.

CHEST CREEK MAJOR HATCHES

Insect	J	F	M	A	M	J	J	A	S	O	N	D
Black Stone #16			■									
Quill Gordon #14				■								
Hendrickson #14				■								
Blue Quill #18				■								
Tan Caddis #16					■	■	■	■				
Sulphur #16						■						
Light Cahill #14						■						
March Brown #12					■							
Midges #20–24 (green, yellow, white, cream)			■	■	■		■	■	■			
Ants #16–20; Beetles #12–18; Grasshoppers #10–14						■	■	■	■			
Caterpillars #12, 3X long						■	■	■	■			
Other												
Floating Nymphs #16–24 (green, yellow, white)						■						
Yellow Adams #16 & 18							■	■	■			
Mosquito					■	■	■	■	■			

Terrestrial and caterpillar patterns should always be in your fly box.

A beautiful trout stream in southwestern Pennsylvania.

CLEAR SHADE CREEK

In a region blessed with trout water, Clear Shade Creek is only one of a host of trout waters in this beautiful countryside. Somerset County is prone to long, harsh winters and significant snowfall that causes heavy spring runoff, filling streams to the bursting point and delaying some hatches. Flyfishers who don't like the early season crowds find this to their liking since the better fishing happens from late April through mid-June.

Clear Shade Creek runs approximately 8 miles through Somerset County and Gallitzin State Forest. It is the only stream in the county with Flyfishing Only regulations (DHFFO), which run from Windber Reservoir upstream 1 mile. There aren't enough wild or native trout for this to be designated as a wild trout stream, but it is stocked and fishing is good throughout most of the year, with the best fishing from May through June and again in September. As summer progresses, this typical free-stone stream warms up more slowly than others in the area.

The creek starts just off Hollow Road northeast of Ogletown and travels 8 miles before joining Shade Creek. Access is available from SR 56, and the very scenic Babcock State Forest Picnic Area is located along the highway 4 miles east of Windber. The Clear Shade Wild Area and the John P. Saylor Trail are both located south of the highway in the Babcock division of Gallitzin State Forest. Jeep trails provide access along the creek's length.

Above all, this is an aesthetically pleasing area that offers tranquility and relative solitude, especially as the season progresses. As much or more than trout, the beautiful surroundings are enough to make this creek worth visiting.

Clear Shade's hatches are decent but not outstanding. Take gypsy moth caterpillar imitations and inchworms as well as searching patterns, which are a must. Take waders and a long-sleeved shirt since temperatures cool quickly after sunset and warm up slowly in the morning.

CLEAR SHADE CREEK MAJOR HATCHES

Insect	J	F	M	A	M	J	J	A	S	O	N	D
Black Stone #16			▪									
Quill Gordon #14				▪								
Hendrickson #14				▪								
Blue Quill #18				▪				▪				
Tan Caddis #16					▪	▪	▪					
Sulphur #16						▪						
Light Cahill #14						▪						
March Brown #12					▪							
Grannom Caddis #14					▪							
Ants #16–20; Beetles #12–18; Grasshoppers #10–14							▪	▪	▪	▪		
Caterpillars #12, 3X long							▪	▪	▪			
Other												
Streamers #8–12, 3X long (white, brown, olive)				▪	▪	▪	▪	▪	▪	▪		
Floating Nymphs #16–24 (green, yellow, white)						▪	▪	▪	▪	▪		
Yellow Adams #16 & 18							▪	▪				
Mosquito #12 & 14						▪	▪	▪	▪	▪	▪	

Terrestrial and caterpillar patterns should always be in your fly box.

Loyalhanna Creek

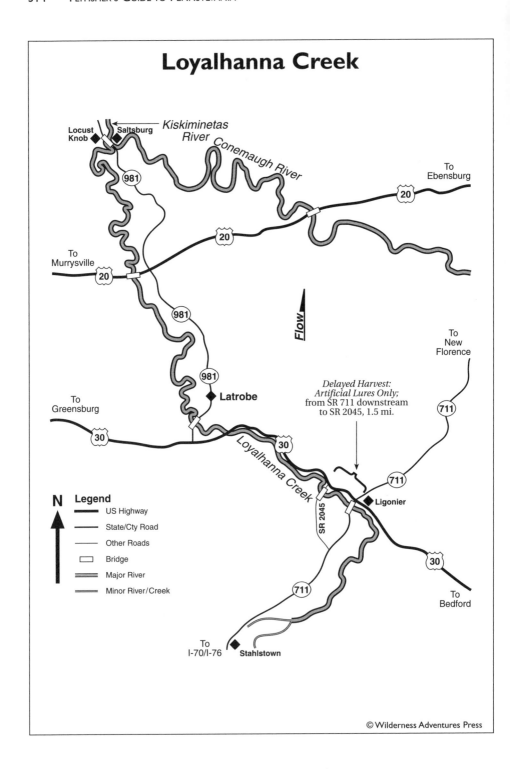

Locust Knob

Saltsburg

Kiskiminetas River

Conemaugh River

To Ebensburg

981

20

20

To Murrysville

20

981

To New Florence

Flow

981

Latrobe

Delayed Harvest: Artificial Lures Only; from SR 711 downstream to SR 2045, 1.5 mi.

711

To Greensburg

30

30

Loyalhanna Creek

711

Ligonier

N

Legend

— US Highway

— State/Cty Road

— Other Roads

▢ Bridge

═ Major River

═ Minor River/Creek

SR 2045

30

711

To Bedford

To I-70/I-76

Stahlstown

© Wilderness Adventures Press

LOYALHANNA CREEK

Not far from the hustle and bustle of Pittsburgh and its suburbs, Loyalhanna Creek offers a beautiful trout fishery that is, surprisingly, not overfished. Found in Westmoreland County, this meandering creek is heavily stocked from Ligonier to just above Latrobe. Loyalhanna's mix of gravel bottom and limestone make it an intriguing place to flyfish, and trout can be extremely selective when the water is low and nearly gin clear.

Karl Power, friend and fellow outdoor writer, took my wife, AnGel, and me to the DHFFO section where large numbers of trout were rising to caddisflies. Contrary to the large, boulder-strewn sections we had stopped to photograph along the way, this section was low and clear. Where the creek is lined with trees, trout stopped chasing caddis and rushed eagerly after a gypsy moth caterpillar imitation. Although there are many sections on the Loyalhanna with long, shallow riffles, there are also unexpectedly deep pools guarded by large boulders.

The DHFFO section is 1.5 miles long, beginning at SR 711 in Ligonier and extending downstream to SR 2045. It is a seasonable stream, and rising water temperatures on its lower reaches can dampen fishing in the summer. However, when we visited this section in late June of the past year, trout were extremely active and feeding heavily despite the low flows caused by what is probably one of the worst droughts in Pennsylvania's history. Despite its warming problems, this proves to me that the creek could fish well into July and beyond depending on weather conditions.

Loyalhanna Creek makes a journey of 7 miles before entering the Conemaugh River in Saltsburg. Its headwaters are found near SR 711 north of Stahlstown. Near

Training the next generation of flyfishers at an early age on the Loyalhanna.
(Photo by A-D Wolf)

Weaver Mill, SR 381 parallels the stream until reaching US 30 near Ligonier. From Latrobe to its mouth, access is available from SR 981. This section turns from marginal trout water to warmwater very quickly.

My suggestion is to take waders along for the entire stream but especially for crossing it or positioning yourself for a proper, drag-free float. As with all special regulation waters, 2- to 4-weight lines are a good choice, and trout will be fussy when the water is thin and clear. Long leaders and light tippets are the rule here.

LOYALHANNA CREEK MAJOR HATCHES

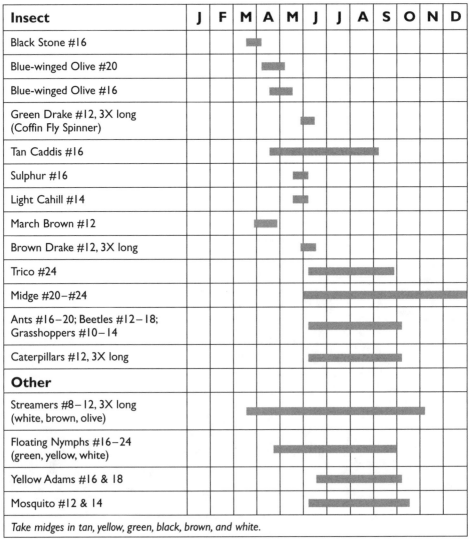

Insect	J	F	M	A	M	J	J	A	S	O	N	D
Black Stone #16			▪									
Blue-winged Olive #20				▪								
Blue-winged Olive #16				▪								
Green Drake #12, 3X long (Coffin Fly Spinner)						▪						
Tan Caddis #16					▪▪▪▪▪							
Sulphur #16						▪						
Light Cahill #14						▪						
March Brown #12				▪								
Brown Drake #12, 3X long						▪						
Trico #24							▪▪▪▪					
Midge #20–#24							▪▪▪▪▪▪▪					
Ants #16–20; Beetles #12–18; Grasshoppers #10–14							▪▪▪▪					
Caterpillars #12, 3X long							▪▪▪▪					
Other												
Streamers #8–12, 3X long (white, brown, olive)				▪▪▪▪▪▪▪▪▪								
Floating Nymphs #16–24 (green, yellow, white)						▪▪▪▪▪						
Yellow Adams #16 & 18							▪▪▪					
Mosquito #12 & 14							▪▪▪▪					
Take midges in tan, yellow, green, black, brown, and white.												

LAUREL HILL CREEK

Laurel Hill Creek has all the right stuff to be an excellent trout stream except cold water throughout the entire summer. The stream begins north of Bakersville and flows south toward Laurel Hill State Park. It traverses 29 miles before entering Casselman Creek in the town of Confluence. State route 31 crosses the stream's upper section, where unnamed forks make the headwaters almost impossible to find. The region's beauty makes any trip here worthwhile.

Trout fishing is rated good before the creek enters the park and a 65-acre impoundment there. As is usual with small impoundments having top water releases, trout fishing below the dam is poor and bass take over. However, Laurel Hill's bass fishing is not is good as it is elsewhere in the state. Both the stream and lake are stocked with trout by the PFBC both early and late in the season.

There are two Delayed Harvest Artificial Lures Only sections that really make this a worthwhile fishery. The first starts at the footbridge in Humbert and runs 1.2 miles through State Game Lands #111 to Paddytown Hollow Run. Better fishing on this section is found where there is more canopy. Due to colder water, the second and more popular section runs 2.2 miles from the Boy Scout Camp in Laurel Hill State Park downstream to road T364.

The creek does have some good, although not abundant, hatches and offers some excellent terrestrial fishing in early summer. The creek's attraction lies in the

Remember to take your time and have fun.

fact that access is not all that good outside of the park, and that helps cut down fishing pressure tremendously. The easily accessible stretches are heavily fished. Since no major roads line the creek, it is best reached from SR 281 via secondary roads.

I like a 4-weight rod to cover all of the available water. Even though the warmwater fishing is adequate, most would choose the Youghiogheny over this stream for bass. Even without the abundant hatches found on most of this area's streams, Laurel Hill Creek is still worth visiting, even if it is primarily a stocked fishery.

LAUREL HILL CREEK MAJOR HATCHES

Insect	J	F	M	A	M	J	J	A	S	O	N	D
Black Stone #16			▪									
Quill Gordon #14				▪								
Blue-winged Olive #16				▪								
Grannom Caddis #14					▪							
Tan Caddis #16					▬▬▬▬▬▬							
Sulphur #16						▪						
Light Cahill #14						▪						
March Brown #12						▪						
Ants #16–20; Beetles #12–18; Grasshoppers #10–14							▬▬▬▬▬					
Caterpillars #12, 3X long							▬▬▬▬▬					
Other												
Streamers #8–12, 3X long (white, brown, olive)				▬▬▬▬▬▬▬▬▬								
Floating Nymphs #16–24 (green, yellow, white)					▬▬▬▬▬▬							
Yellow Adams #16 & 18							▬▬▬▬					
Mosquito #12 & 14							▬▬▬▬▬					
Terrestrial and caterpillar patterns should always be in your fly box.												

YOUGHIOGHENY RIVER

The "Yawk" is one of those rivers that seems to be flowing the wrong way, running north out of Maryland into Pennsylvania at Youghiogheny Lake, which straddles the state line. The town of confluence lies just below the dam, and from there the river proceeds to Ohiopyle, where it becomes wider and deeper. It enters the Monongahela at McKeesport in Allegheny County, which is referred to as "the forks of the Yough."

Coldwater releases from the dam create an excellent trout fishery, and below the tailrace many anglers find success in what can often be deep water. Larger trout are usually taken on weighted nymphs and streamers with a sinktip line even though there can be good hatches here. Because of the river's width and heavy stocking in the stretches just below the dam, there is a lot of early season fishing pressure.

Proceeding toward Ohiopyle, the river becomes wider and deeper, and wading becomes difficult although not impossible. There is a bike trail leading to some good fishing, and the PFBC stocks this area with both adult and fingerling trout. A trophy trout section extends from the Ramcut Run confluence downstream to the Lick Run confluence—remember, the river runs north.

Below this section, the fishery declines rapidly, as the river turns wild and is better suited for whitewater rafting than fishing. From Ohiopyle, there are 9 miles of Class I and II whitewater, suitable for canoes, kayaks, and rafts but not for fishing boats. While I'm sure there are some trout in these raging waters, wading is simply out of the question. Below the whitewater, much of the middle Youghiogheny is more suitable to floating.

Below Connellsville to the river's mouth at McKeesport, the Youghiogheny becomes bigger and warmer and is fished for smallmouth bass and muskie more than trout, although many consider that good trout water extends from Smithton, where the river is stocked, all the way up to the dam.

Access on the upper and middle reaches of this 60-mile river is difficult. There are only a few places where access can be found near a road. The major highways through the area are SR 381 and SR 281. Just below Confluence, the bike trail (converted railroad) is accessible from SR 281. Be sure to have a good map with you.

The Youghiogheny's big water requires 5- and 6-weight lines for trout fishing. A 7-weight is ideal for fishing the tailrace as well as the middle and lower sections. For trout fishing, I prefer a 9-foot rod for a 5-weight. When fishing for bass on the middle and lower sections, I like a 9-foot for an 8-weight. When floating for muskie, I use a 9-foot for a 9-weight with a shock tippet and streamer attached. Although I fish primarily for bass, I go prepared for the possibility of finding the deep holes that hold muskie or finding a muskie feeding. On those occasions, there are only a few moments in which to deliver a fly. Waders are always needed, and some sections are best fished from a boat. Use the Warmwater Fly Box for bass and muskie patterns.

With a good mixture of cold and warmwater, the Youghiogheny offers enough to spend a lifetime exploring and fishing. While traveling on SR 381, consider stopping

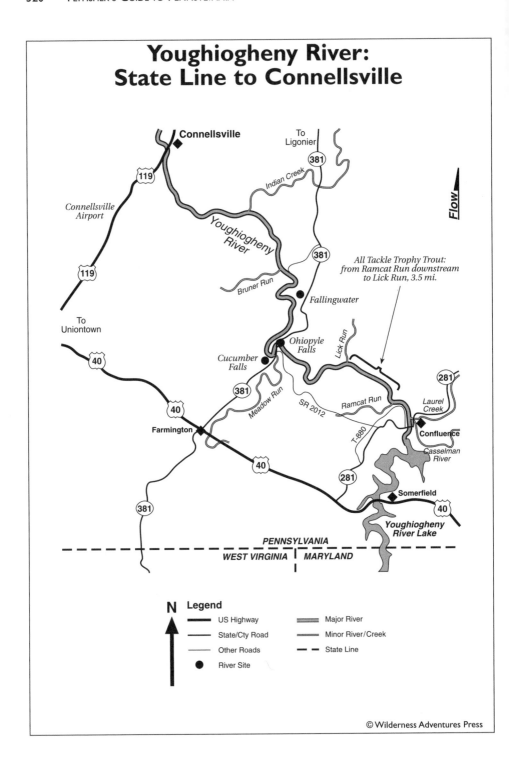

Youghiogheny River:
State Line to Connellsville

Youghiogheny River:
Connellsville to Monongahela Confluence

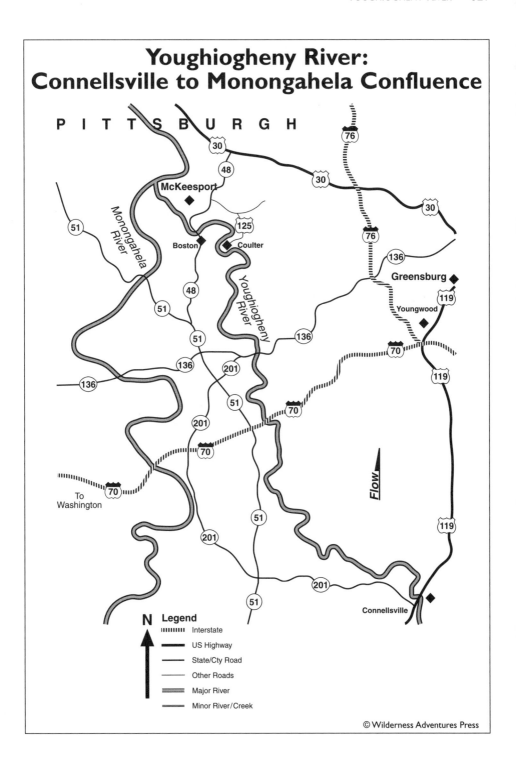

P I T T S B U R G H

McKeesport

Monongahela River

Boston

Coulter

Youghiogheny River

Greensburg

Youngwood

To Washington

Flow

Connellsville

N

Legend

⅄⅄⅄⅄⅄⅄	Interstate
▬▬▬▬	US Highway
———	State/Cty Road
———	Other Roads
▬▬▬▬	Major River
▬▬▬▬	Minor River/Creek

© Wilderness Adventures Press

to see Frank Lloyd Wright's masterpiece, Fallingwater, located between Mill Run and Ohiopyle.

Youghiogheny River Access Sites

Somerset/Fayette Counties

Boston Park Access (PFBC); located under the Boston Bridge
in the Borough of Boston
- Shallow draft, lightweight fishing boats, canoes, and inflatables
- Surfaced ramp and parking

Coulterville Access; Monongahela and Youghiogheny Sportsmen located
off Railroad Street in Coulterville
- Shallow draft, lightweight fishing boats, canoes, and inflatables
- Surfaced ramp and parking

The Lower Youghiogheny River; 7.5 miles of Class III and Class IV whitewater suitable for rafters, kayaks and closed-deck canoes. There is a DER launch site at Ohiopyle State Park along SR 381 at Ohiopyle. This river segment is served by the park-operated Bruner Run Take-Out Area and special regulations govern the use of this river segment. Commercial livery services and guided raft trips are available. Parking is available.

Bruner Run to Connellsville; 8 miles of Class I, Class II and Class III whitewater suitable for canoes, kayaks and rafts. Launching is by special arrangement with Ohiopyle State Park and utilizes a service road at the park's Bruner Run Take-out, 6 miles north of Ohiopyle. There is an excellent coldwater fishery in this river segment and commercial livery services are available. There is a parking area as well. However, this is not a place to wet a line from any sort of craft.

YOUGHIOGHENY RIVER MAJOR HATCHES

Insect	J	F	M	A	M	J	J	A	S	O	N	D
Black Stone #16			■									
Blue-winged Olive #14				■								
Hendrickson #14 (sparse hatch)				■								
Blue Quill #18				■				■				
Tan Caddis #16					■■■■■■							
Sulphur #16						■						
Light Cahill #14						■						
March Brown #12					■							
Caddis #14 (brown, gray, olive, green)						■■■■■						
Midges #20–24 (green, yellow, white, cream)							■■■■■					
Ants #16–20; Beetles #12–18; Grasshoppers #10–14							■■■■■					
Caterpillars #12, 3X long							■■■■■					
Other												
Floating Nymphs #16–24 (green, yellow, white)							■■■■					
Yellow Adams #16 & 18							■■■■					

Terrestrial and caterpillar patterns should always be in your fly box.

DUNBAR CREEK

Dunbar Creek begins near Lookout just a little way from SR 2021 and flows northeast through the town of Dunbar before emptying into the Youghiogheny River at Connellsville. At present it is a good stream that is on its way to becoming a gem. Due to the efforts of the Dunbar Sportsmen's Club and the Chestnut Ridge Chapter of Trout Unlimited, it is recovering well from acid mine drainage in its upper reaches, and stream improvement devices have created a decent pool-to-riffle ratio. Natural reproduction of native brook and wild brown trout is occurring near the stream's headwaters.

I like this stream because of its diversity and natural beauty and am always happy to be on a stream where native brookies might snatch my fly. Large boulders are found throughout the creek's length. For the present, hatches aren't all that great on Dunbar Creek, but as the water keeps improving so will the hatches.

The stream is approximately 7 miles long and has a section designated as DHFFO that runs from the confluence of Glade Run downstream to the stone quarry at SR 1055. In my experience, the better fishing occurs above the Glade Run confluence. PFBC and local sportsmen's groups stock the creek, and when that happens in autumn, this is a delightful destination for fall foliage and fishing.

The author enjoying beautiful Dunbar Creek.

There are some deep pools and long glides in spite of the stream's small size. Waders are best for fishing on Dunbar, and a rod carrying a 4-weight should be just about right.

DUNBAR CREEK MAJOR HATCHES

Insect	J	F	M	A	M	J	J	A	S	O	N	D
Black Stone #16			■									
Quill Gordon #14				■								
Hendrickson #14				■								
Blue Quill #18				■	■				■			
Tan Caddis #16					■	■	■	■				
Sulphur #16						■						
Light Cahill #14						■						
March Brown #12					■							
Blue-winged Olive #20					■	■						
Midges #20–24 (green, yellow, white, cream)						■	■	■	■	■		
Ants #16–20; Beetles #12–18; Grasshoppers #10–14							■	■	■			
Caterpillars #12, 3X long							■	■	■			
Other												
Floating Nymphs #16–24 (green, yellow, white)							■	■	■			
Yellow Adams #16 & 18							■	■	■			

Terrestrial and caterpillar patterns should always be in your fly box.

Camp Run and Indian Creek

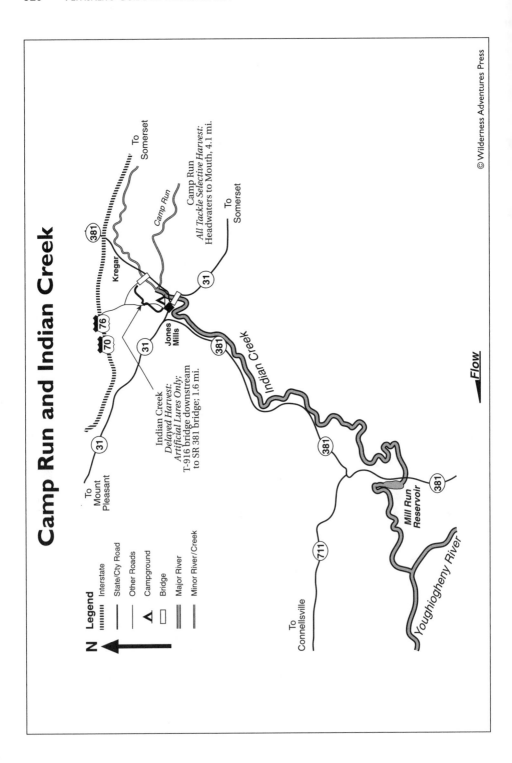

© Wilderness Adventures Press

Camp Run and Indian Creek

When wild trout are calling me to go flyfishing, Westmoreland County doesn't leap to mind as a destination. However, one of the county's streams is classic, native brook trout water in the truest sense: Camp Run, and it's a real jewel.

Overharvest shouldn't become a problem due to the regulations that are in place: All Tackle Selective Harvest on the stream's entire 4.1 miles. Camp Run's native brookies seldom exceed 9 inches in length. It flows into Indian Creek, a stocked trout stream that is within the Roaring Run Natural Area. Camp Run can be found at its confluence with Indian Creek by driving north from Jones Mills on SR 381 toward Kregar.

Stocked throughout spring and fall, Indian Creek's picturesque setting attracts a large number of Pittsburgh residents, as do the other good trout streams in this area. Indian Creek has special regulations along 1.6 miles from the T916 bridge downstream to the SR 381 bridge. The chance to fish small and wild native brook trout on Camp Run as well as larger stocked trout on Indian Creek is an attractive combination. As Indian Creek gets closer to the Youghiogheny River, it becomes a so-so warmwater fishery, compared to others in the area.

Since Camp Run is not a stream requiring exact patterns, searching patterns work well—two of my favorites are the yellow Adams and mosquito. To fish this small

Thin water means long, light leaders.

stream, take hip boots, 3- to 4-weight lines, and rods of your own choice. To fish Indian Creek, take waders.

Brook trout fishing on Indian Creek can be good but is affected by the number of anglers on the stream on any given day. It does hold a fair number of wild browns and native brookies where its coldwater tributaries enter, but mainly, it is fished as a stocked stream.

This portion of the southwest has a number of good native brook trout streams as well as some that hold wild browns. While hatches are not tremendous, the fishing is good. The forest canopy found here calls for some caterpillar patterns, inchworms, and terrestrials.

CAMP RUN & INDIAN CREEK MAJOR HATCHES

Insect	J	F	M	A	M	J	J	A	S	O	N	D
Black Stone #16			▬									
Quill Gordon #14				▬								
Hendrickson #14				▬								
Blue Quill #18				▬				▬				
Tan Caddis #16					▬▬▬▬							
Sulphur #16						▬						
Light Cahill #14						▬						
March Brown #12				▬								
Grannom Caddis				▬								
Ants #16–20; Beetles #12–18; Grasshoppers #10–14							▬▬▬▬					
Caterpillars #12, 3X long							▬▬▬▬					
Other												
Streamers #8–12, 3X long (white, brown, olive)					▬▬▬▬▬▬							
Floating Nymphs #16–24 (green, yellow, white)						▬▬▬▬▬						
Yellow Adams #16 & 18							▬▬▬					
Mosquito #12 & 14						▬▬▬▬						

Terrestrial and caterpillar patterns should always be in your fly box.

MEADOW RUN

Meadow Run, found in Fayette County and beginning above Deer Lake, runs 12.5 miles before entering the Youghiogheny River near Ohiopyle. The Delayed Harvest Artificial Lures Only section is found at the confluence of Laurel Run and flows downstream to its mouth.

The stream has a steep grade that gains enough momentum to be suitable for rafting from the SR 381 bridge downstream. However, there are a lot of pocketwaters and backwater eddies in this rapidly moving stream that make it a good place to cast a brace of wet flies or toss weighted streamers. Although there are good hatches here, the stream's steep grade requires pinpoint casting and a lot of line mending. Meadow Run is stocked in spring and fall, and some trout carry over to the next season.

This is a good sidebar fishery when visiting the Youghiogheny and neighboring streams. The upper reaches are accessible from US 40, both above and below Deer Lake, via State Routes 2008, 2010, and 1055. The lower reaches are accessible from SR 381, which also meets up with US 40.

Meadow Run can be waded but is a bit treacherous in its lower reaches. I usually carry both a sinktip and floating line and prefer a 5-weight line for weighted streamers and nymphs, although 4- and 6-weights will do. Use the hatch chart for Laurel Hill Creek.

Summary of Approved Trout Waters
and Special Regulation Areas for the Southwest

Allegheny County	Section / Regulations
Big Sewickley Creek	
Bull Creek	*DHALO:* 1 mile from the bridge on T-721 downstream to the T-721 bridge in Millerstown
Deer Creek	*DHALO:* 2.1 miles, from SR 0910 bridge at T-678 intersection downstream to the lower boundary of Rose Ridge Golfe Course
Deer Lakes	
Flaugherty Run	
Long Run	
North Park Lake	
Pine Creek	*DHALO:* 1.4 miles, from the abandoned railroad bridge near the T-575 and Duncan Avenue intersection downstream to 150 yards below the SR 4019 bridge

Armstrong County	Section / Regulations
Buffalo Creek	*DHALO:* 3.7 miles, from Little Buffalo Run downstream to 0.6 mile above SR 4035 in Craigsville
Cherry Run	
Cornplanter Run	
Cowansshannock Creek	
Glade Run	
Huling Run	
Patterson Creek	
Pine Creek, North Fork	
Pine Creek, South Fork	
Pine Creek, South Fork North Branch	
Plum Creek	
Scrubgrass Creek	

Beaver County	Section / Regulations
Big Sewickley Creek, North Fork	
Brady Lake Run	
Brady Run, South Branch	
Hereford Manor Lakes (lower & upper)	
Little Beaver River, North Fork	Darlington upstream to the county line
Mill Creek	
Raccoon Lake	
Traverse Creek	

Cambria County   Section / Regulations

Cambria County	Section / Regulations
Beaverdam Run (at Ashville)	
Bender Run	
Ben's Creek	
Blacklick Creek, North Branch	
Chest Creek	*DHALO:* 1.8 miles, from northern Patton Borough line downstream to SR 4022 bridge at Thomas Mills
Duman Dam	
Elton Sportsman's Dam	
Howells Run	
Killbuck Run	
Laurel Lick Run	
Laurel Run	
Laurel Run (near Sidman)	
Laurel Run (near Tannerysville)	
Little Conemaugh River, North Branch	
Little Killbuck Run	
Little Paint Creek	
Noel's Creek	
Slatelick Creek	
Stewart Run	

Fayette County   Section / Regulations

Fayette County	Section / Regulations
Back Creek	
Big Sandy Creek	
Chaney Run	
Dunlap Creek	
Dunlap Creek Lake	
Dunbar Creek	*DHFFO:* 4.1 miles, from the confluence of Glade Run and Dunbar Creek downstream to the stone quarry along SR 1055
Georges Creek	
Indian Creek	
Mountain Creek	
Meadow Run	*DHALO:* 1.7-mile section from the confluence with Laurel Run downstreamto the SR 381 bridge
Mill Run – tributary to Indian Creek	
Mill Run – tributary to Quebec Run	
Mountain Creek	
Virgin Run Dam	

Fayette County (cont.)	Section / Regulations
Youghiogheny River	*All Tackle Trophy Trout:* 3.5-mile section from the confluence with Ramcat Run downstream to the pipeline crossing at the confluence with Lick Run

Greene County	Section / Regulations
Browns Creek	
Duke Lake	
Enlow Fork	
Wheeling Creek, Dunkard Fork	
Wheeling Creek, North Fork Dunkard Fork	
Wheeling Creek, South Fork Dunkard Fork	
Whiteley Lake	

Indiana County	Section / Regulations
Blacklegs Crek	
Brush Creek	
Cush Creek	
Cush-Cushion Creek	
Laurel Run	
Little Mahoning Creek	*DHFFO:* 4 miles, from SR 1034 at Rochester Mills upstream to Cesna Run
Little Yellow Creek	
Mudlick Run	
Repine Run	
Toms Run	
Two Lick Creek, South Branch	
Yellow Creek	

Somerset County	Section / Regulations
Allen Creek	
Beaver Dam Creek	
Beaverdam Run	
Bens Creek	
Bens Creek,South Fork	
Breastwork Run	
Brush Creek	
Casselman River	
Clear Shade Creek	*DHFFO:* 1 mile, from the cable at Windber Water Dam upstream
Cub Run	

Elk Lick Creek	
Flaugherty Creek	
Gladdens Run	
Glade Run	
Jones Mill Run	
Juniata River, Raystown Branch	
Kimberly Run	
Kooser Lake	
Kooser Run	
Laurel Hill Creek	*DHALO:* 2.2 miles, from Laurel Hill State Park at BSA Camp downstream to T-364 *DHALO:* 1.2 miles, from the footbridge on the State Game Lands #111 Road on Humbert downstream to Paddytown Hollow Run
Laurel Hill Lake	
Little Piney Creek	
McClintock Run	
Middle Creek	
Miller Run	
Piney Creek (Big)	
Piney Run	
Shafer Run (near Bakersville)	
Stony Creek	
Whites Creek	
Wills Creek	
Youghiogheny River	*All Tackle Trophy Trout:* 3.5-mile section from the confluence with Ramcat Run downstream to the pipeline crossing at the confluence with Lick Run

Washington County	**Section / Regulations**
Aunt Clara Fork	
Canonsburg Lake	
Dutch Fork Creek	
Dutch Fork Lake	
Enlow Fork	
Kings Creek	
Little Chartiers Creek	
Millers Run	
Mingo Creek	
Templeton Fork	
Ten Mile Creek	From SR 18 downstream to SR 19

Westmoreland County	Section / Regulations
Big Sewickley Creek	
Camp Run	*All Tackle Selective Harvest:* 4.1 miles, from the headwaters downstream to the mouth
Donegal Lake	
Fourmile Run	
Hannas Run	
Hendricks Creek	
Indian Creek	*DHALO:* 1.6 miles, from the T-916 bridge downstream to the SR 0381 bridge
Jacobs Creek	
Keystone Lake	
Linn Run	
Loyalhanna Creek	*DHALO:* 1.5 miles, from SR 711 downstream to SR 2054
Mammoth Lake	
Mill Creek	
Northmoreland Lake	
Roaring Run	
Shannon Run	
Tubmill Creek	
Twin Lake, Lower	

Southwest Hub Cities

Pittsburgh

Population – 369,879

Pittsburgh has a huge number of facilities available. The following is just a small sampling.

ACCOMMODATIONS

Candlewood Suites, 100 Chauvet Drive / 412-787-7770
Clubhouse Inn, 5311 Campbells Run Road / 412-788-8400
Comfort Inn, 2801 Freeport Road / 412-828-9400
Days Inn, 1150 Banksville Road / 412-531-8900
Hampton Inn, 1550 Lebanon Church Road / 412-650-1000
Ironworks Inn, 901 Bingham Street / 412-431-3000
Marriott Hotel, 112 Washington Place / 412-471-4000
Super 8 Motel, 1807 Route 286 / 724-733-8008
Motel 6, 211 Beecham Drive / 412-922-9400
Pittsburgh Motel, 4270 Steubenville Pike / 412-922-1617
Valley Motel, 2571 Freeport Road / 412-828-7100

RESTAURANTS

Jakes Above the Square, 430 Market Square / 412-338-0900
Seventh Street Grille, 130 7th Street / 412-338-0303
The Fresh Fish House, 2102 Murray Street / 412-422-3474
Pittsburgh Steak Company, East Carson Street / 412)381-5505
Café Allegro, 12th Street / 412-481-7788
Primanti Brothers, 3803 Forbes Avenue / 412-621-4444

FLY SHOPS

International Angler, 503 Freeport Road / 412-782-2222
South Hills Rod & Reel, 3227½ West Liberty Avenue / 412-344-8888
The Fly Tyer's Vice, 2225 Swallow Hill Road / 412-276-2831

AUTO RENTAL

Budget Rent-A-Car, 700 5th Ave / 412-261-3320
Dollar Rent-A-Car, PO Box 12107 / 412-262-1300
Enterprise Rent-A-Car, 2229 West Liberty Ave / 412-341-4245
Hertz Rent-A-Car, Greater Pittsburgh International Airport / 412-472-5955
National Car Rental, PO Box 12413 / 412-472-5094
Thrifty Car Rental, 5777 Baum Boulevard / 412-363-7368

AIRPORTS

Pittsburgh International Airport, Landside Terminal #4000 / 412-472-3525

MEDICAL
St. Francis Medical Center, 4117 Liberty Avenue / 412-622-0230

FOR MORE INFORMATION
Chamber of Commerce
700 River Avenue
Pittsburgh, PA 15212
412-322-5015
Website: www.pittsburgh-cvb.org

Somerset
Population – 6500

Accommodations
A Budget Inn, 736 North Center Avenue / 814-443-6441
Days Inn, 220 Waterworks Road / 814-445-9200
Dollar Inn, 1146 North Center Avenue / 814-445-2977
Economy Inn, RR 2 Box 5 / 814-445-4144
Hampton Inn, 324 Laurel Crest Road / 814-445-9161
Super 8 Motel, 125 Lewis Drive / 814-445-8788
Wren Crest Motel, Route 31 West / 814-443-1297

Campgrounds
Hidden Lake Campground, 295 Duck Pond Road / 814-443-2112
Lost Mountain Inc Campground / 814-443-9910
Woodland Campsites Inc, 291 Gilmour Road / 814-445-8860

Restaurants
Grapevine Café, 1640 North Center Avenue / 814-445-6622
Italian Oven Restaurant, 4129 Glades Pike / 814-445-4141
Pine Grill Restaurant, 800 North Center Avenue / 814-445-2102
Pug's Place, 305 East Main Street / 814-444-1988

Fly Shops
Rolling Rock Club (Ligonier) / 412-238-2182
The Fishing Post, 114 North Main Street (Greensburg) / 412-832-8383

Auto Rental
Enterprise Rent-A-Car, 112 Lake Road / 814-443-0700
Hertz Rent-A-Car, 307 Bedford Street (Johnstown) / 814-536-8755
National Car Rental, 479 Airport Road #25 (Johnstown) / 814-536-0079
U-Save Auto Rental, 1177 North Center Avenue / 814-445-3131

Airport
Somerset County Airport, 159 Airport Lane (Friedens) / 814-445-5320
See Pittsburgh

Medical
Conemaugh Memorial Medical Center, 1086 Franklin Street (Johnstown) / 814-534-9000

For More Information
Somerset County Chamber of Commerce
601 North Center Avenue
Somerset, PA 15501
814-445-6431

Coldwater Fly Box

Matching the hatch has almost become a religion for many long-time flyfishermen. In our zeal to identify and match the hatch correctly, we have left a great majority of flyfishers, and particularly "would-be" flyfishers, in our wake. For those who don't live, eat, and breathe the sport, getting immersed in the technicalities of flyfishing makes it seem far too difficult to be fun.

Beginners can invest so much time and energy into mastering a single haul and a drag-free float that attempting to learn the complexities of hatches makes flyfishing seem more like work than fun. Experienced flyfishers all too often overwhelm beginners with too much technical information. If a beginning flyfisher calls a cream mayfly a white rather than a light cahill, don't make him feel foolish or stupid for not knowing the exact name. In actuality, it could be any of several species of mayflies—more species and subspecies are found on streams than any one flyfisher could ever hope to identify. Many fly shop owners and fly tiers would agree. In fact, it takes an expert and a laboratory to identify specific species of mayflies, caddis, or stoneflies correctly.

This book is not intended as a scientific guide to the hatches of Pennsylvania streams. Rather, it is a guide to Pennsylvania streams and what hatches you might expect to find on them. But it is important to remember that as conditions change, hatches change, also. A stream that has been rehabilitated and has cleaner water than previously might have fewer or different hatches. For example, some nymph species require silt to bury in, and when a river has been cleansed of silt, the hatch can disappear.

Recently, I was talking with a group of flyfishermen and expressing my concern about nonpoint pollutants becoming a problem. I nearly fell over when one gentleman began to explain that silt was good for a river. "The white fly, you know, is a silt-burying nymph, and the hatches are becoming greater with each passing year," he explained. My concern is for the overall health of a stream, and I am certain that many hatches are never seen on heavily silted waters that are nearly devoid of fish.

Certainly, many flyfishers will continue to examine and determine the fly species they see on a river. If that means a simple identification and a simple name, such as the light cahill, that is sufficient for many flyfishers. But those who do want to examine and accurately label hatches provide good information for everyone who pursues fish with a fly rod in hand.

Our constant pursuit to imitate the natural insect is endless and, for many, as much fun as the fishing itself. Rarely does a year go by that I do not try to tie a fly that imitates an insect or baitfish a little better than patterns that are readily available. Taking my creations from the tying bench to the water, whether finding success or failure, is fun and has made my fishing days more productive.

Here I offer a shortened list of flies that should be in a coldwater fly box—many should be placed in a warmwater fly box as well. To illustrate this point, one afternoon on the thin waters of the Susquehanna River, I took a dozen or more smallmouth bass that were rising to and feeding heavily on a Trico spinnerfall. I have learned since that time that this was not a fluke, and taking bass over 17 inches on a size 24 fly is now an annual occurrence.

Dry Fly Patterns

My fly box has a wide variety of patterns for trout. Some are tied to resemble mayflies, caddis, and some stonefly adults, although the small black stone (#16) is the one most likely to be encountered. While there are many patterns on the market, I find it more useful to know the water I am going to fish. If it is filled with heavy riffles, I use a pattern that is a general imitation rather than a perfect facsimile of the natural. I might incorporate calf tail wings and tail and three hackles in order to see the fly, something that can be more important than an exact imitation. I know that trout do not have a long time to look over a pattern, so it is best to be able to see the fly at all times.

However, as a lover of slow moving pools, I normally use one hackle in my dressing of duns or use a comparadun.

Spinner Imitations

I almost always tie these with poly wings and thin bodies and split tails to make them ride properly. I am very particular about how I tie a sulphur spinner—it has to have an orange egg sack. This has proven itself to be a reliable pattern over the past 20 years.

Green Drake

My green drake pattern is different than most. I like to use peccary (wild pig) for split tails and cut wings from dyed imitation wood duck that has a yellowish-green tinge. I prefer to tie it on a 3X long, dry fly hook, produced by Mustad.

Yellow Adams

The yellow Adams has had a permanent place in my fly box for well over 25 years. I tie it in sizes 14 to 16, with the 16 being my all-time favorite. This pattern is a good representation of the sulphur dun, and if you split the wings into an almost downward position, it serves as a spinner as well. It is a good representation of many hatches in Pennsylvania, and some claim that it works well for caddis hatches, as well. I have fished this pattern over enough finicky trout to know that it works. In passing the pattern on to others, I have received many reports of an excellent catch rate when using the fly.

Grizzly Caddis

You will see the tan caddis on many of the hatch charts in this book. I have found that they appear on almost all the state's trout streams and often go unnoticed. Again, this is an extremely important pattern that I carry at all times. I prefer the grizzly caddis with a few turns of a single grizzly hackle and no more than six hackle fibers for a wing, and a tan body. This is a great pattern in size 16. When fishing the larger, early season caddis that are found on may freestones in sizes 12 and 14, I prefer to use a more standard pattern with 8 strands of deer hair for a wing. Carry a full compliment of caddis in a variety of colors and sizes. Be sure the hackle has been cut straight across, even with the barb of the hook, so that the fly rides flush and allows the wing to support it.

Fur Nymphs

I love natural fur for dry flies, wets, emergers, and most of all, nymphs. There are many reasons for choosing fur over synthetic materials. It is easy to dub; it has a life-like quality when fished (some claim that it breathes); and it is buggy looking. I prefer simple nymphs that cover the range of insects within the streams I am fishing. The muskrat nymph and hare's ear nymph have taken more fish for me than any other nymphs I have fished. The two colors correctly match most of the naturals, and I use the underfur for bodies. Guard hairs for the thorax have proven extremely successful over the years. One of my favorite patters is a muskrat nymph on a size 8, 3X long streamer hook. I use chain eyes and a mallard wing for a casing. I also tie a similar nymph with light Australian opossum fur and cased with a bronze turkey wing. Again, I like to use chain eyes in all but the smallest of nymphs.

Beadhead Nymphs

Beadheads work extremely well and cover a wide range of insect life available in Pennsylvania streams. These nymphs are particularly good for imitating caddis larva. This pattern is so easy to tie and so versatile, it should prove one thing: "near enough" takes as many, or more, trout than exact patterns. Carry them in all colors.

Streamers

I carry very few streamers in my fly box, because I have found that fishing them more often results in a chase rather than a take. Plenty of early season trout are taken on streamers, but it isn't long until the stocking truck passes and trout begin feeding on naturals. I am fond of marabou streamers and came up with the Wolf's streamer over seven years ago. The streamer has proven itself far too often not to release it here. The fly is tied on a 3X long streamer hook in sizes 8 through 12. It is constructed using pearl tinsel for the body with a slight overwing of sparse cream marabou, and then 10 strands of pearl Flashabou. The Flashabou is then covered with another layer of thin cream marabou and another seven strands of pearl Flashabou, and finally, topped with three strands of green Flashabou. I tie in chain bead eyes. I have had this pattern take fish on nearly every stream I have used it, and have had Yellow Breeches browns take it off the bottom as it lay there without movement. This streamer is extremely underdressed. If it looks too thin, remove still more material. It may also be tied in yellow, brown, and black.

Besides my pattern, I like Matukas with Flashabou added and variations of the muddler. When tying or buying a streamer, I believe flash, tied in with either Krystal

Flash or Flashabou, makes a world of difference. A long time friend and fishing companion, Pete Ryan, has a streamer that also deserves mention here, the Instigator.

Pete Ryan and I have fished together for over 25 years, and I can tell you his enthusiasm for flyfishing has not dwindled in all that time. In fact, it may have increased. Pete, a dentist, is president of the God's Country Chapter of Trout Unlimited and one heck of a good flyfisherman.

Ray Jobe, Pete, and I have shared many fishing waters together, so when the pair first showed me the Instigator, I remarked that it looked like a girdle bug, better suited for bluegill than trout.

I was teasing, of course, and when Pete first introduced the fly in *Fly Fisherman* magazine a few years ago, it was high time to try the pattern. Ray Jobe, an expert nymph fisherman, vouched for the fly, and I now am ready to admit that it has more than proven its worth over the years.

The key ingredients to Pete's fly are flash and movement. The movement is accomplished with materials that include latex legs. I'm convinced, without a shadow of a doubt, that the moving parts of a fly are what makes them a success. Pete's favorite dressing for the fly is as follows: a 3X long streamer hook, brown monocord for thread, white latex legs, and a thorax of brown marabou mixed with four strands of Krystal Flash. The body is created from brown chenille, and the soft hackle is brown partridge, tied collar style. He incorporates nickel-plated barbells for eyes.

Emergers

Emerger patterns come and go like the wind, but I believe that they do have their place and have become extremely important, especially with the increasing amount of special regulation waters in the state, which means educated fish. I believe that we have been fishing emergers in the form of wet flies for many years without knowing what we were trying to represent. I contend that a well tied wet fly is still a good imitation of both an emerger and a drowned dun or spinner. However, whether you choose wet flies, soft-hackles, or any other emerger pattern, I suggest that you add a bit of flash. The finer Flashabou tied into any wet fly streamer or nymph adds to the attraction of the fly. Don't overdo it—a few short strands are all that is needed.

Floating Nymphs

You can see the fish are boiling, but you can't see a spinnerfall or any minute flies on the water. Thinking they might be taking emergers, you have gone through every pattern in your box. The answer in this situation might be floating nymphs. I prefer patterns in size 16 and smaller. My favorite is a white floating nymph with light blue dun tail, split, and a small looped wing case of light gray poly.

I have had such success with floating nymphs that I now carry them in all colors and often fish them through the hatch. I suggest that you fish the imitation one size smaller than the natural.

Terrestrials and Caterpillars

I love fishing terrestrials—and why not? It allows me time on the water from June thru mid-October when others have given up, and the bonus is that I need not match the hatch. The only challenge I have before me is attaching a size 16 beetle to a fine tippet and putting it to the fish with a drag-free float. I might be oversimplifying the procedure a bit, but few trout refuse a spun deer hair beetle when properly presented. I would not go near a stream without them.

I always carry beetles in sizes 12 through 18 and have not found the need to go smaller. I do feel, however, that spun deer hair outfishes all beetle patterns that I have used. My guess is that it might trap water and create air bubbles, but I have fished them with complete confidence and success since the mid-1970s. I also carry ant patterns but rarely use them. On the other hand, many of my fishing partners use ants above all other patterns and have had great success with them. Of course, I carry flying ant patterns for those few blessed days when they appear on the water and wise old trout become suicidal. If you are going to fish terrestrials, you should carry ants and beetles in sizes 12 to 18 and flying ant patterns in size 16.

As a dry fly fisherman, it is hard for me to hate the gypsy moth caterpillar and elm span worms that have invaded the state. Although the gypsy moth caterpillar was thought to be under control, there has been a resurgence of these "pests" in recent years. It really doesn't matter to the fishermen because there have been enough of them, and other caterpillars, to keep the trout on the lookout.

Because of my good fortune with spun deer hair beetles, I began tying my caterpillar imitations with spun deer hair and then simply palmered them with grizzly hackle in the same fashion as a woolly bugger. I trim the hackle underneath, even with the body, and although they are nothing pretty to look at, neither are most caterpillars. I simply don't leave home without them. I tie them on 3X long, light wire hooks in sizes 8 through 12.

Others Patterns

I have a friend who, before we met, fished mostly with a green weenie. He has taken countless trout with them over the years and continues to do so. The green weenie, a simple fly of chenille, is a deadly pattern throughout the year. It is taken for all kinds of caddis larvae and, one must assume, the inchworm—something we have not yet mastered in floating form. The green weenie, egg flies, woolly buggers, and San Juan worms are simply flies that should be carried and that produce trout with great regularity.

I will leave you with one thought. I was well into my fishing career before I had taken a single trout on a regular Adams, a fly that has accounted for more trout than one can imagine. However, I had taken hundreds upon hundreds of fish on the yellow Adams. Finally, I forced myself to fish the fly for well over 45 minutes, until a trout finally took the imitation.

My point is that the fly that you have the most confidence in will be the fly you fish most often. That equates to more fish taken on your favorite fly, or flies, than any other. My reasoning is simple: trout flies are made to imitate the natural as closely as possible, and the pattern you use is a matter of choice. That choice is yours and affects only you and the trout that you are fishing over. Drag-free floats and proper presentation of the fly are nearly as crucial as the choice of fly.

Note: The hatch charts provided throughout this book are broad and compiled for the flyfisher, not necessarily the entomologist. Terrestrials and other productive patterns are included in many of the charts, despite the fact that they are not true "hatches," to give anglers a better feel for what they can expect on each stream.

PENNSYLVANIA'S MAJOR HATCHES

Little Black Stonefly #16–18

Dry Flies	Little black stone
Nymphs/Wet Flies	Beadhead black stone; floating nymphs; lead-wing coachman
Emergers	Soft hackle, beadhead soft hackle
Comments	Early season hatch, March–April

Little Blue-winged Olive #20–22

Dry Flies	BWO parachute; comparadun; olive stillborn; spinner (poly wing or dun wing with olive/brown body)
Nymphs/Wet Flies	Pheasant tail; beadhead pheasant tail; olive floating nymph; lead-wing coachman
Emergers	Olive biot; soft hackle; pheasant tail
Comments	Primary hatch early in season; sporadic hatch throughout season

Quill Gordon #14

Dry Flies	Quill Gordon parachute, rusty spinner
Nymphs/Wet Flies	Dark brown fur nymph; beadhead; Quill Gordon wet fly
Emergers	Light brown soft hackle; beadhead soft hackle
Comments	Early season hatch, March–April

Blue Quill #18

Dry Flies	Blue quill parachute; rusty spinner
Nymphs/Wet Flies	Dark brown fur nymph; beadhead; blue quill wet fly
Emergers	Brown/gray soft hackle; beadhead soft hackle
Comments	Early and late season hatch

Hendrickson #14

Dry Flies	Light Hendrickson (female); red quill (male); comparadun; parachute
Nymphs/Wet Flies	Black to brown fur nymph; beadhead; floating nymph (tan fur/gray poly)
Emergers	Tan soft hackle; beadhead soft hackle
Comments	April and early May hatch

Blue-winged Olive #16

Dry Flies	BWO parachute; comparadun; olive stillborn; poly wing spinner; dun wing spinner
Nymphs/Wet Flies	Pheasant tail; beadhead (gray/brown/olive); lead-wing coachman; olive floating nymph
Emergers	Olive biot; soft hackle; pheasant tail
Comments	Primary hatch in May and June; sporadic throughout season

Light Cahill #14

Dry Flies	Light Cahill; comparadun; parachute; CDC dun; cream body spinnery; cream/yellow poly wing spinner
Nymphs/Wet Flies	Light tan fur nymph; beadhead; cream hare's ear; Light Cahill wet fly
Emergers	Cream soft hackle; beadhead; CDC cream emerger
Comments	Mid-May to mid-June hatch

Gray Fox #12

Dry Flies	Traditional; tan fur parachute; comparadun; spinner (tan body and gray poly wing)
Nymphs/Wet Flies	Pheasant tail; floating nymph (pinkish); tan hare's ear wet fly
Emergers	Tan soft hackle; beadhead
Comments	May hatch

March Brown #12

Dry Flies	Traditional; hare's ear; comparadun; spinner (tan fur and gray poly wings)
Nymphs/Wet Flies	Beadhead hare's ear; tan floating nymph; hare's ear wet fly
Emergers	Soft hackle pheasant tail; pinkish tan soft hackle; beadhead
Comments	April and May hatch

Sulphur #16

Dry Flies	Sulphur thorax; comparadun; spinner (tan fur and gray poly wings); orange and yellow egg sack
Nymphs/Wet Flies	Pheasant tail; floating nymph (pinkish); yellowish sulphur wet fly
Emergers	Soft hackle; pheasant tail; beadhead (pinkish tan body)
Comments	Primarily late Man and June hatch

Green Drake #12, 3X Long

Dry Flies	Eastern green drake; coffin fly (white body and black poly wings)
Nymphs/Wet Flies	Green drake nymph (tan body); soft hackle (striped peacock body)
Emergers	Tan soft hackle
Comments	Mid-May to mid-June hatch

Brown Drake #12, 3X Long

Dry Flies	Brown drake (brown/yellow fur body); spinner (same body with gray poly wing)
Nymphs/Wet Flies	Light tan beadhead; floating nymph; soft hackle (reddish brown slate wing and hackle)
Emergers	Light tan soft hackle
Comments	Late May into June hatch

Cream Cahill #18

Dry Flies	Comparadun (cream color)
Nymphs/Wet Flies	Floating nymph (cream and gray); light cahill wet fly
Emergers	Hare's ear soft hackle
Comments	Like many mayflies, hatches from June through October

Trico #24

Dry Flies	Poly wing RS2 (bunny dun); cluster; sparkle dun; poly wing spinner; Everett's
Nymphs/Wet Flies	Trico nymphs; black to brown floating nymph
Emergers	Poly wing soft hackle
Comments	July through October hatch

White Fly #14

Dry Flies	Traditional; thorax; parachute; comparadun (white); spinner (white/white)
Nymphs/Wet Flies	Tan and white beadhead; floating nymph (white/white with pinkish thorax)
Emergers	Poly wing (grayish white with pink thorax near eye)
Comments	July and August hatch

Midges #20–26

Dry Flies	Griffith's gnat; Travis paramidges
Nymphs/Wet Flies	Crystal midges (suspender, palomino)
Emergers	Lite brite; brassie; disco midge
Comments	Year-round hatch

Caddis #12–18

Dry Flies	Grammon; grizzly; Henryville; CDC; Goddard
Nymphs/Wet Flies	Beadhead; larva; pupa; hen wing soft hackle
Emergers	Glass bead, soft hackle
Comments	April through October hatch

Terrestrials #12–18

Beetles	Spun deer hair beetle; Crowe's beetle
Ants	Black ant (fur, foam, poly); cinnamon ant
Grasshoppers	Dave's hopper; Joe's hopper; Letort
Other	Letort cricket; inchworm; green weenie
Comments	Hatch ranges from June through October

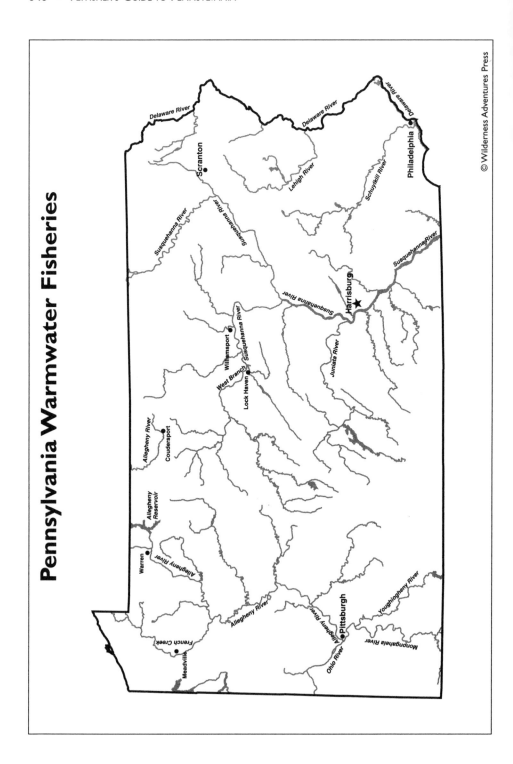

Pennsylvania Warmwater Fisheries

© Wilderness Adventures Press

Pennsylvania's Warmwater Fisheries

Pennsylvania divides its fish into three categories: coldwater (fish that thrive on water temperatures at and below 70 degrees), coolwater (fish that survive and do well in temperatures below and above 70 degrees), and warmwater (fish that do best in temperatures that exceed the 70 degree mark). Trout and salmon are considered coldwater fish, the pike family as cool water, and bass are warmwater. Lakes have the uncanny ability to "turn over," which means that cold water and oxygen content are available at different depths as seasons change. In streams, temperature and oxygen often go hand in hand. Generally, there is less oxygen available in warm water.

It is important to note that all fish in the state can be subjected to extreme water changes throughout the seasons. When fishing for trout, water temperature is especially important in spring, summer, and fall, because a trout's metabolism slows down when the water is too cold as well as too warm.

There are few large streams here that do not include bass in their lower reaches, and as the summer progresses and water warms up, trout move to colder waters and bass move into the warm water the trout have vacated. On many stocked trout streams, there is often a mixture of both smallmouth bass and trout. Trout fishing purists often find the mixing of bass with trout unacceptable.

For years bass have been an indicator that a trout fishery is slipping into a warmwater fishery. However, that is not always the case. On Penns Creek, a world-renowned Class A trout stream with excellent numbers of wild trout, I have taken many smallmouth bass from the same pools in which I have taken wild brown trout in excess of 19 inches. Each time this happened, it was during spring when water temperatures were still in the low 60s. Perhaps we have a lot more to learn about bass, trout, and other fish found in the Keystone State.

While this book attempts to be comprehensive in covering warm, cool, and coldwater fisheries, readers should be aware that Pennsylvania contains 42,000 miles of streams and river and hundreds of lake, making it impossible to cover everything the state has to offer. In general, most streams over 20 miles long that are not polluted hold trout in the upper reaches and smallmouth bass and other species in the lower reaches. However, stream flows during the late 1990s have been severely low due to the longest drought on record for the state, and as of this publication, it is still not known how much this has affected fisheries. By the time you read this, the situation may be quite different.

My best advice is to have a thermometer with you at all times in order to determine what is happening on different sections of a stream. If the water temperature exceeds 70 degrees, move upstream to find trout. For those seeking bass, one of the finest freshwater fish to cast a fly to, the temperature should be in the upper 70s into the 80s.

*Large rivers
generally mean
warmwater flyfishing.*

I have spent as much time flyfishing for bass as I have trout over the past 20 years. At first, I was laughed at and even scorned. Now, I find many of my favorite bass waters containing as many flyfishers as the famed Yellow Breeches, so well known for its trout fishing. As an example of how popular fly-rodding for bass has become, a close friend of mine has forsaken trout fishing entirely and now concentrates solely on bass.

Both fit nicely here, since Pennsylvania offers as much bass water, if not more, than it does trout water, and an angler will find the mixture both exciting and time-consuming. But all flyfishers know that diversity in fishing is a good thing, and with a state that offers so many opportunities, Pennsylvania is hard to turn one's back on.

DELAWARE RIVER

Although the Delaware River now hosts large numbers of striped bass, American shad is still the most popular fish here. Shad runs continue to grow, intensifying in April and May, and the Delaware is the only river in the state where it can be fished. Shad average 4 to 5 pounds, and the state record remains 9 pounds, 9 ounces. Flyfishers have discovered that shad will take a dry fly after spawning, and that small shad flies work well after spring runoff subsides.

The Delaware River is a testament to changing attitudes in Pennsylvania, proving that people and fish can both prosper rather than the old idea that you could have fish or jobs but not both. With Philadelphia cleaning up its portion of the river, stripers and other species are once again making their way up the Delaware River, and fish ranging from 30 to 40 pounds can be taken now. However, it seems the fish are susceptible to chicken liver, and bait fishermen often let them swallow the hook before setting it, resulting in many nonlegal size and released legal fish dying. Anglers are asked to release all stripers, since they are only beginning to come back to the reaches above Philadelphia.

Although the bass fishing is not as good here as it is on the Susquehanna River, the muskie fishing is better. Bass run smaller on average here and seem to be found in pockets rather than in good numbers throughout the entire river. Still, there are enough here to keep the fishing interesting.

American Shad

The largest member of the herring family, American shad are anadromous fish that spend most of their life in the ocean and return each spring to spawn in freshwater rivers. Bucks (males) run up the Delaware River in early spring, and females (roes) follow the bucks shortly thereafter. Spawning takes place when water temperature reaches the 56- to 60-degree range and on or near the surface in pools within the river. Juvenile shad stay and grow in the river throughout the late spring and summer before returning to sea, where they spend the next 3 to 5 years.

An estimated 800,000 American shad migrated up the Delaware in 1998. Shad are now traveling up the Lehigh River from its confluence on the Delaware at Easton. Last year, close to 3,000 shad went up the fish ladder in Easton to spawn in native grounds on the Lehigh River, according to the Delaware Shad Fishing Association.

Shad fishing is definitely an art when pursued with a fly rod. I have taken many with a beadeye streamer with a touch of marabou and a lot of flash. Other patterns consist of no more than thinly wound yarn wrapped with cold wire. There is still much to learn about taking shad with a fly. They move upriver to spawn, not feed, and seem to strike more out of agitation rather than hunger.

Hardware anglers look for river channels, anchor their boat, and then determine the depth at which shad are moving upstream. With waves of shad moving upriver, anglers eventually hook up with fish. The shad dart has long been the most popular lure here, and all hardware anglers had to do was to choose the right color. Now they are being taken on spinners and downriggers, which seem to work even better.

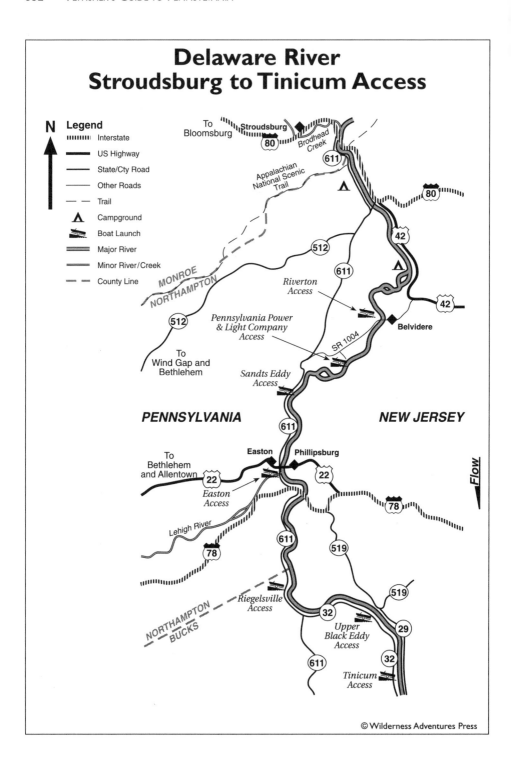

Delaware River
Tinicum Access to Philadelphia County

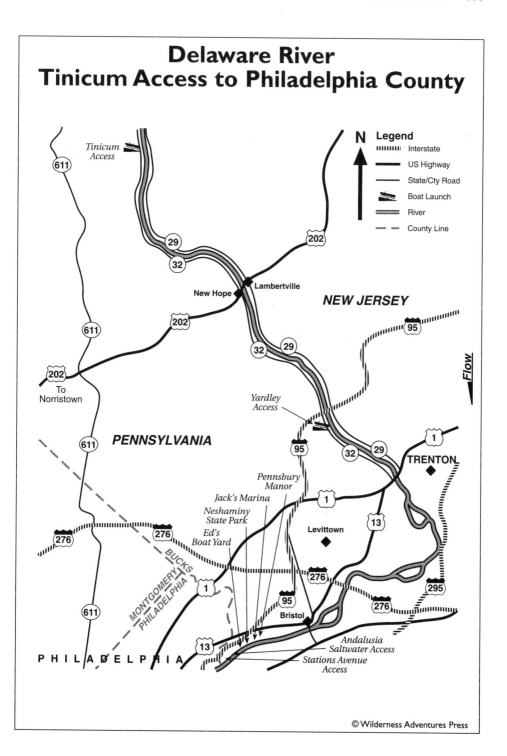

N

Legend
- ‖‖‖‖‖ Interstate
- —— US Highway
- —— State/Cty Road
- Boat Launch
- River
- – – County Line

Tinicum Access

611

29

32

New Hope

Lambertville

NEW JERSEY

202

611

202

To Norristown

95

Flow

PENNSYLVANIA

Yardley Access

611

95

32

29

1

TRENTON

Pennsbury Manor

Jack's Marina

Neshaminy State Park

Ed's Boat Yard

Levittown

13

276

276

BUCKS

MONTGOMERY
PHILADELPHIA

1

276

1

276

295

611

95

Bristol

276

PHILADELPHIA

13

Andalusia Saltwater Access

Stations Avenue Access

© Wilderness Adventures Press

Delaware River
Philadelphia County to Delaware

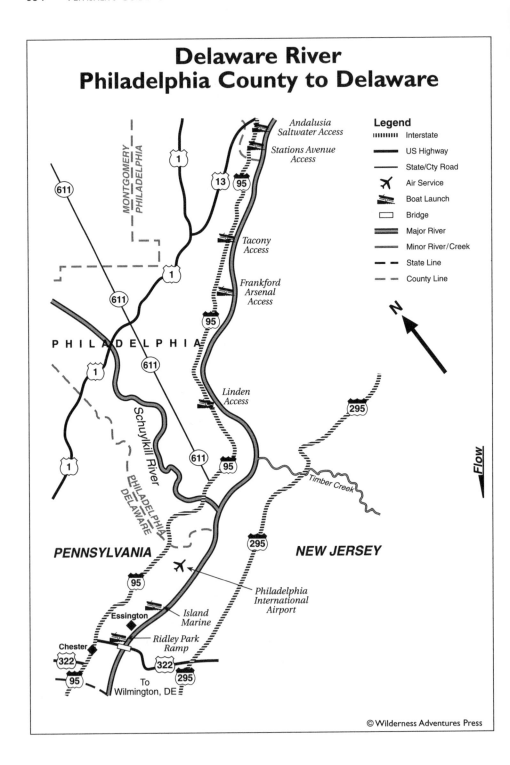

Andalusia
Saltwater Access

Stations Avenue
Access

Legend

‖‖‖‖‖‖	Interstate
▬▬▬	US Highway
────	State/Cty Road
✈	Air Service
🛥	Boat Launch
▭	Bridge
▓▓▓	Major River
═══	Minor River/Creek
▬ ▬	State Line
─ ─	County Line

Tacony
Access

Frankford
Arsenal
Access

PHILADELPHIA

Linden
Access

Schuylkill River

Timber Creek

Flow

PENNSYLVANIA

NEW JERSEY

Philadelphia
International
Airport

Essington

Island
Marine

Chester

Ridley Park
Ramp

To
Wilmington, DE

© Wilderness Adventures Press

Warmwater rivers are often large like the Allegheny and Delaware.

Flyfishers need to cast long lines on most sections of the river, along the channel's edges and into the channel itself. A great place to find shad holding is below riffles at the head of a pool, but getting the fly down quickly enough and keeping it in the strike zone for any period of time is the challenge. The holding water that shad prefer is often deep and flows extremely fast. A lead-core line might get to the fish, and a longer leader will keep the fly off the bottom. Trolling a fast sinking line or allowing the fly to dangle in the current behind a boat will catch shad, but this is not considered flyfishing by most purists, since most consider casting to be an integral part of flyfishing.

Shad, often referred to as "poor man's salmon," have soft mouths and many are lost by setting the hook too hard. Ideal rods for handling this hot, often high-leaping silvery fish, should be 9 feet in length, carrying a 5- or 6-weight line and a reel with 150 yards of backing. The reel must be high quality with an excellent drag system. From a casting standpoint, a 9-foot rod or longer carrying an 8-weight line that allows long casts to be made into the wind might be a better setup.

The better flyfishing is in and around the Delaware Water Gap. There are shallow areas here that allow anglers to stalk a fish just as he would a bonefish on the bay side of the Florida Keys. However, a great disadvantage is that shad are simply moving through and may rest for only minutes at a time at a given spot. If you see a fish, you might be able to get in one cast without spooking it; then a fast retrieve past its nose is in order. This is a fun way to fish, but anglers can expect to have fishless days. The most successful flyfishermen working the upper river sections in and around channels find that sighting fish is a definite plus. If one considers shad fishing to be similar to Atlantic salmon fishing—working hard for a few nice fish—then a trip to the Delaware for shad alone is well worth the effort.

Shad cannot really be considered warmwater fish, since they prefer temperatures in the mid-50s to mid-60s. If water temperature exceeds that in the later part of the season (late May and June), fish early and late, although fishing after dark hasn't met with much success. Spend the daytime hours prowling for bass or muskie when the water warms up.

Wading upstream from the Water Gap is difficult on this large river. A wading staff and common sense are necessary. A guide who can take you to the areas around the channels is the best bet. Most shad are caught closer to the top than many believe; fish the fly 3 feet or more above the river bottom.

It's easy to get information on the shad run by calling the Delaware Shad Hotline to find out where the major run is occurring and what water conditions are like. The numbers are 610-954-0577 or 610-954-0578—don't leave home without this important information.

Stripers, Muskie, and Bass

As warm water becomes prevalent and shad fishing ends, anglers switch to bass fishing using the same techniques as on other bass waters. The best time for bass is from mid-June on.

Muskie are common here and can be found in and around the deeper holes at stream mouths, as well as raiding the shallows during evening hours and again in the morning. Muskie seem to be most active from fall into early winter.

Stripers have become king of the river as pollution cleanup continues. The best action for truly big stripers is the brackish water in the lower portion of Delaware County, but large stripers can now be found throughout the entire river system, at least as far north as the Water Gap. How big? The state record fish is 53 pounds, 13 ounces set in 1989 by Donald Clark, who swore he had hooked larger fish that got away.

With so much variety, the Delaware is a river that shouldn't be missed.

Delaware River Access Sites

Northampton County – 35 miles
Species: Bass, Muskie, Panfish, Shad, Pickerel

Riverton Access (PFBC); on SR 1004 across the Delaware River from Belvedere, NJ
- Undeveloped

Pennsylvania Power & Light Company Access; from Easton to SR 1004, travel toward Belvedere, N.J., until the signs at junction of T-661, take T-661 to access area
- Open to public
- Moderate draft fishing boats, sailboats, and recreational runabout boats
- Recreational boating and fishing
- Beach-type ramp
- Limited Parking

Sandts Eddy Access (PFBC); SR 611 five miles north of Easton
- Parking for 50 cars
- Shallow draft, lightweight fishing boats, canoes, and inflatables
- Boat fishing and float trips
- Surfaced ramp

Easton Access; in Easton on SR 611 at confluence of Delaware and Lehigh Rivers
- Limited parking
- Shallow draft, lightweight fishing boats, canoes, and inflatables
- Boat fishing and float trips
- Surfaced ramp

Delaware Canal; Roosevelt State Park, from Easton to county line at Raubsville; parallels SR 611 along entire length
- Canoes and other hand carry boats only
- No motors permitted
- Float trips
- Beach-type ramp
- Parking available

Bucks County – 60 miles
Species: Bass, Muskie, Panfish, Shad, Pickerel

Riegelsville Access; Intersection of SR 212 and 611
- Allows for easy float to Upper Black Eddy or Tinicum Park ramps
- No launch ramp
- Parking limited to those using the canal
- Hand carry boats only

Upper Black Eddy Access (PFBC); SR 32 just below the bridge
crossing to Milford, New Jersey
- Moderate draft fishing boats, sailboats, and recreational runabout boats
- Boat fishing and recreation
- Surfaced ramp
- Parking available

Tinicum Access (Bucks County Department of Parks and Recreation);
SR 32 at Erwinna
- Moderate draft fishing boats, sailboats, and recreational runabout boats
- Boat fishing and recreation
- Surfaced ramp
- Parking available

Yardley Access (PFBC); River Road, SR 32 at north end of Yardley borough
- Moderate draft fishing boats, sailboats, and recreational runabout boats
- Boat fishing and recreation
- Surfaced ramp
- Parking available

Delaware Canal Access (DER); 423 acres along 60 miles, located
in Roosevelt State Park between Easton and Bristol
- Canoes and other hand-carry boats only
- Recreational boating
- Beach-type ramp
- Parking available

Pennsbury Manor (PFBC, undeveloped), adjacent to Pennsbury Manor
Historical Site; Syefert and Wright, 5th Avenue, Croydon
- Moderate draft fishing boats, sailboats, and recreational runabout boats
- Recreational boating and fishing
- Charge for launching

Neshaminy Creek, Jack's Marina; 1057 Totem Road, Cornwells Heights
- Moderate draft fishing boats, sailboats, and recreational runabout boats
- Recreational boating and fishing
- Surfaced ramp
- Charge for launching

Neshaminy State Park (PFBC); 4th Avenue, Croydon
- Unlimited size boats
- Recreational boating
- Surfaced ramp
- Parking available

Neshaminy State Park Marina (DER); near mouth of Neshaminy Creek
at Croydon on SR 13
- Unlimited size boats
- Recreational boating
- Surfaced ramp
- Parking available

Ed's Boat Yard; 900 Haunted Lane, Cornwells Heights
- Deep draft, high-powered recreational boats
- Recreational boating
- Charge for launching
- Surfaced ramp
- Parking available

Station Avenue Access (Bucks County Parks); Station Avenue in Andalusia
- Deep draft, high-powered recreational boats
- Recreational boating
- Surfaced ramp
- Parking available

Delaware River Tidewater Access (see also Delaware County)
Andalusia, adjacent to Mud Island; Salem Harbor
- Stone and dirt ramp, plus travel lift, charge for launching
- Unlimited size boats
- Recreational boating
- Parking available

Philadelphia County – 18 miles
Species: Bass, Muskie, Panfish, Pickerel, Rock Fish (Striped Bass)

Tacony Access (PFBC); located at Milnor Street and Princeton Avenue;
take Cottman Avenue exit off I-95 to State Road, then to Milnor Street;
located just north of the Tacony-Palmyra bridge
- Concrete launch ramp with adjacent parking lot
- Moderate draft fishing boats, sailboats, and recreational runabout boats
- Recreational boating and fishing
- Surfaced ramp
- Parking available

Frankford Arsenal Access (PFBC); located in the 5600 block of Tacony Street; from the south, take I-95 north to the Bridge Street exit, then Tacony Street north; from the north, take I-95 to the Cottman Avenue exit, then State Road south; State Road turns into Tacony Street; area is south of the Tacony-Palmyra Bridge and north of the Betsy Ross Bridge
- Features a six-lane launch ramp, two floating docks, and large parking lot
- Deep draft, high-powered recreational boats
- Recreational boating
- Surfaced ramp
- Parking available

Linden Access; Linden Avenue and 9100 North Delaware Avenue, owned and maintained by city of Philadelphia
- Three-lane concrete launch ramp with adjacent parking lot
- One floating dock for loading and unloading
- Moderate draft fishing boats, sailboats, and recreational runabout boats
- Recreational boating and fishing
- Surfaced ramp
- Parking available

Delaware County – 12 miles
Species: Bass, Panfish, Pickerel, Muskie, Walleye, Shad, Hybrid Bass

Island Marine; Wanamaker Avenue, Essington
- Ramp and lift available, charge for launching
- Recreational boating PCGO62
- Unlimited size boats
- Parking available
- Gas and oil available

Delaware River Tidewater Anchorage Marina; 401 South Swarthmore Avenue, Ridley Park Ramp (SPCGO64)
- Unlimited size boats, charge for launching
- Recreational boating and fishing
- Surfaced ramp
- Parking available
- Gas and oil available

Delaware River Access; at foot of Flower Street off SR 322 at Commodore Barry Bridge in Chester
- Surface ramp
- Parking available

SCHUYLKILL RIVER

The Schuylkill is the largest tributary of the Delaware River. It changes in size, width, and complexity as it weaves its way over a course of 125 miles through southeastern Pennsylvania. The east and west branches come together at the town of Schuylkill Haven. The source of the east (main) branch is a series of springs in the hills of Tuscarora near the town of Tamaqua.

The Schuylkill has been passed over by fishermen for years due to severe pollution. Mine acid drainage had yellowed its water, poor agricultural practices had turned stretches chocolate, and of course, the pollution at Philadelphia had kept migratory and anadromous fish from running the river.

While many an angler might not change with time, a river can and, more often than might seem possible, does. The Schuylkill has been on the mend for more than 25 years, and the result could be considered nothing less than spectacular—but remember, I said it is on the mend, not completely cured.

Just below Fairmount Dam, located within Philadelphia's city limits, striped bass and American shad gather to find the passageway upriver. Since this area is not very esthetically pleasing, anglers pretty much stay away. From here to where it empties into the Delaware River, the Schuylkill is capable of offering some exciting fishing from May through June.

A nice smallmouth. (Photo by Bob Clouser)

Schuylkill River
Headwaters to Reading

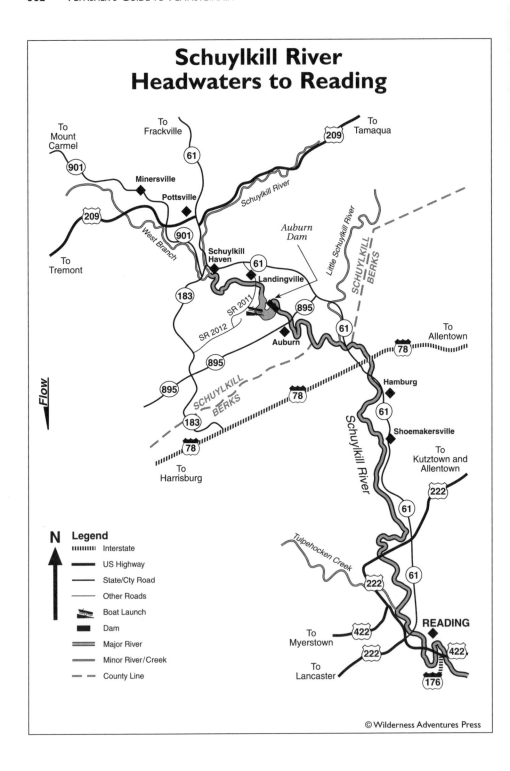

To Mount Carmel

To Frackville

To Tamaqua

209

61

901

Minersville

Pottsville

Schuylkill River

209

West Branch

901

Auburn Dam

Little Schuylkill River

SCHUYLKILL

BERKS

To Tremont

Schuylkill Haven

61

Landingville

183

SR 2011

SR 2012

895

61

Auburn

To Allentown

78

895

SCHUYLKILL

BERKS

78

Hamburg

Flow

895

183

61

78

Shoemakersville

To Harrisburg

Schuylkill River

To Kutztown and Allentown

222

61

Tulpehocken Creek

N

Legend

⊪⊪⊪⊪⊪ Interstate

—— US Highway

—— State/Cty Road

— Other Roads

Boat Launch

Dam

Major River

Minor River/Creek

— — County Line

222

61

READING

To Myerstown

422

222

422

To Lancaster

176

© Wilderness Adventures Press

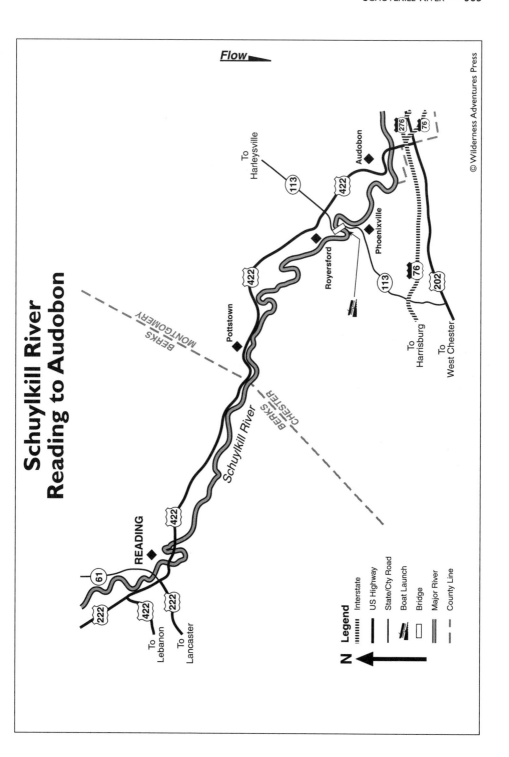

Schuylkill River
Reading to Audobon

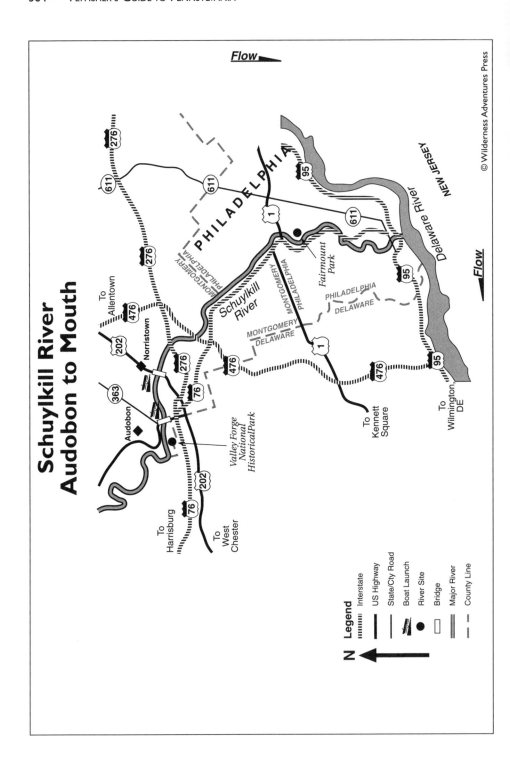

Schuylkill River
Audobon to Mouth

It takes a stiff leader to turn over a popping bug.

As the river flows from the northwest, it becomes a good smallmouth fishery, and most areas can be waded. However, keep in mind that there are nine dams on the river's course, and the river varies with each and every one. There is plenty to explore on this river that offers urban fishing close to home as well as rural getaways. As warmwater flyfishing grows in popularity, the Schuylkill will attract more and more interest. It is a warmwater fisherman's delight, offering opportunities for striper and shad as well as bass and muskie.

The Schuylkill offers good smallmouth flyfishing, with bass averaging a little less than they do on the Susquehanna or neighboring Delaware River. Smallmouth fishing extends throughout the length of the river. One of the river's largest attractions for smallmouth flyfishers is the whitefly hatch that comes off in late July and August. On backwaters in the evening, don't be surprised to find channel catfish willing to take a whitefly, as well.

This is also one of the finest rivers in the state for muskie, especially in Schuylkill County, where purebred muskie have been stocked for years. With its high numbers of muskie above Reading, flyfishers can be assured they are fishing in muskie water. Getting one to take a fly and bringing it to net is another matter. However, the right flies and steel leaders or heavy shock tippets of mono should bring a muskie or two to hand.

Starting in Schuylkill County in the Tuscarora hills near the town of Tamaqua, US 209 follows the river southwest into Pottsville. At SR 61, the river turns south through Schuylkill Haven. From Schuylkill Haven, the river winds its way southeast going

An angler hooks into a smallmouth.

through the town of Auburn and meets with the Little Schuylkill in the Blue Mountains at Port Clinton. From Port Clinton, the river flows south, crossing into Berks County, paralleled by SR 61 down into and through Reading. Below Reading, it takes a hairpin loop north, then south, and then settles on a southeast course along SR 724 crossing into Chester County near Pottstown. It continues southeast along SR 724 into Phoenixville to SR 23.

Continuing alongside SR 23, the Schuylkill flows east into Montgomery County and through Norristown, where it turns southeast. At Conshohocken, the river flows alongside I-76 and forms the Montgomery/Philadelphia County border. Turning south, I-76 continues to run next to the river into Philadelphia County proper until it empties into the Delaware River.

Waders are useful for fishing most of the river. It isn't all that deep, but some portions can be navigated in shallow draft boats.

Schuylkill River Access Sites

Schuylkill County – 10 miles

Auburn Dam Access (PFBC); located on Schuylkill River, south of Landingville between Schuylkill Haven and Auburn. Take SR 2011 from SR 61 near Orwigsburg, proceed south through Landingville, 2.5 miles to ramp
- Moderate draft fishing boats
- Beach-type ramp
- Parking available

Berks County – 37 miles

Chester County

Phoenixville Access (PFBC); off SR 113 bridge
- Shallow draft, lightweight fishing boats, canoes, and inflatables
- Surfaced ramp
- Parking available

Montgomery County – 22 miles

Valley Forge Park Access; near Betzwood on SR 363, at Flat Rock Dam in Lower Marion Township
- Shallow draft, lightweight fishing boats, canoes, and inflatables
- Surfaced ramp
- Parking available

Norristown Access; located at the foot of Haws Avenue
- Shallow draft, lightweight fishing boats, canoes, and inflatables
- Surfaced ramp
- Parking available

Philadelphia County – 15 miles

Strawberry Mansion Bridge (Fairmount Park Commission); located on Kelly Drive at the Strawberry Mansion Bridge; owned by the city of Philadelphia and maintained by the Fairmount Park Commission
- Shallow draft, lightweight fishing boats, canoes, and inflatables
- Wooden boat ramp
- Parking available

LAKE WALLENPAUPACK

Lake Wallenpaupack borders Pike and Wayne Counties and is located in the center of the Pocono Mountains. It was built by the Pennsylvania Power and Light Co. in 1925 for electric generation.

The first time I visited this lake I was ill prepared for what was in store. I arrived in the afternoon with two rods, one an 8-weight and the other a 9-weight. I hadn't brought heavy mono for shock tippets or wire because I was in search of bass the next morning. Toward evening, as I sat in front of the fireplace, strong winds and rain blew in and the water pounded against the shore. Afraid that the whipped up water would ruin my fishing the next day, I donned my raincoat and trod down the shoreline to try my luck in the storm. I wore deck shoes that were more suited for a boat deck than a muddy, rocky shoreline. As it is with so many inveterate flyfishers, a swirl in the backwater lily pads was all that it took to make me forget the conditions. Another roll and I knew that I had a muskie before me in the tangle of lily pads and weedbeds.

Landing the large fish would not be easy; maybe impossible, but that only made it more interesting. I could tell that this spot wasn't heavily fished—it was too shallow for boats and the mud bottom wouldn't support a wading angler. Such conditions are favorable for holding and retaining fish. It was the muskie's dinnertime, and I'm sure

A well-rounded selection of bass, muskie, and northern pike flies.

it had no concern about being disturbed. I found a brightly feathered yellow streamer and tied a 4/0 hook directly to 10-pound test.

Once again, the muskie rolled through the lily pads, and I rolled a cast into a slight opening ahead of it. I stripped the line in short 1-inch jerks, and the muskie rolled and took the fly. It ran through the pads and into open water where, with little thought, I waded in after it. It was a good plan—getting to the edge of the lily pads would give me a chance at landing the fish...if the tippet held. I ignored the fact that I had left one shoe 10 steps behind and that I was knee deep in mud—the fish was losing and the tippet holding. Then the fish ran through a bunch of pads, decorating my line and leader like a Christmas tree. I lost the fish and almost allof the leader...and I lost three more after that.

However, despite the "what-the-heck-happened-to-you" questions back at the cabin the next day, I enjoyed superb smallmouth fishing the next day, and that evening we watched a local expert land a nice striped bass on a 10-weight outfit. If that's not enough to make you want to wet a line here, the largest brown trout taken from the lake weighed 17 pounds, not bad for a state where the record holder is 17 pounds, 14 ounces.

The lake encompasses 5,700 acres, and the fishing ranges from shorelines filled with weedbeds to rocky and boulder strewn. Smallmouth fishing is excellent, muskie fishing is good, and the chance of hooking into a striper is good as well—30 pounds and up have been reported. The PFBC has been stocking purebred stripers into the lake for over 10 years. Some northerns inhabit the lake as do pickerel, perch, bluegills, and crappie. The better fishing is in spring and fall. Trout love the shoreline haunts then, especially near any one of the lake's many feeder streams—and these are not stocked trout, by the way. Bass fishing is good throughout the summer, but better after Labor Day when recreational boats retire from the lake until the next year. Recreational boats have a tendency to take over the lake during summer.

Striped bass fishing, either by wading or by boat, is best at night during the summer and again in the fall when boat traffic slows down. Stripers haunt the shallows in the evening and early morning during the fall but love the deeper water close to the dam.

Trout are not an everyday occurrence here, and this shouldn't be considered a prime destination for trout anglers. However, patience pays off in larger trout than are normally found throughout the state.

Muskie fishing is best later in the year, from October until ice-over. But muskie can be found raiding the shallows at any time of the year.

I like an 8-weight for bass and a10-weight outfit for stripers and muskies on this lake. A 6-weight is ideal for chasing trout, panfish, or crappie, and I prefer longer rods, but anything from an 8-foot on up will do. The lake is easily found along SR 507. See the warmwater fly box section for fly patterns.

Lake Wallenpaupack Access

PP&L has established and maintains four lakeshore campsites, each with its own launching area, parking, sanitary and laundry facilities. Three such campsites are located off SR 507 in Pike County. They include Ledgedale at the extreme south end of the lake; Wilsonville, at the northeast end; and Ironwood Point, northeast of Ledgedale. The fourth area is in Wayne County, off SR 590 in Caffrey Park.

- Deep draft, high-powered recreational boats
- Gas and oil available
- Launch charges apply
- Surfaced ramp
- Parking available

In addition to the PP&L sites, there are also commercial public launches located along the 52 miles of shoreline, including:

Mountain Bay, White Beauty View, Seely's, and Walt's Landing

- Deep draft, high-powered recreational boats
- Gas and oil available
- Launch charges apply
- Beach-type ramp
- Parking available

BLUE MARSH LAKE

Located near the town of Bernville in Berks County, Blue Marsh Lake is a large Army Corps of Engineers project that encompasses 1,150 acres. The lake is rather difficult to fish, although the species mix is interesting and diverse enough to attract any flyfisher's interest. Until recently, most flyfishers dismissed the idea of fishing large impoundments such as this—and a flyfisher climbing into a boat with nothing but a fly rod and vest crammed with odd-looking patterns will still get some strange looks from other anglers.

Blue Marsh Lake's two most sought after species are largemouth bass and stripers that were planted here in the hope that they would add heft to the weight of inland fish. Stripers found in Pennsylvania's stillwaters have never been a pushovers, and although they occasionally feed on the surface, that is the exception rather than the rule. The more serious striper fishermen fish at night, and that only adds to the challenge of casting a fly line from a boat more suitable for a chairbound angler.

Whenever I fish an impoundment in search of bass, I begin during the late afternoon hours, casting into the shallows wherever structure might be found. It could be a patch of lily pads, a boulder-strewn shoreline with a steep dropoff, or something as simple as a piece of woody debris. The shoreline holds a lot of information about a lake. When fishing before the cooler evening hours, make note of the areas in which fish were caught and return later in the evening.

The shoreline should bring to hand a lot of small bass—a sign that the lake is doing well in recruitment of year classes. You may also be surprised at how many large bass come to hand—a good 5-pound largemouth took a small yellow popper here on a July afternoon when the sun was bright. However, this lake does not provide a lot of lakeside canopy, and the majority of fish are taken from 7pm to dark or during the early morning hours before water skiers and jet-skis start combing the water. Schedule a trip before July 4 and again after Labor Day when fishing can be superb due to less recreational use of the lake. Blue Marsh produces some excellent bass and an occasional striper.

I prefer to fish popping bugs constructed of cork or closed cell foam. The colors can vary, but all anglers should carry a selection of bugs ranging in color from white to chartreuse. That means yellow, black, and green. Also, make sure that your fly box includes sliders to represent minnows and other forms of baitfish as well as conclave-faced poppers that attract larger bass. When working shorelines with steep dropoffs, streamers with lead eyes are an excellent option. Bob Clouser of Middletown has designed an entire series of Clouser minnows that work for all species of fish from stripers to smallmouths. Leadeyes coupled with a sinktip line help probe the dropoffs that occur close to the shoreline on this lake.

Two rigs are necessary—one for stripers and another for small and largemouth bass. A striper rod should be at least 9 feet in length and carry a 10- to 12-weight line. I prefer a fast action rod that can deliver the goods from a long distance. Double hauls are a necessity when idling a boat on the far outside edge of a school. Saltwater anglers

A smallmouth that took a popping bug.

have the edge in experience with casting and turning over large flies. My choice for bass would be a 9- to 9½-foot rod designed to carry an 8-weight line. The line weight is needed to turn over the wind resistant bugs and flies that are needed here.

Extra spools to complement one loaded with an intermediate sinking line might be needed. I have found that steelhead lines that sink the first 30 feet at a rapid rate work better than any others. Stripping baskets are a wonderful addition on most boats that have more moving and stationary parts than the types of skiffs you will find in the Keys, that are designed specifically for flyfishermen.

It can be difficult to find guides who operate on Pennsylvania's lakes as they are few and far between. Those that do guide on lakes are more likely to cater to bait and spin fishermen.

Blue Marsh Lake has plenty of character, having backwater coves and progressing from a narrow, river-like area upstream to a good-sized lake at the dam. Regulations are for Big Bass, meaning that bass fishing is allowed from January 1 to April 16 and then again on the second Saturday in June until the following mid-April opener that always ends before trout season begins. Minimum size during the open season is 15 inches, and the creel limit is 4 per day. There is a lot of fishing pressure on the state's lakes, so releasing fish is extremely important. Most bass lakes are reproducing and replenishing the lake on their own, although stocking is done to give lakes a jump start or to improve sagging year classes.

I have found Blue Marsh to fish extremely well, and that means an abundance of bass as well as some very large bass that bring great excitement. I have also found Blue Marsh to be a lake that runs hot and cold, and the fishing here can be disrupted at times by recreational boaters. If you fish the lake during summer, the upper reaches are the best bet for bass, and stripers are most likely to be found close to the dam after dark.

The lake is located along SR 183 between Bernville and Reading, and it has easily found access areas—two owned by the Corps of Engineers and one by the PFBC. All have paved ramps and facilities, and a swimming area is maintained by the Corps. This lake allows large boats with unlimited horsepower.

Bass Flies
- Popping bugs #4-8 in yellow, black, green, chartreuse, and white
- Clouser or lead-eye minnows #2-8
- Crayfish patterns of your choosing #2-8, 3X long, green or brown back
- Lefty's Deceiver #2-8, 3X long
- Comet #4 and 6, 3X long, orange

Striper Flies
- Lefty's Deceiver #2/0-2, white with red collar
- Clouser's Minnow #2/0-2, white over red
- Glass Minnow #1/0-2

Bass also feed on hatches of mayflies and caddis. For a complete hatch chart of this area see Tulpehocken Creek.

West Branch Susquehanna River

The upper reaches of the West Branch Susquehanna serve as an example of what can happen to a beautiful river when it becomes so polluted with acid mine drainage that it might never recover. At this point, even though efforts are being made to clean it up, the West Branch Susquehanna will not return to a clean, pure waterway in our lifetime, if at all. While canoers and kayakers use this part of the river for recreation, it isn't a worthy fishery.

But rather than dwell on the negative, let's concentrate on the sections of river that are fishable. Where clean water from Bald Eagle Creek enters, the fishery recovers nicely near Lock Haven in Clinton County. Bald Eagle's high alkalinity neutralizes the acid mine drainage that damages the river above this point.

From this point to where it joins the North Branch at Sunbury, the fishing becomes consistent. While it isn't large water here, it is large enough for smallmouth and muskie fishing. A small dam backs up enough water to allow recreational boating, and a warmwater fishery begins in the heart of trout country.

The combination fishery is established here, where a good bass is in the 17-inch range. As it flows northeast toward Williamsport, the river's dual nature becomes more established. Residents and visitors enjoy this marriage of trout and bass water, and Williamsport is definitely a flyfishing-oriented community.

Regulations allow bass to be harvested at 12 inches rather than the 15 inches required below the Fibradam at Sunbury. Many who fish this part of the river feel that a higher minimum would improve this section tremendously. The average fish taken here is between 9 and 12 inches, a lower average size than below the Fibradam.

The river is a wonderful mixture of pools and riffles with the large boulders and shelves that are so characteristic of the entire river. Bass are found in the abundant pocket water created by all the boulders, as well as in deeper pools as summer progresses.

Fishing can be done by wading or from a canoe or shallow draft johnboat, and with so much water to cover, a guide is highly recommended. This is a delightful stretch of river without the pressure that the lower reaches encounter. There may be fewer large fish, but smallmouth of all sizes are a wonderful fly rod fish.

The same tactics and gear apply as on the main stem, although lighter lines can be used here. Trout fishing equipment will work for most fishing situations, as much of this river is sheltered, unlike the larger waters below the Fibradam, where casting under windy conditions is a concern.

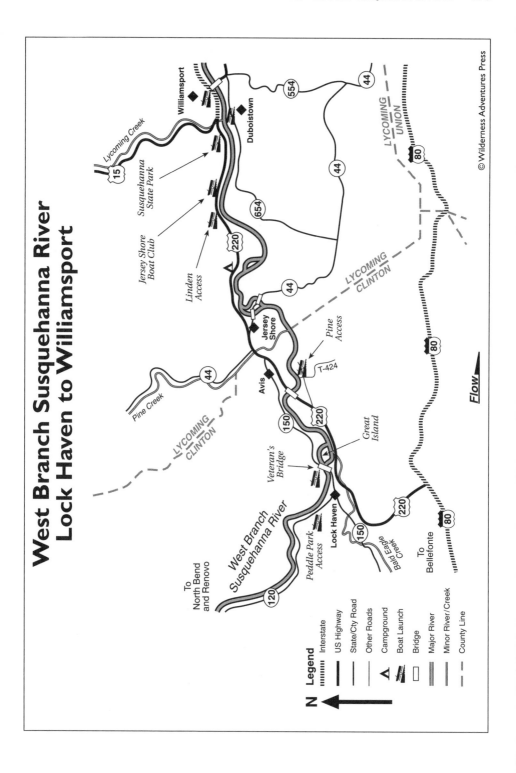

West Branch Susquehanna River
Lock Haven to Williamsport

Williamsport

Duboistown

Lycoming Creek

15

554

44

LYCOMING
UNION

80

© Wilderness Adventures Press

Susquehanna
State Park

Jersey Shore
Boat Club

Linden
Access

220

44

654

LYCOMING
CLINTON

Jersey
Shore

Pine
Access

T-424

80

Pine Creek

44

Avis

150

220

Great
Island

LYCOMING
CLINTON

80

Flow

West Branch
Susquehanna River

Veteran's
Bridge

Lock Haven

150

Bald Eagle Creek

To
Bellefonte

220

80

To
North Bend
and Renovo

Peddle Park
Access

120

Legend

- Interstate
- US Highway
- State/Cty Road
- Other Roads
- Campground
- Boat Launch
- Bridge
- Major River
- Minor River/Creek
- County Line

N

West Branch Susquehanna River
Williamsport to Susquehanna Confluence

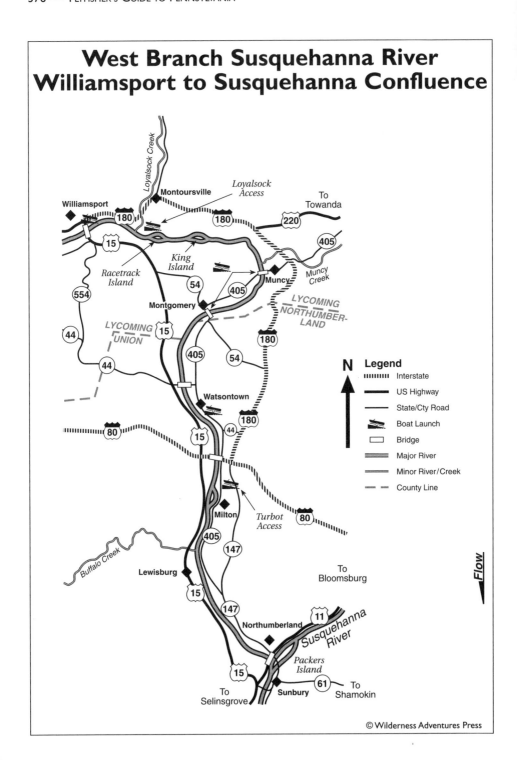

Legend

- ‖‖‖‖‖ Interstate
- ▬▬ US Highway
- ── State/Cty Road
- ⇜ Boat Launch
- ▭ Bridge
- ▬▬ Major River
- ══ Minor River/Creek
- ─ ─ County Line

© Wilderness Adventures Press

West Branch Susquehanna River Access Sites

Clinton County

North Bend Access (PFBC); turn at Four Seasons Motel in North Bend off SR 120
- Undeveloped access for canoes and other handcarry boats only
- Float trips
- Peddle Park Access (PFBC) - SR 120, one mile north of Lock Haven
- Shallow draft, lightweight fishing boats, canoes, and inflatables
- Boat fishing and float trips
- Surfaced ramp
- Parking available

Lock Haven Access; located on the north side of Veterans Bridge in Lock Haven, along SR 120
- No horsepower restrictions
- Moderate draft fishing boats, sailboats, and recreational runabout boats
- Recreational boating
- Surfaced ramp
- Parking available

Pine Access (PFBC); north end of T-424 off L.R. 18013, 1.5 miles shouth of McEllhattan
- Shallow draft, lightweight fishing boats, canoes, and inflatables
- Boat fishing and float trips
- Beach-type ramp
- Parking available

Lycoming County – 40 miles
Species: Bass, Muskie, Northern Pike, Panfish, Pickerel

Linden Access (PFBC); three miles west of Williamsport on US 220
- Moderate draft fishing boats, sailboats, and recreational runabout boats
- Recreational boating and fishing
- Surfaced ramp
- Parking available

Jersey Shore Boat Club; at Angler's Club, 3 miles west of Williamsport on US 220
- Moderate draft fishing boats, sailboats and recreational runabout boats; charge for launching
- Recreational boating and fishing
- Beach-type ramp
- Parking available

Susquehanna State Park Access (DER); access to river (lake) created
by Hepburn Street Dam; maintained by City of Williamsport
- Moderate draft fishing boats, sailboats, and recreational runabout boats
- Recreational boating and fishing
- Surfaced ramp
- Parking available

West Branch Motor Club; Duboistown at foot of Summer Street, off SR 654
- Deep draft, high-powered recreational boats; charge for launching
- Recreational boating and
- Gas and oil available
- Surfaced ramp
- Parking available

Williamsport; at Arch Street Bridge, north shore of river, US 15 or 220
- Moderate draft fishing boats, sailboats, and recreational runabout boats
- Recreational bating and fishing
- Beach-type ramp
- Parking available

Loyalsock Access; Loyalsock Township off Canfield Lane
- Undeveloped

Muncy Access; off SR 405 at West Branch Susquehanna River bridge,
3 miles south of Muncy
- Shallow draft, lightweight fishing boats, canoes, and inflatables
- Boat fishing and float trips
- Beach-type ramp
- Parking available

Montgomery Access (PFBC); SR 405 at Montgomery Park
- Shallow draft, lightweight fishing boats, canoes, and inflatables
- Boat fishing and float trips
- Surfaced ramp
- Parking available

Union County – 22 miles
Species: Bass, Muskie, Panfish, Pickerel, Walleye

Northumberland County – 20 miles
Species: Bass, Muskie, Panfish, Pickerel, Suckers, Walleye

Watsontown Access (PFBC); in Watsontown, at bridge on West Brimmer Avenue
- Shallow draft, lightweight fishing boats, canoes, and inflatables
- Boat fishing and float trips
- Beach-type ramp
- Parking available

Turbot (Milton) Access (PFBC); approximately two miles north of Milton off SR 405
- Shallow draft, lightweight fishing boats, canoes, and inflatables
- Boat fishing and float trips
- Beach-type ramp
- Parking available

NORTH BRANCH SUSQUEHANNA RIVER

Much like trout water, the river produces smaller fish in the areas above the Fibradam than below it. That is not to say that large fish cannot be taken in these river sections, for they are, but to a trout fisherman, this is more like a native brook trout stream, smaller in size, with less food, and thus smaller fish. No one is certain what effect the 15- inch minimum size requirement, in place from the Fibradam downstream, will have on this lengthy river section, but the results should be interesting.

The mainstem, referred to as the North Branch, runs into the state in Susquehanna County and then flows back into New York before entering the state again in Bradford County. Then it flows through Wyoming, Luzerne, Lackawanna, Columbia, Montour, and into Northumberland County to join the West Branch at the Sunbury Pool at Sunbury.

Smaller waters, for the most part, require shallow draft boats. The most common boat in use is a johnboat with a 10-horespower motor or a larger jet drive.

There are small impoundments along the river's course that little affect the river, the more important diversions will be covered in this book. It is a warmwater fishery that covers some 55-miles above the Fibradam at Sunbury.

This river provides excellent canoe tripping for the flyfisherman and has far less anglers than does the lower reaches under the Big Bass regulations. However, this river section should not be lightly dismissed. It offers muskie, some decent hatches, and good bass fishing with the possibility of taking a 20-inch plus smallmouth.

Pennsylvania's number one smallmouth river, the Susquehanna.

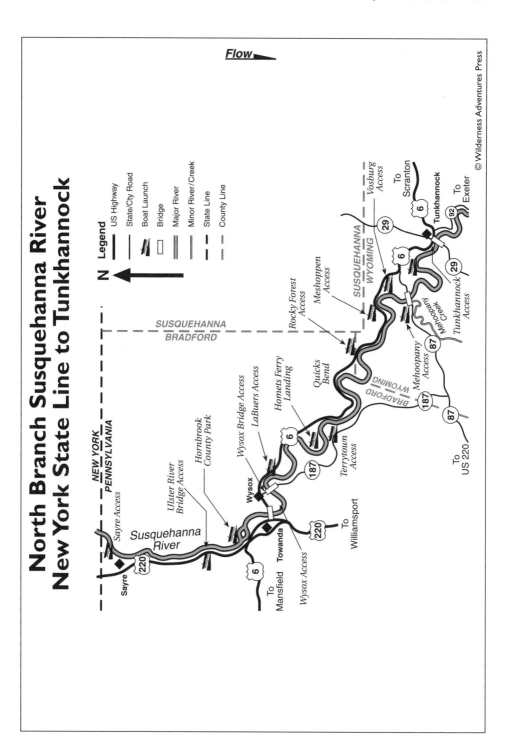

North Branch Susquehanna River
New York State Line to Tunkhannock

Flow

© Wilderness Adventures Press

Legend
N
US Highway
State/Cty Road
Boat Launch
Bridge
Major River
Minor River/Creek
State Line
County Line

To Scranton
To Exeter
Tunkhannock
92
6
29
Vosburg Access
29
SUSQUEHANNA
WYOMING
6
Meshoppen Access
Mehoopany Creek
Tunkhannock Access
87
Mehoopany Access
Rocky Forest Access
SUSQUEHANNA
BRADFORD
187
87
BRADFORD
WYOMING
To US 220
Quicks Bend
Homets Ferry Landing
Terrytown Access
LaBuers Access
Wysox Bridge Access
6
187
Hornbrook County Park
Wysox
NEW YORK
PENNSYLVANIA
Ulster River Bridge Access
220
To Williamsport
Towanda
220
To Mansfield
6
Wysox Access
Susquehanna River
Sayre Access
220
Sayre

North Branch Susquehanna River
Below Tunkhannock to Danville

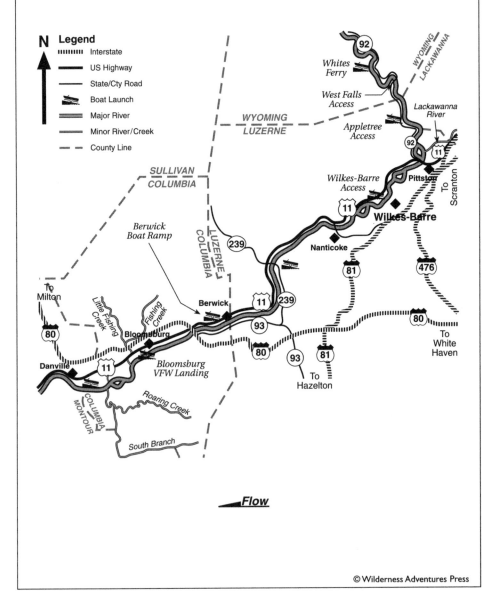

© Wilderness Adventures Press

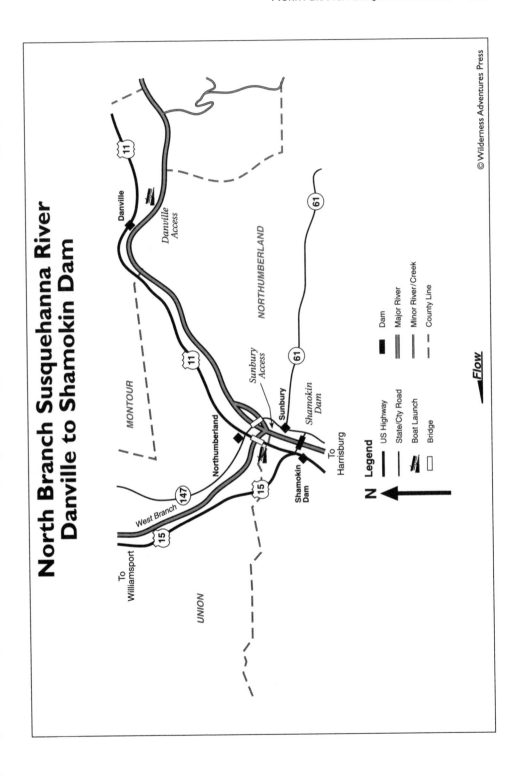

North Branch Susquehanna River
Danville to Shamokin Dam

© Wilderness Adventures Press

Legend

US Highway
State/Cty Road
Boat Launch
Bridge

Dam
Major River
Minor River/Creek
County Line

N

Flow

A Susquehanna River smallmouth.

Bass are found in the pocket waters and along the shelves that are an integral part of the river, and in the deeper pools as summer progresses. This is a beautiful river section and cannot be ignored. This area is for those who want a slow scenic trip with plenty of smallmouth along the way and the occasional muskie that likes the deeper holes created by a long list of feeder streams along the river's course.

Flies and tactics addressed under Susquehanna apply here.

North Branch Susquehanna River Access Sites

Susquehanna County – 15 miles
Species: Bass, Muskie, Panfish, Pickerel, Walleye

Oakland Access (PFBC); Two miles north of Oakland on SR 92
- Shallow draft, lightweight fishing boats, canoes, and inflatables
- Boat fishing and float trips
- Beach-type ramp
- Parking available

Great Bend Access (PFBC); take US 11 or I-81 to Hallstead, then east on SR 1010 about 5 miles
- Shallow draft, lightweight fishing boats, canoes, and inflatables
- Boat fishing and float trips
- Beach-type ramp
- Parking available

Great Bend Boro (PFBC); Boro of Great Bend, east end of Spring Street
- Undeveloped

Bradford County – 46 miles
Species: Bass, Muskie, Panfish Pickerel, Suckers, Walleye

Sayre Access (PFBC); two miles northeast of Sayre on SR 1043
- Shallow draft, lightweight fishing boats, canoes, and inflatables
- Boat fishing and float trips
- Surfaced ramp
- Parking available

Ulster River Bridge; at village of Ulster on US 220
- Shallow draft, lightweight fishing boats, canoes, and inflatables
- Boat fishing and float trips
- Beach-type ramp
- Parking available

Hornbrook County Park; two miles north of Towanda, east side of river
- Shallow draft, lightweight fishing boats, canoes, and inflatables
- Boat fishing and float trips
- Beach-type ramp
- Parking available

Wysox Access (PFBC); two miles south of Towanda
- Shallow draft, lightweight fishing boats, canoes and inflatables
- Boat fishing and float trips
- Beach-type ramp
- Parking available

Wysox Bridge Access; at Wysox, SR 187
- Shallow draft, lightweight fishing boats, canoes, and inflatables
- Boat fishing and float trips
- Beach-type ramp
- Parking available

LaBuers Access; one and one half miles south of Wysox bridge on SR 187
- Canoes and other handcarry boats only
- Boat fishing and float trips
- Beach-type ramp
- Parking available

Bradford County Outboard Motor Club; SR 187
- Moderate draft fishing boats, sailboats, and recreational runabout boats
- Boat fishing and recreation
- Beach-type ramp
- Charge for launching

Homets Ferry Landing; 5 miles north of Wyalusing off US 6 and SR 409, east side of river
- Shallow draft, lightweight fishing boats, canoes, and inflatables
- Boat fishing and float trips
- Beach-type ramp
- Parking available

Terrytown Access (PFBC); at Terrytown on SR 187
- Shallow draft, lightweight fishing boats, canoes, and inflatables
- Boat fishing and float trips
- Surfaced ramp
- Parking available

Wyoming County – 39 miles
Species: Bass, Muskie, Panfish, Walleye

Rocky Forest; US 6 to Laceyville, west on SR 4006
- Shallow draft, lightweight fishing boats, canoes, and inflatables
- Boat fishing and float trips
- Beach-type ramp
- Parking available

Meshoppen Access; off US 6
- Shallow draft, lightweight fishing boats, canoes, and inflatables
- Boat fishing and float trips
- Beach-type ramp
- Parking available

Vosburg; US 6 to Russell Hill, west on T-506
- Shallow draft, lightweight fishing boats, canoes, and inflatables; charge for launching
- Boat fishing and float trips
- Beach-type ramp
- Parking available

Mehoopany; SR 87
- Shallow draft, lightweight fishing boats, canoes, and inflatables; charge for launching
- Boat fishing and float trips
- Beach-type ramp
- Parking available

Tunkhannock Access (PFBC); on River Street (SR 29)
- Suitable for small boats only
- Shallow draft, lightweight fishing boats, canoes, and inflatables
- Boat fishing and float trips
- Surfaced ramp
- Parking available

Whites Ferry (PFBC); six miles south of Tunkhannock
- Undeveloped

West Falls Access (PFBC); one block south of SR 92 bridge on River Road, in village of West Falls
- Shallow draft, lightweight fishing boats, canoes, and inflatables
- Boat fishing and float trips
- Beach-type ramp
- Parking available

Luzerne County – 42 miles
Species: Bass, Muskie, Panfish, Walleye

Appletree Access (PFBC); on SR 92, six miles north of Pittston bridge
- Shallow draft, lightweight fishing boats, canoes, and inflatables
- Boat fishing and float trips
- Surfaced ramp
- Parking available

Wilkes-Barre Access; at Market Street bridge in Wilkes-Barre
- Shallow draft, lightweight fishing boats, canoes, and inflatables
- Boat fishing and float trips
- Surfaced ramp
- Parking available

Columbia County – 24 miles
Species: Bass, Muskie, Panfish, Pickerel, Walleye

Berwick Boat Ramp; travel south on Warren Street in Berwick to river. Turn right and follow River Road to steel gate, through gate area 100 yards to ramp
  • Shallow draft, lightweight fishing boats, canoes, and inflatables
  • Boat fishing and recreation
  • Beach-type ramp
  • Parking available

Bloomsburg VFW Landing; off US 11
  • Parking for 15 cars
  • Shallow draft, lightweight fishing boats, canoes, and inflatables
  • Boat fishing and recreation
  • Beach-type ramp

Montour County – 10 miles
Species: Bass, Muskie, Panfish, Pickerel, Walleye

Danville Boat Club; at Danville, US 11
  • Charge for launching

Danville Access (PFBC); located 0.5 mile east of Danville on SR 2006 (old US 11)
  • Shallow draft, lightweight fishing boats, canoes, and inflatables
  • Recreational boating and fishing
  • Surfaced ramp
  • Parking available

Northumberland County – 12 miles
Species: Bass, Muskie, Panfish, Pickerel, Walleye

Sunbury Access Area (PFBC); along SR 147 at south end of Sunbury

The Susquehanna River

The Susquehanna is the sixteenth largest river in the United States. Its headwaters are located at Otsego Lake near Cooperstown in central New York state. It flows through New York, Pennsylvania, and Maryland, ending in the Chesapeake Bay at Havre de Grace.

What an amazing smallmouth river! Consider the fact that an estimated 248 miles of the main branch, all considered a warmwater fishery, flow through 10 counties within the state, from the New York state line to the Maryland state line. Add to that the West Branch's 99 miles and the North Branch's 173 miles, and you have one huge watershed. This waterway was made for smallmouth, and flyfishers who enjoy casting dry flies, popping bugs, and streamers to an eager lot of good-sized fish.

The best fishing is found over the 170- mile stretch from the Fibradam (Shamokin Dam) near Sunbury downstream to Holtwood Dam because of the 15-inch minimum size limit imposed on this stretch.

A good friend and fellow flyfisher, Wayne Foust, and I found the river to our liking back in the early 80s. There were few long rods waving over the river then, and bait/spin fishermen laughed at the sight of us casting Gaines poppers to rising fish. But after we had taken a good number of limit-sized bass, the laughter would cease.

The scenic Susquehanna—fish above and below the shelves for smallmouth.

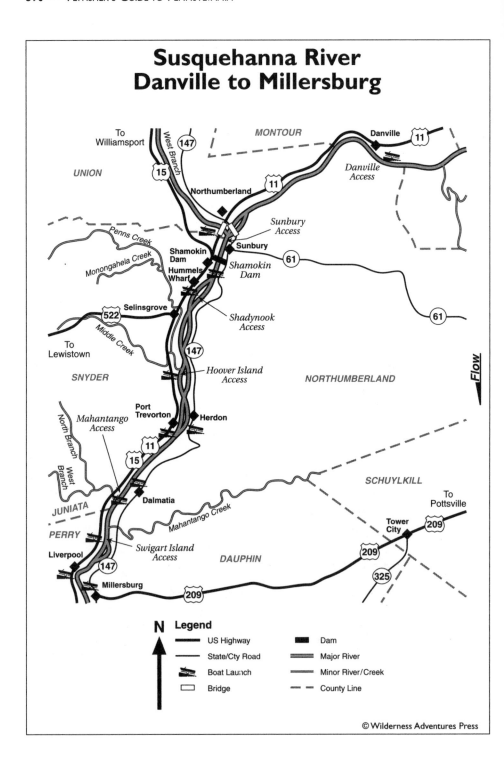

Susquehanna River
Danville to Millersburg

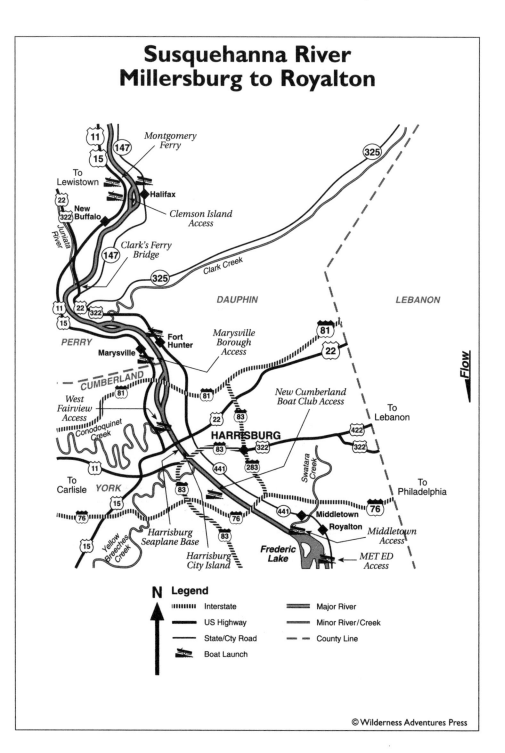

Susquehanna River
Millersburg to Royalton

Montgomery Ferry

To Lewistown

Halifax

New Buffalo

Clemson Island Access

Juniata River

Clark's Ferry Bridge

Clark Creek

DAUPHIN

LEBANON

PERRY

Fort Hunter

Marysville

Marysville Borough Access

CUMBERLAND

West Fairview Access

Conodoquinet Creek

New Cumberland Boat Club Access

To Lebanon

HARRISBURG

To Carlisle

YORK

Swatara Creek

To Philadelphia

Harrisburg Seaplane Base

Yellow Breeches Creek

Harrisburg City Island

Frederic Lake

Middletown

Royalton

Middletown Access

MET ED Access

Flow

N Legend

||||||| Interstate

——— US Highway

——— State/Cty Road

🚤 Boat Launch

═══ Major River

══ Minor River/Creek

– – County Line

© Wilderness Adventures Press

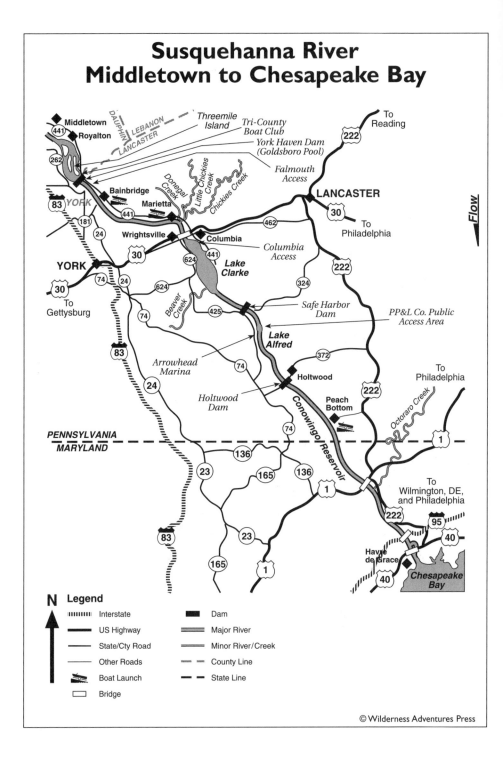

Susquehanna River
Middletown to Chesapeake Bay

Middletown
Royalton
Threemile Island
Tri-County Boat Club
York Haven Dam (Goldsboro Pool)
Falmouth Access
To Reading
Bainbridge
Marietta
LANCASTER
To Philadelphia
Wrightsville
Columbia
Columbia Access
YORK
Lake Clarke
To Gettysburg
Beaver Creek
Safe Harbor Dam
PP&L Co. Public Access Area
Lake Alfred
Arrowhead Marina
Holtwood
Holtwood Dam
To Philadelphia
Peach Bottom
Octoraro Creek
PENNSYLVANIA
MARYLAND
Conowingo Reservoir
To Wilmington, DE, and Philadelphia
Havre de Grace
Chesapeake Bay

Flow

Donegal Creek
Little Chickies Creek
Chickies Creek

N Legend

Interstate	Dam
US Highway	Major River
State/Cty Road	Minor River/Creek
Other Roads	County Line
Boat Launch	State Line
Bridge	

© Wilderness Adventures Press

Bass were not yet a flyfishing attraction in the state, and anglers thought less of them than trout. Anglers loaded their stringers with bass that barely measured over 9 inches in length, and we would sigh nearly every evening when bass of 16 to 20 inches were dragged from the river with a metal stringer attached. Because of its width and length, the Susquehanna was viewed by many as an endless bass factory, much like the West's buffalo herds at the end of the last century. As bass fishing became more popular, anglers started to complain that they were catching nothing but "dinks," which was their name for bass below the legal size. Anglers who had spent a lifetime on the river watched its decline with little hope that things would improve.

As the Army-green johnboats started to crowd the river, more complaints were heard—many of them from the same anglers who had taken a string of 6 bass each time they fished. Many anglers who were unhappy about the river's conditions realized that it would take a concerted effort to get things changed. Thus, the Smallmouth Bass Alliance was formed, and anglers from Maryland and surrounding states quickly joined in their efforts.

Rick Hoopes, who was in charge of the warmwater fishery unit at the time, viewed these events as a window of opportunity to introduce increased size limits. Hoopes' insight and knowledge were instrumental in changing the river's regulations. Between his efforts and those of the Smallmouth Bass Alliance, the river is enjoying increased attention and is being maintained as a premier smallmouth bass fishery. When bringing a smallmouth to hand on the Susquehanna, remember the effort that was put into this river's health and release the fish.

This river is nothing less than amazing, and I have been fortunate enough to cover much of its special regulation areas. In my 20 years of fishing the Susquehanna, my favorite of all warmwaters, I have probably only scratched the surface of its marvels.

The river is complex enough that I highly recommend newcomers hire a guide, especially for those who want to wade. The river bottom is full of ledges, boulders, and deep holes that can surprise the unsuspecting angler. An excellent stretch is located just below the dam at Sunbury downstream to Clark's Ferry Bridge (US 22/322). Access from the west bank is plentiful along US 11/15, which parallels the river its entire length. There are vertical shelves quartering upstream that often lead to a channel that is 10 to 15 feet deep, and there is deep water holding on both sides of the shelves before joining the channel. This is precarious wading—never do so alone.

Bass are found in good numbers throughout this stretch of water, however, the famous whitefly hatch is not as thick here as it is along the eastern bank from the town of Halifax downstream. The hatch occurs in force on the lower reaches of the stream and up the Juniata. It begins in mid-July and extends for three weeks and, on many nights, comes in blizzard proportions. There are many other hatches here, as well, although none that bring bass to the surface like the whitefly.

However, many mayfly and caddis hatches can be found here during spring and throughout the summer months. Most bass will take a cork or foam popping bug as "close enough," but bass can be as fussy as trout at times—I have used emerger patterns, floating nymphs, and large stonefly nymphs as well. Wayne has

The Susquehanna River near Dauphin.

had many a successful evening fishing a Clouser's crayfish with a green back and white stomach. I have also found that a Comet streamer dressed with an orange body and red hackle also gets their attention.

Above Clark's Ferry, the water is clearer and there are no algae blooms. This is the point at which bass are beginning to respond to the new 15-inch minimum size limit. From Clark's Ferry, downstream to the Dock Street Dam, fishing remains topwater oriented, although there are times when wading becomes difficult and dangerous because an algae bloom during the heat of summer causes rocks to be slippery. The Juniata serves as spawning ground for many of the bigger bass found here and is a mainstay of the river.

Muskies have been introduced throughout much of the river system, and in this area, a few muskie can be picked up, many just downstream from the Juniata's mouth. Access here is a bit more difficult, but johnboats equipped with jet drives work best if you are not into paddling a canoe.

This is a fascinating section of river, and the fishing is often superb. Because of shallow water laced with boulders and ledges that run nearly straight across the river in most places, the islands of "duck grass" provide a sanctuary for small bass and bait fish. This combination brings large bass crashing into the shallows around them. Large bass hold in the cuts off ledges and in deeper holes that are a short swim from the grass beds they often raid during morning and evening.

Streamer patterns, with or without leadeyes, work well along the beds and within the deeper holes. Bass feed early and late, although even large fish can be coaxed to a popping bug or a popping bug designed as a slider when bass raid bait schools.

Most anglers mark the third week of July as whitefly hatch time. The fly is easily imitated with a white Wulff in the dun stage or a spun deer hair body or closed foam body with calf tail wings. The river here is full of pocket water and ledges that create oxygen and a constant food supply for bass.

And there are other dry fly opportunities as well. Once in mid-August I found what looked to be small fall fish dimpling the surface and found 30 rises on a flat stretch of water above a small, shin-deep shelf. I cast a size 16 cahill above the first rise form and got no response and kept getting refusal after refusal, which is unusual for fall fish. Taking another look at the air, I found balls of Tricos over the water, so I changed leaders, finding one that was tapered to 6X, the smallest I had with me. I knotted a Trico spinner to the business end. The refusals stopped and 20-plus small-mouth later, I stood in amazement as I could still see small rises up and down the river. My best fish was close to 18 inches and my smallest around 12.

That doesn't mean that bass are sipping Tricos all the time, but there are cahill hatches that are second to none. I don't believe anyone has charted all the hatches found here because many occur too early before the water recedes and warms to be fished effectively and bass just aren't that fussy—-most of the time.

From the Dock Street Dam to Holtwood, fishing conditions change again. Some wading is available, but this water is better fished from a stable johnboat. Here, top-water fishing slows and a Clouser's deep minnow is the ticket. Bob Clouser's fly shop is located downstream in the small town of Royalton, just outside the city limits of Middletown.

Bob has fished the river his entire life and has developed many patterns for bass now found in most fly catalogs. He guides almost daily from mid-June into October and has been instrumental in keeping the river from being overfished and educating others about the value of smallmouth bass. He has developed patterns based on his experience here, and most work as well on saltwater fish as they do on bass. The deep holes of 5 feet or more that are found on this stretch are more likely to hold big bass than the shallower water bass hold upstream. The whitefly will bring bass to the surface, and at times, they turn on to popping or foam bugs, but the majority of the better fish are taken from the deeper holes here.

A smallmouth taken on a dry fly.

A stable casting platform is desirable, and most bass will take right after the strip retrieve as the streamer begins to fall. Many fish are missed because an angler doesn't detect the strike. From the right vantage point, fish can often be seen taking the fly, which makes setting the hook at the proper time that much easier.

From Dock Street Dam down to the Goldsboro pool, fishing is outstanding, and anglers catch and, fortunately, release good numbers of bass. Both Bob and his son, Bob Jr., guide here, and you could not ask for better guides.

There are also muskie throughout the river system. Large saltwater streamers with either 40- to 50-pound monofilament for a shock tippet or wire leader material from Orvis are needed to land some of the large muskie that reside here. It takes time and patience to catch muskie on a fly, but it can be accomplished. Keep in mind that the best muskie fishermen who use hardware on this river and fish over a hundred times a year, consider a 50-fish year excellent. If you want to give muskie a try, it is best to take some large streamers, shock tippet, and an 8- to 9-weight rod with a reel having 200 yards of backing.

Avoid Dock Street Dam at all costs—it is a deceptively mild looking, low head dam that takes lives each and every year. The city of Harrisburg is looking at alternatives to it. In the meantime, a fish of any size is not worth your life or another's.

Equipment for the Susquehanna

Rods: 8½ to 9½ feet

Line: 7- to 9-weight; floating, weight forward. Fibradam (Shamokin) to Dock Street Dam: weight forward, and sinktip from Dam to Goldsboro pool.

Waders: Felt soles from Fibradam to Clarks Ferry. Cleated or studded waders might be necessary in midsummer from Clarks Ferry downstream. Wade with a partner, use a guide whenever possible, and wading staffs are a good idea.

Boats: Shallow draft boats with stable casting platforms, canoes, and stable kayaks. Jet drive motors or extra sheer pins needed.

Flies: Popping bugs, # 4, 6 & 8, sliders, and "popping" bugs, foam or cork. Colors: green, yellow, lime green, and white. Mayflies: whitefly, cahill, blue-winged olive, Isonychia, sizes 10 and 12. Caddis: deer hair wing, caddis, tan, brown, yellow and green sizes 10 and 12. Streamers, Clouser's minnow, Lefty's deceiver, Comet, Dahlberg divers, Popovics pop lip shiner and muddler minnow, sizes 2 to 6. Others: leech and crayfish patterns and woolly buggers.

Warning: River must measure 3.5 or less at Harrisburg for safe wading. River levels found on the internet at: www. pa.water.usgs.gov.

Susquehanna River Access Sites

Northumberland County

Northumberland Boat Club; opposite Northumberland on US 11
- Shallow draft, lightweight fishing boats, canoes, and inflatables; charge for launching
- Boat fishing and recreation
- Beach-type ramp
- Gas and oil available

Sunbury Access (PFBC); along SR 147 at south end of Sunbury Snyder County

Shamokin; off US 11 and 15 at 8th Street
- Shallow draft, lightweight fishing boats, canoes, and inflatables
- Boat fishing and float trips
- Surfaced ramp
- Parking available

Shadynook (PP&L); located at Hummel's Wharf on US 11 and 15
- Shallow draft, lightweight fishing boats, canoes, and inflatables
- Boat fishing and float trips
- Surfaced ramp
- Parking available

Hoover Island Access (PFBC); located 3.5 miles south of Selinsgrove on US 11 and 15
- Shallow draft, lightweight fishing boats, canoes, and inflatables
- Boat fishing and float trips
- Beach-type ramp
- Parking available

Herdon Access; off SR 147 in town of Herdon
- Canoes and other handcarry boats only
- Boat fishing and float trips
- Beach-type ramp
- Parking available

Port Trevorton; US 11 and 15
- Shallow draft, lightweight fishing boats, canoes, and inflatables
- Boat fishing and float trips
- Beach-type ramp
- Parking available

Dalmatia Access; off SR 147 in town of Dalmatia
- Canoes and other handcarry boats only
- Boat fishing and float trips
- Beach-type ramp
- Parking available

Mahantango Access (PFBC); four miles south of Port Trevorton along US 11 and 15
- Shallow draft, lightweight fishing boats, canoes, and inflatables
- Boat fishing and float trips
- Surfaced ramp
- Parking available

Perry County

Swigart Island Access (PGC); three miles north of Liverpool, off US 11 and 15
- Car top boats; shallow draft, lightweight fishing boats, canoes, and inflatables
- Boat fishing and float trips
- Beach-type ramp
- Parking available

Liverpool Access (PFBC); on US 11 and 15 in Liverpool, undeveloped

Montgomery Ferry Access (PFBC); located in village of Montgomery's Ferry on US 11 and 15
- Shallow draft, lightweight fishing boats, canoes, and inflatables
- Boat fishing and float trips
- Beach-type ramp
- Parking available

Clemson Island Access (PGC); located about 1.3 miles north
of New Buffalo, off US 11 and 15
- Shallow draft, lightweight fishing boats, canoes, and inflatables—cartop boats
  are recommended because the ramp is unstable
- No sanitary facilities
- Boat fishing and float trips
- Beach-type ramp
- Parking available

Marysville Borough Access; south Main Street at western end
of Rockville railroad bridge
- Recommend cartop boats only; shallow draft, lightweight fishing boats,
  canoes, and inflatables
- Boat fishing and float trips
- Surfaced ramp
- Parking available

Dauphin County

Millersburg Access (PFBC); located on SR 147, west end of Moore Street
- Shallow draft, lightweight fishing boats, canoes, and inflatables
- Boat fishing and float trips
- Surfaced ramp
- Parking available

Halifax Access (PFBC); on SR 147, west end of Moore Street
- Shallow draft, lightweight fishing boats, canoes, and inflatables
- Boat fishing and float trips
- Surfaced ramp
- Parking available

Fort Hunter Access (PFBC); located on Front Street, Harrisburg, north of Rockville
Bridge; from US 22/322 take Fishing Creek Exit to river, turn left
- Shallow draft, lightweight fishing boats, canoes, and inflatables
- Boat fishing and float trips
- Surfaced ramp
- Parking available

Middletown Access (PFBC); located at the foot of Union Street in Middletown,
where the Swartara Creek enters the Susquehanna River
- Moderate draft fishing boats, sailboats, and recreational runabout boats
- Recreational boating and fishing
- Surfaced ramp
- Parking available

MET ED Access (Metropolitan Edison Company); located along SR 441 south of Royalton in the vicinity of the Middletown rapids
- Moderate draft fishing boats, sailboats, and recreational runabout boats
- Recreational boating and fishing
- Surfaced ramp
- Parking available

Tri-County Boat Club; located along SR 441 north of the entrance to Three Mile Island nuclear generating plant
- Moderate draft fishing boats, sailboats, and recreational runabout boats
- Recreational boating and fishing
- Surfaced ramp
- Gas and oil available
- Parking available

Cumberland County

West Fairview Access (PFBC); off US 11 at the Conodoquinet Creek
- Shallow draft, lightweight fishing boats, canoes and inflatables
- Boat fishing and float trips
- Surfaced ramp
- Parking available

Harrisburg Seaplane Base; Wormleysburg, at west end of Walnut Street Bridge on upstream side
- Moderate draft fishing boats, sailboats, and recreational runabout boats; charge for launching
- Boat fishing and recreation
- Surfaced ramp
- Gas and oil available
- Parking available

Harrisburg City Island; reached via Front Street in Harrisburg on east side or US 11 and 15 on west side of river
- Free public access
- Swimming facilities on city Island (located at Cumberland/Dauphin County Line off Walnut and Market Street Bridges)
- Moderate draft fishing boats, sailboats, and recreational runabout boats
- Boat fishing and recreation
- Surfaced ramp
- Parking available

New Cumberland Boat Club Access; located at the end of Fifth Street in the borough of New Cumberland
- Shallow draft, lightweight fishing boats, canoes, and inflatables; charge for launching
- Boat fishing and recreation
- Surfaced ramp
- Gas and oil available
- Parking available

Lancaster County

Falmouth Access (PFBC); one mile below York Haven Dam along SR 441—rocky area, use caution!
- Shallow draft, lightweight fishing boats, canoes, and inflatables
- Boat fishing
- Surfaced ramp
- Parking available

Bainbridge Access; foot of Race Street—Rocky area, use caution!—there are other areas where small craft can be launched from shore, although it may be difficult during low water
- Shallow draft, lightweight fishing boats, canoes, and inflatables
- Boat fishing
- Surfaced ramp
- Parking available

Marietta Access (PFBC); south end of borough of Marrietta, developed in 1989

Columbia Access (PFBC); just south of SR 462 in Columbia
- Other launching areas privately-owned or maintained by boat clubs
- Shallow draft, lightweight fishing boats, canoes, and inflatables
- Boat fishing
- Surfaced ramp
- Limited parking facilities available

PP&L Co. Public Access Area; at the mouth of Pequea Creek just off SR 324—Use caution when water levels are low!
- Picnic area and children's playground
- Shallow draft, lightweight fishing boats, canoes, and inflatables
- Recreational boating and fishing
- Surfaced ramp
- Parking available

Arrowhead Marina; on opposite side of Pequea Creek from PP & L area
- Moderate draft fishing boats, sailboats, and recreational runabout boats; charge for launching
- Recreational boating and fishing
- Surfaced ramp
- Oil and gas available; groceries; snack bar; boat rentals
- Parking available

Peach Bottom Marina; take Peach Bottom Road west off US 222, approximately 3 miles north of the Maryland state line
- Mooring over summer months
- Hoist available at boat house
- Moderate draft fishing boats, sailboats, and recreational runabout boats; charge for launching
- Recreational boating and fishing
- Surface ramp
- Gas and oil available, groceries, fishing supplies, bait

YORK HAVEN DAM/LAKE FREDERIC

The first of four dams on the Susquehanna River below the city of Harrisburg, this dam is often referred to as the Goldsboro pool, and it is extremely difficult to determine where the river stops and the lake begins. Access to this lake also gives access to the river in Dauphin, York, and Lancaster Counties.

York Haven Dam provides some excellent fishing for smallmouth and the occasional muskie. It is a recreational dam and the first "silt catcher" below the Fibradam (Shamokin) at Sunbury. The water here changes dramatically from a free-running river with large boulders and gravel to a silty bottom that often becomes knee deep and more. This is not an area to wade.

The better fishing is found upstream of the pool, where the rocks and natural habitat of smallmouth are found. Muskie can be located in the deeper waters near the dam.

Because this area is heavily used in summer by recreational craft, including water skiers and jet-skis, serious anglers head upstream where structure is more prevalent or to one of the islands. A 15-inch minimum size limit governs this lake.

Lake Frederic Access Sites

York County

Goldsboro Access (PFBC); from I-83, take SR 262 to Goldsboro. Pass through the town square, cross the railroad tracks and immediately turn left.
- Moderate draft fishing boats, sailboats, and recreational runabout boats
- Recreational boating and fishing
- Beach-type ramp
- Parking available

Goldsboro Marina; located east of Goldsboro; turn right after crossing the railroad tracks
- Moderate draft fishing boats, sailboats, and recreational runabout boats; charge for launching
- Recreational boating and fishing
- Beach-type ramp
- Parking available
- Gas and oil available

City Public Access; within borough limits
- Moderate draft fishing boats, sailboats, and recreational runabout boats
- Recreational boating and fishing
- Beach-type ramp
- Parking available

A striped bass/white bass hybrid.

York Haven Access; south (downstream) side of mouth of Conewago Creek. BPN33
- Shallow draft, lightweight fishing boats, canoes, and inflatables
- Boat fishing and recreation
- Beach-type ramp
- Parking available

Saginaw Access ; from Mt. Wolf follow SR 929 east 1.5 miles to village of Saginaw; access is located through railroad underpass off Second Street
- Shallow draft, lightweight fishing boats, canoes, and inflatables
- Boat fishing
- Beach-type ramp
- Parking available

Dauphin County

MET ED Access (Metropolitan Edison Company); located along SR 441 south of Royalton in the vicinity of the Middletown rapids
- Moderate draft fishing boats, sailboats, and recreational runabout boats
- Recreational boating and fishing
- Surfaced ramp
- Parking available

Safe Harbor Dam/Lake Clarke

Lake Clarke is shared by both recreational boater and anglers. However, the amount of water available here allows anglers to probe the shallows and around the islands where the water is too shallow for recreational use. Access is widely available to unlimited horsepower boats.

The lake can be demanding, but the bass most frequently inhabit the rocky shoreline and areas with quick drop-offs and large boulders that are in 10-15 feet of water. Here, a boat is a must. Also sink-tip lines as well as full sinking lines. The shorelines will produce bass that will rise to top water popping bugs and, for those, you will need a floating line. Two rods, reels and extra spools are a good idea if you want to fish this 650-acre impoundment.

Besides bass, muskie and stripers are always a possibility. Your fly box should include some larger streamers for both. If you are after a certain species, then you should try your best to target that species. The problem arises when stripers, white bass/striped bass hybrids, start swelling the waters in a feeding frenzy. I carry a 9-foot, 9-weight, just in case, and fish a 9-foot for an 8-weight for smallmouth bass.

This lake will take some exploring and I am more concerned with boat traffic ruining my fishing than where I fish on any given day. This is a fine impoundment with a lot of good water.

I would suggest the rock outcroppings, the shoreline and around the islands when fishing for bass. Most often stripers will not be that far away, either.

This lake is best fished from mid-June through mid-October.

Boat rentals are available on many lakes.

Lake Clarke Access Sites

Wrightsville Access (PFBC); at Wrightsville along SR 624, approximately 100 yards below the SR 462 bridge; located in the extreme backwaters of the dam and suitable for small boats only
  • Shallow draft, lightweight fishing boats, canoes, and inflatables
  • Boat fishing and recreation

Susquehanna Boat Works Marina; from Wrightsville, turn right (south) on SR 624; go approximately 3 miles, turn left on Boat House Road
  • Deep draft, high-powered recreational boats; charge for launching
  • Recreational boating and fishing
  • Beach-type ramp
  • Parking available
  • Gas and oil available

Lake Clarke Marina; approximately 0.1 mile south of Susquehanna Boat Works Marina
  • Deep draft, high-powered recreational boats; charge for launching
  • Recreational boating and fishing
  • Surfaced ramp
  • Parking available
  • Gas and oil available

Long Level Marina; from Wrightsville, turn right (south) on SR 624; go approximately 4.5 miles to marina at the mouth of Cabin Creek
  • Deep draft, high-powered recreational boats; charge for launching
  • Recreational boating and fishing
  • Surfaced ramp
  • Parking available
  • Gas and oil available

Safe Harbor Water and Power Company; from Wrightsville, turn right (south) on SR 624; go approximately 5 miles to where 624 turns to the right. Do not make the turn, continue straight for 0.5 mile
  • Deep draft, high-powered recreational boats
  • Recreational boating and fishing
  • Beach-type ramp
  • Parking available
  • Picnic tables
  • Sanitary facilities

HOLTWOOD DAM/LAKE ALDRED

Flyfishers who have a boat or use the services of a guide will find this lake offers a mixed bag of opportunities. Covering 2,400 acres, the lake is where the 15-inch minimum size limit for smallmouth bass ends on the Susquehanna. The lake holds smallmouth and largemouth as well as muskie and stripers.

Although striped bass here are usually a hybrid and do not grow all that large, averaging 5 pounds, they are often caught coincidentally when fishing for bass.

Again, the rocky shoreline and boulder-laden areas of the lake are the best areas for smallmouth. Silt-laden shallow waters also produce some nice-sized smallmouth, and deeper water brings stripers to hand.

Because the water is deeper here, the opportunity for hooking up with a good smallmouth decreases, and it will take an intermediate sinktip and lead core, along with a floating line, for consistent success. However, there are greater opportunities for stripers and muskie, and that can offer a flyfisher some welcome diversity.

I have found this lake to run hot and cold, while others find excellent fishing here fairly consistently. Knowing the lake is a big plus, which is why a guide's services are important, at least for the first time. Carry the same flies suggested for the Susquehanna River.

The access areas are plentiful, and for those who like the challenge of flyfishing a lake, this one will provide much of interest.

Lake Aldred Access Sites

Pennsylvania Power and Light Company Access Areas
York Furnace Access; at mouth of Otter Creek; take SR 74 south from Red Lion to SR 425; turn left (east) on 425 for about 4.3 miles to access area on right
- Picnic tables and sanitary facilities
- Deep draft, high-powered recreational boats
- Recreational boating and fishing
- Surfaced ramp
- Parking available

Pennsylvania Power and Light Access; near York Furnace at Indian Steps; take SR 74 south from Red Lion to SR 425 to access area
- Deep draft, high-powered recreational boats
- Recreational boating and fishing
- Surfaced ramp
- Parking available

CONOWINGO RESERVOIR

This is the last stop on the Susquehanna River before it enters Maryland. Because it blocks passage for anadromous fish from Chesapeake Bay, this impoundment has been the center of controversy for years. American shad that had once made spawning runs throughout much of the Pennsylvania River system were effectively cut off. However, the dam now has fish lifts, and all upstream dams will have either lifts or passageways completed by 2002. It has been an uphill battle, but shad are now starting to appear throughout the Susquehanna. Although still protected from recreational and commercial fishermen within the state, the day may come when the Susquehanna is once again a shad river.

This is a large lake, over 6,000 acres, and extremely deep. While smallmouth fishing is marginal, there is the possibility of hooking into stripers, since purebred and hybrid stripers both exist here. Bass fishing is confined to small areas, but stripers can be on top at any time and place, and muskie are rather common. A guide is highly recommended, and a well-rounded fly selection is needed for fishing all depths. The lake is controlled and managed by both Pennsylvania and Maryland.

Conowingo Reservoir Access Sites

Muddy Creek Access (PFBC); take SR 74 south from Red Lion; turn left (east) on SR 372; at the western end of the Norman Wood Bridge, turn right (south) and go approximately 1.5 miles; turn left (east) into access area
- Deep draft, high powered, recreational boats
- Recreational boating and fishing
- Surfaced ramp
- Parking available

PINCHOT LAKE (CONEWAGO LAKE)

Pinchot Lake in York County has one of the finest largemouth populations in this region. Lake surveys indicate that populations of largemouth in this lake of only 340 acres are exceptional in both number and size. With access areas on both sides of the lake, it receives heavy fishing pressure. The electric motor-only regulation has been good for the lake, although it makes it difficult to cover thoroughly in a single day.

I have fished the lake with some degree of regularity over the years but never as often as I would like. One particular afternoon, some years ago, I was probing the shoreline in a canoe. Wind was giving me difficulty in handling the canoe and my fly rod. I had gone to the lake after hearing reports that anglers were doing well on the PFBC stocked striped bass hybrids. One man told me the fish were surface feeding during the evening hours, so I thought I would give it a try, even though others that day weren't having much success.

I fought the wind and probed the shoreline with a homespun sunfish imitation I tied onto a 4/0 hook that included leadeyes. It wasn't a completely foolish act to cast the heavily dressed fly into a near gale force wind since I knew that muskie were present in good numbers as well.

I chose a 9-foot rod that carried a 9-weight slime line and moved the canoe into a sheltered shoreline where streamside vegetation and root systems fingered their

A point on Pinchot Lake.

way into the lake's lapping waters. Topped off with an Orvis knotted leader tapered to 10-pound test, I was prepared for few strikes, if any.

The bulky fly landed next to the exposed roots of an old oak that would succumb to the eroding bank in a few short years, and I patiently allowed the fly to sink out of sight. When it settled, I began to pull the line in a short erratic manner, moving it two to three inches at a time. The second pull brought a tight line and a hard strike. I set the hook on the unknown creature, which did not reveal its identity until it went airborne some 60 feet from where it took the fly. I nearly rolled the canoe at the sight of the leaping, outsized largemouth. It was a hefty fish in the 6-pound class, the best I had taken from this lake. The wind was blowing the canoe in circles, and the fish took three more long runs and three more leaps before I brought it to hand. I quickly photographed the fish before releasing it. As I paddled to shore, the first clap of thunder told me it was time to leave.

This small lake is known both as Pinchot Lake and Conewago Lake and is owned by the Department of Conservation and Natural Resources (DCNR). Gifford Pinchot State Park, named after Governor Pinchot, has picnic areas, and the lake has designated swimming areas and boat rentals in the day-use area that closes at sunset. There are other ramps surrounding the park that allow fishing after dark, but no rentals are available.

This a great lake to fish and, although extremely popular, doesn't get overcrowded with boats except on weekends. Shore fishing is extremely difficult, as is wading—a johnboat or canoe are needed to fish this lake properly. Although the lake is advertised as both a muskie and northern pike fishery, as well as largemouth, it is rare to find a northern here, and muskie are few and far between. The striper program has been forgotten, although many claim that a remnant population still exists.

I highly recommend this as a largemouth lake, although I have picked up a number of smallmouth along one particular shoreline. The lake is under Big Bass Regulations that have helped fish achieve growth beyond the 15-inch minimum size limit. The better bass I have taken seem to feed on bluegill and sunfish populations, so the flies I tie for this lake are large and bulky. With today's modern rods as well as the proper line and leader combinations, it is not difficult to create a wind-resistant streamer with a lot of bulk.

Clouser's minnows and leadeyes of varying weights work well here as they do on all bass waters, and leech and crayfish patterns are a must. Because I love topwater action, I work the lake surface with popping bugs in various sizes ranging from 2 to 8, because the smaller sizes of white or yellow popper have worked better than any others. I have taken many 5-pound fish here on bugs, and those with concave faces and cork bodies seem to work on most lakes.

This means fishing the shorelines carefully and methodically, covering the rises that occur on the lake itself. Concentrating on the shoreline during morning and evening and in the small coves during the day brings amazing results. Pinchot (Conewago) Lake is located on SR 177 between Lewisberry and Rossville and can be reached via I-83.

Driftwood Branch Sinnemahoning Creek

Here on the Driftwood Branch my friend and fishing partner, Harry Karns, had a fishing revelation that would change the way he fished forever. While I had fished the stream many times above Emporium in Cameron County and found the trout fishing to be excellent, we were in search of bass in a pool that Harry knew held them in good numbers and size.

Harry was insistent about where and how to fish bass and claimed that a fly rod, while excellent for catching trout, would hopelessly handicap my ability to catch bass. I'm convinced that where water depth is not a limiting factor and where the water has any degree of clarity, a fly rod is the most proficient fishing method no matter what the species. So when I grabbed some large nymphs and a box of popping bugs, Harry simply laughed and shook his head. As we drove along SR 120, he teased me that I would be sorry and that he had brought an extra spinning rod along, just in case.

We found one of Harry's favorite pools, and he immediately began searching the shallows for crayfish—he seemed to enjoy collecting bait as much as fishing. While he was occupied with that, I strung my rod, attached a size 6 muskrat nymph with bead eyes, then waded into the stream and found some waist-deep pockets of water. I cast the large nymph on a 9-foot with a 7-weight. When the nymph hit the water and I began my slow retrieve, a bass came into view. A good dozen bass followed the imitation and, on the drop, rushed to take it. This fishing was ridiculously easy since

A nice smallmouth from the Driftwood Branch of the Sinnemahoning.

Driftwood Branch Sinnemahoning Creek

To
Smethport

*Delayed Harvest:
Flyfishing Only;
from Shippen Township
Building downstream to
SR 120, 1.4 mi.*

46

To
Saint
Marys

120

120

155

To
Port
Allegany

Emporium ◆

120

Legend

━━━ State/Cty Road

═══ Major River

━━━ Minor River/Creek

McNuff Branch

Flow

Hunts Run

*All Tackle;
Select Harvest*

120

Driftwood Branch

Bennett Branch

555

120

Driftwood

872

To
Austin

120

Sinnemahoning Creek

120

To
Renovo

© Wilderness Adventures Press

I could see the fish take. Before Harry had found enough crayfish to start fishing, I had already taken eight bass.

Each small pocket of water was loaded with eager fish, and the muskrat nymph became battered and torn around the bead chain eyes, and the thread became exposed. I was so engrossed with this wonderful fishing that I hadn't kept track of how many fish I had taken, but Harry did—he counted 128.

When the action slowed up toward evening, tan caddis began to hover over the water, and the fish were no longer interested in my muskrat nymph. So I switched to a dry fly, a size 14 tan caddis with deer hair wing, and when it hit the water, bass came after it one after another. Harry had only been able to muster an occasional bass with his live crayfish, so when the fish turned to surface feeding, he simply sat on the bank and watched in awe. From that point on, Harry has used nothing by a fly rod for all species, and I have returned to the Driftwood Branch many times to fish for bass.

Fishing begins a mile or two below Emporium and continues close to 15 miles downstream before acid mine runoff at Sterling Run virtually kills the stream. SR 120 parallels the stream from Emporium to Sinnemahoning.

Take waders, an assortment of popping bugs, leech patterns, large stonefly nymphs, and streamers in size 6—I like Matukas in olive and white. Pay attention to any and all hatches—hatches aren't for trout alone, and in a stream situation, fish rise freely to a good hatch or spinnerfall. For a hatch chart, see the Driftwood Branch in the coldwater description.

Bass average 12 to 14 inches, with many 15 inches and above, and taking one close to 20 inches is possible.

GEORGE B. STEVENSON DAM

Located in Sinnemahoning State Park, this small dam slows the First Fork Sinnemahoning into stillwater. Although stocked with trout, the section from the dam downstream to Sinnemahoning Creek must be considered a warmwater fishery. During the mid-70s, the lake was heavily fished for trout but not bass. The release of muskie created some interest in the lake and tailwaters, but it didn't last long. A few short years ago, fishing for bass on this hallowed north country trout water would have been laughed at. But with the growing popularity of fishing for bass on a fly, all that has changed.

Even back in the 1970s, my good friend, Norm Brooks, and I were fishing bass with a fly rod here. We fished the lake weekly through the summer and into early fall. We both loved top-water action and fished nothing other than popping bugs in white and yellow. We fished our pattern exclusively on a size 6 hook and never failed to take a good number of bass in an evening of fishing. We worked the bugs tight against the shoreline and then let them sit before beginning a slow retrieve and stop that brought both smallmouth and largemouth leaping over the calm waters.

We used to laugh and create such a commotion while pursuing the bass that the park ranger would stop to see what we were up to. He would shake his head and rub his forehead stating, "I've never seen anything like this before." He became so interested in our fishing that he took to watching us through binoculars.

One evening, while working the far shore, we got into a number of largemouth, and as we made our way back to the parking lot found that he had been anxiously awaiting our arrival. "Were you guys catching largemouth?" he asked. We nodded that we were, and he was nearly speechless. "Those are the first largemouth I have seen caught in this lake for over 20 years!"

The lake is a decent trout lake as well, especially near the upper end. I hooked a large brown there one evening that was perhaps the largest brown I had ever hooked in the state. The fish took off after inhaling the fly—a popping bug of all things—and ran line so swiftly off my single action reel that I feared losing the line and 75 yards of backing. Despite my efforts to keep up with an electric trolling motor, the brown surfaced and then turned and ran toward the boat. I reeled madly but could not do so quickly enough, and the slack line was all the large trout needed to escape.

This is a small lake of 142 acres located at the southern end of the state park. It is a good warmwater fishery with good populations of both largemouth and small-mouth bass.

Clouser minnows, leech patterns, and comets with an orange tail and red hackle work well here. However, I continue to use popping bugs in yellow and white with a concave face—a tradition that brings a lot of fish to hand and rekindles the memory of a great friend who passed on far too early.

Stevenson Dam is easily accessible from SR 872, and parking and a paved ramp are available in the park. The lake is limited to electric motors only.

*A selection of warmwater flies, including
a Clouser's deep-diving minnow in the back.*

JUNIATA RIVER

The Juniata is a medium-sized river with so much flyfishing to offer that it would take a life-time to discover it all. It is a gentle, meandering river, extending through four counties before emptying into the Susquehanna River a mile below Amity Hall at Duncannon. It is an excellent smallmouth fishery throughout its length, and one of the finest, if not the best, river muskie fisheries in the state.

One of the Juniata's attractions is that, from mid-June into late September when bass fishing is at its best, the river can be fished by wading or from small, shallow draft boats and canoes. The river is so long and full of smallmouth that its bass come readily to a wide variety of popping bugs, streamers, leech patterns, and crayfish patterns. A 50- to 60-bass day is not uncommon.

As with all good fishing water, fishermen have favorite spots to fish, and these places can be more difficult to fish than other areas that receive less pressure. But one of the attractions on the Juniata is that access is easily found its entire length.

The addition of Big Bass regulations, which do not allow taking fish under 15 inches, has been well accepted, and with each passing year, the average fish size has become larger. It now requires a 20-inch bass to raise an eyebrow when, only a few short years ago, 16 or 17 inches was considered large.

This is a medium-sized river, averaging over 200 feet in width, and there are larger pools, especially in the lower reaches. The river has some silt-bottom flat pools that extend for 500 yards or more, and in these areas, the fishing might be stale. It's best to find the rocky, boulder-strewn areas that are best suited for smallmouth and deeper pools (12 to 15 feet) when searching for muskie.

For those who want to float and fish, be aware that the Juniata holds some surprises in the form of fast water and narrow passages that require excellent maneuvering skills. From my own experience, it is usually best to portage these areas. Two friends and I capsized an excellent craft as we maneuvered through a narrow opening guarded by large boulders the size of bread trucks. I lost an excellent rod and reel and a very expensive Nikon camera and lens to the 15-foot deep pool. It was a careless mistake that can happen all too easily on this river.

This river's nature changes frequently, and one can be lulled by the gentle flow and then suddenly become panic-stricken trying to maneuver through some treacherous waters. But it is not a whitewater river by any stretch of the imagination, and by remaining calm and taking a few precautions, the river can be navigated safely.

Although the average bass are a little smaller on the Juniata than on the Susquehanna (the best bass water in the state), the new regulations will ensure that this river can maintain a good crop of fish on its own. Spring smallmouth spawning success is often judged by the number of bass that are electroshocked by the PFBC.

The river has also been used to reintroduce shad into the Susquehanna River system. Fingerling shad implants have proved their worth by opening passageways for American shad throughout the river system.

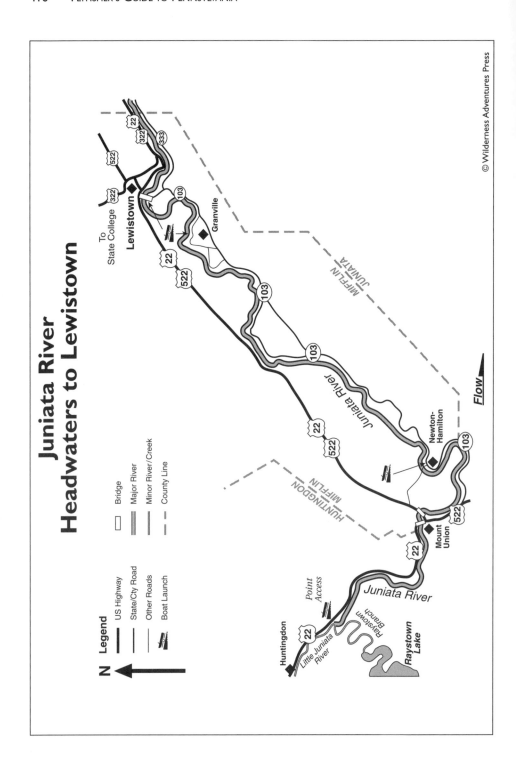

Juniata River
Headwaters to Lewistown

Legend

- US Highway
- State/Cty Road
- Other Roads
- Boat Launch
- Bridge
- Major River
- Minor River/Creek
- County Line

© Wilderness Adventures Press

Flow

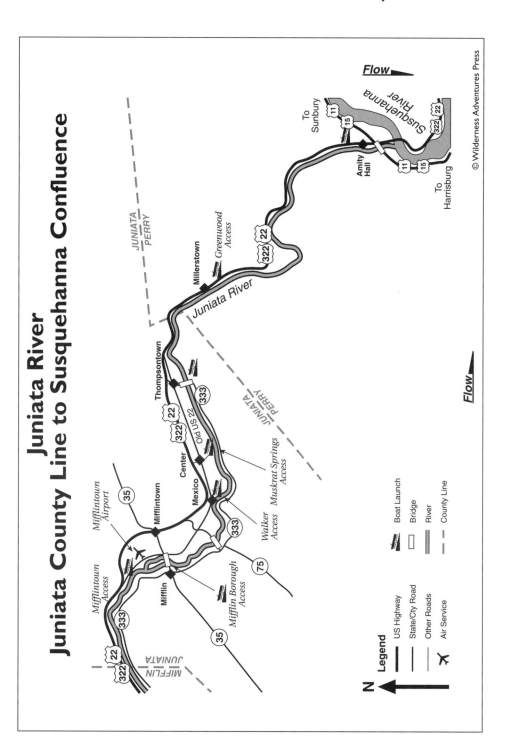

This largemouth bass took a popping bug.

This is perhaps the second best river in the state when flyfishing for bass. The Allegheny is coming on strong as a smallmouth fishery near the city of Pittsburgh. The main difference is that larger craft are required on the Allegheny, while on the Juniata, smaller craft and wading make this a nearly perfect river to flyfish.

The river does have inherent problems—it is bordered by farm country along much of its course, and this causes the river to rise and become chocolate-colored quickly, virtually shutting down any fishing. Rain can put flyfishing on hold from 3 day to weeks, depending on the amount of rainfall in the entire region—rising rivers to the north can affect river stages to the south.

Before traveling to the Juniata, it is important to call for a river update to make sure it is fishable. Fortunately, those who have a computer or access to one can get river updates on the net at "www.pa.water.usgs.gov." As a guide to whether wading is appropriate on the Susquehanna and Juniata, the river stage at Harrisburg should be at 3.5 or less. Track the stages to be certain that water rises are not occurring on the Juniata or any of its tributaries.

Juniata River Access Sites

River access is available throughout it's length. Boating accesses are as follows:

Huntingdon County – 23 miles
Species: Bass, Muskie, Panfish, Chain Pickerel, Walleye

Point Access (PFBC); located off US 22, east of Huntingdon
- Shallow draft, lightweight fishing boats, canoes, inflatables, and small outboards
- Boat fishing and float trips
- Surface ramped
- Parking available

Mifflin County – 35 miles
Species: Bass, Muskie, Panfish, Walleye

Newton-Hamilton Access (PFBC); located at Newton-Hamilton on SR 103
- Shallow draft, lightweight fishing boats, canoes, and inflatables
- Boat fishing and float trips
- Surface ramped
- Parking available

Granville Access (PFBC); located 3 miles west of Lewistown off SR 103, look for PFC directional signs
- Shallow draft, lightweight fishing boats, canoes, and inflatables
- Boat fishing and float trips
- Surface ramped
- Parking available

Victory Park; on Third Street in Lewistown
- Canoes and other handcarry boats
- Boat fishing and float trips
- Beach-type ramp
- Parking available

Juniata County – 22 miles
Species: Bass, Muskie, Panfish, Walleye, Sucker
Access areas listed are suitable for small outboards only

Mifflintown Access (PFBC); located 0.5 miles west of Mifflintown airport on SR 3002 (old US 22)
- Shallow draft, lightweight fishing boats, canoes, inflatables, and small outboards
- Boat fishing and float trips
- Surface ramped
- Parking available

Mifflin Borough Access; downstream from SR. 35 bridge
- Shallow draft, lightweight fishing boats, canoes, inflatables, and small outboards (cartop boats only)
- Boat fishing and float trips
- Surface ramped
- Limited parking

Walker Access (PFBC); located at Mexico on SR 3002 (old US 22)
- Shallow draft, lightweight fishing boats, canoes, inflatables, and small outboards
- Boat fishing and float trips
- Surface ramped
- Parking available

Muskrat Springs Access (PFBC); located at village of Center, 2.5 miles east of Mexico on SR 3002 (old US 22)
- Shallow draft, lightweight fishing boats, canoes, inflatables, and small outboards
- Boat fishing and float trips
- Surface ramped
- Parking available

Thompsontown Access (PFBC); located 0.5 miles south of Thompsontown on SR 333
- Shallow draft, lightweight fishing boats, canoes, inflatables, and small outboards
- Boat fishing and float trips
- Surface ramped
- Parking available

Perry County – 18 miles
Species: Bass, Muskie, Panfish, Chain Pickerel, Sucker, Walleye

Greenwood Access (PFBC); located 2.5 miles south of Millerstown, off US 22 and 322 and old SR 22
- Shallow draft, lightweight fishing boats, canoes, and inflatables
- Boat fishing and float trips
- Surface ramped
- Parking available
- Sanitary facilities

Amity Hall Access (PFBC); in the village of Amity Hall, off US 11 and 15 and US 22 and 322; approximately one-quarter mile north of the old Amity Hall Restaurant and Truck Stop
- Shallow draft, lightweight fishing boats, canoes, and inflatables
- Boat fishing and float trips
- Surface ramped
- Parking available
- Sanitary facilities

Green Valley Campgrounds; off US 22 and 322 at Midway exit, north on old US 22 about one-quarter mile
- Shallow draft, lightweight fishing boats, canoes, and inflatables
- Boat fishing and float trips
- Parking available
- Gravel ramp
- Camping facilities

RAYSTOWN LAKE

Raystown Lake in Huntingdon County is famous for its striped bass fishery—it has claimed the state record for landlocked striper since 1994. Robert Price's 53-pound, 13-ounce fish was nothing new and unusual at Raystown Lake—records have been made and broken here nearly annually. Having withstood the challenge of new records longer than most, one might think that Price's prize striper would discourage those who chase such records. However, local guides and resident anglers are smug in the fact that they know there are larger stripers in the lake, and many claim to have lost fish bigger than Price's. Stripers have been raiding the points and shallows of Raystown Lake for years in pursuit of gizzard shad, smelt, and alewife.

Most anglers, not just fly enthusiasts, find this lake very complex to fish—it is simply too deep in many areas and many of its coves aren't shallow enough for good flyfishing. Striper fishing is best in spring and again in the fall after recreational use slows down and the water temperature cools down. Stripers are most easily taken at night when they are near the surface.

Most of the lake trout and stripers have taken to feeding just above the treetops that still remain in the lake. The most successful striper fishermen dangle live brown trout just above those treetops in 40 to 60 feet of water during the summer months, which means flyfishermen will find this tactic of no use—there just isn't a lead core line that can sink that fast or a fly rod designed to handle a meal that size yet. From the shore, the lake drops off quickly and dramatically, and quick sinking lines and intermediate sinking lines are a necessity.

Private and public access are good on this 8,300-acre lake that has been maintained primarily by stocking. It is known to contain large muskie, decent-sized lake trout, some landlocked salmon, as well as largemouth and smallmouth bass. Raystown Lake also gave up the state record landlocked Atlantic salmon, a 10-pound, 14.5-ounce fish taken by Timothy Grace of Huntingdon, a guide on the lake. Walleye, panfish, and pickerel are abundant as well, and there are some northern pike, too. In spite of its complexity and depth, I wouldn't want to go a year without visiting this lake.

Check out the spillway or tailrace water for stripers, smallmouth, and a host of other good fish. Leroy Patterson of Huntingdon took the state record brown trout there in 1993—it weighed 17 pounds, 14.5 ounces. It's probably no coincidence that all the record fish have been taken by area residents—locals know that this is a good fishery and have the experience to know when and where to fish.

Surveys conducted by the Pennsylvania Fish and Boat Commission in 1999 revealed that the lake's population is better than it has been in many years. There is little more that can be said, other than that this is an excellent fishery. Pennsylvania's deep lakes and fast flowing waters are challenging fly waters, but more and more flyfishers are learning to fish them and manufacturers are developing new equipment to meet their needs.

Access is easily found along SR 26 on the west as well as various state roads on its east side. Administered by the U.S. Army Corps of Engineers, the lake is 30 miles long and is the largest within the state. A variety of recreational opportunities are provided in 13 public use areas, including boat launches, marinas, camping, picnicking, swimming, and access areas for fishermen. The impoundment is open to all types of boating, but several areas have been limited to "slow, minimum height swell speed" craft. There are no horsepower restrictions. For more information, contact: Manager, Raystown Lake, U.S. Army Corps of Engineers, RR 1, Hesston, PA 16647, telephone 814-658-3405.

Trough Creek State Park on the east side can be reached by traveling 16 miles south from Huntingdon along SR 26, then 5 miles east along SR 994 near the village of Entriken.

Some anglers prefer unpowered boats, even on the largest lakes.

OPOSSUM CREEK LAKE

As one of my favorite getaways, Opossum Lake's attraction is its setting in rural Cumberland County. It is a place where a heron can often be seen standing near one of the launch ramps, and the electric motors-only regulation guards its tranquility. By the time trout anglers have left for cooler water, it is an ideal getaway. Opossum is basically a bass and muskie fishery, and its panfish have increased enough in population and size that the PFBC will be lifting the conservation regulations that have been placed on the lake. Big bass regulations will remain in place when the new regulations take effect, which will be at the time this book is published. But anglers should always check the Summary Book that is issued with their fishing license to be certain. Regulations can change very quickly in Pennsylvania, often in a matter of months.

The late Harry Fox, so well known as a trout fisher on the fabled Letort, spent hours on end at Opossum Creek Lake working his handmade wooden lures over the quiet waters. Many claimed that the muskie population was gone after the lake was drawn down in 1991 for repairs. But one evening after that I watched Harry work magic with those wooden lures. Harry was unaware of my presence, and I saw him take three muskies and raise two others in just one hour.

After he waded to shore—that's right, he simply waded off the near shoreline into waist-deep water—I asked him how he had done. In Harry's most congenial and gentleman like manner, he responded, "Okay, nothing spectacular." Anyone who has fished for muskie in this state can tell you that hooking and raising that many fish in such a short period of time is an amazing feat. But Harry, an extremely honest man, told me it was a common night of fishing for him, and he was a little disappointed that he did not hook any big ones, even though the three he landed and released all exceeded the 36-inch minimum size limit.

I find flyfishing for muskie can be compared to permit fishing on tropical flats. Muskie seldom feed and will follow a fly to the rod tip and then sink out of sight. Although patterns are important, I have taken muskie on flies designed for steelhead as well as tarpon. That means hooks can range in size from 3 to 6. As for color, I've used everything from pure white saddle hackles to a red-bodied fly with gray squirrel tail for a wing...and I'm talking about muskie in the 30-pound range.

Once hooked, a muskie that has attained a reasonable size will do just about anything it pleases. Many fish are lost when the fly is taken and the hook is not set properly, while others are lost on the first leap. And then there are the ones I have broken off in fear of losing my fly line and over 200 yards of backing. That means that I have lost more fish than I have landed—and I've landed quite a few over the years. The muskie I have taken at Opossum Creek Lake can be counted on one hand, and those I have lost would take two hands and a few toes to boot.

When I fish Opossum, I take two rigs: a 9-foot for a 10-weight and a 9-foot for an 8-weight. I rig the heavier rod with a shock tippet, and the lighter is a bass rod. The last muskie I lost there was raiding the shallows as evening fell, and it took a slider popping bug that I worked over a school of fleeing baitfish. I just knew that a large

Deer hair bass bug.

fish was corralling the baitfish into the shallows with frenzied leaps, and I simply cast a white slider past the school and worked it fast and furiously over and through the school. My reward was a giant swell and then a large roll. Then I saw the large, long-toothed fish swim away with a speck of white planted firmly in its jaw. I felt the weight for a millisecond before the sharp teeth sliced my 8-pound test tippet. A size 6 popping bug without a shock tippet hardly annoys a muskie of any size.

But the lake holds more than muskie. Points and coves, as well as woody, debris-littered areas, hold good numbers of bass. On this relatively small lake (only 59 acres), I learned that even during broad daylight bass hide in the most shallow water imaginable as long as there is sufficient cover.

On one day of a hot July weekend, I traveled to Opossum Creek Lake and found a good number of fishermen combing my favorite areas. To get away from the crowd,

I chose a shallow cove littered with stumps and fallen trees. My small popping bug had barely settled along the first stump when a good-sized largemouth took my offering in a hurried rise. Five legal fish later, all of which were returned to the water unharmed, I found that my Zodiac raft had drifted into water so shallow that no draft remained. I spotted a fallen tree in 2 feet of water and laid the bug tight against it. A bass came out from beneath it and took the bug readily. I cast from the base of the tree to the top and picked up 6 more legal fish, with at least two approaching 19 inches in length.

I studied a backwater wash and noted a little "nervous" water, so shallow that I thought it had to be a bluegill making small wakes. I made a challenging cast over three lily pads and into a small pocket of open water. If it were a bluegill, I would have to set the hook hard and hope that it cleared the pads before becoming entangled in the stems.

I shot my cast into the open pocket and the water exploded. I set the hook with a hard sweeping motion toward me, and a 25-inch largemouth leaped over the pads and was landed after a few more heart-stopping leaps. So this lake, with its weed and lily pad-choked source, its points, small coves, and fingerlike extensions, is worth the effort. The area near the spillway also holds some extremely large bass. If fishing the shoreline, fish near the edges of the weed line. Cover the coves and fingers well, and if you're really intent on a muskie, try the weed-choked area near the lake source— it's the best area for a hook-up and also the most difficult to land a large fish.

Opossum Lake is located in Cumberland County and can be found 6 miles northwest of Carlisle by following the signs on SR 641. There are restroom facilities, two paved ramps, and ample parking at the lake.

This lake is managed for bass and is stocked heavily with trout during the months of April, May, and June. However, this is a warmwater fishery, so most fly-fishers come here to take advantage of the bass and muskie fishing, considering the many major limestones that are found within a half-hour's drive from the lake. This lake does have sections that can be waded, but a bottom with a great deal of silt and quick dropoffs can be hazardous. I suggest that this lake be fished from a small boat or canoe. The main access areas close at dark.

The lake is managed primarily for largemouth and panfish, which are the major forage fish. Whether fishing for bass or muskie, take patterns that imitate sunfish.

FRENCH CREEK

More like a river in places, French Creek is in need of repair like so many of Pennsylvania's larger watersheds. However, the fishing here can be superb for warmwater species, such as smallmouth, largemouth, northern pike, and muskie. Since the PFBC stocks all counties with purebred muskie, this could become one of the premier muskie waters in the state.

It is one of the largest and perhaps most overlooked streams for warmwater species within the state. The stream provides habitat for over 80 species of fish and 26 species of freshwater mussels, more than any other stream in Pennsylvania, according to the Department of Environmental Protection.

French Creek's problems include nonpoint source pollution from farm and highway runoff, sewage treatment plant discharges, malfunctioning onlot septic systems, erosion, sedimentation and silt formation, chemical spills, nonnative species, and loss of buffer strips along its banks. The creek now has many friends who are working to reverse these problems and prevent further pollution on this important fishery.

The French Creek Project, based at Allegheny College in Meadville, has been working long and hard on this stream. For more information, check out their website at http://www.alleh.edu.

French Creek begins in Chautauqua County, New York, and extends 117 miles south through northwestern Pennsylvania to its confluence with the Allegheny River at Franklin in Venango County. The 1,270-squaremile watershed constitutes 11 percent of the drainage basin for the Allegheny River.

Most of the stream must be fished by boat, but there are sections of the stream that can be waded with extreme caution. This long and winding watershed deserves a look. From its mouth near Franklin, where it enters the Allegheny River, US 322 follows the stream to Meadville. From there US 6 tracks the stream northeast from Meadville to Indian Head, where secondary roads follow it for a few miles to Union City Lake. Follow the creek north to the state line by taking SR 8 from US 6. Route 8 continues north to SR 8 and 89, then the West Branch can be followed on SR 430 and 426.

The stream can be waded in many parts of Erie County and can be waded again in the upper reaches of Crawford County. Good access is found along the length of the river. This good warmwater stream might help you hook up with that muskie you've been after.

A 9-foot rod carrying an 8-weight line should take care of angling needs. The lower reaches may require a sinktip or sinking line to reach the depths in some of the deeper pools. See Warmwater Fly Box for a list of flies and other important items.

French Creek

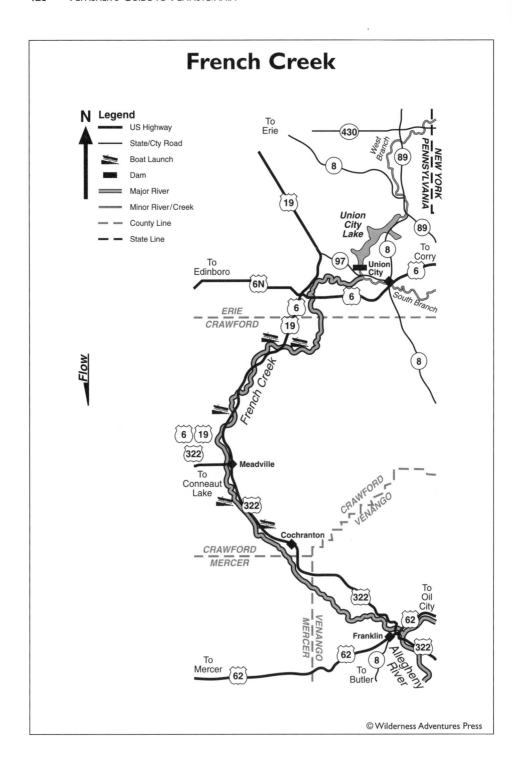

© Wilderness Adventures Press

ALLEGHENY RIVER

From its source, a small spring seep a few miles north of Coudersport, it is difficult to imagine that the Allegheny River flows 325 miles and drains 11,778 square miles. Having covered the coldwater portion of the river in the North Central chapter, we now turn to the river below Allegheny Reservoir, which flows 200 miles before it joins the Monongahela River in Pittsburgh to form the Ohio River. The river passes through Allegheny National Forest, State Game Lands, the Allegheny National Wild and Scenic River corridor, as well as a number of Pennsylvania communities.

This river is as diverse as the landscape that surrounds it. A river that begins by supporting coldwater species and then becoming warmwater habitat is not that unusual here. However, a stream of this length, supporting a fishery of some sort throughout its entire course, is indeed unusual.

From the Allegheny Reservoir (Kinzua Dam) southwest, the river, except for an exceptional tailrace fishery created by the dam, becomes a wonderful warmwater fishery. The tailrace waters and the large brown trout that reside in a short distance of coldwater fishing below the dam evaporate into a warmwater fishery of great worth and value.

The PFBC stocks muskie within the dam and in the river from the dam downstream throughout the entire northwest portion of the state. Once the river reaches the southwest, tiger muskie, along with the purebred muskie and striped bass hybrids, are also stocked by the PFBC.

Fishing the northwest portion of the river often involves shallow draft boats and rafts. As it enters the southwest, inboards and high horsepower fishing boats that are lifted through locks and dams become more common.

The river's lower reaches in the southwest have been virtually ignored as good bass and muskie water due to pollution. However, conditions have changed rapidly since stringent water quality regulations have been put in place, and because this has happened so fast, most anglers are unaware of the opportunities that now exist here. At least one officer of the PFBC feels that the river is now full of fish that have experienced virtually no angling pressure, especially no flyfishing pressure.

Big water, truly big water, seems to frighten local flyfishermen whose experience has been limited to small trout streams and small lakes filled with panfish. And I'll say it once again: Many anglers are missing out on some excellent fishing because they fear to reach beyond their comfort range. There are miles upon miles of "big city" flyfishing available in this area of the state, and it is safe to assume that a vast majority of the bass, striper, and muskie that swim here have never seen a popping bug or streamer.

The reasons for the reluctance to fish here are many: not liking to fish within sight of a city; not knowing what equipment to use; and the fact that there are few guides for the river. However, that should change in the future. Already many hardware

Allegheny River
New York State to President Access

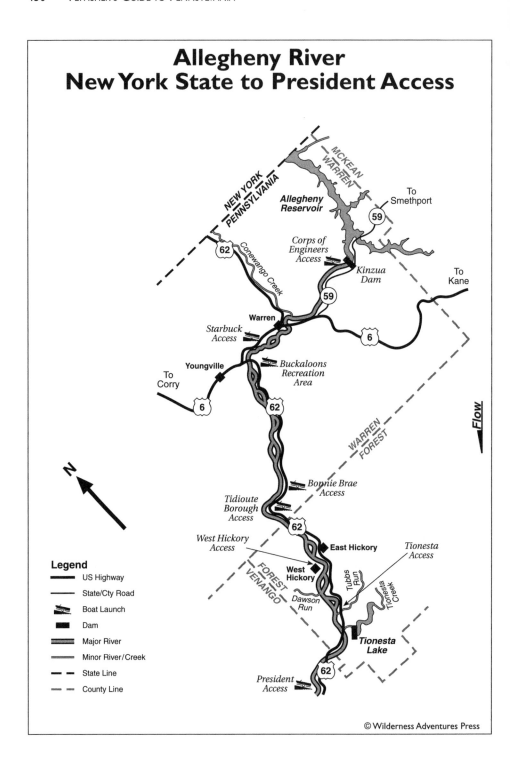

Legend

▬▬▬	US Highway
────	State/Cty Road
⛵	Boat Launch
▰	Dam
▬▬▬	Major River
────	Minor River/Creek
▬ ▬	State Line
─ ─	County Line

© Wilderness Adventures Press

Allegheny River
President Access to East Brady

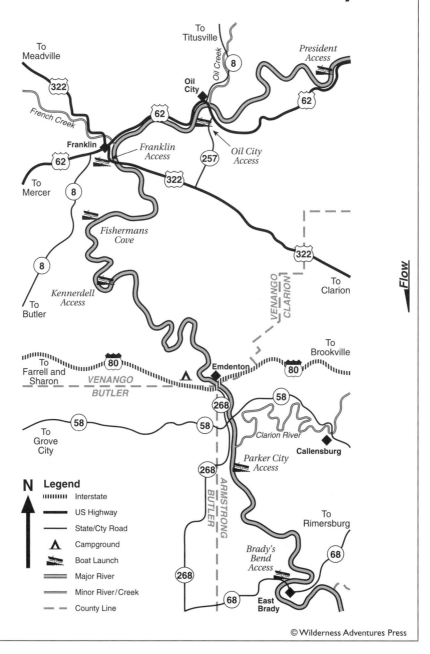

To
Titusville

President
Access

To
Meadville

8

322

Oil
City

62

62

French Creek

Franklin

62

Franklin
Access

257

Oil City
Access

To
Mercer

8

322

Fishermans
Cove

8

322

To
Clarion

VENANGO
CLARION

Flow

Kennerdell
Access

To
Butler

To
Brookville

To
Farrell and
Sharon

80

VENANGO
BUTLER

Emdenton

80

58

268

58

To
Grove
City

58

58

Clarion River

Callensburg

Parker City
Access

268

ARMSTRONG
BUTLER

To
Rimersburg

N Legend

|||||||| Interstate

US Highway

State/Cty Road

Λ Campground

Boat Launch

Major River

Minor River/Creek

County Line

Brady's
Bend
Access

68

268

68 East
Brady

© Wilderness Adventures Press

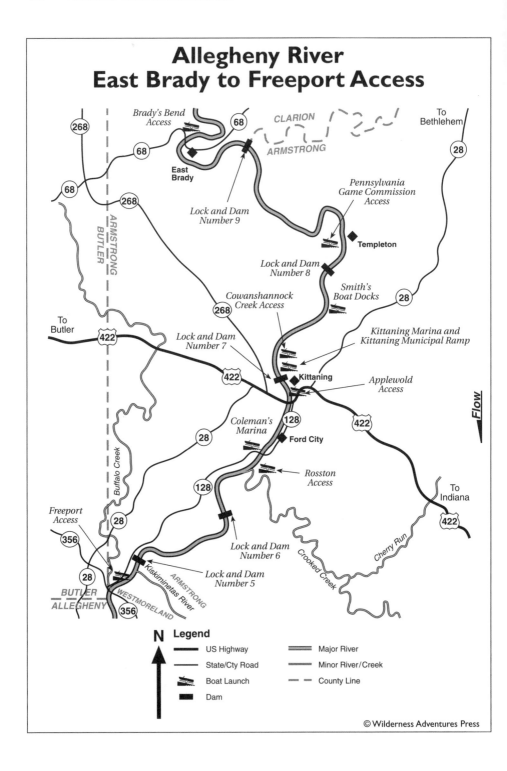

Allegheny River
East Brady to Freeport Access

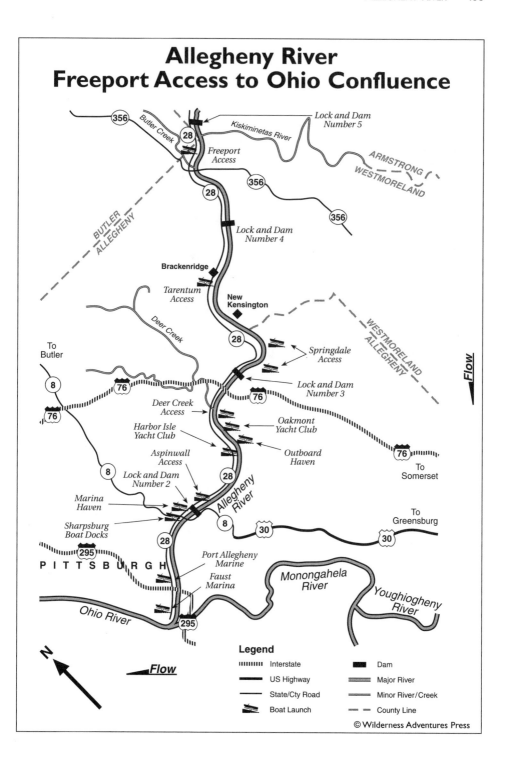

Allegheny River
Freeport Access to Ohio Confluence

356

Butler Creek

28

Kiskiminetas River

Lock and Dam
Number 5

Freeport
Access

ARMSTRONG
WESTMORELAND

28

356

356

Lock and Dam
Number 4

BUTLER
ALLEGHENY

Brackenridge

Tarentum
Access

New
Kensington

Deer Creek

To
Butler

28

Springdale
Access

WESTMORELAND
ALLEGHENY

8

76

Lock and Dam
Number 3

76

76

Deer Creek
Access

Oakmont
Yacht Club

Harbor Isle
Yacht Club

76

To
Somerset

Aspinwall
Access

Outboard
Haven

8

Lock and Dam
Number 2

28

Allegheny
River

To
Greensburg

Marina
Haven

8

30

30

Sharpsburg
Boat Docks

28

295

P I T T S B U R G H

Port Allegheny
Marine

Faust
Marina

Monongahela
River

Youghiogheny
River

Ohio River

295

Flow

N

Flow

Legend

|||||||	Interstate	▬	Dam
▬▬	US Highway	≈≈≈	Major River
—	State/Cty Road	—	Minor River/Creek
Boat Launch		– – –	County Line

© Wilderness Adventures Press

Largemouth bass and pike are often attracted to gaudy flies—don't be afraid to experiment.

anglers are finding bass along islands and visible structure and are becoming more knowledgeable about the shipping lanes to avoid commercial traffic.

Flyfishers will appear on the river as the word gets out that the fish are there—all it will take is to see schools of striped bass hybrids working the water's surface. And equipment is available—much like that used for saltwater fishing. Floating lines work in many areas, while lead-cores might be needed in others.

Fishing is best accomplished by boat, preferably a good-sized one for this portion of the Allegheny. Rods of 9 feet or longer, carrying 8-weight lines, both floating and sinking, are needed. Extra spools should be taken for a reel capable of carrying 150 feet of backing.

A series of eight locks and dams that make the Allegheny navigable through deep pools from Pittsburgh to East Brady allow access to over 70-plus miles of fishing water—water that is providing better fishing with each passing year. Today, according to the Pennsylvania Fish and Boat Commission, the lower Allegheny is home to 46 different species of fish and is a popular sport fishery for smallmouth bass, walleye, sauger, white bass, rock bass, channel catfish, muskie, largemouth bass, and striped bass hybrids.

The river is still in the recovery process—mine drainage still pollutes the Kiskiminetas River, which enters the Allegheny 30 miles upstream from where the three rivers meet in Pittsburgh. But improvements are being made there, as well.

Through Allegheny County, SR 28 follows the river northeast and SR 128 follows it in Armstrong County to the town of Kittaning. From there take secondary roads off SR 28/66 and SR 68 farther north. State route 268 then parallels the river into Venango County. Between Franklin and Oil City, take SR 8, and in Warren and Forest Counties, US 62 runs next to the river until Rogerville, where SR 59 picks the river up to Kinzua Dam.

Consult the Warmwater Fly Box for your choice of flies.

Allegheny River Access Sites

Warren County – 31 miles

Corps of Engineers Access; immediately below Kinzua Dam
- Shallow draft, lightweight fishing boats, canoes, and inflatables
- Boat fishing and float trips
- Surfaced ramp
- Parking available

Starbrick Access; in Starbrick, turn right at traffic light onto US 6, then left on River Road; 2 blocks to access
- Shallow draft, lightweight fishing boats, canoes, and inflatables
- Boat fishing and float trips
- Surfaced ramp
- Parking available

Buckaloons Recreation Area (Allegheny National Forest); go to the junction of US 62 and 6; at the south end of the bridge, turn west
- Shallow draft, lightweight fishing boats, canoes, and inflatables
- Boat fishing and float trips
- Surfaced ramp
- Parking available

Bonnie Brae Access (PFBC); US 62, 2 miles north of Tidioute Bridge
- Shallow draft, lightweight fishing boats, canoes, and inflatables
- Boat fishing and float trips
- Surfaced ramp
- Parking available

Tidioute Borough Access (PFBC); in Tidioute, at foot of Johnson Street
- Shallow draft, lightweight fishing boats, canoes, and inflatables
- Boat fishing and float trips
- Surfaced ramp
- Parking available

Forest County – 15 miles

West Hickory Access (PFBC); East end of West Hickory Bridge on US 62
- Shallow draft, lightweight fishing boats, canoes, and inflatables
- Boat fishing
- Surfaced ramp
- Parking available

Tionesta Access (PFBC); 1 mile north of Tionesta on US 62 at the Tionesta Fish Hatchery
- Shallow draft, lightweight fishing boats, canoes, and inflatables
- Boat fishing
- Surfaced ramp
- Parking available

Venango County – 60 miles

President (PFBC); 1 mile south of Hunter Bridge on SR 537
- Undeveloped

Oil City Access (PFBC); on east shore at Oil City, foot of Wyllis Street
- Shallow draft, lightweight fishing boats, canoes, and inflatables
- Boat fishing and float trips
- Surfaced ramp
- Parking available

Franklin Access (PFBC); in Franklin between 3rd & 4th Streets along Elk Street; south off SR 322 Bridge
- Shallow draft, lightweight fishing boats, canoes, and inflatables
- Boat fishing and float trips
- Surfaced ramp
- Parking available

Fishermans Cove (PFBC); located approximately 10 miles downtown of Franklin on the right bank (west) of the Allegheny River; travel south from Franklin on old SR 8 to the intersection with Sandy Creek; follow the old railroad bed (township road) on the right bank (south) of Sandy Creek to the intersection with Fishermans Cove Road; turn right onto Fishermans Cove Road and travel approximately 300 yards to the access
- Shallow draft, lightweight fishing boats, canoes, and inflatables
- Boat fishing and float trips
- Beach-type ramp
- Parking available
- Minimal development

Kennerdell (PFBC); at Kennerdell off SR 3008
- Undeveloped

Allegheny River (DER & WPA Conservancy); camping permitted on islands and near Kennderell (Danner Rest Stop)

Armstrong County – 60 miles

Parker City Access (PFBC); located at bridge (Parkers Landing)
- Shallow draft, lightweight fishing boats, canoes, and inflatables
- Surfaced ramp
- Parking available

Brady's Bend Access (PFC); across from East Brady off SR 68 at west side of bridge
- Deep draft, high-powered boats
- Surfaced ramp
- Parking

PA Game Commission Access; Game Lands #287 at Templeton; take SR 28/66 north of Kittanning for 6 miles to SR 1034; go 2.5 miles to SR 1031; continue south to end of village of Templeton
- Moderate draft fishing boats
- Surfaced ramp
- Parking available

Smith's Boat Docks; Mosgrove, off SR 1033
- Deep draft, high-powered boats; charge for launching
- Surfaced ramp
- Parking, gas, and oil available

Cowanshannock Creek Access (PFBC); take SR 1033 north of Kittanning, approximately 1 mile
- Moderate draft fishing boats
- Surfaced ramp
- Parking available

Kittanning Marina; north of Water Street, at Colwell
- Deep draft, high-powered boats; charge for launching
- Surfaced ramp

Kittanning Municipal Ramp; Mulberry Street, Kittanning
- Deep draft, high-powered boats
- Surfaced ramp
- Parking available

Applewold Access (PFC); west shore, 1.5 miles south on SR 3001, or take Linde Air Products Road off old US 422 in West Kittanning beneath new US 422 bridge
- Deep draft, high-powered boats
- Surfaced ramp
- Parking available

Coleman's Marina; at Rosston; off T-842, one mile south of Ford City
- Moderate draft fishing boats
- Surfaced ramp
- Parking, gas, and oil available

Rosston Access (PFBC); located 2 miles south of Ford City Bridge off T-862 at mouth of Crooked Creek. Good take-out spot for float trip on Crooked Creek
- Moderate draft fishing boats
- Parking available

Freeport Access (PFBC); Water Street, Freeport
- Moderate draft fishing boats
- Surfaced ramp
- Parking available

Westmoreland County (no accesses)

Allegheny County – 24 miles

Tarentum Access (PFBC); In Tarentum, off SR 28, under SR 366 Bridge
- Moderate draft fishing boats
- Surfaced ramp
- Parking

Springdale Access (PFC); foot of Butler Street in Springdale
- Shallow draft, lightweight fishing boats, canoes, and inflatables
- Beach-type ramp

Springdale Access (PFC); Colfax Street, Springdale
- Moderate draft fishing boats
- Surfaced ramp
- Parking available

Deer Creek Access (PFBC); off SR 28 at 2526 Wenzel Drive, Harmarville
- Moderate draft fishing boats; charge for launching
- Beach type ramp
- Parking, gas, and oil available

Oakmont Yacht Club; in Oakmont off Allegheny River Boulevard at Washington Avenue to California Avenue ramp
- Deep draft, high-powered boats
- Limited parking
- Surfaced ramp
- Gas and oil available

Outboard Haven; off Allegheny River Boulevard at Arch Street in Verona
- Moderate draft fishing boats; charge for launching
- Surfaced ramp
- Parking, gas, and oil available

Harbor Isle Yacht Club; off SR 28, No. 1 River Road at Blawnox
- Unlimited size boats, hoist; *charge for launching
- Beach-type ramp
- Parking, gas and oil available

Aspinwall Marina, Inc.; off SR 28, 285 River Avenue, Aspinwall
- Unlimited size boats; charge for launching
- Marine hoist
- Surface ramp
- Parking, gas, and oil available
- Charge for launching (usually indicates a commercial area, but note also, that all boats launched on state park waters must possess either a PA registration or a launch permit obtained from the park office.

Marina Haven; off SR 28 to 19th Street in Sharpsburg
- Moderate draft fishing boats; charge for launching
- Surfaced ramp
- Parking, gas, and oil available

Sharpsburg Boat Docks; off SR 28 to 13th Street in Sharpsburg
- Moderate draft fishing boats
- Beach-type ramp
- Parking, gas, and oil available

Port Allegheny Marine; Pittsburgh (Fox Chapel), off Rt. 28 to Squaw Road and Old Freeport Road
- Unlimited sized boats; charge for launching
- Handicapped Facilities
- Gas and oil available
- No ramp
- Hoist-type launching only

Faust Marina; 300 River Avenue East, foot of 9th Street Bridge, Pittsburgh
- Moderate draft fishing boats, *charge for launching
- Parking limited
- Surfaced ramp
- Beach-type ramp
- Gas and oil available

Kinzua Dam

The largest dam in the state, Kinzua is a 12,000-acre impoundment that provides excellent fishing for a wide variety of game fish, and its tailrace fishing has become superb.

My first visit to Kinzua (Allegheny Reservoir) was more years ago than I would like to mention. We had decided to fish early and, upon our arrival, large brown trout were feeding at the mouth of Sugar Run. I promptly began casting a small streamer to the hefty fish swimming into the tributary as dawn broke into full light. By then I had hooked, and promptly lost, four browns over 20 inches. The area was filled with lily pads, and it seemed that the large browns had a plan—take the fly, run to the lily pads, and wrap my fragile leader around them. When they tired of the game, they simply swam away up the small feeder stream.

On the lake, bass began rising in the backwater bay. A white Gaines popping bug took bass after bass, fish that fed much like stripers or bluefish, herding minnows into the shallows and along the points. Working the bug over the bass as fast as possible did the trick, and I caught more average-sized smallmouth than I could count. None of the smallmouth were very big, but large boils did prove that bigger bass than I was catching were around.

When the action slowed down, I maneuvered my old johnboat within casting distance of the shoreline and took bass everywhere that looked like smallmouth

Allegheny Reservoir.

water. As I worked the shoreline, I noted another flyfisher working the same stretch I was. We were far enough apart not to interfere with one another.

I paused for a moment when the other angler hooked an outsized muskie. He was poorly equipped with an automatic reel attached to a fiberglass rod. The drag system was far too tight for a fish that size, but he was able to handle the fish through a series of half-hearted leaps. But, as muskie are prone to do, it ran for the boat and then went beneath it. The man could not let out enough line to maneuver it around the boat and lost the fish and the rod in a sickening snap. He looked up at me, smiled, and then laughed, "At least I know they are here!"

Kinzua is an excellent flyfishing impoundment with enough backwater coves to allow one to escape the midsummer pleasure boaters. The dam boasts the state record northern, a 33-pound, 8-ounce fish, taken in 1980, and, surprisingly, a 17-pound, 9-ounce walleye taken the same year.

Fed by the Allegheny River, the reservoir offers some excellent tailrace fishing for trout. The PFBC stocks the lake with fingerling lake trout, muskie, and walleye.

A boat is necessary for fishing, and boat rentals are available. I suggest a rod carrying an 8-weight for bass, a 6-weight for trout, and a 9-weight coupled with a shock-tippet for muskie and northerns.

Kinzua Dam is a concrete gravity dam with an earthen abutment on the right side. The maximum height above the streambed is 179 feet. The dam's overall length is 1,877 feet and is located on the Allegheny River about 8 miles above Warren on US 6. Consult the Warmwater Fly Box for your fly selection.

Kinzua Dam Access Sites

McKean County

Dunkle Corners; from US 6 in Kane, take SR 321 north for 11.7 miles and make a left turn onto Forest Service Road #601; the ramp is an abandoned blacktop road suitable for small fishing-type boats
- Shallow draft, lightweight fishing boats, canoes, and inflatables
- Parking available

Kiasutha; from US 6 in Kane, take SR 321 north 9 miles to Forest Service Road #262 (known as Longhouse Scenic Drive). Turn left onto road #262 and go 1.7 miles
- Camping available
- Unlimited boat size
- Surfaced ramp
- Parking available

Elijah Run; from US 6 in Kane, take SR 321 north 9 miles to Forest Service Road #262 (known as Longhouse Scenic Drive). Turn left onto road #262 and go 7.1 miles
- Unlimited boat size
- Surfaced ramp
- Parking available

Willow Bay; from US 6 in Kane: take SR 321 north 19.7 miles to SR 59, turn right onto 59 and go east 2.2 miles to SR 59 and 321 junction; turn left onto SR 321 and go 14.5 miles to SR 346; turn left onto road #602 and go 1.5 miles to launching ramp.

From US 219 and US 6 junction at Lantz Corners: take US 219 north for 8.5 miles to SR 59. Turn left onto SR 59 and go 6.2 miles to SR 321. Turn right onto SR 321 and go 14.5 miles to SR 346. Turn left onto 346 and go 1.5 miles to Forest Service Road #602 and go 1.5 miles to launching ramp.

From Bradford: take SR 346 at junction of US 219 north of the city and go west on SR 346 for 16.9 miles to Forest Service Road #602 (1.5 miles past junction with Rt. 321). Turn left onto road #602 and go 1.5 miles to launching ramp.

- Camping available
- Unlimited boat size
- Surfaced ramp
- Parking available

Warren County

Dew Drop Launch; take SR 59 north from Warren; turn right at Casey bridge or Forest Service Road #262 (Longhouse Scenic Drive); launch and campground is on the left, about 3 miles from SR 59

Wolfe Run Marina; located off SR 59, just south of Cornplanter bridge
- Private marina, restaurant
- Boat rentals, bait and ample parking
- Fee area

Roper Hollow Access ; take SR 1013 north from Warren to Scandia; turn right on T-615, which leads to launch area
- Unlimited boat size
- Surfaced ramp
- Parking available

Webbs Ferry; take L.R. 61037 north from Scandia to 0.5 mile south of New York state line
- Unlimited sized boats
- Surfaced ramp
- Parking available

LAKE ERIE

Smallmouth bass of 5 pounds are quite common in Lake Erie, which will more than likely capture the next smallmouth record for Pennsylvania. It already has many other state records, such as chinook, 28 pounds, 15 ounces; coho, 15 pounds, 5 ounces; lake trout, 27 pounds, 13 ounces; palomino, 11 pounds, 10 ounces; and steelhead, 19 pounds, 2 ounces.

Lake Erie holds a wide variety of game fish: walleyes, often found in the shallows during spring, that are extremely fond of yellow streamers tied on 2/0 hooks; muskie in the fall; northerns in the spring; and even lake trout that seek out the shallows in spring and fall.

The lake's size as well as the size of boats found on it can be intimidating for flyfishers. Many of the charter boats are designed for trolling and use downriggers to probe the depths. There aren't many guides or boats that cater to flyfishing anglers, either.

However, Pennsylvania does have 40 miles of shoreline with opportunities for the wading flyfisher. I have taken many large steelhead a short cast from shore next to tributaries. Smallmouth bass crowd the rocky shore in spring and can be reached easily with a lead core or fast-sinking line. Smallmouth can also be seen surface feeding just offshore. So wading can be productive if that is your only option. I usually use a 9-weight with a floating line when wading because of the wind and because many fish along the shore can be taken with a floating line.

A charter boat on Lake Erie.

That said, a boat would be ideal for flyfishing on Lake Erie. Because it is so large, finding fish can pose problems, but fishing around structure can help, especially structure that is suited to whatever species is being sought. With everything imaginable to offer, Lake Erie is much too overlooked as a flyfishing venue. If fished in the same manner as bays and estuaries using 9- and 10-weight lines, this would be a wonderful place for flyfishers to explore. Be warned that Lake Erie is a shallow body of water, and at the first sign of bad weather, one should head for shore or the dock.

To cover a variety of depths and to address the difficulty in locating fish, I use three rods for Lake Erie, ranging in line weight from 8 to 10. I use a floating line on my 8-weight outfit, a fast-sinking line on my 9-weight, and a lead core on my 10-weight. I often use Clouser's minnows or lead eyes in various weights to reach the depths. Because of the lake's size, the better locations for individual species have not yet been charted.

See the Warmwater Fly Box for your selection. Also see the section on Lake Erie steelhead in the Northwest Pennsylvania chapter for a selection of steelhead flies.

Lake Erie Access Sites

Walnut Creek Access (PFBC); located in Fairview Township, four miles west of Erie off SR 5 (east side of Walnut Creek at the mouth); overnight mooring is available (May 15–October); Administration building is manned from early spring to fall; open 24 hours a day.
- Deep draft, high-powered recreational boats
- Surfaced ramp
- Parking available

Lake City; off SR 5, at the mouth of Elk Creek
- Privately-owned ramp with camping facilities; launching charges apply

Raccoon County Park Access; six miles west of Lake City off SR 5
- Picnicking and sanitary facilities available without fee
- Moderate draft fishing boats, sailboats, and recreational runabout boats
- Beach-type ramp
- Parking available

Charley's Boat Livery; one mile east of Sixteenmile Creek

Safe Harbor Marina (PFBC); located 2.5 miles east of the intersection of SR 5 and 89
- Full service marina: mooring, parking, fuel sales, repairs, food, launch ramps; no fee

Shades Beach; six miles east of Erie off SR 5 with picnicking, camping and sanitary facilities
- No fee launching
- Moderate draft fishing boats, sailboats, and recreational runabout boats
- Beach-type ramp
- Parking available

City of Erie Sites

Chestnut Street Access; located two blocks west of State Street, which terminates at the Public Dock
- Moderate draft fishing boats, sailboats, and recreational runabout boats
- Surfaced ramp
- Parking available

East Avenue Access; located at the foot of East Avenue
- Moderate draft fishing boats, sailboats, and recreational runabout boats
- Surfaced ramp
- Parking available

Erie Public Dock; on either side there are six marine dealers with hoists for large and small boats and dockage with complete supply of marine services
- Unlimited size boats; charge for launching
- Gas and oil available
- Surfaced ramp
- Parking available

East Boat Livery; located east of Perry monument
- Rental boats
- Unlimited size boats
- Surfaced ramp
- Parking available

Lampe Marina; located at the foot of Wayne Avenue. Extended in the city of Erie
- Deep draft, high-powered recreational boats
- Surfaced ramp
- Parking available

Presque Isle State Park; three large ramps and four smaller ones on the Presque Isle Bay side and one on the lake side. Smaller ramps are located off the parking lots on the peninsula. The larger ramps (all free) include:
- Niagara Ramp: 0.25 mil east of the administration building
- Marina Ramp: East of main Marina on West Fisher Drive
- Logan Ramp: Northeast of Perry Monument

The main marina on West Fisher Drive has two hoists and seasonal boat dockage, as well as overnight dockage (fee). The hoists area designed to accommodate boats up to 45 feet in length.

Presque Isle Bay

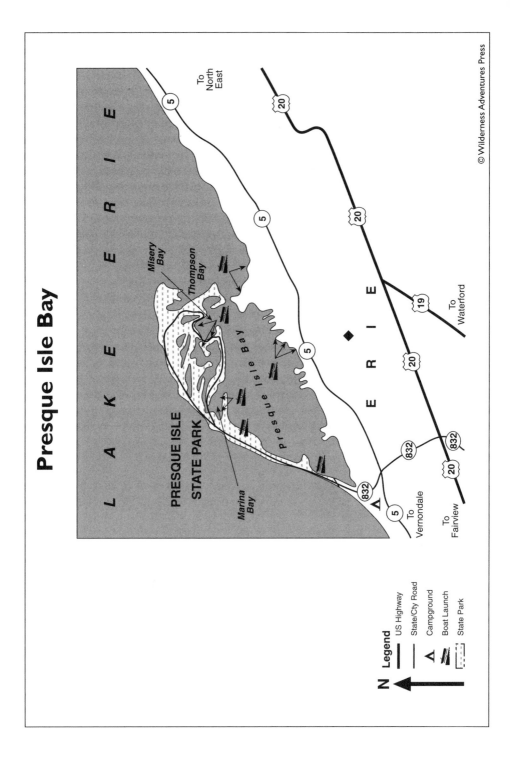

© Wilderness Adventures Press

PRESQUE ISLE BAY

Presque Isle Bay is an area I absolutely love—the bay is shallow enough to wade and has enough vegetation to hide muskie and pike, as well as smallmouth and largemouth bass. Recent surveys by the PFBC indicate that the bay holds more largemouth than smallmouth, and if one looks at the area, it is quickly obvious that the weedbeds and silt bottom are better suited for largemouth.

Average size of smallmouth in the bay is smaller than in Lake Erie, but they are big enough to keep anyone's interest. I have brought many smallmouth and largemouth to the surface and broken off more muskie than I landed at Presque Isle. As autumn approaches, steelhead and coho wander in and out of the bay and add extra excitement to the fishing. In addition to the great fishing there is a breathtaking view—a combination that is pretty hard to beat.

Presque Isle State Park encompasses 3,200 acres in Erie County and can be reached by SR 832 or by boat. The road system within the park forms a loop approximately 14 miles in length. The neck of the peninsula is attached to the mainland 4 miles west of downtown Erie.

Both nonpowered and registered powered crafts are permitted. Internal combustion engines are prohibited in the interior lagoons, which are defined as the continuous body of water between Misery Bay and Marina Bay, excluding Grave Yard Pond. A boat rental concession, located in the Grave Yard Pond area, provides a variety of powered and nonpowered crafts. Beaching of boats along Presque Isle shoreline is permitted, except at the Gull Point Special Management Area (between April 1 and November 30) and within 100 feet of designated swimming areas. A slow minimum height swell speed must be observed within all park waters, which include all waters within 500 feet of the shoreline.

If you are visiting the area, it is important to know that weather can change quickly, affecting conditions on the bay and the lake. When weather changes, the shallowness of the lake creates dangerous conditions. Wading anglers should note weather changes as well. DCNR suggests that anglers heed all weather notices and listen to channel 16, the Coast Guard Emergency Channel, or a VHS radio for current boating conditions. I have visited often enough to know that any sign of bad weather means it's time to head for the dock or wade ashore. I have been caught in bad weather, both in a boat and while wading, and I cannot stress the importance of heeding all signs of bad weather approaching. If it passes, resume fishing.

When wade fishing, I take a 9-foot rod suited for a 9-weight line. I use overhand loops to connect my tippets to the popping bugs I love to use. If a muskie shows up, I simply back the leader off and bug off and replace it with a streamer already rigged with a shock-tippet. I use 40-pound mono with an overhand loop as well. The exchange is quick and easy, even when wading in waist deep water. It has worked for a good number of the muskie and northern pike I have taken here.

I fish the edges of weedbeds with popping bugs the better part of the day and then change over to a large streamer with a shock tippet, reworking as many beds as

A lot of Flashabou helped convince this stillwater largemouth bass.

possible before day's end. This strategy has resulted in many successful hookups with both bass and muskie.

Fish early and late in the season, since tourist traffic is heavy during summer. If I had a choice, I would fish this beautiful area from September on. For more information concerning the park contact: Presque Isle State Park, Department of Conservation and Natural Resources, PO Box 8510, Erie, PA 16505, 814-8337424 or Erie Chamber of Commerce, 1006 State Street, Erie, PA 16505, 814-4547190. See the Warmwater Fly Box for your fly selection.

Boat Launches: A total of five launching areas are available which can accommodate various sized craft. The Vista Launch is recommended for small watercraft. The Niagara Launch has two ramps and can accommodate small to medium size craft. The West Pier Launch area is the largest facility with four launching ramps and is recommended for larger watercraft. The Lagoon Launch area can accommodate small to medium size craft, although the southern launch in this area is intended for small craft only.

PYMATUNING LAKE

A lake covering 13,500 acres and straddling the border of two states is nothing to sneeze at. Three-fourths of the reservoir is located in Pennsylvania's Crawford County and the remaining portion is in Ashtabula County, Ohio. Pymatuning State Park borders most of the lake in Pennsylvania.

As in most of the state's lakes, the fishing on Pymatuning can vary from year to year, depending on year classes of fish. For example, muskie numbers dropped dramatically in the early 1990s but are now on the rebound, and the chances of taking a good-sized muskie are excellent. According to the PFBC surveys, this lake has an abundance of muskie, and a lot of them are large—one taken in 1999 measured 47 inches, a large fish anywhere. The PFBC continues to stock this lake with both muskie and walleye—yes, walleye can be taken on a fly rod—and bass and northern pike fishing are good as well. If there is a problem here, it is finding fish with a 10-horsepower boat on such a large lake. Wading opportunities are limited due to the lake's depth. For those unfamiliar with the lake, do not attempt to wade it.

From the east and west, the park is accessible by US 6 and 322, and SR 18, 285, and 58. Nonpowered boats and boats to 10 horsepower are permitted. Boats with a motor in excess of 10 horsepower are permitted, but the motor cannot be used. There are three Pennsylvania boat marinas where floatboats, motorboats, rowboats, canoes, and motors can be rented.

Fishing licenses issued by either Ohio or Pennsylvania are honored anywhere on the lake, but only Ohio licensed fishermen can fish from the Ohio shore and Pennsylvania licensed fishermen from the Pennsylvania shore. Common species of fish in the lake include walleye, muskellunge, crappie, perch, bluegill, and largemouth and smallmouth bass.

Bass fishing is good for both largemouth and smallmouth, but one needs to find the areas where they hang out. Smallmouth are found in rocky areas, while largemouth are often found in silty backwaters, including coves. I fish this lake with a 9-foot for a 9-weight most of the time and have found good fishing along the shoreline and in small coves.

I love topwater fishing, mostly with floating lines, but fly lines with the first 30 feet sinking help when bass are hanging off shore. As with any place where muskie or northern pike are found, I use a second rod rigged with wire leader or heavy monofilament shock-tippets.

This is a good lake for those who have time to explore it, and for those who don't, the fishing can be disappointing at times. Still there is little doubt that this is a good lake that can yield good bass and those toothy critters to flyfishers willing to make the effort.

Pymatuning has year-round bass fishing with a creel limit of 8 and a minimum size of 12 inches. Both the creel and size limit are far too liberal to sustain an excellent fishery. Because of that, the reservoir has to be rated as no better than good.

Camping: With 657 campsites in three areas, Pymatuning is one of the largest camping areas in the Commonwealth. Approximately half of the campsites have electric hookups. Modern tent and trailer camping areas are available in the Jamestown, Tuttle, and Linesville campgrounds. In addition, an organized group camping area is available for groups of up to 400 people. Campsite permits may be obtained at the contact stations in the three camping areas. Reservations can be made and are recommended for Jamestown and Tuttle campgrounds as well as the organized group camping area. Reservations may be made by calling 888PAPARKS.

Cabins: 25 modern rental cabins are available for yearround use. Six of these cabins meet the Americans with Disabilities Act standards for accessibility. Cabins have a furnished living area, kitchen/dining area, toilet/shower room and two or three bedrooms. Occupants must bring linens, towels, cookware and tableware.

Advance reservations are required and can be made by calling 888PAPARKS. For additional information and up to the minute fishing conditions contact: Department of Conservation and Natural Resources, Pymatuning State Park, 2660 Williamsfield Road, Jamestown, PA 16134; telephone 724-932-3141.

Check the Warmwater Fly Box for flies.

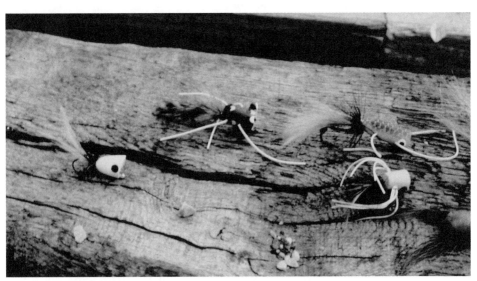

A collection of bass flies and bugs.

CONNEAUT LAKE

This lake is one of the very best smallmouth and muskie lakes I have been privileged to fish. It has an excellent combination of shoreline structure and shallow mounds within the lake and is ideal water for flyfishing. The chances of taking a good bass here are excellent and battling a muskie very good.

Despite the fact that it is only 925 acres, the habitat is great and the fishing is hard to beat. A boat is needed to get around on this lake, one of the most overlooked in the state. It is nearly 3 miles long, varies from a mile to 2 miles wide, and is 90 feet at its deepest point. A depth finder is a must, since deep water can turn to shallow flats and humps quickly. Bass grow well and in large proportions. Although Conneaut Lake doesn't look impressive at first glance, it has all the components that make a superb fishery.

The state record muskie of 54 pounds, 3 ounces was taken at Conneaut back in 1924, and it has proven impossible to top. The record for white bass, 3 pounds, 4 ounces, was also set here in 1996. I mention state records only to prove what the lake is capable of producing. In this era of catch and release, I'm certain that many fish that could have qualified for state records have been released. Muskie fishing is well above average here, and smallmouth fishing is great...this is one good lake that should not be passed up, as so many anglers do on their way to Lake Erie.

Take an 8-weight rod for bass and a 9 or 10 for muskie and northerns. Keep one rigged with a large streamer and a shock tippet for covering the shorelines at dusk and into the evening with popping bugs.

The PFBC stocks muskie, yellow perch, walleye, and white bass at Conneaut, mostly as fingerling. See Warmwater Fly Box for flies and poppers.

This lake is easy to find by taking US 6/322 west of Meadville to the lake.

Conneaut Lake Access Sites

PFC access; area at northwest corner of lake off SR 618
- Unlimited horsepower, deep draft, high-powered recreational boats; charge for launching
- Launching, mooring, and parking facilities available
- Surfaced ramp
- Commercial docks and launching area available
- Gas and oil available
- No fees

LAKE ARTHUR

At 3,225 acres, Lake Arthur is a tremendous fishery found in Butler County that is home to bass, muskie, northern pike, and hybrid striped bass. The lake, found within the confines of Moraine State Park, has a lot to offer a serious flyfisher. The park is situated in some beautiful country and isn't far from Pittsburgh.

The lake is well known for its largemouth fishery, and muskies are extremely abundant. The pike fishing is excellent as well, and there are not that many good pike lakes within the boundaries of Pennsylvania. It is well known for truly big largemouth bass and is regulated under the Big Bass Program by the PFBC. An extremely productive method for largemouth is to toss popping bugs along the shoreline and points.

Careful wading is possible in many areas, and bass, muskie and northerns are all possible. The area's quietness is maintained by special boating regulations that allow nothing larger than a 10-horsepower motor.

Volunteers, lead by the PFBC, have been busy placing structure within the lake that has helped attract fish to particular areas. Fortunately for flyfishers who are new to the lake, maps can be purchased that show these locations. The maps, which show fish habitat project locations, water depths, and specific features of the lake, are available at the park office, marina office, and the gift shop at McDanel's Boat Launch.

The lake impoundment is located in northwestern Pennsylvania south of the I–79 and I–80 intersection. Two state routes pass through Moraine State Park: US 422 running east/west and SR 528 running north/south. To reach the South Shore Recreation Area, take the South Shore Exit from US 422. To reach the North Shore from US 422, take the North Shore Exit. There is no access to the North Shore from US 422 headed east from I–79, so take the South Shore Exit, get onto US 422 west and take the North Shore Exit.

The chance of taking northern pike and muskie on Lake Arthur is good to excellent, and a big largemouth is above average compared to most of the state's lakes. Lake Arthur is a good lake for flyfishing because its depth is not that great. Striper action, as well as pike and muskie, is best during spring and fall, and largemouth fishing is good throughout the entire summer. There are those who feel the fishing isn't as good as it once was, but I feel it is an ideal flyfishing lake. Even when summer recreational traffic is high, there is plenty of water for a flyfisher to cover and some good wading possibilities.

My rod preference for Lake Arthur is one 9 feet or more in length with medium to fast action and carrying an 8- or 9-weight line. Both a floating and a sinktip line are needed here, and an intermediate sinking line is a good choice in summer.

I have taken everything from muskie to stripers with a Grandt rod having a weight-forward line, floating or sinking, and it has handled all of them well. But whenever there is a mixed bag of fish available, as there are at Lake Arthur, I take a rod that is suitable for 8-, 9-, or even 10-weight lines. I rig the heavier rod with a shock tippet of wire or heavy mono attached to 10- to-12-pound test Maxima tippet material. I prefer Maxima material because it is stiff and can turn over the heavier bugs and leadeyes needed for fishing this lake.

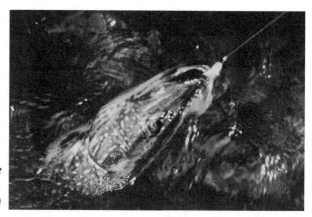

This northern pike took a streamer. (Photo by Karl Power)

When stripers are chasing baitfish on top, I either change the rod or the fly on an 8-weight. I prefer an 8- or 9-weight when wading since casting a 10-weight or heavier can be too laborious. I base my selection of rod on what fish are visible or when I know muskie are present in a particular area.

Lake Arthur Flies

- Popping bugs, # 2 thru #6. Foam and Cork- sliders, flat and conclave face. Yellow, white, black, chartruse, green (lime), brown and black.
- Floating Minnows: 2, 3x long thru 6, 3x long. A wide variety of colors (my favorite is a white deer hair wing and head over a white spun rabbit fur body) with marabou tail. Tie in pearl Flashabou.

Same pattern with brown wing and olive or tan body. Same pattern with yellow wing and pearl tinsel body; green wing with tan or olive body; black wing with black or white, or tan body.

- Deep diving minnows: 4/0 thru #4. Chartruse and white, brown and white, black, white and white. White and yellow. Be sure to use Krsytal Flash or Flashabou.
- Lefty's Deceiver: 4/0 thru #4. White and Yellow and Grizzly and Ginger Grizzly variations.
- Crayfish Pattern of you choice: 2 thru #8; my favorite is Clouser's Crayfish, Green back with white body.
- Black Leech Pattern of your choice. It seems that we still do not have a perfect leech pattern.
- Dragon Fly adults and emergers.

Add a touch of red to all you streamer patterns.

For additional information on cabins or the lake contact: Department of Conservation and Natural Resources, Moraine State Park 225 Pleasant Valley Road, Portersville, PA 160519650; Park Office: 724-3688811, Marina: 724-368-9346

KEYSTONE LAKE

This Keystone Lake should not be confused with the one found in Keystone State Park that is in Westmoreland County. Armstrong County's Keystone Lake is a much larger and better fishery. The impoundment is owned by Keystone Power Company and is stocked by the PFBC with trout throughout the year as well as muskie and walleye. It is also an excellent smallmouth bass fishery and does contain some northern pike, lake trout, and panfish.

Covering some 1,000 acres, it is a lake well worth fishing for its plentiful supply of smallmouth bass and, to a lesser degree, largemouth bass. Fishing along the shoreline can produce excellent results with a popping bug or floating minnow. Karl Power, a well-known outdoor writer and radio broadcaster in the area who fishes the lake frequently, claims the lake is best fished closer to the dam due to the old-growth pines that were placed there years ago for additional structure.

The lake varies greatly from rocky shoreline to mud-bottom bays, where largemouth like to hang out. The lake also has steep dropoffs that require sinktips and medium sinking lines to reach the depths.

A 9-foot rod carrying an 8-weight line is nearly perfect for this lake, and prowling the shallows in the evening and morning is the best bet. This rod or an additional rod with shock-tippet and streamer in place will take care of any muskie or pike that might be encountered.

The lake is protected by a 10-horsepower limit for boats, which limits recreational boating and maintains the excellent fishing found throughout the year. Sections of the lake can be waded, but using a boat is a much better way to cover the water and a safer one as well.

Keystone is about an hour and a half from Pittsburgh along SR 210, three miles north of Elderton. Check the Warmwater Fly Box for a selection of flies for this lake.

Keystone Lake Access Sites

Atwood Access; SR 210 at Atwood
- Shallow draft, lightweight fishing boats, canoes, and inflatables
- Surfaced ramp
- Parking available

Rural Valley Access; south from SR 85 between Rural Valley and NuMine
- Shallow draft, lightweight fishing boats, canoes, and inflatables
- Surfaced ramp
- Parking available

Sagamore Access; off SR 210 south of Sagamore
- Walk-in access to fishing waters—no boats
- Beach-type ramp
- Parking available

In addition, there are two parking lots off SR 210.

OHIO RIVER

One of the "three rivers" used to promote the city of Pittsburgh for decades, the Ohio River has, like the other two, been shunned by flyfishers as too polluted to be worthwhile. But, like the others, it too is on the mend, although it has a long way to go before its water can be called clean. The introduced striped bass hybrids (locally known as Kentucky bass) have thrived to the point that they are now seen chasing baitfish across the river.

Here at Pittsburgh, the Ohio River begins its approximately 1,000 mile journey west to the Mississippi River. Within the boundaries of Pennsylvania, however, the river flows for less than 50 miles and is heavily used by barges and commercial traffic.

From the point in Pittsburgh to the Ohio/West Virginia state line, the return of the fishery has gone mostly ignored. It does not have the proper trimmings to be a destination spot for most flyfishermen. But as industry and sewage treatment plants continue to comply with stringent regulations, the river will become more and more popular.

While there are muskie and bass available, the striped bass hybrids really attract anglers. The Ohio isn't an ideal flyfishing river, but it does have enough to be worth a visit. A boat is pretty much essential to fish on the Ohio, and as with any major waterway, it can be hazardous. Take a rod, preferably a 9-foot, that will carry an 8-weight line.

Following the course of the Ohio River is not difficult. From Pittsburgh, follow SR 65 northwest as it crosses into Beaver County at Ambridge. This road continues to follow the river to Rochester and Beaver, where the Beaver River joins it. From there, SR 68 follows the river west, escorting it into West Virginia and Ohio.

Use the Warmwater Fly Box for your fly selection.

Ohio River Access Sites

Allegheny County

Sutey Marina; off River Avenue in McKees Rocks; on back channel at Brunot Island, downstream from Chartiers Creek
  - Moderate draft fishing boats
  - Gas and oil available
  - Surfaced ramp
  - No parking

C & E Marina; off SR 65 at end of Dawson Avenue, in Glenfield
  - Deep draft, high-powered boats; charge for launching
  - Gas and oil available
  - Surfaced ramp
  - Parking available

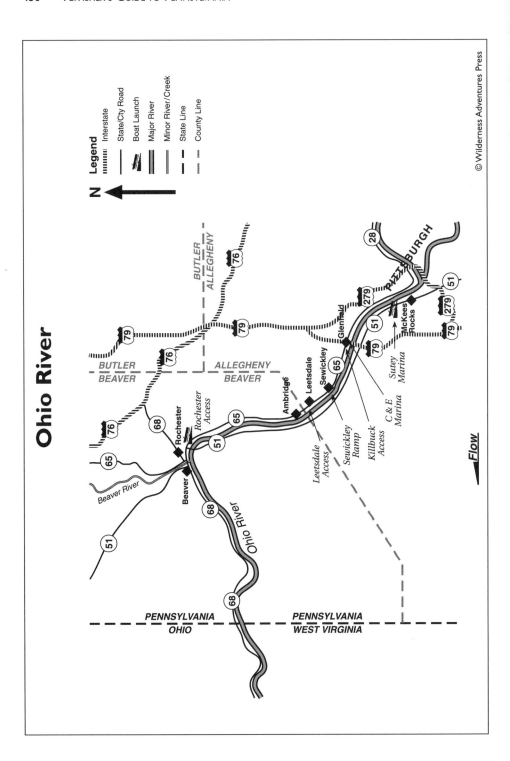

Ohio River

Killbuck Access (PFBC); cross viaduct in Glenfield. East along railroad tracks to access area
- Undeveloped, no facilities

Sewickley Ramp; off SR 65, end of Chestnut Street in Sewickley
- Shallow draft, lightweight fishing boats, canoes, and inflatables
- Surfaced ramp
- Limited parking

Leetsdale Access (PFBC); SR 65 at Leetsdale
- Deep draft, high-powered boats
- Surfaced ramp
- Parking available

Beaver County

Rochester Access (PFBC); located off SR 65 at foot of Pleasant Street and New York Avenue (railroad overpass) in Rochester
- Shallow draft, lightweight fishing boats, canoes, and inflatables
- Surfaced ramp
- Parking available

THE MONONGAHELA RIVER

The Monongahela River is the last of the three famous rivers that join in Pittsburgh and possibly the best for flyfishing. The wealth of this river is its smallmouth bass fishery. Although other species of fish exist here, smallmouth are the main attraction. By the time it reaches the three rivers, the Monongahela has to be considered a huge river, measuring over 350 yards wide.

Locally called the "Mon," the river begins in Pennsylvania, then crosses the state line before flowing north from West Virginia back into Pennsylvania close to Point Marion and forming the Greene/Fayette County line. It is quickly joined by the Cheat River and becomes a full-blown river at this juncture.

From this point to Pittsburgh, the river is known for its abundance of smallmouth bass, joined by northern pike and muskie. Its only drawback is a lack of guides, which is true of many of the larger rivers where flyfishing is still relatively new. Two areas of the river that are highly regarded by outdoor writer Karl Power as "very good fishing for bass" are the Fredericktown and Brownsville areas along the Fayette/Washington County line.

What makes this river extremely attractive to flyfishers is that small fishing boats can be used throughout its entire length. Along with the excellent smallmouth fishing, the introduction of hybrid stripers has further increased the river's attraction. The PFBC stocks the river with striped bass hybrids, tiger and purebred muskie, and walleye. Striped bass and purebred muskie stocking at this time is limited to Allegheny and Washington Counties.

A long, flowing body of water, the river extends approximately 275 miles through four counties. Fishing varies from deep pools, especially at the mouths of the Cheat and Youghiogheny Rivers, to shallow stretches of water. Fishing is best done with a floating line in some areas, but others require a sinktip of 14 feet or, in places, a quick sinking line. I suggest a 9-foot rod carrying an 8- or even a 9-weight line. An ideal situation is to have two rods, one with a floating line and another with a high density sinking line.

Northern pike.

Monongahela River
Point Marion to Brownsville

WASHINGTON

40

West Brownsville
Access

43

88

East Fredericktown-
East Millsboro Access

Brownsville

88

WASHINGTON

GREENE

Fredericktown

166

40

Ten Mile Creek
County Park
Access

Millsboro

Raystown Branch
Access

88

Sunset
Marina

Dry
Tavern

Rices
Landing

FAYETTE

To
Uniontown

GREENE

166

21

To
Waynesburg

88

21

21

21

To
Uniontown

Masontown

88

166

119

166

Point Marion
Access

Dunkard Valley
Marina

88

119

Scott
Motorboat
Sales

N
Legend

US Highway
State/Cty Road
Boat Launch
Major River
Minor River/Creek
State Line
County Line

PENNSYLVANIA
WEST VIRGINIA

Point
Marion

119

Cheat River

Flow

© Wilderness Adventures Press

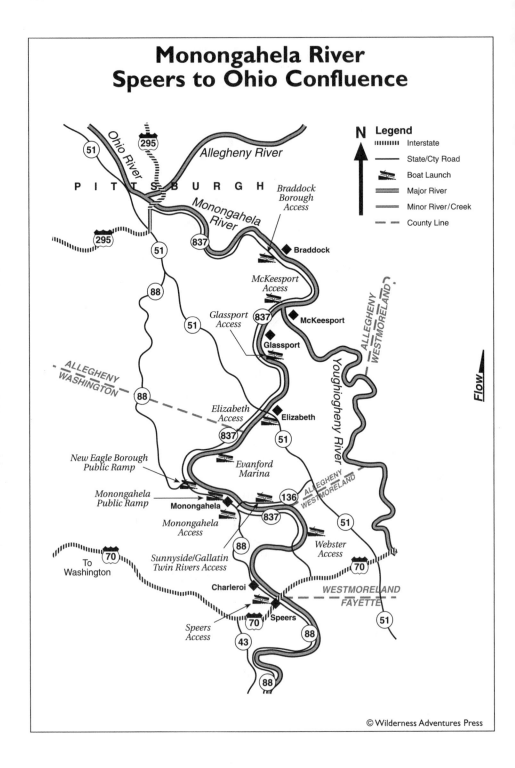

Monongahela River
Speers to Ohio Confluence

Legend

‖‖‖‖‖	Interstate
——	State/Cty Road
⚓	Boat Launch
══	Major River
——	Minor River/Creek
– – –	County Line

Ohio River

Allegheny River

P I T T S B U R G H

Monongahela River

Braddock Borough Access

Braddock

McKeesport Access

Glassport Access

McKeesport

Glassport

Youghiogheny River

ALLEGHENY / WESTMORELAND

ALLEGHENY / WASHINGTON

Elizabeth Access

Elizabeth

New Eagle Borough Public Ramp

Evanford Marina

Monongahela Public Ramp

Monongahela

ALLEGHENY / WESTMORELAND

Monongahela Access

To Washington

Sunnyside/Gallatin Twin Rivers Access

Webster Access

Charleroi

WESTMORELAND / FAYETTE

Speers Access

Speers

Flow

© Wilderness Adventures Press

From West Virginia, SR 88 runs close to the river to New Eagle, where SR 837 then continues to follow the river to its confluence with the Allegheny and Ohio Rivers in Pittsburgh.

Consult the Warmwater Fly Box for a selection of flies.

Monongahela River Access Sites

Charge for launching usually indicates a commercial area, but note also that all boats launched on state park waters must possess either a PA registration or a launch permit obtained from the park office.

Greene County – 20 miles

Dunkard Valley Marina; Dunkard Crossing at SR. 88 Bridge
- Moderate draft fishing boats
- Gas and oil available
- Parking available

Rices Landing (PFBC); one mile east of Dry Tavern, off SR 88
- Shallow draft, lightweight fishing boats, canoes, and inflatables
- Surfaced ramp
- Parking available

Raystown Branch Access; Ten Mile Creek at SR 88 Bridge
- Deep draft, high-powered boats
- Gas and oil available

Sunset Marina; Ten Mile Creek at SR 88 Bridge
- Deep draft, high-powered boats; charge for launching
- Gas and oil available
- Surfaced ramp
- Parking available

Fayette County

Scott Motorboat Sales; off SR 88 at Point Marion
- Deep draft, high-powered boats
- Gas and oil available
- Surfaced ramp
- Parking available

Point Marion (PFBC); Point Marion borough, off SR 88 near glass company and city parking area, just below Lock #8 on left side of river looking upstream
- Deep draft, high-powered boats
- Surfaced ramp
- Parking available

East Frederickstown (PFBC); East Millsboro, adjacent to county ferry. Two miles south of Maxwell; seven miles upstream from Brownsville
- Deep draft, high-powered boats
- Surfaced ramp
- Parking available

Washington County

Ten Mile Creek County Park Access (on Ten Mile Creek); take SR 88 for one mile south out of Millsboro to SR 4023 (Millsboro to Clarksville Rd.); go one mile toward Clarksville to access area along north side of Ten mile Creek; owned by Washington County Park Commission
- Moderate draft fishing boats; charge for launching
- Surfaced ramp
- Parking available

West Brownsville; under I-40 (high level) bridge; use SR 88 into West Brownsville, then follow the railroad tracks to I-40 bridge
- Moderate draft fishing boats
- Surfaced ramp
- Parking available

Speers Access (PFBC); located one mile south of Charleroi at Speers off SR 88 (look for PFBC directional signs)
- Deep draft, high-powered boats
- Gas and oil available
- Surfaced ramp
- Parking available

Monongahela Access; south end of Monongahela off SR 837 at foot of Nelson Street
- Deep draft, high-powered boats
- Surfaced ramp
- Parking available

Monongahela Public Ramp; off SR 88 on 2nd Street in Monongahela
- Shallow draft, lightweight fishing boats, canoes, and inflatables
- Surfaced ramp
- Parking available

New Eagle Borough Public Ramp; off SR 88/837 at Howard Street
- Moderate draft fishing boats
- Surfaced ramp
- Parking available

Westmoreland County

Webster Access; in Webster, off SR 906, two blocks north of Webster Bridge
- Moderate draft fishing boats
- Beach-type ramp
- Parking available

Allegheny County – 40 miles

Sunnyside/Gallatin Twin Rivers; foot of Maca Road off SR 136, Forward Township
- Moderate draft fishing boats
- Beach-type ramp
- Parking available

Evanford Marina; 3 miles south of Elizabeth on Bunola Road off SR 51
- Unlimited boat size; charge for launching
- Surface ramp
- Parking available
- Gas and oil available

Elizabeth Access; City of Elizabeth, foot of Market Street
- Unlimited boat size
- Surface ramp
- Parking available

Glassport Access; City of Glassport, foot of Harrison Street
- Boat fishing
- Beach-type ramp
- Parking available

McKeesport Access (PFBC); off SR 148, foot of Atlantic Avenue at confluence with Youghiogheny River
- Moderate draft fishing boats
- Surface ramp
- Parking available

Braddock Borough Access; at foot of 11th street in Braddock
- Moderate draft fishing boats
- Surfaced ramp
- Limited parking

Pittsburgh South Side Access; City of Pittsburgh, foot of 18th Street off East Carson Street
- Unlimited sized boats
- Surfaced ramp
- Parking available

Monongahela Parking Wharf, Pittsburgh (downtown); off Boulevard of Allies
- Moderate draft fishing boats; charge for launching
- Surfaced ramp
- Parking

BIG BASS PROGRAM

Special regulations affecting bass fishing have been established on selected waters within the Commonwealth. The regulations apply to largemouth, smallmouth, and spotted bass in the waters listed below. Approved trout lakes that are in the Big Bass Program are closed to all fishing from March 1 until the opening day of trout season, unless listed in the Select Trout Stocked Lake Program (indicated by (*) below).

Season: January 1 to April 16 and June 12 to December 31
Minimum size: 15 inches
Daily limit: 4 (combined species)
Inland Regulations apply to all other species

Waters Governed by These Regulations

County	Water
Allegheny/Westmoreland	Allegheny River, pool 3, from Lock and Dam #4 at Natrona downstream to and including Lock and Dam #3 at Acmetonia
Armstrong	Keystone Lake
Beaver	Lower Hereford Manor Lake*
Berks	Blue Marsh Reservoir Hopewell Kaercher Creek Lake
Bedford	Shawnee Lake
Blair	Canoe Creek Lake (State Park) to include two small ponds and race way adjacent to Canoe Creek Lake*
Bucks	Nockamixon Lake (State Park)
Butler	Glade Run Lake* Lake Arthur (Moraine State Park)
Carbon	Mauch Chunk Lake
Chester	Chambers Lake Marsh Creek Lake (State Park)
Clarion	Kahle Lake

Dauphin/Perry/Juniata/
  Snyder/Northumberland/
  Lancaster/Cumberland/York
	Susquehanna River from Holtwood Dam upstream to the Fibradam near Sunbury

Erie	Lake Erie and Presque Isle Bay
Fayette	Mill Run Reservoir

Indiana	Yellow Creek Lake (State Park)
Jefferson	Kyle Lake
Juniata/Perry	Juniata River (18.5 miles) from the SR 0075 Bridge at Port Royal downstream to Newport SR 0034 Bridge
Lackawanna	Lackawanna Lake (State Park)*
Lancaster	Speedwell Forge Lake
Lebanon	Memorial Lake (State park)
Luzerne	Frances Slocum Lake (State Park) Harris Pond Lake Lily*
Lycoming	Rose Valley Lake
Mercer	Shenango Lake
Montour	Lake Chillisquaque
Perry	Holman Lake (State Park) Juniata River from mouth upstream to the Route 11/15 Bridge near Amity Hall
Somerset	Lake Somerset
Venango	Justus Lake*
Washington	Cross Creek Lake
Westmoreland	Keystone Lake (State Park)* Upper Twin Lake
Wyoming	Stevens Lake
York	Lake Marburg (State Park) Pinchot Lake (State Park) Lake Redman Lake Williams

Warmwater Fly Box

The warmwater fly box includes flies for bass, muskie, northern pike, stripers, and shad. The more folks pursue warmwater and coolwater species, the more fly boxes we will carry. The greatest inventor of warmwater flies within the state, and perhaps the nation, has been Bob Clouser, who guides flyfishers and runs Clouser's Fly Shop near Middletown.

Bob is responsible for the Clouser's Crayfish, the Deep Diving Minnow, Clouser's Floating Minnow, and now Darters, Clouser Style©. Bob makes his newly released darter in olive, purple, and blue. With the demand for warmwater flies on the rise, I'm impressed with Bob's conscientious effort to test and retest every fly that he develops.

In talking with him and discussing flies and patterns, we agreed that many flies are ineffective because of the way they are fished. A good fly will not produce if not fished properly.

Although plenty of fish have been taken on crayfish patterns while hanging haplessly at the tail of a whitewater riffle, the pattern is far more effective when fished near the bottom with quick, short retrieves.

For example, Bob states, "According to state studies, the darter is just as prevalent as the crayfish in many of our streams. This makes it a top food choice for smallmouth bass."

I'm pleased to announce the release of the new Darter, Clouser Style© in this book and tying instructions can be found at the end of this section. All patterns should be fished to imitate the life form they are intended to represent.

The Warmwater Selection
- Clouser's Crayfish or a crayfish pattern of your choosing . . . . #4–8
- Dahlberg's Diver in various colors . . . . #2–4
- Lefty's Deceivers in various colors . . . . #2/0–4
- Gaines Poppers or other cork body popping bugs,
  concave face and sliders, in white, chartreuse, lime green,
  yellow and black
  - Bass . . . . #4–6
  - Stripers, muskie and northern . . . . #1/0–4
- Clouser's floating minnow . . . . #4–8
- Deer hair floating minnow . . . . #4–8
- Darters Clouser Style© in olive, purple, and blue . . . . #4–8
- Comet in orange, yellow, and red . . . . #4–8
- Popovics Pop Lip Shinner
- Leech patterns . . . . #4–8
- Tabory's Sea Rat . . . . #4–8
- Conehead minnow . . . . #2–8

- Bonito Bunny . . . .#2–8
  When fishing for northerns, muskie, or stripers, the above flies
  may be tied on sizes 4/0–4. Stainless steel saltwater hooks
  are preferred to give added depth and durability. Most of the
  above are tied
  on long shanks or wide gap hooks.
- Woolly buggers with Krystal or Flashabou added,
  and bead or lead eyes in brown, green, white, olive, black . . . .#4–10
- Dragonfly, emergers, and adults (3X long, light, wire hooks) . . . . . .#10–12

Mayflies and Caddis

Warmwater species do key in on hatches, particularly smallmouth bass. The following is a list of hatches and/or patterns to be aware of.

- White fly
- Light cahill
- Quill Gordon
- Mosquito
- Brown and slate drake and spinners
- Blue-winged olive
- Hare's ear
- Caddis: deer hair wing, caddis, tan, brown, yellow, and green #10–12

Use whatever flies appear in the headwaters or tributary streams. It is more than likely that you will encounter the hatch on the warmwater streams below the headwaters or in the warmwater river into which they flow.

Body Materials for Dry Flies

On the larger rivers and lakes where bass are found, mayflies are an important food source, but the ability of traditional dry flies to float has been a problem. It has been my experience that bass are far less fussy than trout, and I normally fish an imitation that is one size larger than the natural I am trying to imitate. For years I fished Wulff patterns and still find them useful. However, aging eyes and the long casts often required on larger rivers made it imperative that I see the fly in the fading light of evening when many hatches occur.

I began to use spun deer hair for bodies and calf tail wings. Later, many of us began experimenting with different fly bodies. I know Bob Clouser produces many dry flies with foam bodies. Two years ago, Jim Yurejefcic of South Mountain Tackle began tinkering with the concept, working first with the yellow Adams I had shown him, and then the white fly. Jim, an excellent fly tier and rod builder, came up with the idea of twisting closed cell foam cylinders for a dry fly body. I had seen them used on hopper patterns but not on dry flies.

The fly works extremely well for bass and creates a high floating dry fly, spinner, and floating nymph pattern. The secret is in the stretching and twisting of the foam.

It would seem that foam, closed cell foam especially, has a great future in fly tying circles. I just wish we had a few more colors available to us.

The warmwater fly box is expanding with each passing year. Still in its infancy, the streamers and other imitations could already fill a school bus. For northerns and walleye, I am extremely fond of a yellow streamer of saddle hackle with a lot of Krystal flash. I'll stop here, because the list is endless.

As in all fishing, match the fly as closely as possible and work the streamers as though crippled or as they would behave in their natural environment. When fishing dry flies and nymphs, drag-free floats are a must.

Proper presentation is the key to all flyfishing success.

Clouser Darter©: Tying Instructions

Clouser Darter©

Hook	Mustad 3366 or other brand equivalent in sizes 2, 4, or 6
Eyes	Metallic eyes, 1/30 or small, for 2 and 4 size hooks and 1/50 or extra small for size 6 hook
Thread	Size 6/0 Uni-Thread, color matched to the body color of the fly
Ingredients	Calf tail or deer tail fiber, Krystal Flash and Flashabou

Clouser Purple Darter©

Step 1 — Secure the hook in the fly tying vise. Attach the tying thread to the hook 1/3 the distance behind the eye of the hook and make a bump at this position with the tying thread.

Step 2 — Select a pair of hourglass shaped metallic eyes and attach them to the hook shank with cross wraps behind the bump of tying thread. Note: the metallic eyes should be snug against the bump of tying thread and also lashed with cross wraps snugly to the shank of the hook.

Step 3 — Move tying thread to the rear of the hook, behind the metallic eyes, by spiral wrapping the thread to the area directly above the point of the hook. Then spiral wrap tying forward to the rear of the metallic eyes.

Step 4 — Cut a section of purple calf tail hair fibers, at least one half to two times the length of the hook shank. About the thickness of a wooden match. Lay the bundle of calf tail hairs on top of the hook shank with the butts touching the rear portion of the metallic eyes. Tie the fibers down by spiral wrapping the thread to the rear of the hook, just above the hook point, and then wrap the thread forward to the rear of the eyes. This procedure should attach the tail portion of the darter.

Step 5 — Move the tying thread forward of the metallic eyes and spiral wrap the shank of the hook to the rear of the hook eye. Cut a bundle of olive calf tail hair, about the thickness of a wooden match. The length of the calf tail hair can be at least one half to two times the length of the hook shank.

Step 6 — Tie the bundle of olive calf tail hair down at the point forward of the eyes and then move the tying thread to the rear of the eyes and finish tying the bundle of olive calf tail at this position. After the hair is bound down, move the tying thread forward of the eyes to a point at the rear of the eye of the hook.

Step 7 — Turn hook upside down in the tying vise and cut 6 to 10 strands of black Krystal Flash. Tie the strands in on top of the shank in front of the metallic eyes only, making sure the length of the Krystal Flash extends out the rear of the fly at least one full length longer than the calf tail fibers. This gives the fly a flash tail effect. Repeat this step by using 6 to 10 strands of purple Flashabou, tying it down on top of the black Krystal Flash at the point where the black Krystal Flash is attached.

Step 8 — Cut a bundle of olive calf tail about the same thickness as a wooden match and, the same length as in step 5 and tie it down on top of the hook shank in front of the metallic eyes, making a neat cone shaped head. Coat all exposed thread with a coat or two of a heavy base head cement.

The Clouser's Darter© is now complete.

Fly Shops by Region

Northeast

BRADFORD COUNTY
Wright's Wholesale Tackle
Baltimore Pike & Bishop Avenue
Springfield, PA 19064
610-284-5522

CARBON COUNTY
Gary's Flies
363 Chestnut Street, Box 211
Mertzown, PA 19539
610-682-6255

Gary's Sport & Tackle
Barbara Court
Saylorsburg, PA
570-992-6837

COLUMBIA COUNTY
Benton Sports Center
Main Street
Benton, PA 17814
570-925-6001

Fishing Creek Outfitters
Box 314, Gabriel Road
Benton, PA 17814
570-925-2709

Valley Fishing & Hunting
136 Main Street
Catawissa, PA 17820
570-356-2434

LUZERNE COUNTY
Back Mountain Outfitters
Rt. 118 Lehman Corners
Dallas, PA
570-675-1055

Dick Ackourey & Sons Fly Den
95 Kelly Street
Luzerne, PA 18709
570-287-2999

Evening Hatch Flyfishing Shop
Rt 940 East
White Haven, PA 18661
570-443-0772
E-mail: thehatch@epix.net

Morning Dew Anglers
2100 West Front Street
Berwick, PA 18603
570-759-3030

MONROE COUNTY
AA Pro Shop
HC1, Box 1030
Blakeslee, PA 18610
800-443-8119

Al Caucci Flyfishing
38 Chestnut Ridge
Tannersville, PA 18372
570-629-2962

Alpha Sporting 'N' Gun Shop
U.S. Highway 209
Sciota, PA
570-992-7026

Blakeslee Sport Shop
PA. Highway 115
Blakeslee, PA
570-646-2670

Dunkelberger's Sports Outfitters
585 Main Street
Stroudsburg, PA 18360
570-421-7950

Family Bait & Tackle Shop
624 North Courtland Street
East Stroudsburg, PA
570-4216918

JC's Fish & Game
Main Street
Tobyhanna, PA
570-894-1420

Silver Springs Outfitters
RR3, Box 657, Lobach Lane
Kunkeltown, PA 18058
610-381-3631

Skytop Fishing Lodge
1 Skytop
Skytop, PA 18357
800-345-7759

West End Gun & Sport Inc.
US Highway 209
Kresgeville, PA
610-6814117

Windsor Fly Shop
348 North 9th Street
Stroudsburg, PA 18360
570-424-0938

MONTOUR COUNTY
Nestor's Sporting Goods
2510 MacArthur Road
Whitehall, PA 18052-3896
610-437-0341

NORTHUMBERLAND COUNTY
Penns Creek Fly Fishing Services
146 East Sunbury Street., Rt. 61
Shamokin, PA 17872
800-858-8564

PIKE COUNTY
Angler's Roost & Hunter's Rest
106 Scenic Drive #A
Lackawaxen, PA
570-685-2010

Dennis's Sport Shop
U.S. Route 6
Shohola, PA
570-296-6283

Inn Sport Shop
PA Highway 402
Pecks Pond, PA
570-775-0441

Ironwood Point Sport Shop
PA Highway 507
Greentown, PA
570-857-0677

Sisters Country Sports Shops
PA Highway 739
Dingmans Ferry, PA
570-828-2929

Sportsman's Rendezvous
113 West Harford Street
Milford, PA
570-296-6113

Thom Rivell's Flyfishing
6 Greentown Plaza #507
Greentown, PA 18426
570-676.4446

SULLIVAN COUNTY
Renniger's Country Store
PO Box 99,PA SR8 7
Hillsgrove, PA 18619
570-924-3505

WAYNE COUNTY
Delaware River Fly Shop, Inc.
HC 1, Box 1061
Starlight, PA 18461
570-635-5983

Heberling Sport Shop
P.O. Box 73
Prompton, PA
570-253-1801

Hemlock Gun Shop
PA Highway 590 and Crane Road
Lakeville, PA
570-226-9410

Hunter's Gallery
PA Highway 590
Hamlin, PA
570-689-7898

Northeast Flyfishers
923 Main Street
Honesdale, PA 18431
570-253-9780

River Essentials
HC1, Box 1025
Starlight, PA 18461
570-635-5900

Wallenpaupack Sport Shop
Rt. 6 & Rt. 590 West
Hawley, PA
570-226-4797

WYOMING COUNTY
Ron's Flies
RR1 Box, 1092
Rt 92 North
Nicholson, PA 18446
570-942-6333

Southeast

BERKS COUNTY
Angler & Archer Outfitter
1400 Lancaster Avenue
Kenhorst, PA 19607
610-777-6118

Blue Mountain Outfitters
2001 Bernville Road, Rt. 183
Reading, PA 19601
610-372-6970

TCO Tulpehocken Creek Outfitters
2229 Penn Avenue
West Lawn, PA 19609
610-678-1899

BUCKS COUNTY
Covert & Moore
3118 Fretz Valley Road
Perkaise, PA 18944
215-795-2274

Dave's Fisherman's Shop
Rt. 611
Doylestown, PA
215-766-8000

Nestor's Sporting Goods, Inc.
99 North West End Boulevard
Quakertown, PA 18951
215-529-0100

Quinby's Gun Shop
Rte. 313
Dublin, PA 18917
215-249-1144

CHESTER COUNTY
Chip's Bait & Tackle
325 East Gay Street,
Cambridge Square D-3
West Chester, PA 19380
610-696-3474

Custom Trophies & Fly Tackle
25 Rust Leaf Lane
Levittown, PA 19055
215-945-0646

Orvis Downington
Brandywine Square Shopping Center
Downington, PA 19335
610-873-8400

DELAWARE COUNTY
The Sporting Gentleman
306 East Baltimore Avenue
Media, PA 19063
610-565-6140

LANCASTER COUNTY
Evening Rise Fly Anglers Shop
4182 Old Philadelphia Pike, Box 446
Paradise, PA 17529
717-768-3020

Kinsey's Outdoors
Steel Way Drive
Mount Joy, PA 17552
717-653-5524

Quiet Times Fly Shop
288 Hess Road
Quarryville, PA 17566
717-768-0951

Trout Run Sports
438 North Reading Road
Ephrata, PA 17522
717-738-2525

LEHIGH COUNTY
Brandywine Outfitters
200 West Lincoln Way, Rt.30
Exton, PA 19341
610-594-8008

Dale Clemens Custom Tackle
444 Schantz Spring Road
Allentown, PA 18104
610-395-5119

Little Lehigh Fly Shop
Fish Hatchery Road
Allentown, PA 18103
610-797-5599

ProAm Fishing Shop
5916 Tilghman Street
Allentown, PA 18103
610-395-0885

MONTGOMERY COUNTY
Anglers Pro Shop
3361 Bethlehem Pike
Soudertown, PA 18964
215-721-4909

Delaware River Anglers
228 Davisville Road
Willow Grove, PA 19090
215-830-9766

Eyler's Fly & Tackle
895 Penn Street
Bryn Mawr, PA 19010
610-527-3388

Fly Fishing Forever
Germantown Pike & Valley Forge Road
Fairview Village, PA 19409
610-631-8990

French Creek Outfitter
1414 South Hanover Street, Rt. 100
Pottstown, PA 19465
610-326-6740

The Fly Fishing Shop
528 Fox Road
Glenside, PA 19038
215-887-1523

PHILADELPHIA COUNTY
Becks Sport Shop
7113 Rising Sun Avenue
Philadelphia, PA 19111
215-342-0930

Chestnut Hill Country Store
8605 Germantown Avenue
Philadelphia, PA 19118
215-242-9332

On the Hook
524 Cresheim Valley Road
Wyndmoor, PA 19118
215-836-5950

SCHUYLKILL COUNTY
Custom Flies
866 Roosevelt Street
Hazelton, PA 18201
570-454-4554

Ed's Fly Shop
317 Mauch Chunk Street
Pottsville, PA 17901
570-622-1814

Wilderness Trekker
RD. 1, Box 1243C
Orwigsburg, PA 17961
570-366-0165

Northcentral

CENTRE COUNTY
Appalachian Ski & Outdoors
324 West College Avenue
State College, PA 16801
800-690-5220

Flyfishers Paradise
2603 East College Avenue
State College, PA 16801
814-234-4189
www.flyfishersparadise.com

CLEARFIELD COUNTY
Dan's Pro Shop
6 DuBoise Area Plaza
DuBoise, PA 15801
814-371-1365

Jim's Sport Center
26 North Second Street
Clearfield, PA 16830
814-765-3582

CLINTON COUNTY
Kettle Creek Tackle Shop
HCR 62, Box 140, SR 144
Renovo, PA 17764
570-923-1416

ELK COUNTY
Smith's Sport Shop
10 Erie Avenue
St. Marys, PA 15857
814-834-3701

LYCOMING COUNTY
Angler's Supply House
811 South Market Street
South Williamsport, PA 17702
570-323-7564

Blair's Sporting Goods
1508 Memorial Avenue
Williamsport, PA 17701
717-322-4739

Brown & Waldman Bass Pros
2303 Lycoming Creek Road
Williamsport, PA 17701
570-322-2277

Country Store Fly Shop
Route 44
Waterville, PA 17776
570-753-8241

E. Hille's Anglers Supply
815 Railway, POB 996
Williamsport, PA 17701
800-326-6612

Fred Reese Trout Shop
220 Thompson Street, Box 698
Jersey Shore, PA 17740
570-398-3016

Slate Run Tackle Shop
Route 414, PO Box 1
Slate Run, PA 17769
570-753-8551

MCKEAN COUNTY
True Life Fly Co.
1005 West Main Street
Smethport, PA 16749
814-887-1974

NORTHUMBERLAND COUNTY
SEE NORTHEAST LISTINGS

POTTER COUNTY
Big Moores Run Lodge
RD3, Box 204A
Coudersport, PA 16915
814-647-5300

Cross Fork Tackle Shop
Main Street, Box 261
Cross Fork, PA 17729
570-923-1960

Northern Tier Outfitters
15 Fairview Avenue
Galeton, PA 16922
814-435-6324

TIOGA COUNTY
Cooper's Sporting Goods
15 West Wellsboro Street
Mansfield, PA 16933
570-662-3429

Davis Sporting Goods
9 Charleston Street
Wellsboro, PA 16901
570-724-2626

UNION COUNTY
Campus Cycle & Fly Fishing Center
223 Market Street
Lewisburg, PA 17837
570-524-2998

Southcentral

CUMBERLAND COUNTY
Angling Adventures
328 Zion Road
Mt. Holly Springs, PA 17065
717-486-7438

Cold Springs Anglers
419 East High Street, Suite A
Carlisle, PA 17013
717-245-2646

Green Spring Fly Shop
202 Steelestown Road
Newville, PA 17241
717-249-0709

Yellow Breeches Outfitters
2 First Street, Box 200
Boiling Springs, PA 17007
717-258-6752

DAUPHIN COUNTY
Clouser's Fly Shop
101 Ulrich Street
Middletown, PA 17057
717-944-6541

FRANKLIN COUNTY
Dave's Sports Center
1127 North Easton Road, Rt. 611
Doylestown, PA 18901
215-766-8000

Falling Spring Outfitters
3813 Old Scotland Main Street
Scotland, PA 17254
717-263-7811

Mike Heck's Trout Guides
532 Bracken Drive
Chambersburg, PA
717-261-0070

HUNTINGDON COUNTY
Six Springs Fly Shop
HC-01, Box 13
Spruce Creek, PA 16683
814-632-3393

Spruce Creek Outfitters
Route 45, P.O. Box 36
Spruce Creek, PA 16683
814-632-3071

MIFFLIN COUNTY
The Feathered Hook
Box 84, Main Street
Coburn, PA 16832
814-349-8757

YORK COUNTY
Bob's Hackle Farm
Road #1, Box 84
New Park, PA 17352
717-382-4402

Old Village Fly Shop
25 South Main Street
Shrewsbury, PA 17361
717-235-9020

Otter Creek Rec. Area
Rt. #1, Box 243
Airville, PA 17302
717-862-3628

Sport-About Penn Outfitters
2709 Queen Street
York, PA 17403
717-741-4343

Northwest

CLARION COUNTY
J & L Sporting Goods
RD#2 Rt. 66 5miles north of I 80
Shippenville, PA 16254
814-226-8211

Redbank Flyfisher's
214 Broad Street
New Bethlehem, PA 16242
814-275-4410

CRAWFORD COUNTY
Conneaut Lake Tackle
110 Water Street
Conneaut Lake, PA 16316
814-382-6095

The Fly Fisherman's Shop
Monroe Valley Rd #1, Box 263
Fredricksburg, PA 17026
717-865-5712

ERIE COUNTY
Erie Sport Store
701 State Street
Erie, PA 16501
814-452-2289

Erie Sport Store
3702 Liberty Liberty Plaza
Erie, PA 16508
814-868-0948

Erie Sport Store
124 East 8th Street
Erie, PA 16508
814-459-1328

Lakes, Ponds, Streams Fly Shop
8236 Perry Hwy
Erie, PA 16509
814-864-3269

FOREST COUNTY
Forest Country Sports Center
311 Elm Street
Tionesta, PA 163530098
800-458-6093

LAWRENCE COUNTY
Neshannock Creek Fly Shop
Main Street, PO Box 310
Volant, PA 16156
(724-533-3212

VENANGO COUNTY
Oil Creek Outfitters
RR 3 Box 114
Titusville, PA 16354
814-677-4684

Southwest

ALLEGHENY COUNTY
Drury's Buffalo Valley Outfitters
Rd #1 Box 398A
Natrona Heights, PA 15065
888-792-3395

Hoey's Fly Fishing Shop
9200 Old Perry Hwy
Pittsburgh, PA 15237
412-364-2850

International Angler
503 Freeport Road
Pittsburgh, PA 15215
412-782-2222

Pete's Outdoor Store
305 West State #A
Kennett Square, PA 19348
610-444-0482

South Hills Rod and Reel
3227½ West Liberty Avenue
Pittsburgh, PA 15216
412-344-8888

The Fly Tyer's Vice
2225 Swallow Hill Road
Pittsburgh PA 15220
412-276-2831

ARMSTRONG COUNTY
Kiski Angler Fly Shoppe
114 Market Street
Leechburg, PA 15656
724-845-9171

Transue's Tackle
321 Butler Road
West Kittanning, PA 16201
724-543-2971

INDIANA COUNTY
Indiana Angler
218 Grandview Avenue
Indiana, PA 15701
724-463-2011

SOMERSET COUNTY
Hart's Sporting Center
Route 403 South
Tire Hill, PA 15905
814-288-5099

WESTMORELAND COUNTY
The Angler's Room Fly Shop
1 mile north of Kingston Dam, Rt. 217
Latrobe, PA 15650
724-537-0683

The Fishing Post
114 North Main Street
Greensburg, PA 15601
412-832-8383

Rolling Rock Club
Rt. 30 East
Ligonier, PA 15658
724-238-9501

Pennsylvania Fish and Boat Commission Regional Law Enforcement Headquarters

Northeast Region
Box 88
Sweet Valley, PA 18656
Phone 717-477-5717
Fax 717-477-3221
Counties Bradford, Carbon, Columbia, Lackawanna, Luzerne, Monroe, Montour, Northumberland (north of SR 147), Pike, Sullivan, Susquehanna, Wayne, Wyoming

Southeast Region
Box 8
Elm, PA 17521
Phone 717-626-0228
Fax 717-626-0486
Counties Berks, Bucks, Chester, Delaware, Lancaster, Lehigh, Montgomery, Northampton, Philadelphia, Schuykill

Northcentral Region
Box 187
Lamar, PA 16848
Phone 717-726-6056
Fax 717-726-3912
Counties Cameron, Centre, Clearfield, Clinton, Elk, Jefferson, Lycoming, McKean, Northumberland (west of SR 147), Potter, Snyder, Tioga, Union

Southcentral Region
1704 Pine Road
Newville, PA 17241
Phone 717-486-7087
Fax 717-486-8227
Counties Adams, Bedford, Blair, Cumberland, Dauphin, Franklin, Fulton, Huntingdon, Juniata, Lebanon, Mifflin, Perry, York

Northwest Region
11528 SH 98
Meadville, PA 16335
Phone 814-337-0444
Fax 814-337-0579
Counties Butler, Clarion, Crawford, Erie, Forest, Lawrence, Mercer, Venango, Warren

Southwest Region
236 Lake Road
Somerset, PA 15501
Phone 814-445-8974
Fax 814-445-3497
Counties Allegheny, Armstrong, Beaver, Cambria, Fayette, Greene, Indiana, Somerset, Washington, Westmoreland

Headquarters
3532 Walnut Street, PO Box 67000
Harrisburg, PA 17106-7000
Phone 717-657-4518

Tackle and Equipment

Flyfishing equipment has improved dramatically. There are now lighter rods and reels than ever before and lines, leaders and tippet material that is stronger and smaller in diameter than in the past. A properly equipped angler, with the right instruction, will learn to cast farther and more accurately than when I first picked up a cumbersome bamboo rod with an automatic reel attached. Flyfishing equipment, including rods, reels, lines, clothing that allows freedom for casting, waders and wading shoes, continues to improve with each passing year.

Coldwater

Coldwater is the designation for water that holds trout in the Keystone state. This term is rather loosely applied to all streams and lakes that are stocked with trout. Those streams include many waters that warm above the trout's tolerance level.

Lines

Throughout this book, references are made to line weights that I have found suitable for the waters I fish. I prefer 4- to 5-weight lines, with a rod to match, for almost all of the trout fishing I have found in Pennsylvania. That does not mean that a 6-weight is out of bounds for larger rivers and lakes or that it may not double nicely as a bass rod for the shad fishing and the bluegills that are in abundance here.

I prefer weight-forward lines, which can be called any number of things depending upon the manufacturer. Weight-forward, rocker taper lines with a heavier taper at the front of the line before becoming thin in the last 10 feet or so, allow one to "shoot" line in small stream situations. They are well suited for fishing Pennsylvania's trout waters, where there is not enough room for backcasts, and on larger waters. The fewer false casts, the better, when fishing, and the weight forward line allows this. Over 98 percent of my trout fishing is accomplished with floating lines.

Leaders and Tippets

Leaders, in my opinion, should never be less than 9 feet in length when fishing dry flies.

As a firm believer in proper presentation, which normally requires drag-free floats, I fish the finest tippet the fly allows. Most would consider my tippets too light, but the lighter the tippet, the less drag. If the tippet begins twisting continually while casting, it is too small for the fly. I rarely fish anything less than 6X tippets when trout fishing. I find that I am able to cast even a size 10, 3X long caterpillar pattern with 6X without any problems. I do make some adjustments in my casting to do so, including a little more "umph" during my forward cast and a longer pause at the end of my backcast. Do whatever it takes to make the fly roll over properly. If it does not, tie on a heavier tippet.

I like knotted leaders and usually make my own or purchase Orvis knotted leaders. As of this writing, manufacturers haven't produced a knotless leader that would help turn a fly "over" properly. One other problem I have with knotless leaders is that, after removing numerous flies, I am never certain what stage of the leader to tie on a tippet or what diameter the tippet should be at that point. All leaders should be tapered—if that sounds too simplistic, consider that a the majority of anglers who experience casting problems because "the fly is sitting too close to the fly line" are using straight, nontapered leaders.

Rods

The majority of my trout fishing is conducted with a 9-foot rod designed for a 4 weight line. On larger streams and when fishing high water, most often in the early part of trout season, I use a 9-foot designed for a 5-weight line. I have two rods that I use 95 percent of the time — a custom rod, designed for me by South Mountain Tackle, and a Sage. However, Orvis, Winston, LL Bean, Loomis, Cabela's, and many others companies manufacture rods that perform beautifully.

The move toward rods with much faster action is disturbing. They are fine for warm water, but when trout fishing, these rods often throw a loop too tight to lay a fly down gently. In order to cast them properly in all types of situations, the casting stroke must be altered in order to keep the tag end of the leader from catching the midsection of the leader as it unrolls. In the East, where casts rarely exceed 40 feet, most trout anglers prefer medium to medium fast action rods.

Reels

I do like good reels for trout fishing, and there are many on the market. Teton and Orvis CFOs have proven their worth to me over the years. Scientific Angler, Pfluger, Abel, STH, and Marryat all produce excellent trout fishing reels. Cortland reels and outfits are also excellent combinations for the money expended and will do the job for trout. Combination outfits have, with few minor exceptions, proven their worth beyond beginner outfits. When the time comes to upgrade, these outfits can be kept for spares.

Warmwater

Warmwater is a term used to describe all streams, lakes, and impoundments that hold species other than trout. This term is used for nearly all lakes within the state, even though we have many lakes stocked with trout. The same lakes are also stocked with warmwater species. The trout placed into the majority of the state's stillwaters are, with minor exceptions, placed there on a "put-and-take basis." The same lakes are often stocked with warmwater fingerlings of bass, muskie, walleye, stripers and/or striper hybrids. As summer begins, these lakes are truly warmwater fisheries.

Cool water is a term used for water that holds fish preferring water temperatures somewhere between bass and trout, such as northern pike. We have few waters of this nature, and the term is seldom used any longer. For the sake of simplicity, we have divided the book into coldwater and warmwater sections.

The primary difference between warmwater fishing and coldwater fishing is the equipment needed—primarily rods, reels, lines, tippets, and flies. The Warmwater Fly Box will give you a description of flies needed for all warmwater species.

Rods

Fly rods for warmwater differ from coldwater in many ways. While it is possible to fish many lakes, river, and streams with a 6- or 7-weight outfit, in time, this can be a disadvantage. After fishing warmwater for 25 years, it has become apparent to me that an 8-weight outfit is the right ticket for warmwater species. I have settled on a 9-foot rod carrying an 8-weight line. The Grandt has served me well on all warmwater lakes and rivers and doubles as a saltwater rod for bonefish, blues, and small tarpon.

Rods capable of casting heavier lines are required equipment for the serious warmwater angler for many reasons: Longer casts are required; the wind is often a big factor; flies do not need to be presented as carefully; and last but not least, are the new lead- and metallic-eyed flies that, at times, require a "chuck-and-duck" cast.

A trout rod will work on smaller bass waters or when a white fly hatch transpires, but in time, a heavier outfit will be necessary. Not having the right equipment limits the ability to fish for warmwater species under the wide variety of waters in which they are found. Remember that warmwater includes muskie and pike. Larger fish like these will require a rod with some backbone.

Rods can range from medium fast to fast action for warmwater.

Leaders and Tippets

Warmwater flyfishing requires stiff leader and tippet material. I prefer Maxima in order to turn over the wind-resistant and weighted flies most often incorporated in warmwater fishing.

From the many clinics I have taught and from guiding, I have found that most flyfishers do not use heavy or stiff enough leaders. Trout leaders used for warmwater fishing just don't do the job. You can test this by trying to do a backcast with a leader that is too light with a wind-resistant popping bug or weighted streamer attached — the leader will collapse on the backcast.

Maxima is a stiff monofilament leader that turns over heavier flies with ease. I also have had a lot of luck with Orvis saltwater leaders. Despite my love of fine tippets for trout, I fish bass and other warmwater species with 10-pound test tippets the majority of the time. If a hatch comes off, I go down to a tippet testing 6 pounds.

Heavier leaders and tippets help when pulling bass from weedbeds and lily pads, and bass are not that leader-shy. I rarely use a leader under 10 feet, including my permanent butt section, when fishing surface flies and poppers. While I do not believe that bass are leader shy, I do not believe they are stupid either. They rarely tolerate a fly line that is too close to the fly.

Subsurface flies need to be fished with shorter leaders, and in order to get the fly to the proper depths, leaders of 6 to 7 feet will help get the fly down. This is especially important in deeper water and when fishing sinktips and full-sinking lines.

Lines

Lines are as important in warmwater fishing as they are in coldwater. Cortland makes an exceptional line, and Orvis, Scientific Angler, and Wulff all have lines that are in the ballpark. I personally don't like "bug tapers," but I admit that I haven't tried all brands. The bug tapers I have used do not turn over the fly and fall too heavily on the water. Weight-forwards are, by far, my favorite. Here you want to be able to shoot line to cover the water. On rivers and lakes, longer casts are required. Average casts for warmwater are 60 feet or more, and a good line is essential. Learning to double haul also helps.

A floating line is needed for 75 percent of warmwater flyfishing. The rest of the time, a sinktip of 10 to 14 feet will serve well. An intermediate sinking line works well, and if a "slime line" could be designed that would work well in colder weather, I would use it in a minute.

When fishing the warmwater lakes, an intermediate to fast-sinking line and a lead-core are needed to probe the depths for stripers when they are not on top. But the majority of flyfishing can be done with a floating line.

Continuing my list, I would have a sinktip and sinking lines, and the last of the lines on my list would be a lead-core.

Reels

For warmwater a good drag system is a must. Any medium or light saltwater reel will do the job well and will also work in saltwater. I have fished so many different reels in warmwater that it is a tough call on which one served me best. I do like Abel, Teton, STH, Billy Pates, Islander, and Orvis reels.

I prefer larger reels, as lightweight as possible with a good drag system—something that can hold a 9-weight line and 200 or more yards of backing. When buying a warmwater reel, consider that the same reel can be used for steelhead, chinook, and saltwater fishing.

Warmwater and Coldwater Essentials

Sunglasses

Polarized sunglasses are a must. Action Optic and Smith top the list as makers of the better sunglasses I have worn. They both allow you to see fish and also cut down on the glare from the water that can bring on a headache at day's end.

Magnifiers

Flip Focals have proven to be one of those things I could not live without. They can be pinned to your cap and flipped up under the bill when not in use. They are made with different magnifications, so be certain that the one you buy fits your needs. I see no need for struggling to tie a fly to a tippet when these are available in nearly every fly shop for a very modest price.

Waders

I now wear waders almost 100 percent of the time. When fishing in hipboots, I have far too often waded too deep. Neoprene waders are excellent for cold weather. At this time, I am using Orvis waders that have held up well for nearly three years. I wear them in the spring and fall, and because of the newer design that allows me to roll them down to the waist, I find them extremely comfortable and warm.

The newer breathable waders are a welcome improvement. I have been more than pleased with my Dan Bailey breathable waders. Many others also manufacture these, and I have heard from friends that most are dependable and reliable. If I had to choose one, it would probably be a breathable wader. You can always dress warmly underneath for coldwater fishing.

Forceps

I would not consider fishing without a pair of forceps. They allow me to pinch barbs down on purchased flies. I pinch all my barbs down when tying my own, and they are an absolute must when removing hooks to release fish.

Clippers

Carry at least two pair for changing flies, tippets, and trimming knots. I would feel lost without them.

Flashlight

It is a rare day when I come off the water before dark. The mini-mag flashlight is a good choice. Carry two since the odds are that the batteries will die when coming off the shelves of the Susquehanna, for example. Taking time to change batteries on the river without the aid of another light is no fun. The gooseneck light is excellent for changing flies and will help you find your way off the river in a pinch.

Fishing Vest

A short wading vest is desirable in Pennsylvania waters. When choosing a vest, be sure there are plenty of pockets and that the pockets, both inside and out, are large enough to carry the bigger boxes often used to hold warmwater flies. The better vests are sold through Bailey's, Orvis, Columbia, Cabela, and LL Bean.

Rain Gear

There is no doubt that Gore-tex rain gear is the best available for all conditions — the price tag is well worth it. Recently, I bought a Hodgeman fishing coat that doubles as a raincoat. It is a great product, and I have worn it fishing extensively for two years. A raincoat that can be rolled up and placed in the back of your vest is a good choice — just don't forget that it's there. I did this a few years ago when the rain forced me to walk off the Yellow Breeches. I was drenched when I returned to the Jeep and simply sat inside with all my gear on. It was when I leaned back in the seat that I felt the raincoat lumped in the back of my vest.

Stream Thermometer

The most overlooked tool in flyfishing, the stream thermometer is an absolute essential item here. Freestone streams may be cold water one day and warm water the next. Water temperatures should dictate where you fish. If the water temperature is in the mid-70s, move upstream or into the tributaries when fishing for trout.

Odds and Ends

- Line cleaner is a must. Clean your line as often as possible, it will help with your casting and save you money in worn lines and fly rod guides.
- Always carry a bottle of water.
- Snacks will keep you on the water when an unexpected hatch arrives.
- Split shot designed for flyfishing.
- Gink or other fly floatant.
- Extra clothes—an extra pair in the car could save you from hypothermia.
- Sweater or jacket. Evenings cool quickly—keep one with you on the stream or in your vehicle.

Pennsylvania Fish Species

Brook Trout

The brook trout, *Salvelinus fontinalis*, is the only trout native to Pennsylvania. It is then fitting that the "brookie" is the official state fish. Although some argue that it might actually be a char, you will never hear it mentioned as anything other than a trout.

Within Pennsylvania, the native brookie is found most often in the cold tributary brooks and headwaters of our larger streams. Because the brook trout shows no tolerance for warm water, preferring water temperatures of 65 degrees or less, it has been relegated to the smaller streams of the state. Flyfishers find them in the often brush-choked tributary streams, where the fish is quite elusive and well aware of a misplaced shadow. However, they are not selective feeders, and if the approach and presentation are correct, a brook trout is likely to take your offering. Native brook trout seldom exceed 10 inches in length, with the average fish around 5 to 7 inches.

Stocked brook trout are generally easy to take, resistant to acid precipitation, and most often exhibit a larger girth than length. The current state record is a 7-pound giant taken from Fishing Creek in Clinton County in 1996.

Brook trout are easily distinguished from the other trout species by their colorful appearance. The exhibit a dark olive green back mottled with dark vermiculations that extend to a square tail. The square tail, rather than a forked one, is a dead giveaway that it is a brookie. The sides are lighter than the back and have red spots with blue halos. Most consider the "wormy markings" to be a better indicator of the species. Reddish fins feathered in white and rich orange bellies also help with identification. The final touch is the orange belly that is prevalent on nearly all the native fish. When spawning, the brook trout's colors make it impossible not to identify this fish properly. The colors of freshly stocked fish are far more muted.

Brook trout spawn from mid-September to December, depending on where they are found within the state. Eggs are hatched in late winter to early spring. Although

Brook Trout

the size of the species and the small streams in which they are found keep them from being the flyfisher's favorite trout, all anglers awestruck by their beauty.

Brown Trout

The brown trout, *Salmo trutta*, is a longtime favorite of flyfishers. This species is more adaptable to warm water and seems to be more disease resistant than brook or rainbow trout. Although it has been argued that they compete with brook trout for habitat and food, few would argue that this trout is the mainstay of Pennsylvania fisheries.

Brown trout were introduced from Europe, and a second strain, referred to as Loch Leven browns, came from Scotland. It is difficult to distinguish the differences of the two types, and they are mostly lumped together as simply brown trout. The Letort reportedly holds Loch Leven browns that have reached enormous proportions.

The brown trout is dark or golden brown on top. Wild fish and carryover fish almost always display a red adipose fin. The sides are yellowish brown with yellow spots (stocked fish), and red spots are found on carryover and wild trout. The belly is yellowish to white, depending on how long the trout has been in the stream or if it is spawning. The fins are tarnished yellow and often have white feathering.

Spawning begins in October in the northern regions of the state and as late as January in the south. Eggs hatch in the spring.

Known to be the most difficult trout to catch and thus available to anglers throughout the entire season on many waters, the brown trout is a favorite here. The average fish is a little over 10 inches, but 20-inch browns are not uncommon. The current state record is 17 pounds, 14.5 ounces taken from the Raystown Lake Spillway in Huntingdon County in 1993.

Brown trout feed readily on the surface, which accounts for their popularity among flyfishers. Browns live longer than the other two species and hold over well after stocking wherever water is suitable for year-round survival.

Brown Trout

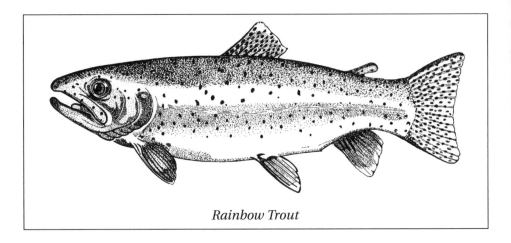

Rainbow Trout

Rainbow Trout

Rainbow trout, *Oncorhynchus mykiss*, are not native to Pennsylvania. Rainbows have self-sustaining wild populations from California north to Alaska. They are used primarily as stocked fish here, with only a few streams recording natural reproduction.

The Pennsylvania Fish and Boat Commission has adapted the rainbow to a fall spawning fish, although they naturally spawn in spring. In doing so, they have been able to achieve a better growth rate within the hatchery systems and now comprise nearly half of all fish stocked within the state.

Rainbows are used in what has been termed "put-and-take fisheries." These fisheries place stocked trout in streams, which are then taken by anglers. Turning downstream upon release has not helped the fish establish itself here. By heading downstream, they inadvertently run into warm water that is above their tolerance level. No matter, rainbows are spectacular fighting fish, usually found in many streams until mid-June when they rather mysteriously disappear.

Rainbows are easily distinguished from brook and brown trout by coloration that includes a pinkish to red stripe that runs from the head to the base of the tail. The degree of color varies from fish to fish. They are dark to light green in color, most often darker on top than on the sides, and have white to cream-colored bellies.

Rainbows have black dots covering them from head to tail, including the cardinal fin.

"False spawning" often occurs on many limestone streams. I have witnessed them on beds in the "Run" that feeds the Yellow Breeches in late November. Some natural reproduction may occur, but it is rare.

Although the average rainbow runs 9 to12 inches, the size seems to depend mainly on the Fish and Boat Commission. When they have excess brood stock or have older spawning females that are past their prime, they are stocked into our streams. The current state record came from Jordan Creek in Lehigh County. The fish weighed 15 pounds, 6.25 ounces and was taken in 1986.

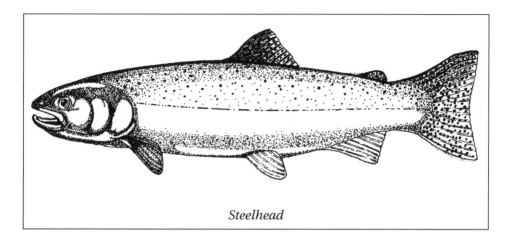

Steelhead

Steelhead

When the Pennsylvania Fish and Boat Commission began stocking steelhead in Lake Erie, they were actually rainbow trout. At first considered "lake run rainbows," they achieved tremendous size while feeding in the food-rich water of Lake Erie. Years later, additional strains of fish have been added, and true steelhead now start running into the lake's tributary streams as early as mid-September. Because of the addition of strains that include Michigan stocks and a Skamania strain raised in New York, the runs have increased in numbers and frequency.

Runs that depend on water temperature and tributary stream flows that are sufficient enough to allow spawning runs now begin in September, and fish continue to pour into the tributaries in November and December. Actual spawning of these fish takes place from March through April.

The Commission's Fairview hatchery artificially spawns steelhead from the lake in an effort to keep the risk of whirling disease at a minimum. Besides fish that migrate from New York and Ohio, Pennsylvania also stocks steelhead after holding them in hatchery facilities for a year. They normally spend two years in the lake before running the tributaries to spawn, adding another stock of fish from natural reproduction. Unlike many species of salmon, steelhead do not die after spawning.

Steelhead are large by any standard, averaging 6 to 8 pounds with a 10-pound plus fish not extraordinary. The current state record is 19 pounds, 2 ounces, taken from Lake Erie in 1992.

Identification of the species is nearly the same as the rainbow, although they are usually more silver in color and are more streamlined than the rainbow found in most of our streams. The lateral stripe is somewhat less obvious than the nonmigratory rainbow, but I have seen them with incredible color. It is pretty safe to assume that a rainbow taken from one of Lake Erie's tributaries, weighing 5 pounds or more, is actually a steelhead.

Palomino Trout

The palomino was first introduced into Pennsylvania waters in 1967. It is a "novelty" trout that stands out like a plate of gold wherever it is placed. A hybrid mix between a golden trout and rainbow, this fish is found only where it has been placed by the Fish and Boat Commission.

Palominos are nearly the same color as a palomino horse, with the rainbow's lateral stripe of reddish pink. Of course, this hybrid does not reproduce and rarely stays in the streams or lakes where it is placed for any period of time because they are easy to spot by anglers as well as avian and land-roving predators.

Palominos average 14 to 16 inches, 18- to 20-inch fish are not all that rare. They are popular fish for many anglers and draw attention wherever they are placed. They fight well when hooked and are often hard to capture. They do not seem prone to surface feeding. The current state record is an 11-pound, 10-ounce fish taken from Lake Erie in 1986.

Smallmouth Bass

Smallmouth bass, *Micropterus dolomieui*, are found in nearly all but the coldest brooks in the state. Smallmouth bass were originally found only in the Great Lakes drainage and Ohio watershed. Today they rival trout as the most popular game fish found in the Commonwealth.

Stocking of the species is now limited to new lakes and areas where populations need a boost. Stocked as fingerlings, smallmouth are stocked for the purpose of creating a reproducing and self-sustaining population. They have taken over areas where trout were once the only species found. Tolerant of warmer water temperatures, smallmouth may be found in good numbers throughout the state's larger river systems, in the lower reaches of nearly all trout streams, and within most lakes.

Smallmouth Bass

Smallmouth are easy to distinguish from other species, with a bronze cast that is darker on the back and vertical bars of black. They also have three dark vertical bands beginning near the eye and extending to the gill plate.

If in doubt, the upper jaw is a dead giveaway when compared to a largemouth because it does not extend beyond the eye. Smallmouth also have two dorsal fins and cream-colored bellies.

Bass can be taken throughout the year, but they prefer water temperatures between 60 and 80 degrees. Feeding activity slows when the temperature rises above or below these margins, although ice fishermen frequently take smallmouth.

A spring spawner, the bronzeback spawns from May through early June, when water temperatures normally climb into the 60- to 70-degree range. Eggs incubate and hatch within two to nine days. Bass are truly wild fish and rise freely in shallow waters. They prefer gravel bottoms, whereas largemouth prefer areas that have more silt. The average smallmouth size is somewhere between 9 and 12 inches, although all year classes should be found in good smallmouth fisheries. Recent regulations placed on some streams and a good number of lakes have helped increase the average size.

Bass of 15 inches in these areas are not uncommon, and fish ranging from 17 to 19 inches are becoming more abundant. A fish over 20 inches is considered a good fish.

The current state record smallmouth bass is 8 pounds, 8 ounces, taken from Scotts Run Lake, Berks County, in 1997.

Largemouth Bass

Largemouth bass, *Micropterus salmoides*, are now found in many lakes and slower moving streams or rivers within the state. The fish love the top-water bugs tossed by flyfishers and are attracting a lot of attention.

Because of the shorter growing season, bass here do not normally achieve the size of largemouth found in the southeastern United States, but many bass in the 2- to 3-pound range are found within the state.

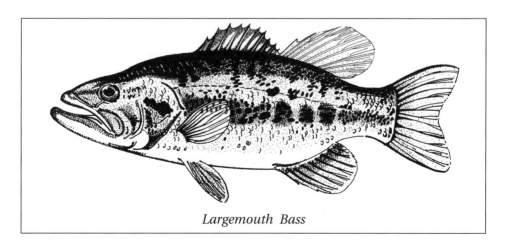

Largemouth Bass

Largemouth bass are slow growing fish here and require seven or more years of growth to attain good size and weight. The 15-inch minimum size limit placed on many lakes should help fish to reach an older age than they have in the past.

The fish is black to dark green on its back, muting to lighter green on its side. The belly is cream to dull white in color. A lateral line runs from the head to tail. However, the easiest way to identify a largemouth is to look at the upper jaw, which always extends beyond the eye. For those familiar with bass, this large mouth is another method of telling it apart from the smallmouth.

Largemouth spawn during spring and early summer, when water temperatures reach 62 to 65 degrees, usually in May and June. Eggs hatch in seven to ten days. Largemouth like warm water and prefer to feed in waters of 20 feet or less, making them an excellent fish for lake fishing. The current state record is 11 pounds, 3 ounces, taken from Birch Run Reservoir in Adams County in 1983

Striped Bass

Striped bass, *Morone saxatilis*, exist in Pennsylvania in three forms. The marine species is once again making its way up the Delaware River now that pollution near Philadelphia is dissipating. With the completion of passageways around dams on the Susquehanna River, anglers should be seeing them in this watershed, as well.

Purebred stripers have also been stocked in many lakes throughout the state and have fared well. The most notable results have been in Raystown Lake and Lake Wallenpaupack, which have produced large purebred fish.

The Pennsylvania Fish and Boat Commission has also introduced hybrids of white bass, *Morone chrysops*, and striped bass. This hybrid does not attain the weight of pure stripers, averaging 5 to 6 pounds. Although rarely mentioned as a game fish here, the striper's future looks bright.

Once a striper is hooked, it isn't difficult to identify due to its tremendous fighting ability. Smaller stripers are in the 5-pound range, while better fish are usually 20 pounds, and 40-pound fish are widely available. Flyfishers are beginning to realize that stripers will take a fly designed for saltwater and are adjusting their equipment and tactics to take one of the largest game fish to be found within the state.

The back of the striper is black, the side is silvery, and the belly is white. Black, unbroken stripes line the body of a purebred, while broken, less distinctive lateral stripes are found on the hybrid. They have two dorsal fins that are separate from one another and close to the same length. The front one is spiny while the rear dorsal fin is soft.

Marine stripers spawn in the spring in freshwater above the tidal waters. Peak spawning begins when water temperatures reach 60 to 68 degrees. The floating eggs hatch in two to three days.

Within the lake systems, there is no recorded natural reproduction, and the Fish and Boat Commission stock these impoundments with young fish to ensure that there will be solid year classes in the years to follow. Of course, there is no reproduction of the white bass/striped bass hybrid.

Striped bass state records are recorded in two categories, marine and land-locked. The current marine state record is 53 pounds, 13 ounces, taken from the Delaware River, Delaware County, in 1989. The landlocked record rivals the marine record and currently is 53 pounds, 12 ounces, taken from Raystown Lake, Huntingdon County, in 1994. Most believe that these records will be broken in the near future.

American Shad

American shad, *Alosa sapidissima*, were responsible for the formation of the Pennsylvania Fish and Boat Commission in 1866. At one time a prolific fish within the Susquehanna watershed and a source of income and food for those who lived along the river, this shad fishery came to an abrupt end when dams stopped the runs short of natural spawning grounds.

The addition of hydroelectric dams halted the runs below the Pennsylvania state line. After years of negotiating, the final dam passageways should bring the shad back to the Susquehanna watershed in coming years.

The return of the American shad to this river system after 144 years of continuous effort is an historical event. Insofar as fishing is concerned, American shad are currently found only in the Delaware River watershed. The majority of shad fishing takes place on the Delaware River itself, and flyfishers are adapting their techniques to take shad on the fly rod.

The largest member of the herring family, shad average 5 to 6 pounds and have olive to bluish backs with very silver sides. The belly has sawtoothed belly scales, the dorsal fin is short, and the tail is deeply etched. Shad runs begin when water temperature reaches 50 degrees, usually in early April on the Delaware. They come in waves until early June at which time the female releases buoyant eggs that hatch in six to ten days. Adult shad remain in the river system and seem to feed heavily before returning to sea. Juvenile shad depart for the sea after two to three months and return to spawn in three to five years.

The current state record shad was taken from the Delaware River in Pike county. Taken in 1986, the fish and weighed 9 pounds, 9 ounces.

Muskellunge

The muskie, *Exos masquinongy*, is the bully of Pennsylvania waters. Native to the Ohio River and Lake Erie watersheds, it is now scattered throughout the state.

Muskie are solitary fish and love shallow water and weedbeds, making them easily available to flyfishers, although they are not easy to catch. Known as "the fish of a thousand casts," locating a fish is more than half the battle of capturing one.

Pennsylvania streams and lakes also contain a good number of tiger muskellunge, *Esox lincius*, a hybrid cross of purebred muskie and male northern pike. Both exhibit the same characteristics, although the hybrid does not reproduce in the wild.

Muskies have extremely long sleek bodies, usually light green to tan in color and having distinctive dark vertical broken bars filtering down their sides. Both the cheek and gill cover are scaled only on the upper half. The head is slim and narrows toward a mouth filled with razor-sharp teeth, which require the use shock-tippets when fishing for this species.

The anal and dorsal fins are set far back on the muskie, with only a short gap between the fins and the tail. The muskellunge is a spring spawner, beginning when water temperatures reach 48 to 56 degrees. The eggs hatch within eight to 14 days.

These fish easily reach 20 to 35 pounds within the Keystone State's waters, and fish exceeding 40 pounds and 50 inches are not all that uncommon. However, the state record fish, taken from Conneaut Lake, Crawford County, in 1924, does seem like an unbeatable record—the 54-pound, 3-ounce fish has held the top spot since 1924.

Pennsylvania's Wild Trout Streams

Pennsylvania is blessed with a number of wild trout streams, many of which are native brook trout streams and others that hold wild brown trout. Both are the last strongholds of the wild and native trout found here.

While perusing this book, you will notice that many of the more famous streams are stocked waters. With the drought of the past few years, we can ill afford to lose the remaining wild trout streams found here. Many groups are intent on maintaining the resource via stream monitoring and careful planning. We need to support these groups.

Without knowing how heavily these streams will be fished, it is extremely important that these special and precious waters be treated kindly. That means packing out everything that you packed in.

I feel these waters should all be under special regulations with stringent policies set forth for flies only and/or single hooked lures. Barbless hook regulations would help as well. By including this list, I have taken on the responsibility of possibly causing harm to this resource. Overfishing could present problems, both social and biological.

However, there is a part of me that believes in mankind. A prime example is an unofficial survey that showed the majority of anglers have been releasing the majority of their catch. That fact helped the Pennsylvania Fish and Boat Commission decide to reduce the creel limit on trout from 8 per day to 5.

Flyfishers are, for the most part, a conservation-oriented group of anglers, and I hope and believe that the vast majority will release all the trout they catch on these fragile streams. Yes, some of our brook trout streams have a lot of stunted fish, but no studies have been made to prove that reducing numbers of fish in these streams will help the growth rate.

Many of these streams have been labeled "sterile," but trout have flourished here despite the lack of abundant food—if not in size, then in number.

I ask all of you to release every fish you catch on these waters. I firmly believe that if we err on the side of caution, fish can always be culled if they become too abundant. However, an overfished stream will take years to recover, if it ever does.

As anglers, it is our responsibility to take care of all the waters that have been so kind to us. I believe that trout genetics are extremely important. The continual inbreeding of hatchery trout has not helped strengthen our wild trout populations. Brown trout that were introduced here were a far superior form than we find today.

Wild trout waters are special places and are not renewed by hatchery-bred fish. I have been asked not to share the names of these streams with you, even though they are public information. Since they are not managed to protect wild trout, it is up to anglers to treat these streams as such and release all fish and not subject them to overfishing.

It is my hope that as the number of flyfishers increases there will be more pressure to place stringent regulations that will guarantee that these streams are not overcrowded and overfished. There are few, if any, secret spots remaining, and I firmly believe that sharing these waters is a necessity—not to do so would be selfish and self-serving. Trout waters need all the help they can get.

For anglers who have never fished these streams before, you can help by practicing catch and release on all wild trout waters and by becoming educated about what is necessary for wild trout to survive. These streams are more than a place to fish—they are places to be explored and treasured. I hope that you will prove me right to include this list and show that flyfishers are true defenders of wild trout.

A complete list of waters that the Commission is designating as Class A Wild Trout Waters is as follows:

Stream	Limits	Length (miles)
ADAMS COUNTY		
Antietam Creek East Branch	From headwaters downstream to Waynesboro Reservoir Adams	2.5
BEDFORD COUNTY		
Carbaugh Run	From headwaters downstream to Carbaugh Run Reservoir	1.6
Potter Creek	From Route T-609 bridge downstream to mouth	3.3
Yellow Creek	From Keagy Dam breast downstream to dam breast at Waterside	1.4
BERKS COUNTY		
Beaver Run	From headwaters downstream to mouth	3.1
Bieber Creek	From SR 2026 Bridge/Boyers Junction downstream to Dam at SR 1021 / T-593 Junction	2.2
Furnace Creek	From headwaters downstream to 930 meters upstream from SR 4044	2.8
Hay Creek	From headwaters downstream to SR 0082 at Geigertown	6.4
Perkiomen Creek NW Branch	SR 1022 downstream to SR 2069	4.9
Peters Creek	From headwaters spring downstream to the mouth	0.75
Pine Creek	From headwaters downstream to mouth	6.0
Six Penny Creek	From headwaters downstream to mouth at Schuylkill River	3.7
Swamp Creek	From headwaters downstream to dam in Bechtelsville	2.6
UNT Perkiomen Creek NW Branch	From headwaters downstream to mouth	2.4
UNT to Six Penny Creek	From headwaters downstream to mouth	1.7
Wyomissing Creek	SR 222 downstream to dam pool downstream of Wyomissing Boulevard	2.4

BERKS/LEHIGH COUNTIES

Perkiomen Creek	From headwaters downstream to SR 1010 at Hereford	5.3

BLAIR COUNTY

Clover Creek	From LR 7009 bridge near Larke downstream to mouth	6.0
Piney Creek	From mouth of Poverty Hollow Run downstream to mouth at Gannister	6.2
Tipton Run	From headwaters downstream to upper limit of slackwater at Tipton Reservoir	2.5
Tipton Run	From dam at Tipton Reservoir downstream to mouth	4.6

BLAIR/CENTRE COUNTIES

Big Fill Run	From confluence of Big Fill Run and Wolf Run downstream to mouth	4.7

BLAIR/HUNTINGDON COUNTIES

Fox Run	From headwaters downstream to mouth	2.4

BRADFORD COUNTY

Chilson Run	From headwaters downstream to mouth	1.6
Deep Hollow	2.87 upstream of mouth downstream to mouth	2.9
Millstone Creek	From headwaters downstream to Deep Hollow Run	3.5
Pine Swamp Run	From headwaters downstream to mouth	2.3
Sugar Run	From headwaters downstream to mouth	3.2

BUCKS COUNTY

Cooks Creek	From confluence with Silver Creek downstream to SR 4075 bridge	3.7
Cooks Creek	SR 4075 bridge downstream to mouth	2.2
UNT Cooks Creek (SilverCreek)	From a spring 0.5 upstream of mouth downstream to mouth	0.5
UNT Cooks Creek (Coon Hollow Run)	From headwaters downstream to mouth	2.5

CAMBRIA COUNTY

Bens Creek	From headwaters downstream to the Portage Water Authority Backwater	2.7
Conemaugh River, Little South Fork	From headwaters downstream to Beaverdale Reservoir	2.0
Sandy Run	From headwaters downstream to mouth	2.2

CAMERON COUNTY

Bailey Run, Little	From headwaters downstream to mouth	1.4
Black Stump Hollow	From headwaters downstream to mouth	2.2
Bronson Run	From headwaters downstream to mouth	2.3

CAMERON COUNTY (CONT.)

Brooks Run	From confluence of left and right branches downstream to SF RD bridge 2.9 km upstream mouth	1.6
Canoe Run	From headwaters downstream to mouth	3.1
Colbert Hollow	From headwaters downstream to mouth	1.8
Cowley Run	From confluence of East and West Branches downstream to mouth	0.9
Finley Run	From headwaters downstream to Forest Road Bridge 2.1 upstream from mouth	2.5
Grove Run	From headwaters downstream to mouth	5.8
Hunts Run	From McNuff Branch downstream to mouth	4.7
Lick Island Run	From confluence with Gravelly Run downstream to mouth	1.4
McNuff Branch	From headwaters downstream to mouth	5.1
Miller Run	From headwaters downstream to mouth	2.2
Norcross Run	From headwaters downstream to mouth	3.0
Sinn-Portage Creek	From confluence with Parker Run downstream to confluence with Cowley Run	2.5
Sinnemahoning Creek Driftwood Branch	From headwaters downstream to confluence with Elk Fork	6.8
Square Timber Run	From headwaters downstream to mouth	3.7
Whitehead Run	From headwaters downstream to mouth	2.5

CARBON COUNTY

Aquashicola	Bridge on T-372 downstream to Chicola Lake	2.4
Black Creek	From Weider Tract downstream to mouth	3.0
Hickory Run	From Sand Spring Run downstream to mouth	1.6
Little Bear Creek	From headwaters downstream to confluence with Big Bear Creek	1.9

CENTRE COUNTY

Benner Run	From headwaters downstream to first tributary below Pine Haven Camp	2.0
Black Bear Run	From headwaters downstream to Black Bear Reservoir	3.7
Bougher Run	From headwaters downstream to mouth	3.0
Buffalo Run	From headwaters downstream to bridge at SR 3008	5.5
Buffalo Run	From SR 3008 bridge in Fillmore downstream to mouth	6.7
Cedar Run	From headwaters downstream to mouth	2.9
Elk Creek	From headwaters downstream to Stover Gap Road	1.5

Elk Creek	From Stover Gap Road downstream to the spring approximately 0.8 west of SR 0445 and SR 874 intersection	5.8
Elk Creek	From the spring 9.8 km upstream of mouth downstream to mouth	6.1
Fields Run	From headwaters downstream to mouth	4.9
Galbraith Gap	From headwaters downstream to mouth	3.2
Laurel Run	From Whetstone Run downstream to the mouth	2.09
Lick Run	From headwaters downstream to mouth	2.5
Little Fishing Creek	From spring 6.8 km above T-420 downstream to 1.2 km below T-470 in Mingoville	6.5
Logan Branch	From 135 m upstream T-371 bridge downstream to Axemann Spring	1.6
Logan Branch	From Axemann Spring downstream to mouth	2.0
Muddy Creek	From headwaters downstream to mouth	3.6
Nittany Creek	From I-80 eastbound bridge downstream to mouth	2.9
Penns Creek	From confluence with Elk Creek at Coburn downstream to .6 km downstream from confluence with Swift Run	7.0
Pine Creek	From headwaters downstream to bridge on Stony Run Road	3.7
Pine Creek	From SR 2018 bridge downstream to mouth	1.5
Rock Run	From headwaters downstream to the confluence with Middle Branch of Rock Run	1.4
Rock Run, Middle Branch	From headwaters downstream to mouth	2.7
Smays Run	From headwaters downstream to mouth	1.1
Spring Creek	From SR 3010 bridge downstream to Thorton Spring at SR 0026 bridge	2.0
Spring Creek	From Thorton Spring downstream to 2.0 km below T-376 bridge	3.1
Spring Creek	From 2.0 km below T-376 bridge downstream to upper limit of Fisherman's Paradise	5.5
Spring Creek	Fisherman's Paradise	1.0
Spring Creek	From downstream limit of Fisherman's Paradise downstream to RR trestle 100 yds above dam in Bellefonte	3.7
Spring Creek	Lamb Street bridge in Bellefonte downstream to mouth	2.3
Spruce Creek	From private road south of Rock Spring downstream to Centre/Huntingdon county line	2.0
Thompson Run, Unit #3	From headwaters at Duck Pond downstream to mouth	0.9

CENTRE COUNTY (CONT.)

Tomtit Run	From headwaters downstream to 300 m upstream from mouth	3.8
Trim Root Run	From headwaters downstream to mouth	2.5
Wallace Run	From confluence of North Branch downstream to UNT at Gum Stump	2.0

CENTRE/CLEARFIELD COUNTIES

Moshannon Creek	From headwaters downstream to Roup Run	5.0

CHESTER COUNTY

Little Valley Creek	From tributary upstream of SR 0202 bridge downstream to mouth	1.7

CHESTER/MONTGOMERY COUNTIES

Valley Creek	From SR 0029 downstream to mouth	7.0

CLEARFIELD COUNTY

Jack Dent Branch	From headwaters downstream to first Jack Dent Road bridge	1.8

CLEARFIELD COUNTY

Simeling Run	From headwaters downstream to mouth	2.5
Amos Branch	From headwaters downstream to mouth	4.7
Barney Run	From headwaters downstream to mouth	4.7
Bear Run	From headwaters downstream to mouth	2.7
Beaver Dam Run	From confluence of Left Fork and Right Fork downstream to mouth	1.6
Boggs Hollow	From headwaters downstream to mouth	5.2
Burns Run	From headwaters downstream to mouth	3.8
Calhoun Branch	From headwaters downstream to confluence with Trout Run	2.5
Camp Run	From headwaters downstream to 3.1 km upstream from mouth	1.9
Cedar Run	From headwaters downstream to mouth	5.6
Cranberry Run	From headwaters downstream to mouth	2.9
East Kammerdiner Run	From headwaters downstream to Keller Reservoir	1.7
Ferney Run	From headwaters downstream to mouth	4.6
Fishing Creek	From 0.3 above the T-350 bridge downstream to Sink Hole below SR 2007 bridge	5.3
Fishing Creek	From 200 yards above SR 0880 bridge downstream to bridge at Tylersville Fish Culture Station	3.4
Fishing Creek	From Tylersville Fish Culture Station downstream to Flemings Bridge (SR 2004)	5.2
Fishing Creek	From Flemings Bridge (SR 2004) downstream to Cedar Run	9.8

Gann Run	From headwaters downstream to mouth	1.3
Gottshall Run	From headwaters downstream to mouth	2.0
Henry Run	From headwaters downstream to mouth	3.7
Hunter Hollow	From headwaters downstream to mouth	1.5
Hyner Run, East Branch	From headwaters downstream to mouth	3.3
John Summerson Branch	From headwaters downstream to mouth	2.4
Love Run	From headwaters downstream to mouth	1.8
Mill Run	From headwaters downstream to Crabapple Hollow	2.6
Montour Run	From headwaters downstream to mouth	3.2
Rattlesnake Run	From headwaters downstream to confluence with Wildcat Hollow	3.8
Rauchtown Creek	SR 0880 upstream Gotshall Run upstream to confluence with Rockey/Krape	1.2
Ritchie Run	From headwaters downstream to mouth	3.2
Rock Run	From headwaters downstream to polluted spring approximately 630 m downstream from confluence with Wild Cat Hollow	3.9
Shingle Branch	From headwaters downstream to 2.4 km upstream from mouth	3.3
Swamp Branch	From headwaters downstream to confluence with East Branch of Big Run	3.4
Trout Run	From confluence Greene & Calhoun Branch downstream to mouth	2.4
Two Mile Run	From headwaters downstream to confluence with Middle Branch of Two Mile Run Middle Branch	2.7
Young Womans Creek	From Beechwood Trail downstream to State Forest property line	5.5

COLUMBIA COUNTY

Fisher Run	From headwaters downstream to the mouth	2.8
Furnace Run	From headwaters downstream to mouth	1.4
Klingermans Run	From headwaters downstream to mouth	2.4
Lick Run	From headwaters downstream to mouth	4.1
Little Fishing Creek	From headwaters downstream to SR 4032	4.3
Roaring Creek	From headwaters downstream to mouth of Lick Run	6.0
Tenmile Run	From headwaters downstream to T-409	3.0

CRAWFORD COUNTY

Shirley Run	From SR 1032 bridge downstream to SR 0089 bridge	2.0
Sugar Creek, East Branch	From SR 0428 bridge downstream to mouth	3.5
Big Spring Creek	From source downstream to old Thomas Dam	0.6

CRAWFORD COUNTY (CONT.)

Letort Spring Run	From Letort Spring downstream to southern edge of Letort Spring Park	1.7
Letort Spring Run	From southern edge of Letort Spring Park downstream to sewage treatment plant	1.9
Trindle Spring Run (Silver Springs)	From a spring source near Silver Spring meeting house downstream to mouth	0.9

ELK COUNTY

Dents Run	From headwaters downstream to mouth	10.5
Little Dents Run	From headwaters downstream to mouth	2.0
Spring Run	From confluence with Stoney Brook downstream to confluence with UNT 600 m downstream of Elk State Forest boundary	2.3
Straight Creek, South Fork	Headwaters downstream to mouth	4.6
Vineyard Run	From headwaters downstream to Spring Creek Horton Twp line	2.4
Beaver Run	From bridge on T-778 downstream to mouth	4.7
Trout Run	From Twitchell Road downstream to mouth	2.3

FAYETTE COUNTY

Buck Run	From headwaters downstream to 2.3 km above mouth	1.7

FRANKLIN COUNTY

Antietam Creek, West Branch	From headwaters downstream to SR 0997	3.4
Bear Valley Run	From headwaters downstream to mouth	3.7
Broad Run	From headwaters downstream to 4.6 km upstream of mouth at shale pit	5.3
Broad Run	From shale pit downstream 1.6 to Tree Farm Lane Bridge	1.6
Falling Spring Branch	From source at spring downstream to T-515 bridge	1.3
Falling Spring Branch	From T-515 bridge downstream to T-519 bridge	0.5

HUNTINGDON COUNTY

Spruce Creek	Lower body PSU exp area upstream to upper body PSU exp area	0.5
Standing Stone Creek, East Branch	Dam at Greenwood Furnace State Park downstream to mouth	9.2

JUNIATA COUNTY

Lost Creek	From headwaters downstream to SR 0235 bridge	3.4
Lost Creek	From SR 0235 bridge downstream to SR 0035 bridge	5.1
UNT to Willow Run	From SR 0035 bridge in Peru Mills downstream to confluence with Willow Run	1.1

Willow Run	From confluence of Willow Run and UNT downstream to T-314 bridge crossing	3.6
Willow Run	From T-314 bridge downstream to SR 0850 bridge	2.5

JUNIATA/MIFFLIN COUNTIES

Spectacle Run	From headwaters downstream to mouth	2.9

LACKAWANNA COUNTY

Ash Creek	From SGL #135 downstream to mouth	1.9
Greene Run	From headwaters downstream to mouth	4.9
Kellum Creek	From headwaters downstream to mouth	2.5
Lackawanna River	From the ups Carbondale city line downstream to Gilmartin Street	6.7
Lackawanna River	From Gilmartin Street downstream to Depot Street	3.1
Lackawanna River	From Depot Street downstream to Mellow Park Footbridge	0.7
Lackawanna River	From Mellow Park Foot bridge downstream to Route 347	1.1
Lake Run	From headwaters downstream to the mouth	1.1
Panther Creek	From headwaters downstream to mouth	2.8
Rattlesnake Creek	From lower bridge on SR 0690 downstream to mouth	2.2
Roaring Brook	From headwaters downstream to upper limit of Hollisterville Dam	3.2
Roaring Brook	Hollisterville Dam downstream to Elmhurst Reservoir	3.9
Spring Brook	Watres Dam downstream to Nesbitt Reservoir	2.7

LANCASTER COUNTY

Conowingo Creek	From headwaters downstream to SR 3005	5.5
Segloch Run	From T-596 Y T-548 intersection downstream to SR 1026 bridge	2.2
UNT to Conowingo Creek	From headwaters downstream to the mouth	1.6
UNT to Trout Run	From headwaters downstream to confluence with Trout Run	1.9

LANCASTER/LEBANON COUNTIES

Shearers Creek	From headwaters downstream to powerline near county line	1.7

LEHIGH COUNTY

Cedar Creek	From SR 1019 bridge downstream Lake Muhlenberg	1.1
Lehigh Creek, Little	From T-476 downstream to the confluence with Spring Creek	1.6
Trout Creek	From first bridge on Dixon St downstream to mouth at Little Lehigh Creek	1.6

LUZERNE COUNTY

Arnold Creek	From headwaters downstream to SR 0118	2.3
Arnold Creek	SR 0118 downstream to mouth	2.7
Butternut Run	From headwaters downstream to mouth	1.5
Fades Creek	From pipeline crossing downstream to mouth	1.7
Huntington Creek	From headwaters downstream to 300 m upstream T-575	2.7
Lick Branch	From headwaters downstream to the mouth	2.5
Little Schickshinny	From T-429 downstream to mouth	2.5
Mitchler Run	From headwaters downstream to the mouth	1.9
Oley Creek	From headwaters downstream to SGL #187 boundary near Dennison township line	1.0
Pikes Creek	From headwaters downstream to upper most arm of Pikes Creek Reservoir	3.7
Shingle Run	From source downstream to confluence with Huntington Creek	1.7
Solomon Creek	From headwaters downstream to confluence with Pine Creek	2.4

LYCOMING COUNTY

Aughanbaugh Run	From headwaters to mouth	0.9
Bear Run	From headwaters downstream to mouth	4.7
Big Run	From headwaters downstream to mouth	1.6
Callahan Run	From headwaters downstream to mouth	1.9
Dog Run	From headwaters downstream to mouth	0.9
Engle Run	From headwaters downstream to mouth	4.9
Flicks Run	From headwaters downstream to mouth	3.2
Grays Run	From T-842 downstream to mouth	2.2
Hagerman Run	From headwaters downstream to mouth	2.4
Hawk Run	From headwaters downstream to mouth	3.2
McMurrin Run	From Sand Spring downstream to sink near T-030	4.0
Mill Run	From headwaters downstream to mouth	3.8
Miller Run	From headwaters downstream to mouth	3.9
Morgan Valley Run	From headwaters downstream to mouth	1.2
Potash Hollow	From headwaters downstream to the mouth	2.9
Ramsey Run	From headwaters downstream to mouth	2.7
Slate Run	From confluence with Francis Branch and Cushman Branch downstream to mouth	7.1
Trout Run	From headwaters downstream to mouth	6.9
UNT – Fourth Gap	From headwaters downstream to mouth	3.0
White Deer Hole Creek	From headwaters downstream to T-384 bridge	4.7
Wolf Run Noon Branch	From headwaters downstream to mouth	2.0

MCKEAN COUNTY

Lewis Run	From headwaters downstream to mouth	5.0
Tunungwant Creek, East Branch	From confluence of Pigeon Run downstream to Main Street bridge in Lewis Run	3.0
Tunungwant Creek, East Branch	From Main Street bridge in Lewis Run downstream to T-331 bridge in Lewis Run	1.0
Tunungwant Creek, East Branch	T-331 bridge at Howard downstream to SR 4002 bridge	3.5

MCKEAN/POTTER COUNTIES

Allegheny Portage Creek	Confluence with Brown Hollow downstream to confluence with Scaffold Lick Run	1.6

MIFFLIN COUNTY

Frog Hollow (Alexander Springs Run)	From headwaters downstream to mouth	1.1
Honey Creek	From Alexander Caverns downstream to mouth	3.8
Kishacoquillas Creek	From Yeagertown RR bridge downstream to Mill Road bridge	2.4
Long Hollow Run	From confluence with UNT near T-741 intersection downstream to the mouth	1.9
Tea Creek	From spring at SR 0322 bridge downstream to mouth	1.1

MIFFLIN/UNION COUNTIES

Penns Creek	600 below the confluence with Swift Run downstream to 0.3 mi. Downstream from confluence with Cherry Run	3.6

MONROE COUNTY

Appenzell Creek	From SR 3018 at Neola downstream to mouth	4.0
Broadhead Creek, Middle Branch	From headwaters downstream to confluence with Broadhead Creek	3.2
Cranberry Creek	Lake outlet at Cresco downstream to T-590 bridge	3.1
Devils Hole Creek	From separated SGL #221 border downstream to SGL #221 border	1.8
Devils Hole Creek	From upper boundary of SGL #221 downstream to lower boundary of SGL #221	1.4
Devils Hole Creek	From SGL #221 downstream to mouth	1.1
Dotters Creek	From Monroe/Carbon Co. border downstream to confluence with UNT below Jonas	1.9
Dotters Creek	From confluence with UNT below Jonas downstream to bridge on T-442	2.4
Middle Creek	From 0.25 km above T-444 downstream to mouth	4.9
Mill Creek	From Headwaters downstream to SGL #221 border	1.9
Pohopoco Creek	From Bridge on SR 3016 downstream to SR 0209 Bridge in Kresgeville	8.0

MONROE COUNTY (CONT.)

Poplar Run	Delaware State Forest	2.5
Singer Run	From SGL #127 downstream to mouth	1.0

NORTHAMPTON COUNTY

Bushkill Creek	From Dam at Binney & Smith factory downstream to Easton Heights Dam	1.7
Bushkill Creek	From SR 2019 bridge downstream to SR 2019 and SR 2036 Int	1.3
Frya Run	From spring 1 mile up from mouth downstream to mouth	1.0
Monocacy Creek	From SR 0987 bridge downstream to SR 0248 bridge	1.9
Monocacy Creek	From Gertrude Fox conservation area downstream to Illicks Mill Dam	1.9
Nancy Run	From bridge on SR 3007 downstream to mouth	1.6
Saucon Creek	From confluence Black R downstream to SR 0412	2.1
Roaring Creek, South Branch	From SR 2024 downstream to T-335 bridge	3.0

PERRY COUNTY

Shaeffer Run	From Couch Road Bridge at 2nd narrows downstream to Tuscarora St. Forest boundary	3.9

PIKE COUNTY

Bushkill Creek	From Bushkill Swamp downstream to Delaware State Forest boundary	2.7
Pond Eddy Creek	From 2.2 above mouth downstream to mouth	2.2
Sawkill Creek	From confluence with Sloat Bank downstream to mouth	1.3
Toms Creek	From Delaware Water Gap NRA boundary downstream to mouth	2.1

POTTER COUNTY

Beech Run	From headwaters downstream to mouth	1.9
Big Moores Run	From headwaters downstream to confluence with Knickerbocker Hollow	3.4
Big Moores Run	From confluence with UNT at Bluecoat Trail downstream to 2.9 km above mouth	1.6
Big Nelson Run, Left Branch	From headwaters downstream to mouth	4.0
Birch Run	From headwaters downstream to mouth	5.3
Cherry Run	From headwaters downstream to mouth	2.1
Commissioner Run	From headwaters downstream to mouth	1.7
Cross Fork Creek	From confluence with Rhulo Hollow downstream to 400 m downstream from T-416	5.4
Dingman Run	From headwaters downstream to mouth	4.0
Dry Run	From headwaters downstream to mouth	3.6
Dwight Creek	From headwaters downstream to mouth	2.4

Elevenmile Creek	From headwaters downstream to T-379 (Turkey Path Rpad)	4.5
Francis Branch	From headwaters downstream to the confluence with Kramer Hollow	4.0
Freeman Run	From confluence with Postal Weight Hollow downstream to confluence with Bark Shanty Hollow	2.2
Freeman Run, West Branch	Headwaters downstream to confluence with Gas Well Hollow	3.2
Freeman Run, West Branch	Gas Well Hollow downstream to mouth	2.7
Genesee Forks	From confluence of Baldwin & Lehman Hollow downstream to confluence with California Creek	2.6
Genesse Forks	From confluence with California Creek downstream to mouth	5.1
Genesse River, Middle Branch	From headwaters downstream to T-450 bridge near Gold	3.6
Genesee River, West Branch	From T-410 bridge downstream to confluence with Rose Lake Run	2.4
Germania Branch	From Straight Run downstream to mouth	2.2
Hammersley Fork	From headwaters downstream to confluence with Bell Branch	6.9
Indian Run	From headwaters downstream to mouth	2.5
Johnson Brook	From headwaters downstream to SGL boundary above Thunder Run	3.5
Kettle Creek	From Billings Branch downstream to confluence with Long Run	7.9
Long Run	From confluence with Lechler Branch downstream to mouth	4.9
Lushbaugh Run, Right Branch	From headwaters downstream to mouth	2.9
Lyman Run	From headwaters downstream to confluence with Splash Dam Hollow	1.5
Lyman Run	From confluence with Splash Dam Hollow downstream to Lyman Lake	3.8
Mill Creek	From bridge at Coudersport County Club downstream to mouth	5.9
Nelson Branch	From headwaters downstream to mouth	5.2
Ninemile Run	From headwaters downstream to confluence with Commission Run	2.2
Ninemile Run	From confluence with Commissioner Run downstream to mouth	3.9
Oswayo Creek	From lower hatchery property line downstream to confluence with Clara Creek	5.5
Phoenix Run	From confluence with Little Phoenix Run downstream to mouth	5.3

POTTER COUNTY (CONT.)

Pine Creek	From headwaters downstream to confluence with Buckseller Run	3.7
Pine Creek	From confluence with Buckseller Run downstream to confluence with Genesee Forks	4.8
Prouty Run	From confluence with Ford Hollow downstream to mouth	2.9
Reed Run	From confluence with Reed Run Rt Fk downstream to mouth	1.8
Sawmill Run	From headwaters downstream to mouth	2.3
Schoolhouse Run	From headwaters downstream to the mouth	1.9
Sinn Creek, East Fork	From headwaters downstream to Dolliver Trail	2.5
Sinn Creek, East Fork	From confluence with Wild Boy Run downstream to confluence with Camp Run	2.9
Sliders Branch	From headwaters downstream to mouth	3.9
Splash Dam Hollow	From headwaters downstream to mouth	2.7
Stony Lick Run	From headwaters downstream to mouth	3.2
Wildboy Run	From headwaters downstream to mouth	2.4
Windfall Run	From headwaters downstream to mouth	6.1

SCHUYLKILL COUNTY

Bear Creek	Headwaters downstream to 500 m below Jct T-895/T-594	3.4
Beaver Creek	From headwaters downstream to the bridge on the lane off of SR 1013	1.5
Catawissa Creek, Little	From headwaters downstream to T-431	2.1
Cold Run	From headwaters downstream to the confluence with Beaver Creek	2.7
Crooked Run	From headwaters downstream to mouth	4.4
Crooked Run, Little	From headwaters downstream to mouth	1.7
Davis Run	From headwaters downstream to mouth	1.2
Messers Run	From Lofty Rs downstream to Blue Head Rs	2.4
Negro Hollow	From headwaters downstream to mouth	1.1
Owl Creek	From headwaters downstream Tamaqua Reservoir	0.25
Owl Creek	Tamaqua Reservoir downstream to mouth	1.7
Rattling Run	From headwaters downstream to mouth	1.8
Trexler Run	From headwaters downstream to mouth	3.0
Tumbling Run	Headwaters downstream to Silver Creek Reservoir	5.1

SCHUYLKILL/BERKS COUINTIES

Rattling Run	From headwaters downstream to mouth	3.9
Schuylkill RL	From headwaters downstream to mouth	1.8

SCHUYLKILL/LUZERNE COUNTIES

Raccoon Creek	From headwaters downstream to mouth	3.2

SOMERSET COUNTY

Allwine Creek	From headwaters downstream to mouth	1.9
Beaverdam Run	From outflow of pond near Daley downstream to SR 1018 bridge downstream of SGL #228	3.2
Enos Run	From headwaters downstream to the mouth	1.2
Higgins Run	From coal tipple at RM 1.37 downstream to mouth	1.4
Laurel Run	From PA/MD state line downstream to 300 m downstream of T-331 bridge	2.9
Laurel Run	From 300 m downstream of T-331 bridge downstream to the mouth	5.5
UNT to Beaverdam Creek	From headwaters downstream to the mouth	1.8
Zehner Run	From PA/MD border downstream to mouth	1.4

SULLIVAN COUNTY

Deep Hollow Run	From headwaters downstream to mouth	2.4
Fishing Creek, West Branch	From headwaters downstream to Hemlock Run	2.5
Hoagland Branch	From headwaters downstream to SR 0154 bridge	2.2
Swanks Run	From headwaters downstream to mouth	1.6
Tamarack Run	From headwaters downstream to mouth	3.7
UNT Painter Run	From headwaters downstream to mouth	1.9

TIOGA COUNTY

Apple Tree Hollow	From headwaters to mouth	2.4
Asaph Run Rt	Confluence with Bear Wallow Bridge & Roberts Bridge downstream to confluence with Asaph Run	1.7
Baker Branch	From headwaters downstream to mouth	3.9
Baldwin Run	From headwaters downstream to mouth	4.7
Billings Branch	From headwaters downstream to mouth	2.5
Bohen Run	From headwaters downstream to mouth	1.3
Canada Run	From headwaters downstream to mouth	3.2
Cedar Run	From headwaters downstream to confluence with Buck Run	3.6
Cedar Run	From confluence of Buck Run downstream to Fahnestock Run	2.8
Cushman Branch	From headwaters downstream to confluence with Bear Run	3.7
Cushman Branch	From confluence with Bear Run downstream to mouth	0.6
Elk Run	From headwaters downstream to Thompson Hollow	1.1
Elk Run	From confluence with Thompson Hollow downstream to mouth	5.4

TIOGA COUNTY (CONT.)

Fahnestock Run	From headwaters downstream to confluence with Cedar run	4.5
Fourmile Run	From confluence with Right and Left Branch downstream to mouth	2.0
Francis Branch	From Francis Rd bridge at confluence with Kramer Hollow downstream to mouth	1.7
Jemison Run	From headwaters downstream to T-559	2.4
Mill Run	From headwaters downstream to mouth	2.7
Nickle Run	From headwaters downstream to mouth	4.1
Straight Run Rt Branch	From headwaters downstream to mouth	2.0

TIOGA/LYCOMING COUNTIES

Cedar Run	From Fahnestock Run downstream to mouth	4.6

UNION COUNTY

Buffalo Creek, North Branch	From headwaters to outflow of Mifflinburg Reservoir	7.0
Cherry Run	From 4.3 km above mouth downstream to mouth	2.7
Weikert Run	From Little Weikert Run downstream to mouth	2.9

VENANGO COUNTY

Cherry Run	From bridge at T-599 downstream to bridge in Plumer Borough	3.3
Porcupine Creek	1.1 km upstream of Norway Run downstream to 1.7 km upstream from mouth	1.1
Porcupine Creek	1.7 km upstream from mouth downstream to mouth	1.1

WARREN COUNTY

Caldwell Creek, West Branch	From confluence of Three Bridge Run downstream to mouth	2.9
Fourmile Run	From headwaters downstream to confluence with the North Branch	3.3
Spring Creek	From 600 m downstream of SR 3001 bridge downstream to mouth	2.1

WAYNE COUNTY

Faulkner Brook	From first unnamed lake upstream from mouth downstream to mouth	1.8
Sherman Creek	From 0.5 km above SR 4043 & T-673 Intersection downstream to PA/NY border	2.7
Stiles Creek	From source downstream to confluence with East Branch Dyberry Creek	2.5

WESTMORELAND COUNTY

Camp Run	From Headwater Ponds downstream to mouth	4.1
Furnace Run	From headwaters downstream to mouth	2.3

Laughlintown Run	From confluence with Furnace Run downstream to mouth	2.2
Powdermill Run	From headwaters downstream to confluence with Loyalhanna Creek	4.7
Tub Mill Creek	From headwaters downstream to Tub Mill Reservoir	4.1
WYOMING COUNTY		
Stone Run	From headwaters downstream to mouth	2.9
Sugar Hollow Creek	From headwaters downstream to mouth	4.5
YORK COUNTY		
Cordorus Creek	From SR 3047 bridge downstream to SR 0116 bridge	3.3
Rambo Run	From headwaters downstream to first UNT above T-557	1.9
UNT-Rambo Run	From headwaters downstream to first UNT above T-641	3.0

Afterword

Pennsylvania has produced more than its share of legendary flyfishers. It is a long list, and each one on the list has contributed to the lore of flyfishing. And in their passing, we have lost great friends and advocates of flyfishing. One who comes quickly to mind is Charlie Wetzel, one of the first to study stream entomology in the state. His book, *Trout Flies*, is a classic.

I was first introduced to Charlie when I was but a mere lad of five or six years. To me then and even now he was more a student of the art of flyfishing—he was one heck of a good flyfisherman. Charlie and my grandfather were best of friends, and that meant a great deal to them.

My string of Pennsylvania flyfishing acquaintances began back then and continues to this day—Charlie Fox, Vince Marinaro, Eddie Koch, Jim Bashline, Charlie Meck, Bob Clouser, and George Harvey, to name but a few. There are "experts" among us who have never put pen to paper about flyfishing or tied a fly to persuade a trout to take it. Charlie Fox, for example, was not a fly tier. There were many others who influenced me over the years—many men and women in Pennsylvania have devoted their lives to flyfishing.

Undoubtedly, there will be more and more flyfishers searching for the perfect pattern, rod, reel, line, tippet material, and waders. We have well over 800 mayfly species in North America and far more patterns to imitate them. While roaming the Pennsylvania countryside in search of waters far removed from the rigors of daily life or while simply stealing away for the final hours of the day along a trout or bass water, it is important to simply have fun. For some, flyfishing is a lifetime addiction that brings great satisfaction, and to others, flyfishing is another way to while away some time in a tranquil and enjoyable environment.

I admit to having found satisfaction in taking trout from a slow-moving glide—a trout with a pea-sized brain but with far greater instincts than I possess—but my goal is not to conquer my quarry. I have taken great pleasure in watching a bass rush for a popping bug from the shadowed sanctuary of a fallen tree in a backwater cove of a lake; finding a muskie in a deep hole carved by an incoming tributary; hooking and losing a fish on three occasions and then having it come to hand after taking a saltwater-sized streamer, only to release it and watch it swim into the shadowed depths. But I don't feel that I have "defeated" the fish, rather I have gained knowledge in my pursuit. I view flyfishing as an endless search for knowledge of the habits and habitat of these species.

The Resource

Perhaps it is obvious, but it bears repeating: Without clean water, there are no fish to cast flies to. In this heavily industrialized state, we are fortunate to be richly blessed with an abundance of both cold and warmwater fisheries. However, we are plagued with the sins of the past: heavy metals, PCBs, Clorodane, and Myrex, are but a few of the things that pollute our waters. But we are making progress as many of the large plants that stood on the banks of our waters closed down, mine acid drainage has decreased and rivers are coming back to life with cleaner water.

This doesn't mean that our waters are safe, though. The worth of our fisheries is still measured in dollars and cents, and if a polluting industry comes calling with the promise of jobs, we must prove that the recreational value is worth more. We should be able to accomplish both industrial and recreational use of water with the proper measures put in place and enforced.

I was representing the God's Country Chapter of Trout Unlimited in the late 1970s, when the Army Corps of Engineers was planning to extend a "flood control" channel that had proven to be detrimental to trout. When I asked a spokesman for the Corps if the extension would damage the fishery even more and also flood more homes downstream, he became irate, screaming, "What do you want, jobs or fish?" My reply was, "Both." The Corps has changed dramatically since then and now frowns on damming rivers for short-term gain.

The drought of 1999 has provided more emphasis on the essential need for clean water—once again showing that something good can come out of something bad. The realization that we need water to drink became more apparent as a million gallons of water was pumped daily from the lower Susquehanna to provide water for Baltimore. The Delaware Bay tidal basin was drawing water all the way up into Pennsylvania's freshwater streams, and many home wells went bone dry.

As of this writing, trout have been stocked by the Fish and Boat Commission from hatcheries laced with PCBs, and you will find fish advisories in the "Summary Booklet" issued with a fishing license. Like many states, Pennsylvania is suffering from chemical, bacterial, metal, and nonpoint pollution. But great strides to remedy the situation have been made, and you might have noted while reading this book, that nearly all streams, lakes, and rivers have a conservation group monitoring and protecting them. Pennsylvania flyfishers have always led the way in conserving coldwater resource and are now turning to warmwater resources, as well.

It is with great faith that I have written this book: faith that those who fish our waters will enjoy them and treat them as the precious resource they are. Today, the fact that the number of flyfishers is increasing means that there are more voices being raised to protect our streams. As more and more fishermen have united to preserve the Atlantic salmon, the chances of realizing that goal have improved. Those involved in the struggle have discovered that it is necessary to resist the urge to move on to "greener pastures" when water quantity and quality decrease. It is at these times that more effort needs to be put into fixing the problems. The greener pastures are shrinking, so we need to protect what we have.

As my late boss and past executive director of the Pennsylvania Fish and Boat Commission said when faced with the problems of acid precipitation and the feeling among some staff members that acid resistant trout were the answer, "Damn it, I don't want a Band-aid approach to this problem!" Ralph Abele was a great leader, and in his position as executive director of the PFBC, he put his career on the line daily to protect the state's water resources. We need more like him, and Ken Sink and Dr.

Goddard come to mind as others who have contributed a great deal to the health of our waters.

Finally...

Flyfishing, above all else, should be fun. I wrote this book with both the hardcore and the casual flyfisher in mind. This is a guide to the better streams, lakes, and rivers, and I hope, instructional about what flies to carry and what hatches to expect. I have tried to provide as much detail as possible. I also hope that I have aroused your curiosity enough to give some of these Pennsylvania fisheries a look. Personally, I can't pass a stream or a lake without stopping to look, at the very least.

Flyfishing is more than a sport to me, and I believe that it is worthwhile for anyone to expand their fishing opportunities beyond trout. I have taken all the species I have written about and many more that I have not. For example, channel catfish will rise to a dry fly when the white fly hatch is on, and I have taken some very large browns with a cork popping bug when fishing for bass.

Walleye have come to my fly on many occasions, and I have taken them on dry flies in Canada. I am almost certain that they will rise to a dry fly here in Pennsylvania, as well, under special circumstances. Carp have been crowding our waters for as long as I can remember, and a 20-pounder is common. Despite their resemblance in feeding habits to the red drum of saltwater fame, they are mostly ignored by flyfishers.

There is no sound reason why flyfishers can't enjoy fishing for all the state's species. Taking fish of any type requires confidence and skill. Trout will always be an integral part of flyfishing, but smallmouth bass here are a close second.

While there will always be those who pursue flyfishing obsessively, there are now many more who simply want to fish without becoming so technical that it is no longer fun. And if it's not fun, why are we doing it at all?

Index

A

Abele, Ralph   513
Adams County   223, 257, 492, 496
Aldred, Lake   407
Alexander Caverns   250, 505
Alexandria, PA   235
All Tackle Selective Harvest   1, 179, 185–186,
    260, 327, 334
All Tackle Trophy Trout   2, 124, 137, 177,
    332–333
Allegheny College   427
Allegheny County   319, 330, 435, 438, 455,
    463, 477
Allegheny National Forest   173, 175, 429,
    435
Allegheny Reservoir (*see also* Kinzua Dam)
    271, 429, 435, 440–442
Allegheny River
    Coldwater section   98–102, 184–185
    Warmwater section   271, 273, 299, 427,
        429–441, 464
Allentown, PA   55, 57, 61, 89–90, 267, 473
Altoona, PA   233
Alvin Bush Dam   159
Ambridge, PA   455
Americans with Disabilities Act   450
Annville, PA   253, 255
Approved Trout Waters   2–3, 44–49, 84–88,
    113, 179–187, 257–263, 296–299, 330–334
Armstrong County   330, 435, 437, 454, 478
Army Corps of Engineers   4, 79, 109, 371,
    373, 422–423, 435, 513
Arthur, Lake   452–453, 464
Audobon, PA   363–364

B

Babcock State Forest   312
Bailey Run   163, 165, 185, 497
Baker Creek   99
Bald Eagle Creek   179, 238–241, 258, 262,
    374
Bashline, Jim   71, 99, 512
Bass
    Big Bass Program   452, 464–465
    Hybrid   360
    Kentucky   305, 455

Largemouth (*Micropterus salmoides*)
    55, 81, 371, 407, 409–410, 413–414,
    418, 422, 426–427, 434, 447–449, 452,
    454, 464, 491–492
    description of   491–492
Rock   xv
Smallmouth (*Micropterus dolomieui*)
    8, 25, 55, 159, 203, 235, 243, 247, 271,
    319, 339, 349, 361, 365–366, 369, 372,
    374, 380, 384, 389, 393, 395–396, 403,
    405, 407–408, 410–411, 413–415, 418,
    422, 427, 434, 440, 443, 447, 449, 451,
    454, 458, 464, 466–467, 490–492, 514
    description of   490–491
Striped (*Morone saxatilis*)   7–8, 346, 351,
    359, 361, 365, 369, 371, 373, 404–405,
    407, 409–410, 422, 429, 434, 452, 455,
    458, 481, 492–493
    description of   492–493
White (*Morone chrysops*)   271, 305,
    404–405, 434, 451, 492
Bath, PA   63, 87
Beaver County   330, 455, 457
Beaver River   297, 330, 455
Beaver Run   44, 85, 180, 257, 281, 297, 496,
    502
Bedford County   243, 245, 257, 496
Bedford, PA   243–245, 257, 337, 464, 479,
    496
Bellefonte, PA   150, 189, 499
Belvedere, NJ   357
Berger, Paul   147
Berks County   57, 66, 79, 84, 366–367, 371,
    472, 491, 496
Berwick, PA   388, 470
Bethlehem, PA   55, 59–60, 63–64, 473, 477
Big Bass Program   452, 464–465
Big Bushkill Creek   28
Big Mill Creek   173–175, 181–182
Big Run   126, 181–183, 261, 501, 504
Big Spring Creek   216–218, 258, 501
Big Spring State Park   203
Birch Run Reservoir   492
Black Creek (Hayes Creek)   32–33, 47, 498
Blair County   233–235, 239, 258, 497
Bloomsburg, PA   39, 388

Blue Marsh Dam   79
Blue Marsh Lake   81, 371–373
Bluegill   342, 410, 426, 449
Boiling Springs, PA   205, 211, 258, 476
Borie Branch   161
Brandywine Creek   70–73, 85
Bright, Alan   152
Bristol, PA   358
Brodhead Creek   29–31, 46
Brooks, Joe   159
Brooks, Norm   169, 413
Brown bullhead   xv
Brownsville, PA   458–459, 462
Bruner Run   322
Bucks County   84, 357–359, 472, 497
Bulls Head Branch   218, 258
Burbot   xv
Bureau of Forestry   95
Bushkill, PA   16
Butler County   296, 452

C

Caldwell Creek   276–279, 296, 299, 510
Caldwell Creek, West Branch   279
Callicoon, NY   15
Cambria County   309, 331, 497
Cameron County   171, 179, 411, 497–498
Camp Run   184–185, 326–328, 334, 500, 508, 510
Canadohita Lake   273
Cannonsville Reservoir   13
Canoe Creek   232–234, 258, 296, 464
Canoe Creek Lake   233, 464
Carbon County   35, 44, 59, 470, 498
Carbondale, PA   19, 51, 503
Carlisle, PA   213–214, 264–265, 426, 476
Carp   97, 514
Carter, President Jimmy   151
Casselman Creek   317
Catch-and-Release   1, 3, 23, 32, 35, 39, 44–45, 47, 57, 87, 120, 122, 135, 137, 139, 147, 151, 155, 158, 179, 187, 199, 205, 207, 209, 211, 214, 217, 235, 240, 259–262, 273, 277, 279, 289, 299, 451, 496
Catfish, channel   365, 434, 514
Catfish, flathead   xv
Catskill Mountains   8
Cedar Creek   65, 86, 503
Cedar Run   116, 119, 145, 181, 183, 186, 498, 500, 509–510

Centre County   71, 132, 137, 179–180, 187, 191, 474, 498, 500
Chambersburg, PA   225, 227, 266, 476
Chartiers Creek   333, 455
Cheat River   458
Cherry Run   137, 140–141, 186–187, 262, 330, 505–506, 510
Chesapeake Bay   389, 392, 408
Chest Creek   180, 309–311, 331
Chester County   66, 68, 85, 366–367, 473, 500
Chickies Creek   78, 86
Children's Lake   205, 211
Cisna Run   203, 262
Clara Creek   507
Clarion County   296, 477
Clarion River   176–178, 181, 183–184
Clark, Donald   356
Clarke, Lake   405–406
Clarks Creek   198–203, 259
Clear Creek   178–179, 182
Clear Shade Creek   312–313, 332
Clear Shade Wild Area   312
Clearfield County   180, 309, 474, 500
Clinton County   181, 189, 374, 377, 474, 486
Clouser Darter   468–469
Clouser, Bob   361, 371, 395, 466–469, 512
Coatesville, PA   71
Coburn, PA   124–125, 137, 476, 499
Codorus Creek   219–221, 263
Coldwater Fly Box   339–347
Coles Creek   39
Columbia County   37, 39, 44, 388, 470, 501
Columbia, PA   273, 298, 380, 401, 479, 484
Conemaugh River   315, 331, 497
Conewago Creek   223–224, 257, 261, 404
Conewago Lake (*see also* Pinchot Lake) 409–410
Confluence, PA   317, 319, 321, 324
Conneaut Creek   291, 296
Conneaut Lake   302, 451, 477, 494
Connellsville, PA   319–322, 324
Conodoguinet Creek   259
Conowingo Reservoir   408
Conservation Lakes   2
Cook Forest   178
Cool Spring Creek   284, 298
Coudersport, PA   99, 101, 106, 113, 166–167, 188, 429, 475, 507
Crappie, black   xv

Crawford County   273, 291, 296, 427, 449, 477, 494, 501–502
Crooked Creek   181, 289, 438
Cross Fork Creek   154–157, 185, 506
Croydon, PA   358–359
Cumberland County   3, 79, 153, 205, 213, 217, 258, 400, 424, 426, 476

D

Danville, PA   382–383, 388, 390
Dauphin County   201, 203, 259, 399–400, 404, 476
Dauphin County Anglers Club   201
Deer Lake   329
DeHart Reservoir   199, 201
Delaware   47, 55, 64, 67, 84–85, 261, 358, 479, 506
Delaware Bay   7–8, 513
Delaware County   67, 85, 356, 359–360, 473, 493
Delaware River
    Coldwater section   7–17, 21, 28, 50, 59, 61, 71, 472–473
    Warmwater section   351–355, 357, 359–361, 365–366, 492–493
    West Branch   13
Delaware Shad Hotline   356
Delaware Water Gap   16, 47, 355–356, 506
Delayed Harvest Artificial Lures Only (DHALO)
    2, 35, 44–46, 48–49, 64, 71, 79, 83–85, 87–88, 116, 118, 126, 129, 163, 173, 177, 179–181, 183–185, 227, 253, 259–262, 273, 281, 284, 297–298, 309, 317, 329–331, 333–334
Delayed Harvest Flyfishing Only (DHFFO)
    1, 25, 28, 46, 48–49, 57, 66, 75, 77, 85–86, 132, 171, 177, 179, 181, 183–185, 187, 199, 201, 218, 223, 229, 257–259, 263, 277, 279, 298–299, 307, 312, 315, 324, 331–332
Department of Conservation and Natural Resources (DCNR)   32, 273, 410, 447–448, 450, 453
Dismal Run   67, 85
Donegal Creek   77–78, 86
Donegal Fish and Conservation Association   77
Downington, PA   71, 85, 473
Downsville Reservoir   13
Drake Well Museum   273, 298

Driftwood Branch Sinnemahoning Creek
    Coldwater section   163–172, 179, 498
    Warmwater section   411–413
Duboistown, PA   378
Dunbar Creek   324–325, 331
Dunbar Sportsmen's Club   324
Dyberry Creek   20, 25, 27, 48, 510

E

East Branch Antietam Creek   229
East Fork Sportsmen   163
East Stroudsburg, PA   29, 52, 471
Easton, PA   61, 87, 351, 357–358, 476, 506
Eel, American   xv
Elevenmile Creek   507
Elk County   171, 173, 181–182, 190, 475, 502
Elk Creek
    Lake Erie tributary   289, 444
    Northcentral   124–125, 137, 177, 179, 498–499
Elmhurst Reservoir   23, 45, 503
Emporium, PA   171, 179, 411, 413
Erie County   289, 291, 293, 297, 427, 447, 477
Erie, Lake   271, 285–295, 443–448, 451, 464, 489–490, 493
Erie, PA   190, 295, 300–301, 303, 444–448, 475, 477, 479
Everett, PA   243, 346

F

Fairmount Dam   361
Falling Spring Greenway Association   225
Falling Springs Branch Creek   225–227, 229, 259
Fallingwater   322
Fayette County   329, 331–332, 458, 461, 502
First Fork Sinnemahoning Creek
    3, 161–167, 179, 185, 233, 281, 413
Fisherman's Paradise   147, 150, 180, 499
Fishing Creek
    Northcentral   101, 143–146, 179, 181, 185, 486, 499–500
    Northeast   37–40, 45, 47, 509
Flick, Art,   120
Fly Shops by Region   470–478
Forest County   297, 436, 477
Fort Indiantown Gap   203
Foster Joseph Sayer Lake   151
Fourmile Creek   293
Foust, Wayne   389

Fox, Charlie 213–214, 512
Fox, Harry 424
Francis Branch 120–121, 186, 504, 507, 510
Francis E. Walter Dam 60
Franklin County 476, 502
Franklin, PA 337, 427, 435–436, 479
Frankstown Branch Juniata River 232–233, 235–237, 258
Frederic, Lake 403
Fredericktown, PA 458
French Creek
  Southeast coldwater 66–67, 85
  Northwest warmwater 297–298, 427–428
French Creek Project 427
French Creek State Park 66
Fritz, Bill 79
Fulton County 260

G
Galeton, PA 107, 111, 115, 188, 475
Gallitzin State Forest 312–313
Gar, longnose xv
Genesee River 112–113, 507
George B. Stevenson Dam 163, 165, 413–414
Gertrude Fox Conservation Center 63, 87
Gifford Pinchot State Park 410
Glade Run 296, 324, 330–331, 333, 464
Grace, Timothy 422
Grand Valley, PA 277
Grave Yard Pond 447
Gray's Run 122–123, 183
Gray's Run Hunting Club 122, 183
Green Spring Creek 218, 258
Greene County 332, 461
Gull Point Special Management Area 447

H
Hallstead, PA 385
Hammersley Fork 95, 156, 189, 507
Hancock, NY 8, 13
Harrisburg, PA 86, 91, 201, 203, 264, 266–269, 396–397, 399–400, 403, 418, 479
Harvey, George W. 95, 512
Havre de Grace, MD 389
Hawley, PA 21, 472
Hayes Creek 32–33
Hazleton, PA 83
Hemlock Run 203, 262, 299, 509
Henry Lake 23

Heritage Trout Angling 1, 57, 86, 120–121, 149, 155, 180, 185–186, 214, 217, 227, 258–259
Hershey, PA 251–252
Hickory Run 32–35, 44, 297, 498
Hickory Run State Park 32–33, 35, 44
Hollidaysburg, PA 235
Hollister Dam 23
Holtwood Dam 389, 407, 464
Honesdale, PA 14, 21, 25–26, 48, 50, 472
Honey Creek 249–250, 262, 505
Hoopes, Rick 393
Hopewell Lake 66
Huntingdon County 235, 243, 245, 247, 260, 419, 422, 476, 487, 493, 499, 502
Huntingdon, PA 153, 195, 229–230, 269, 423, 479, 497
Hunts Run 171, 179, 498

I–J
Illick's Mill Dam 63, 87
Indian Creek 87, 326–328, 331, 334
Indian Mountain Lake 35
Indiana County 307, 332, 478
Jackson, Larry 253
Jefferson County 182
Jobe, Ray 342
John P. Saylor Trail 312
Jones Mills, PA 327
Juniata County 247, 261, 417, 419, 502
Juniata River 228, 242–243, 247, 257–258, 415–421, 465

K
Kane, PA 51, 441–442
Karns, Harry 411
Kepone 147
Kettle Creek 95, 97, 154–156, 158–160, 166, 181, 185, 189, 233, 474, 507
Kettle Creek Watershed Association 158, 160, 166
Keystone Lake 334, 454, 464–465
Keystone State Park 454
Kinzua Dam 271, 429, 435, 440–442
Kittaning, PA 435
Kock, Eddie 512

L
Lackawanna County 45–46, 503
Lackawanna River 18–19, 23, 45, 47–48, 503

Lackawanna River, West Branch   47
Lackawanna, PA   18–19, 21–23, 45–48, 51, 59, 380, 465, 479, 503
Lackawaxen River   20–22, 25, 46, 48
Lamar Fish Hatchery   145
Lamprey   xv
Lancaster County   75, 77, 85–86, 401, 473, 503
Lancaster, PA   91, 403, 464–465, 472, 479
Latrobe, PA   315–316, 478
Laurel Hill Creek   317–318, 329, 333
Laurel Hill State Park   317, 333
Laurel Run   179–180, 182, 186, 260–262, 329, 331–332, 499, 509
Lawrence County   281, 297–298, 477
Lebanon County   203, 253, 255, 261
Lehigh County   57, 61, 86, 473, 488, 503
Lehigh River   23, 32, 35, 45–46, 57, 59, 61–64, 351
Letort   4, 199, 205, 212–215, 217, 227, 255, 258, 347, 424, 487, 502
Letort Regulars   213
Letort Spring Park   214, 258, 502
Lewistown, PA   416, 419
Lick Run   151, 182, 319, 331–333, 499, 501, 505, 508
Ligonier, PA   315–316, 337, 478
Little Chest Creek   309
Little Juniata River   228–231, 239, 258, 260
Little Lehigh Creek   56–57, 84, 86, 503
Little Lehigh Flyfishers   57
Little Mahoning Creek   306–308, 332
Little Pine Creek   113, 116–118, 183
Little Sandy Creek   182, 279–280, 298
Little Schuylkill River   82–83, 88
Little Valley Creek   68, 500
Lock Haven, PA   135, 145, 189, 240, 374–375, 377
Lower Woods Pond   26
Loyalhanna Creek   314–316, 334, 511
Loyalsock Creek   47, 128–131, 183
Luzerne County   19, 41, 45, 59, 387, 470, 504
Lycoming County   116, 129, 183–184, 377, 475, 504
Lyman Lake   107–111, 185, 507
Lyman Run   107–109, 111, 185, 507
Lyman Run State Park   107, 111

M

Mahoning Creek   44, 46, 88, 182–183, 332
Manada Creek   251–252, 259

Marburg, Lake   219, 465
Marina Bay   447
Marinaro, Vince   213, 512
Marion Center, PA   307
Marsh Creek State Park   71
Maryland   222, 225, 229, 319, 389, 393, 402, 408
McKean County   101, 184, 188, 441, 475, 505
McKeesport, PA   319, 463
McNuff Branch (Hunts Run)   171, 179, 498
Meadow Run   329, 331
Meadville, PA   302, 427, 451, 479
Meck, Charlie   512
Mehoopany Creek   41–43, 47, 49
Mercer County   279, 281, 298
Mercer, PA   285, 465, 479
Michigan   286, 489
Middletown, PA   259, 267–268, 371, 392, 395, 399–400, 404, 466, 476
Mifflin County   262, 419, 476, 505
Mifflintown, PA   419
Milford, NJ   84, 358, 471
Mill Run   263, 281, 322, 331, 333, 464, 501, 504, 510
Millersburg, PA   383, 390–391, 399
Millheim, PA   125
Misery Bay   447
Monocacy Creek   63–65, 87, 506
Monocacy Watershed Association   63
Monongahela River   429, 458–461, 463
Monroe County   28, 35, 46, 470, 505–506
Montgomery County   87, 366–367, 473
Montour County   46, 388, 471
Montoursville, PA   129, 475
Moore's Run   161
Moraine State Park   452–453, 464
Mosey Wood Pond   32
Mud Run   34–36, 44
Mud Run Natural Area   35
Muddy Creek   84, 86, 222, 263, 296, 408, 499
Muhlenberg, Lake   65, 503
Muncy Creek   47, 126–127, 183
Muskellunge or Muskie (*Exos masquinongy*)   2, 7–8, 15–16, 55, 66–67, 101, 243–247, 271, 305, 319, 351, 356–357, 359–360, 365, 368–369, 374, 377–380, 384–388, 394, 396, 403, 405, 407–410, 413, 415, 419–420, 422, 424–427, 429, 434, 441, 443, 447–449, 451–455, 458, 466–467, 481–482, 493–494, 512
   description of   493–494

Muskellunge, tiger or tiger muskie
(*Exos lincius*)   244, 429, 493
Myrex   147, 512

N

Narrowsburg, NY   16
Neshaminy Creek   84, 358–359
Neshannock Creek   281, 283–285, 295,
   297–298, 477
New Castle, PA   281
New Jersey   7–8, 358
New York   7–8, 11–13, 285–286, 291,
   380–381, 389, 427, 430, 442, 457, 489
Newville, PA   217–218, 264, 476, 479
Norristown, PA   366–367
Northampton County   61, 63–64, 87, 357,
   506
Northcentral Pennsylvania   94–193
Northeast Pennsylvania   6–53
Northumberland County   185, 379–380,
   388, 397, 471, 475
Northumberland, PA   464, 479
Northwest Pennsylvania   270–303

O

Octoraro Creek   74–75, 85–86
Octoraro Lake   75
Ohio   289, 291, 449, 455–456, 489
Ohio River   303, 429, 433, 455–457, 460–461,
   490, 493
Ohiopyle, PA   319, 322, 329
Oil City, PA   273–274, 435–436
Oil Creek   272–275, 296, 298, 477
Oil Creek State Park   273–274, 298
Ole Bull State Park   159
Olyphant, PA   19, 45
Opossum Creek Lake   258, 424–425
Oswayo Creek   103–106, 185, 507
Otter Creek   263, 281, 285, 297, 407, 476
Owl Creek   83, 508

P

Paddlefish   xv
Palmyra Sportsmen's Association   253
Panfish   15–16, 67, 71, 223, 243, 245, 247,
   357, 359–360, 369, 377–379, 385–388,
   419–420, 422, 424, 426, 429, 454
Patterson, Leroy   422
Penns Cave   137
Penns Creek   124, 137–142, 179, 187, 213,
   233, 262, 349, 471, 499, 505

Pennsylvania Fish & Boat Commission
   (PFBC)   3, 8, 57, 63–64, 67, 147, 163,
   171, 213, 235, 243, 422, 434, 479, 488–489,
   492–493, 495, 513
Pennsylvania Game Commission (PGC)   95,
   173, 199, 201, 203, 259, 398–399, 437
Pennsylvania State College   95
Pennsylvania State Experimental Fisheries
   Area   151
Pennsylvania Turnpike   32, 35, 68, 81, 243
Perch, white   xv
Perch, yellow   451
Perry County   203, 262, 398, 420, 506
Philadelphia County   87, 353–354, 359,
   366–367, 474
Philadelphia, PA   52, 55, 67, 71, 91, 266–267,
   351, 360–361, 473, 479, 492
Phoenixville, PA   66, 366–367
Pickerel, chain   15–16, 159, 243, 245, 357,
   359–360, 369, 377–379, 385, 388,
   419–420, 422
Pike County   16, 21, 46, 59, 370, 471, 493,
   506
Pike, Northern   2, 271, 368, 377, 410, 422,
   427, 447, 449, 452–454, 458, 466, 481,
   493
Pinchot Lake   409–410, 465
Pine Creek   46, 84, 88, 113–120, 183,
   185–186, 259, 277, 296, 299, 330, 496,
   499, 504, 508
Pittsburgh, PA   55, 190, 295, 305, 315, 327,
   335–337, 418, 429, 434, 439, 452, 454–455,
   458, 461, 463, 477–478
Pittston, PA   19, 387
Point Marion, PA   458–459, 461
Port Allegany, PA   99, 101, 184, 188
Port Clinton, PA   83, 366
Port Jervis, NY   8
Port Trevorton, PA   398
Potter County   71, 95, 99, 103, 110, 115, 119,
   156, 163, 166, 185–186, 281, 475, 506, 508
Potter County Anglers Club   163
Pottsville, PA   365, 474
Power, Karl   315, 454, 458
Presque Isle   300, 445–448, 464
Presque Isle Bay   445–447, 464
Presque Isle State Park   300, 445, 447–448
Price, Robert   422
Prouty Run   161, 165, 508
Pymatuning Lake   449
Pymatuning State Park   449–450

Q–R

Quittapahilla Creek (the Quitty)   253–256, 261
Quittie Nature Park   253, 261
Raccoon Creek   262, 291, 509
Ramcut Run   319
Rattling Run   83, 508
Rausch Run   203
Raystown Branch Juniata River   242–246, 257, 260, 333, 461
Raystown Lake   243, 245, 260, 422–423, 487, 492–493
Reading, PA   81, 92, 362–363, 365–366, 373, 472
Redbreast   xv
Redear   xv
Redfin   xv
Redline, Harry   152–153, 229
Reed, Leon   8
Renovo, PA   135, 189, 474
Resica Falls Scout Reservation   28
Ridgway, PA   173, 175, 178, 190
Ridley Creek   67, 85
Ridley Creek State Park   67, 85
Rieglesville, PA   357
Roaring Brook   23–24, 45, 183, 186, 503
Roaring Run Natural Area   327
Robert Mellow Park   19, 45
Rocheseter, PA   307, 332, 455, 457
Roosevelt State Park   357–358
Rose Valley Lake   113, 465
Run, The (*see also* Yellow Breeches Creek)   205–211, 488
Ryan, Pete   99, 342

S

Safe Harbor Dam   405
Salmon
    Atlantic   356, 422, 513
    Chinook   271, 285, 289, 294, 443, 483
    Coho   271, 285, 289, 294, 443, 447
    Pacific   271, 285
    Pink   289
Sandy Creek   182, 279–280, 296, 298, 331, 436
Sanford Corners, PA   279
Saucon Creek   64, 86–87, 506
Saucon Park   64
Sauger   434
Sayre, PA   385
Schoolhouse Hollow   116, 183

Schuylkill County   83, 87, 365, 367, 474, 508
Schuylkill Haven, PA   361, 365, 367
Schuylkill River   66, 68, 82–84, 88, 361–367, 496
Scotts Run Lake   84, 491
Scranton, PA   19, 23, 50–51
Select Trout Stocked Lake Program   464
Selective Harvest Program   1, 64, 107, 122, 135, 179, 181, 183, 185–186, 219, 221, 260, 263, 327, 334
Sevenmile Creek   293
Shad, American (*Alosa sapidissima*)   7–8, 15–16, 55, 59–60, 137, 351, 355–357, 360–361, 365, 408, 415, 422, 466, 480, 493
    description of   493
Shamokin Dam   389
Shermans Creek   203–204
Shobers Run   243, 257
Sink, Ken   308, 513
Sinnemahoning Creek
    Driftwood Branch
        Coldwater section   163–172, 179, 498
        Warmwater section   411–413
    First Fork   3, 161–167, 179, 185, 233, 281, 413
Sixteenmile Creek   293, 444
Smallmouth Bass Alliance   393
Snitz Creek   253, 261
Snyder County   186, 397
Somerset County   243–245, 312, 332, 337, 478, 509
Somerset, PA   305, 322, 465, 479
Southcentral Pennsylvania   194–269
Southeast Pennsylvania   54–93
Southwest Pennsylvania   304–347
Splash Dam Hollow   107, 185, 507–508
Spring Creek   84, 132, 147–151, 180, 182, 184, 187, 297, 299, 499, 501–503, 510
Spring Creek Fish Culture Station   149
Spruce Creek   29, 71, 151–153, 229–231, 260–261, 269, 476, 499, 502
Spruce Mountain   29
State College, PA   95, 132, 150, 153, 191, 269, 474
Steelhead   59, 271, 285–295, 297, 372, 424, 443–444, 447, 483, 489
    Description   489
Sterling Run   413
Stillwater Lake   19
Stony Creek   44, 87, 203, 259, 261, 333
Stroudsburg, PA   10, 14, 29, 52, 352, 471

Struble Lake 71
Sullivan County 39, 47, 126, 472, 509
Sunbury, PA 374, 380, 388–389, 393, 397, 403, 464, 471
Sunfish, green xv
Susquehanna County 19, 47–48, 380, 385
Susquehanna River
 Main Branch 19, 37–39, 41, 126, 159, 199, 203, 243, 253, 263, 339, 351, 376, 384, 389–408, 415, 464, 492
 North Branch 19, 37–39, 41, 126, 380–388
 West Branch 128–129, 132, 145, 240, 309, 374–380
Swatara Creek 84, 88, 253, 255

T

Tackle and Equipment (overview) 480–485
Tamaqua, PA 83, 361, 365, 508
Tioga County 116, 186, 475, 509–510
Titusville, PA 273–274, 296, 477
Towanda, PA 44, 385
Tower City, PA 199
Treaster Run 250, 262
Trembley, G.L. 95
Trophy Trout Projects 2, 19, 45, 63, 87, 119, 124, 137, 143, 145, 151, 155, 177, 181, 183–184, 186, 217, 319, 332–333
Trough Creek State Park 423
Trout Run 116, 261, 289, 500–504
Trout Unlimited 57, 63, 68, 79, 99, 135, 151, 166, 195, 203, 213, 217, 234, 273, 308, 324, 342, 513
 Blair County Chapter 234
 Chestnut Ridge Chapter 324
 Cumberland County Chapter 213, 217
 God's Country Chapter 99, 166, 342, 513
 Ken Sink Chapter 308
 Little Lehigh Chapter 57
 Monocacy Chapter 63
 Oil Creek Chapter 273
 Tulpehocken Chapter 79
 Valley Forge Chapter 68
Trout
 Brook (*Salvelinus fontinalis*) 3–4, 7, 12, 32, 35, 37, 41, 59, 95–96, 99–100, 103, 105, 107, 109, 117, 119–121, 124, 132, 137, 140, 155–156, 161, 165, 171, 173, 175, 201, 203, 208, 217, 234–235, 247, 249–250, 271, 277, 305, 327–328, 380, 486–487, 495
  description of 486–487

Brown (*Salmo trutta*) 1, 3, 7, 12, 32, 41, 64, 68, 72, 96, 99, 120, 124, 135, 139, 145, 147, 149, 151, 161, 171, 175, 208, 214–215, 239, 247, 279, 324, 349, 369, 422, 429, 440, 487–488, 495
  description of 487
 Golden 490
 Lake 289, 422, 441, 443, 454
 Palomino 271, 289, 347, 443, 490
  description of 490
 Rainbow (*Oncorhynchus mykiss*) 12, 107, 136, 147, 152, 199, 217, 223, 225, 230, 487–490
  description of 488
 Steelhead 59, 271, 285–295, 297, 372, 424, 443–444, 447, 483, 489
  description of 489
Tulpehocken Creek 79–81, 84, 92, 261, 373, 472
Tunkhannock, PA 45, 48–49, 381–382, 387
Turkey Creek 291
Tuscarora Creek 44, 247–248, 261
Twentymile Creek 293
Tylersville Fish Hatchery 143, 181
Tyrone, PA 240, 258

U–V

Ulysses, PA 113
Union County 132, 186, 378, 476, 510
Upper Woods Pond 25, 48
Valley Creek 68, 85, 87, 260–261, 500
Valley Forge National Park 68
Venango County 273–274, 279, 298, 427, 435–436, 477, 510

W

Wallenpaupack, Lake 45, 48, 367–370, 472, 492
Walleye 15–16, 245, 360, 378–379, 385–388, 419–420, 422, 434, 441, 449, 451, 454, 458, 468, 481, 514
Walnut Creek 286, 289, 444
Warmwater Fly Box 466–469
Warren County 299, 303, 435, 442, 510
Warren, PA 299, 303, 388, 435, 441–442, 479, 510
Washington County 333, 458, 462
Waterville, PA 117–118, 120, 183, 192, 475
Watsontown, PA 379
Watts, R.L. 95
Wayne County 12–13, 15, 21, 23, 48, 59, 370, 472, 510

West Virginia   455, 458, 461
Westmoreland County   315, 327, 334, 438, 454, 462, 478, 510
Wetzel, Charlie   135, 137, 159, 512
White Clay Creek   63–64, 85
White Clay Creek Preserve State Park   64
White Clay Watershed Association   63
White Deer Creek   132–133, 180, 187
White Haven, PA   32, 470
Wilkes-Barre, PA   51, 387
Williamsport, PA   129, 192, 295, 374–378, 475
Windber Reservoir   312
Wolf, AnGel   315
Wolfe's Orvis Shop   113

Wrightsville, PA   406
Wyoming County   41, 49, 386, 472, 511

Y

Yellow Breeches Creek   205–211, 259, 263
York County   219, 222, 239, 262, 403, 409, 476, 511
York Haven Dam   401, 403
Yorks, Wayne   37
Youghiogheny Lake   319
Youghiogheny River   305, 319–324, 327, 329, 332–333, 463
Young Woman's Creek   134–136, 181
Yurejefcic, Jim   255, 467

NOTES

WILDERNESS ADVENTURES GUIDE SERIES

If you would like to order additional copies of this book or our other Wilderness Adventures Press guidebooks, please fill out the order form below or call **1-800-925-3339** or **fax 800-390-7558.** Visit our website for the largest online listing of sporting books: **www.wildadv.com**

Mail to: Wilderness Adventures Press, 45 Buckskin Road
Belgrade, MT 59714

☐ **Please send me your quarterly catalog on hunting and fishing books.**

Ship to:
Name _____

Address _____

City _____ State_____ Zip_____

Home Phone_____Work Phone_____

Payment: ☐ Check ☐ Visa ☐ Mastercard ☐ Discover ☐ American Express

Card Number _____ Expiration Date_____

Signature_____

Qty	Title of Book and Author	Price	Total
	Flyfisher's Guide to Colorado	$26.95	
	Flyfisher's Guide to Idaho	$26.95	
	Flyfisher's Guide to Michigan	$26.95	
	Flyfisher's Guide to Montana	$26.95	
	Flyfisher's Guide to Northern California	$26.95	
	Flyfisher's Guide to Northern New England	$26.95	
	Flyfisher's Guide to Oregon	$26.95	
	Flyfisher's Guide to Pennsylvania	$26.95	
	Flyfisher's Guide to Washington	$26.95	
	Flyfisher's Guide to Wyoming	$26.95	
	Total Order + shipping & handling		

Shipping and handling: $4.00 for first book,
$2.50 per additional book, up to $11.50 maximum

NOTES